Dangerous-Game RIFLES

— ❧ —

Terry Wieland

Countrysport Press
Camden, Maine

ALSO BY TERRY WIELAND

A View From A Tall Hill: Robert Ruark in Africa
Spanish Best: The Fine Shotguns of Spain
Spiral-Horn Dreams
The Magic of Big Game

Copyright © 2006 by Terry Wieland

ISBN 0-89272-691-1

Book and Dust-Jacket Design by Lynda H. Mills

Library of Congress Cataloging-in-Publication Data
Wieland, Terry.
Dangerous-game rifles / Terry Wieland.-- 1st ed.
p. cm.
Includes bibliographical references and index.
ISBN 0-89272-691-1 (trade hardcover : alk. paper)
1. Hunting rifles. I. Title.
SK274.2.W54 2006
799.2028'32--dc22

2006000733

Printed at Versa Press Inc., East Peoria, Illiinois

5   4   3   2   1

Countrysport Press
Camden, Maine
www.countrysportpress.com
A division of Down East Enterprise, Inc.
publishers of *Shooting Sportsman* magazine

For David C. Foster, Editor-in-Chief
Gray's Sporting Journal

A fine editor and the best of friends

Table of Contents

Foreword by Robin Hurt

Acknowledgments

Introduction

Section V—Cartridges and Bullets

Section VI—Using the Dangerous-Game Rifle

Section VII—Appendices

Foreword

It was in 1990 that I first met Terry Wieland. The place was Kigozi in Tanzania's western swamp area of the Moyowosi. The purpose was to try some new bullets that were about to come on the market. Jack Carter's Trophy Bonded Bear Claw soft-nosed bullets and his Sledgehammer solid bullets. Terry and I have been friends ever since.

Getting off the plane at Kigozi airstrip was an experienced team, consisting of Terry, Jack Carter, and Finn Aagaard. We were all to hunt together. The idea of using soft-nosed bullets on buffalo was of some concern to me. In East Africa we had traditionally used only solids

Robin Hurt

on buffalo. The reason was quite simply that soft-nosed bullets nearly always broke up and did not penetrate, resulting in a wounded and very angry antagonist to deal with.

I told Terry's group that I had seen an old bull buffalo on the way to the airstrip and was hoping to find him again. Jack Carter was to shoot first, so I asked him to try his rifle to make sure it was properly zeroed, before we set off to look for the buffalo. Jack had a .450 Ackley, and he had loaded it with his soft-nosed Bear Claws. It was with some trepidation that I agreed to him shooting a buffalo with a soft bullet.

We found the bull near where I had left him. He was a fine old animal with a fair, heavy-bossed head of about forty inches. Jack and I stalked up behind an ant hill to within forty yards of our quarry. He was facing us. I set up the shooting sticks as a rest and Jack shot the buffalo perfectly in the center of the chest. The bull stumbled at the shot, turned, and ran ten yards, collapsing with a loud bellow. It was all over in seconds. I was impressed.

My reluctance to use soft-nosed bullets on buffalo was changing quickly. Also impressive was the performance of the .450 Ackley. This cartridge is similar to the

.458 Lott, of which I am a big fan. On dissecting the animal we found the bullet to have penetrated clear through the chest, demolishing the top of the heart and penetrating both lungs through to the middle of the belly. The bullet had mushroomed perfectly and, as far as I could tell, had stayed together 100 percent.

Terry and I continued to test bullets on other buffalo and smaller game with different calibers, and the result was always the same: perfect mushroom and core retention. I was awed, to say the least, and have been an ardent user and fan of Jack Carter's bullets ever since.

In this book, Terry goes into details of heavy-caliber rifles and their bullets. He is a man who does not write by hearsay—he has done it. He has used double rifles of the largest caliber. He has used magazine rifles of the largest caliber. He has experienced many makes of custom bullets on dangerous game. In other words, what he has seen is what he has written about. Too many other writers have relied on mere hearsay; this book is based on fact, and for that is eminently readable.

My personal experience of heavy rifles in the hands of hunters coming on safari has been mixed. In the hands of a good shot, who has practiced, there can be nothing better for use on Africa's dangerous game. But, all too often, I have had clients arrive with a double rifle of large caliber, such as a .470 or .500, believing that merely hitting a buffalo with a big bullet would be enough to put it down and kill it. Nothing could be farther from the truth. No matter what caliber of rifle one uses, shot placement using the right bullet is the most critical factor. I would far prefer to have someone who can shoot a .375 accurately than a .470 inaccurately. My advice to anyone contemplating bringing a large-caliber rifle on safari is that they should practice and be familiar with it beforehand. Also, they must make sure the rifle is fitted with a proper recoil pad, and those who can't shoot open sights accurately should attach a low-power telescope.

My son Derek recently hunted with Terry in the Burko area of Northern Tanzania. The buffalo in Burko are bad news, having a reputation of being extremely aggressive. This is because of the constant disturbance caused by the presence of the Masai people and their cattle, resulting in bad-tempered, testy buffalo. Derek told me that he was impressed by Terry's courage and calmness in a couple of tight corners they got into. Hunting buffalo in Burko is not for the timid and requires the client to listen carefully to instructions and not shoot too hastily, but rather shoot straight. If you wound a buff here, you had better watch out and tackle the follow-up with caution, armed with a rifle of the largest caliber you can handle effectively. By the way, I still insist on using only solid bullets on wounded buffalo. A brain shot is the only effective stopper of a determined charge. For this, a solid can be relied on to fully penetrate the heavy bone surrounding the brain.

For professional hunters, there is always a discussion on which rifle to use—a magazine bolt action, or a side-by-side double. I prefer a double rifle for my own use because I know that if I get into trouble, it is going to be at very close quarters. That second fast shot has gotten me out of trouble on more occasions than I care to think about. The advantage of the double rifle is two very quick shots without having to reload. Those who favor the bolt action will tell you that without the third or fourth shot, they would have had a problem. These charges must have come from a long enough distance, allowing the hunter to work the bolt in time to get all the shots off. My experience of charges has always been at very short range—often under five yards. At the end of the day, one should use the rifle and caliber that he has the most confidence in.

As hunters who care about the animals we hunt, we want to be able to make sure our shots are clean and that the animal does not suffer unnecessarily. Therefore Terry's advice on bullets is crucial. Thank you, Terry, for a most timely book on dangerous-game rifles and cartridges.

Robin Hurt
Maswa, Tanzania

Acknowledgments

Preparation of this book, although I did not know it at the time, began on a 1990 safari with a list of participants that reads like Who's Who of the safari world: Robin Hurt, Tony Henley, Jack Carter, and Finn Aagaard.

Robin Hurt has been a good friend and great supporter ever since, helping in any way possible when I was seeking a way of testing bullets and ammunition. Robin's son Derek, also a fine professional hunter, guided me on my most recent bullet-testing expedition. My safari with Derek, aside from being educational and productive, was also a wonderful experience.

Tony, Jack, and Finn have all departed, but their influence survives. Their dedication to ethical hunting and to the development and use of humane big-game bullets has changed the hunting world, directly or indirectly, and I learned a great deal from each of them. I only wish I'd had the wit and foresight to pay even more attention when I had the chance.

Most of the people who contributed information and photographs to this book receive their thanks within its pages, but some deserve special mention: David Miller of The David Miller Company, maker of some of the world's best bolt-action rifles; Geoff Miller, of John Rigby & Co.; my old German gunmaker, Siegfried Trillus, who taught me a great deal about how a rifle should be made; and Edwin von Atzigen, who carries on Siegfried's tradition of excellent work and his deep understanding of what makes a good rifle.

George Sandmann of the Empire Rifle Company has made it a personal crusade to keep the Mauser 98 alive and well, and to thwart those who would cheapen it. The results speak for themselves, notably in the Empire bolt-action rifle that graces our cover.

Steve Denny of Holland & Holland was, as always, a treasure trove of knowledge about the British gun business.

Among the ammunition people, Larry Barnett of Superior Ammunition has been a good friend for many years and has always gone out of his way to help, especially in sharing his wide knowledge of good bullets and ammunition.

Two colleagues, Craig Boddington and Tom Turpin, were both supportive and generous in sharing their information and experience. Craig is the most experienced hunter among today's writers, and Tom is the current authority on custom-built rifles. Either of them could have (and perhaps should have) written this book, in which case it would have been much better than it is.

Finally, graphic designer Lynda Mills and editor Chris Cornell from Countrysport Press were both devoted and diligent in taking a manuscript and a bushel of photos, and turning them into a genuine book. For that, thank you.

Introduction

A rifle for dangerous game has one highly specialized purpose: To kill a dangerous animal under difficult circumstances.

In ideal conditions, any animal can be killed with almost any rifle. There is no beast on earth, including dangerous ones, that cannot be dispatched with a well-placed bullet from a .30-06. Animals as formidable as elephants and Cape buffalo have, on occasion, been killed with small rifles firing light bullets. Proponents of high-velocity rifles for dangerous game often cite the example of W.D.M. (Karamoja) Bell, one of the greatest of the ivory hunters, who killed more than a thousand elephants with small-caliber rifles.

Because of this debate, it is best to explain immediately which rifles are covered in this book, and why.

Bob Hagel, a big-game guide and firearms writer, once wrote that in hunting you "should not use a rifle that will kill an animal when everything goes right; you should use one that will do the job when everything goes wrong." That is excellent advice for hunting everything from starlings to mastodons, but is especially true regarding animals that bite back.

What is dangerous game? It is an animal that when wounded does not run from the hunter, but attempts to turn the tables and even the score. This includes animals that will attack a human being even though unwounded:

Man-eaters of all sorts—lions in Africa, and grizzly bears in North America. It also includes Cape buffalo, which kill passers-by on a fairly regular basis, not because these animals are wounded, but simply because (we assume) they do not like to be disturbed. Whether an elephant kills a person because it has a toothache or a snare around its leg or feels its young to be threatened is largely academic if you happen to be the person who incurs its wrath.

The smallest animal seriously considered dangerous game—and it is very dangerous indeed—is the leopard. A leopard may be as small as a hundred pounds, and a large one rarely exceeds two hundred, but when wounded it becomes a fury that must be seen to be believed. It is a soft-skinned animal and not difficult to kill; light rifles are often used on leopards with complete success. If the leopard is only wounded, however, and the hunter or his guide goes into the long grass to find it, they do not go in carrying light rifles. They might have a 12-bore loaded with buckshot or slugs, or a double rifle in anything up to .500 Nitro Express, because when the leopard comes (as it surely will unless it has died of its wounds) you want a gun that will stop it in its tracks.

Upon reading this passage in the original draft, Robin Hurt, Africa's foremost professional hunter of modern times, immediately wrote me: "Nowadays, most professional hunters will not use shotguns on wounded leopards because they simply do not have the stopping power afforded by a large-caliber rifle loaded with soft-nosed bullets. Most professional hunters who have been mauled by a leopard were using shotguns and buckshot. I will never use a shotgun on a wounded leopard again," wrote Hurt. "The one time I did, I got badly mauled."

If anything from a one-hundred-pound leopard to a ten-ton elephant is dangerous game, then one would think there would be a wide variety of dangerous-game rifles, but such is not the case.

A dangerous-game rifle is not just for hunting such animals under normal conditions, it is also the rifle taken into the bush after a wounded one. Included are some calibers that are last-ditch stopping rifles, such as the .577 and .600 Nitro Express, simply because they are used only on dangerous game. In the past, the .600 was a highly specialized weapon employed only in dire circumstances—the tool of the professional ivory hunter whose usual hunting rifle might be a .450 NE. Ivory hunting being a thing of the past, any hunting done today with a .600 is by a sport hunter with a large bankroll and a taste for nostalgia. This does not, however, make the .600 any less devastating a cartridge.

This book deals primarily with double rifles and bolt actions, with chapters on single-shots and lever actions. It does not cover such archaic delights as Cape guns, Paradox guns, or 10-bores with buckshot. These have killed a great deal of dangerous game in the past and will probably be used for that purpose in the future. By our definition, however, a dangerous-game rifle is not just one that might be used by a hunting client, but also one that is carried by the professional hunter for backing up the client and dealing with wounded animals. That effectively excludes these ghost guns from the past. In giving short shrift to single-shots, I am torn; I adore single-shot rifles, but the fact is, serious hunters abandoned them as soon as dependable repeaters became either available or affordable. No professional hunter today uses a single-shot in a dangerous situation.

The smallest legitimate dangerous-game cartridge is the .375 Holland & Holland. It has been in use for almost a century and has compiled an extraordinary record of success. Although most professional hunters consider it light for a stopping rifle, there are professional hunters who do use a .375 for this purpose. Also, the .375 is the last word for grizzly bears and Alaska brown bears, and has been standard equipment in Alaska since Winchester first chambered the Model 70 bolt action for the cartridge in 1937. Two comparable cartridges, the .375 Flanged and the 9.3x74R, are included in this volume because double rifles and single shots are commonly chambered for them and they are occasionally used on dangerous game. In fact, a double in .375 Flanged would be excellent for following up a wounded leopard.

* * *

When considering dangerous-game rifles, an inseparable issue is the cartridge itself and, even more important, the bullet it fires. In the end, the factor that determines whether an animal lives or dies, whether he dies quickly or slowly, and whether he goes to his reward alone or takes the hunter with him, is how the bullet penetrates and expands. Hunters today have a vast range of bullets available—far more than in years gone by, when a pursuer of elephants bought a rifle and then accepted whatever ammunition the rifle maker cared to supply.

Today, a hunter has three decisions to make: rifle, cartridge, and bullet. Bullet choice is every bit as important as the other two.

* * *

The evolution of the dangerous-game rifle is like a skein of wool: There are many historical strands that intertwine. The invention and refinement of rifling, the development of action types, progress in bullets and in gunpowder, as well as many lesser factors, all affected each other through the years until gunmakers and hunters arrived at combinations that worked. These historical links are more than merely interesting; they are useful to the man who is trying to decide what rifle to use when going after elephant, Cape buffalo, or Alaska brown bear. Certain rifles gained a following for a reason; it is useful to know what that reason was. If a rifle was largely shunned by serious hunters, it is best to know why before seizing upon a bargain.

From their earliest days, firearms have progressed in three directions: Bore diameters have become smaller; bullets have become lighter; and velocities have become greater. While elephants have become less numerous, they are no smaller, no less truculent (quite the opposite in most places), and no less difficult to kill. Logic tells us these three ballistic trends can go only so far, and beyond that point the smaller, faster, lighter bullets will do the job less well, rather than better.

This leads us smack into the old Jack O'Connor/Elmer Keith debate about velocity versus bullet weight, a debate that has kept campfires in an uproar since the Korean War. Much as I hate to douse such a hot topic, a close look at the writings of both men shows that they never really contradicted each other. Keeping the controversy alive sold magazines, so editors loved it. O'Connor said that if you hit an animal in the right place, a small, fast bullet would do the job well; Keith said yes, but many times you do not hit the right place, so it is best to have a heavier bullet for insurance. Who can dispute either position?

Actually, the debate over velocity versus bullet weight goes back much earlier, to the 1800s, long before nitro-express cartridges ever saw the light of day. It began in 1856, with the introduction of James Purdey's first "express" rifles—relatively small bores (.500) shooting comparatively light (340-grain) hollow-point bullets. These were fine for red stag in the Scottish hills, but inevitably, some hunters took them to Africa and India, and just as inevitably, some of those men did not come back. Sir Samuel Baker, the greatest hunter of the age, felt the high-velocity hollow-points were an abomination when it came to dangerous game, and he said so in print. His sentiments were echoed by Henry Holland, his close friend and gunmaker. The debate, then as now, was framed in terms of weight retention, controlled expansion, and penetration. Elmer Keith was doing nothing but carrying on the fight begun by Sir Samuel Baker.

When it comes to dangerous game, the debate is more than academic, and every professional hunter I know comes down on the side of Baker and Keith. Since you cannot guarantee exact shot placement with a heavy rifle—and even if you could these animals rarely go down instantly with one shot—it is best to have insurance in the form of a heavy bullet with a lot of punch. More than that, you must ensure that the bullet you use will expand well under a range of conditions, hold together under all conditions, and penetrate deeply to destroy tissue and damage the vitals.

* * *

Another debate that has lasted more than a century is the question of whether to select a double rifle or bolt action. When hunting dangerous game, which is better?

There is a short answer to that question: A hunter should use the rifle with which he is most skillful and comfortable. This assumes that relative power is not an issue, and leaves aside questions like cost, versatility, and accuracy. All else being equal, a hunter with a familiar old bolt-action .458 should not set it aside to go into the long grass with a double .470 that is strange to him, just because someone tells him a double is preferable for wounded animals.

I have no personal preference, no strong feelings either way, and no axe to grind. I am an unabashed lover of double rifles, bolt-action rifles, and fine single-shot rifles; I have used them all and hope to again.

For the record, at this writing I have found myself in a tight spot with a dangerous animal exactly twice—once with an incoming Alaska brown bear and once with a charging, wounded Cape buffalo. In both cases, I was armed with a bolt action, and both cases it was the third shot that finally put the animal down. Had I been armed with a double rifle either time, I might not be writing this now. This is not an argument in favor of bolt actions, it is merely fact. Had the rifle been a double, in a major caliber such as the .500 Nitro Express, the bear and the buffalo might have thrown in the towel earlier. But who really knows?

The essential point is that anyone hunting dangerous game should know his rifle as well as humanly possible. It should be an extension of himself. He should be able to load it, operate it, aim and fire it, all without conscious thought. Instinct should take over. Achieving this level of familiarity requires a great deal of practice and, unfortunately, sufficient practice with the big rifle is one thing many hunters lack when they go to Africa. Among themselves, professional hunters tell of clients arriving with rifles they have not even fired and which are not sighted-in—rifles with recoil that frightens them more than the animals do.

It is one thing to buy the largest and most powerful rifle available and hang it on your wall to show your friends. It is quite another to haul the beast to the range week after week and fire a dozen rounds on every outing. I do not know a single big-game hunter who says he gets enough practice with his big rifle. For that matter, even professional hunters rarely practice, although most shoot their rifles on a regular basis.

So the final section of this book deals with the use of a dangerous-game rifle: coping with recoil, loading ammunition for both hunting and practice, making the rifle work properly and well, and learning to use it the same way. It is possible to have fun with a big rifle, but not by putting an endless round of full-power loads through it and developing a severe flinch in the process. That can be worse than no practice at all.

* * *

A man's rifle is a very personal thing. In years gone by, hunters developed mystical relationships with their guns because their lives depended on them.

Today, most hunters own several rifles, each with a specialized purpose. Some we love, some we respect, some are merely tools. The dangerous-game rifle is a throwback to an earlier time, and once a rifle has bailed us out of a tight situation, we develop an affection for it that dates from the Stone Age. As well, preparing a rifle and ammunition for an expedition after elephant or Cape buffalo or Alaska brown bear concentrates the mind wonderfully and leads us to pay special care to every detail and nuance of the rifle's functions.

Let a dangerous-game rifle fail you once and—assuming you survive—you are almost certain to replace it. Let it come through every time, and you will refuse to part with it under any circumstances.

Rarely in modern life does a man develop such a relationship with an inanimate object. But then, who says a dangerous-game rifle is inanimate? I, for one, believe a rifle has a soul that is compounded of equal parts that include the skill of the maker, the love of its owner, and its tally on animals it has faced. Such a rifle carries its soul with it, from owner to owner, outliving many, outlasting them all. I am reminded of a particularly worn and weathered Manton .470 carried by Derek Hurt when I hunted with him in Tanzania. The rifle was made in the early twentieth century and may have been close to a hundred years old when we climbed down into a ravine after two old Cape buffalo bulls. Who knows how many times that rifle had been in a similar situation? Who knows how many Cape buffalo it had faced, how many lions it had killed, how many elephants or wounded leopards it had downed in thick bush?

It is impossible to tell. But pick up that rifle, open its slick action, run your hands over the receiver with its well-rubbed engraving, its color hardening gone, its stock scratched and worn, and it is equally impossible to not feel a connection with all of hunting for the last hundred years.

Terry Wieland
Peterborough, Ontario

Section I

GENESIS

The Rifle to 1898

To me the rifle has always been the most romantic of all weapons. . .
Jack O'Connor

The era of the modern dangerous-game rifle began in 1898, when John Rigby of London introduced the .450 Nitro Express (NE). Everything that went before was merely a prelude to this event—although it was a prelude that lasted almost four hundred years. Until the advent of the .450 NE, no cartridge rifle as we know it was fully adequate for animals as large as elephant under any and all conditions. When the .450 arrived on the scene, everything that went before was rendered obsolete.

It is a strange quirk in the history of firearms that the dangerous-game rifle was almost exclusively a British development because only the British hunted dangerous game on a regular basis. Their empire included India and other parts of the Far East, with tigers, lions, leopards, and other assorted large animals, as well as an ever-increasing share of Africa, with its elephants, Cape buffalo, lions, leopards, rhinoceros, hippos, and crocodiles. There were British army officers who hunted for sport while on leave, but there were also professional ivory hunters, game-control officers, and an increasing number of professional hunting guides. While other countries had colonies, none had the sheer scale of demand that the British gunmakers enjoyed.

Rigby's .450 was a modification of an existing blackpowder cartridge. Charged with the newly introduced smokeless powder, it launched a 480-grain bullet at 2,150 feet per second—performance unheard of up to that time. The addition of smokeless powder was the final piece of a puzzle gunmakers had been piecing together since the first attempt at rifling a barrel almost four hundred years earlier.

The concept of improving accuracy and increasing range by imparting spin to a projectile has been understood for thousands of years—ever since man first put fletching on an arrow. The idea that the same principle would work with a spinning lead ball was not revolutionary, and several gunmakers arrived at it around the same time (circa 1500 A.D.). The chasm between concept and practical application, however, was vast, and no serious progress was made toward a true rifle for the next three hundred years. Similarly, the idea of loading a gun from the breech rather than the muzzle first occurred several centuries before it could be applied in practice.

The problem was that neither rifling nor breech-loading could evolve by themselves. There was no single solution just waiting for the application of one brilliant mind. Instead, many different facets of firearms evolved, bit by hesitant bit, until all came together as a unit. The generally accepted date for when they did so is 1867. In that year, the breech-loading cartridge rifle finally and irrevocably assumed command of the firearms world.

* * *

Between 1500 and 1898, every aspect of firearms technology followed its own meandering path to perfection: barrel steel—from iron, to Damascus, to fluid steel; rifling—shape, depth, and rate of twist; projectiles—lead ball or elongated bullet; bullet material—pure lead, tempered lead or alloy; ignition systems—matchlock, wheel lock, flintlock, cap lock, self-contained cartridge; gunpowder—from black to smokeless. Muzzleloaders eventually gave way to breechloaders. Every one of these factors depends on some or all of the others.

Meanwhile, as gunmakers in Europe fiddled with rifling and lead alloys, hunters and soldiers were heading for parts unknown—India and Africa, in the case of the British—with the need to hunt animals to live. Some hunted ivory, others cleared lions and Cape buffalo off land for cultivation. The Dutch settled the Cape of Good Hope in 1648, and for the next two hundred years hunting big animals was done with muskets, propelling whatever objects could be stuffed down the barrel. Not surprisingly, while many animals died, many hunters did as well.

Those who hunted elephant for survival or profit quickly realized that the more power they had in their hands, the better. With a muzzleloader, the answer was fairly simple: Shove more powder down the bore to increase velocity. And, the larger the bore, the heavier the lead ball that could be thrown from it. The result was the development of behemoth muzzleloaders: 2- and 4-bore guns that fired lead balls weighing up to a half-pound, with up to twenty drams of black powder behind them. A "2-bore" uses a lead ball weighing a half-pound, a "4-bore" uses balls of a quarter-pound, and so on. A four-ounce lead ball is 1,750 grains; 20 drams is 550 grains of black powder. These guns weighed twenty to twenty-five pounds, but even so the recoil was overwhelming. Because they were accurate only in the broadest sense, hunters needed to get to within a few yards of their quarry. And, because they were so close and had only one shot, they insisted on all the power they could get to immobilize the beast and keep from being stomped.

Tales of the old hunters are replete with frightening accounts of encounters with large animals and no less frightening accounts of the effect of recoil.

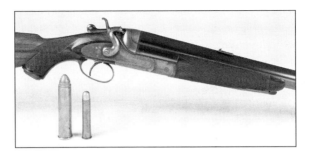

Four-bore single-barrel hammer rifle by Thomas Bland, typical of the huge guns used for dangerous game during the blackpowder era. Heavy bullets with massive charges of powder were the only way to achieve killing power, and the recoil of these beasts was legendary. *Courtesy Holland & Holland*

Frederick Courteney Selous was battered by some poorly made big guns early in his hunting career and developed a flinch that plagued him for the rest of his life. Then there was William Finaughty, an elephant hunter who killed more than five hundred tuskers with muzzleloaders between 1864 and 1875; he sold his old gun when his hunting days were over and recounted its subsequent career, cutting a swath through a succession of owners:

> *The man Horn to whom I sold it very soon had enough of it, and parted with it to a man named Cunningham who, after having his cheek nearly knocked off by the old muzzleloader's terrific kick, sold it to a Mr. Saunders who had his eye damaged for life with it. The last white man I heard of as its proud owner was poor old Blanch, who, I was informed, used to tie a three-pound bar of lead to the muzzle to keep it from jumping up, when fired.*

Finaughty said the gun did its best to knock him out of the saddle (he always hunted from horseback), but he had learned its peculiarities and could counter the recoil to some extent.

> *Still, what could one expect with a gun of that ancient pattern, whose charge was a handful of black powder and a bullet weighing something like a quarter of a pound?*

In spite of the battering, professional ivory hunters were not about to give up their big blasters in favor of any newfangled thing that came along. With few exceptions, they were very conservative in their choice of weapons because they knew that one slip could cost them their lives. Hideous recoil was vastly preferable to being gored or trampled.

* * *

Most accounts of rifle development during this period focus on James Purdey and his coining of the term "express" in 1856 to describe his high-velocity rifles. The express rifles were smaller of bore and lighter of bullet, very accurate with a flat (for the time) trajectory, and they caught the public imagination. However, a parallel and equally important development in the history of dangerous-game rifles was the remarkable partnership that grew up, from 1860 to 1890, between Sir Samuel Baker and the fledgling firm of Holland & Holland.

Sir Samuel White Baker was the greatest sportsman of the Victorian Age. He was a hunter, explorer, and adventurer; he was also a serious naturalist and ballistician, and a prolific author who produced some of the most enduring works on hunting, especially African hunting, ever written.

Baker was born into money in 1821, began hunting virtually from the moment he leapt from his crib, and never stopped. At the age of nineteen, he made his first serious contribution to the world of firearms when he persuaded George Gibbs, the Bristol gunsmith, to make him a rifle the likes of which had never been seen before. At the time, it was believed that only small charges of powder could produce accuracy; Baker believed in big bullets, with bigger charges of powder. His Gibbs fired a four-ounce conical bullet, propelled by 16 drams (437 grains) of black powder. Its rifling consisted of two grooves; the projectile had two corresponding belts and was wrapped in a greased silk patch for smooth passage down the bore. This beast had a thirty-six-inch barrel and weighed twenty-one pounds.

"An extraordinary success attended this rifle, which became my colossal companion for many years in wild sports with dangerous game," Baker wrote, a half-century later, in his valedictory (and perhaps greatest) book, *Wild Beasts and Their Ways.*

In between, Baker hunted tigers in Ceylon, killed elephants from horseback in Africa (armed only with a saber, if you can imagine), was married, widowed, and, during a hunting trip to the Balkans with an Indian maharajah, purchased a companion in a white-slave market. Florence Maria Finnian von Sass became his constant companion, and together they searched for the source of the Nile, hunted throughout Abyssinia, governed the Sudan, fought the slave trade— well, you get the idea.

Baker never lost his deep interest in rifles and what made them work, especially in terms of dangerous game. He was always looking for a better gun and, equally vital, a better bullet.

Meanwhile, in London in 1837, a tobacconist named Harris Holland pursued his own interest in firearms by opening a gun shop in Bond Street. Exactly how Baker and Holland came together is not known, but come together they did, and Holland became Sam Baker's gunmaker. When nephew Henry Holland came into the firm, he and Samuel Baker became close friends, and together they pursued the development of the big-bore rifle for the biggest (and baddest) animals.

In 1869, Baker ordered a rifle from H&H that would become famous in itself: "Baby" or, in Arabic, *Jenab al Mootfah*—"Child of a Cannon"—was H&H rifle No. 1526, a 3-bore that fired a five-ounce (2,187-grain) bullet.

Sir Samuel Baker believed in heavy bullets, especially for elephants, but he hunted all kinds of game—lions, tigers, rhinos, Cape buffalo—and was serious about digging out bullets to see how they had performed. As Purdey's "express" rifles gained adherents, Baker became more than a little skeptical of them.

> *The Express rifle is a term signifying velocity, and this is generally accompanied by a hollow bullet, which is intended to serve two purposes— to lighten the bullet, and therefore to reduce the work of the powder, and to secure an expansion and smash-up of the lead upon impact with the animal. I contend that this smashing up of the bullet is a mistake. . . .*
>
> *If the animal is small and harmless, this should be the desired result. If, on the other hand, the animal should be large and dangerous, there cannot be a greater mistake than the hollow Express projectile.*
>
> *I have frequently heard persons of great experience dilate with satisfaction upon the good shots made with their little .450 hollow Express exactly behind the shoulder of a tiger... I have also heard of their failures, which were to themselves sometimes incomprehensible.*
>
> *A solid Express .577 never fails if the direction is accurate towards a vital part.*

Sir Samuel Baker persuaded H&H to take the military .577 Snider cartridge and lengthen it to 2¾". This became the .577 Express, which Baker eventually settled on as his favorite all-around rifle. It fired a 650-grain lead bullet at 1,650 feet per second (fps). Baker believed that a properly directed .577 would handle anything, including elephant, and he continued to advocate the use of solid lead bullets. For elephant and other large game, the bullets could be hardened; for soft-skinned, smaller game, they could be left as pure, soft lead. The key, as he said repeatedly, was penetration to the vitals—a bullet that held together, mushroomed, and penetrated.

Henry Holland himself echoed these sentiments in his chapter in *Big Game Shooting* in 1894, the year after Baker's death. He quoted Baker liberally, crediting him with many of the developments that had made H&H one of the pre-eminent rifle makers in the world. And, like Baker, he stressed the importance of the bullet—not just the rifle, or the cartridge—and how it performed on impact. For those who insisted on hollow points, Holland advocated the use of bullets with smaller cavities, which increased the weight, reduced the velocity, and made the bullet tougher, all at the same time.

* * *

The theory and practice of bullets and bores was one thing. The rifles themselves were another.

In 1851, at London's Great Exposition, French gunmaker Casimir Lefaucheux exhibited the first break-action shotgun and pinfire cartridges. Joseph Lang seized upon the idea, and within a few years break-action guns were being produced—and improved upon—by English makers. Each of the features we take for granted today had to be invented and perfected, including the locking system, the hinge pin, extractors and ejectors, the cartridge itself, hammerless operation and a cocking system for the internal tumblers. It is amazing, but all of these were developed in the space of just a few decades.

The first documented self-contained cartridge was the .22 rimfire (now known as the .22 Short), introduced by Smith & Wesson in 1857. The road from a gun that could handle the .22 Short to the .600 Nitro Express was obviously a long one. Once the .22 was established, however, progress came in a flood. By 1867, the cartridge rifle had, for smaller and less truculent game at least, largely supplanted the muzzleloader. In long-range matches, cartridge rifles proved they could hold their own with muzzleloaders in the accuracy department, and they were far faster to reload.

Neither the break-action gun nor the self-contained cartridge was really developed when James Purdey produced his "express" rifle in 1856. It was a relatively small bore for the time—.450 or .500—and had two rifling grooves; originally, these were muzzleloaders and achieved their great velocity by reducing the weight of the bullet. One way to reduce weight was to give the bullet a hollow point which, combined with the extra velocity, made it expand violently upon impact. The result was some astonishing kills. Soon, Purdey express rifles were being used to shoot red stag in the Scottish hills. The name remained even as muzzleloaders gave way to breechloaders.

Black powder was still the propellant, however, and it carried limitations. No matter how much you stuffed into a cartridge case, it was impossible to get velocities much above 1,800 fps. Bullets were all pure lead, or hardened lead of some sort. Powder fouling and lead fouling were both serious problems.

By 1870, the largest black-powder cartridge in use in England was Baker's .577. It was a big cartridge—a 650-grain lead bullet, propelled by 190 grains of black powder—adequate for soft-skinned, (albeit highly dangerous) animals such as lions and tigers, but not considered really enough for elephants in all hands, under all conditions. Even as late as 1894, hunters heading to Africa were advised to take double rifles in calibers such as the .500 BP Express for smaller game, but a single-shot 4-bore or 2-bore—preferably a hammer gun—for the big stuff.

In 1894, in a chapter in the Badminton Library volume *Big Game Shooting*, Sir Frederick Jackson, a noted British hunter in East Africa, described his favorite battery:

> *A single 4-bore rifle, weighing 21 lbs., sighted for 50, 100, and 150 yards,*
> * *shooting 12 drams of powder and a spherical bullet.*
>   *A double 8-bore rifle, weighing 15 lbs., sighted for 100 and 200 yards,*
> * *shooting 12 drams of powder and a spherical bullet.*
>   *A double .500 Express, sighted for 100 and 200 yards, bored for long*
> * *bottle-shaped cases, 'Magnum,' shooting 6 drams of powder and long*
>   *bullets of three kinds—solid, small-hole, and copper-tube.*

* * *

Progress in rifle design came in leaps. Once the principle of a hinged, break-action gun was established, a means was needed to bolt it shut. James Purdey invented the double underlug, which became the standard method of bolting side-by-side guns. It was a breakthrough. With the underlug established, the question became how to operate it quickly and smoothly.

The first approach was an underlever of some sort, and gunmakers experimented with various designs. From a double-rifle point of view, the most successful and desirable was the Jones underlever, invented by Henry Jones. It pivots to the side to release the barrels. The locking point is a shallow screw thread that cams the barrels down and locks them tight, and also cams them up to release them. The great advantage of the Jones underlever is that it is mechanically positive and does not depend on springs. As well, it can be operated in absolute silence if need be. Hunters of elephants who might find themselves surrounded by truculent beasts prized that feature very highly, and the Jones underlever continued in use long after the top lever (or "snap action") had become standard on shotguns and most other rifles.

Similarly, hammers remained on big rifles long after smaller guns had been converted to hammerless operation. Hammers could also be operated in absolute silence, and by cocking just one hammer at a time, double discharges were prevented.

All of this feverish development took place between 1850 and 1898. Double rifles evolved in step with double shotguns. This was the heyday of driven shooting in England, with steady demand for improved guns and intense competition among landowners (who raised the birds), guns (who shot them), and gunmakers (who made it all possible). Hence, the speed at which all of these developments took place is not surprising.

Most improvements applied to what we now know as "sidelock" guns—firearms that are descended directly from flintlocks and external-hammer caplocks. The sidelock was (and remains) the aristocrat of double guns and rifles. A "hammerless" sidelock is not really hammerless; it has a tumbler, or internal hammer, which is cocked mechanically as the gun is opened using one of several systems. Some early hammerless models also had small pins that projected out through the side plates, mechanisms that allowed the shooter to cock or uncock the gun manually, but these never caught on.

As rifles became larger and more powerful, sidelock designs for rifles began to evolve in directions slightly different from those taken by shotguns. The actions became heavier and stronger, with certain features designed either to withstand recoil or to stand up to the greater strain of firing cartridges of much higher pressure. Obvious features include bolsters—the elbow-shaped bulge of extra metal down each side of the standing breech and along the action bar that is frequently seen on rifles and also on many Continental shotguns. And there were sideclips—little ears of metal projecting from the sides of the standing breech; they fit into bevelled edges of the barrels and theoretically prevent the barrels flexing from side to side on firing.

Older hammer guns have what are now called "back-action" locks—that is, the plate extends back along the wrist of the stock, and the mainspring is positioned behind the hammer. Newer hammer guns have a "bar action," in which the mainspring is in front of the hammer, and the forward portion of the plate and the spring are inset into the action bar. Obviously, a gunmaker has a choice of whether to weaken the wrist of the stock or the bar of the action in order to accommodate the mainspring. For rifles, with their greater pressure and torque, most gunmakers prefer to sacrifice a bit of the wood of the wrist, and then strengthen it in another way. Consequently, back-action sidelocks became the accepted standard for double rifles (although this is not a universal rule).

The two most common ways of strengthening the wrist of a double rifle were to give rifles a full pistol grip, which is thicker than the traditional English straight stock, and to lengthen the top strap down the grip and up over the comb. Henry Holland said this was originally Samuel Baker's idea—another example of how practical field experience was put to use by English gunmakers. Similarly, the lower tang from the trigger guard was often extended down the pistol grip and married to the metal grip cap. These two long strips of metal reinforced the grip and gave it greater strength to withstand recoil. Stockmakers say inletting these tang extensions is enough to give one a serious drinking problem, especially when working with an exhibition-grade walnut stock worth thousands of dollars, a case where a slight miscalculation will render the blank worthless.

The Anson & Deeley boxlock action—an inside view of the Westley Richards classic. Simple, strong, and eminently adaptable, when it was introduced in 1875 the A&D revolutionized gunmaking in general and riflemaking in particular. *Courtesy Westley Richards*

Today, these features are generally found only on best-quality custom rifles, but in the halcyon days of the late 1800s—when gunmakers' skills were great, their pride in their work was greater, and labor costs were low—they were routinely used even on rifles made for the trade or to be crated up and sent to the colonies.

* * *

The most significant single development in double-rifle mechanisms took place in 1876, when two gunmakers employed by Westley Richards of Birmingham started with a blank sheet and designed, from the ground up, a completely new action for side-by-side double guns. William Anson and John Deeley looked at the existing state of the art, which was the breech-loading, break-action hammer gun, and envisioned an action that would have its hammers inside the frame, hammers that would be cocked automatically when the action was opened.

The resulting design, British patent #1756, came to be known as the Anson & Deeley boxlock, and in the 130 years since it was introduced, it has become the most-manufactured mechanical device in history. A&D boxlocks have been produced in dozens of countries and have been in continuous production throughout that time. It is impossible to estimate accurately how many million have been made. Although the vast majority of these have been shotguns, a large number have been double rifles in calibers ranging from .22 rimfire to .600 Nitro Express.

The A&D boxlock revolutionized double-gun design, but not because it immediately displaced all the hammer guns then in use. Far from it: External hammer guns remained popular for years thereafter. The boxlock's barrel-cocking feature, however, could be adapted to hammer guns, and was in several ways. First came the self-cocking hammer gun, a delightful variation of which—alas—there are all too few in existence. It takes but a moment's thought to realize all the advantages inherent in such a design, especially for the big-game hunter: having two barrels instantly ready to fire after reloading; being able to carry a loaded rifle with the hammers down or at the half-cock position (very safe when using gunbearers and more than one rifle); and being able to cock and fire one barrel at a time, if the rifle developed a tendency to double (always a possibility, especially under rough conditions).

More significant, however, the A&D cocking mechanism provided the opportunity to move the hammers from the outside of the sideplates to the inside, thereby creating the modern sidelock. Although the Prince of Wales (later King Edward VII) described a hammerless gun as "a spaniel without ears," and stuck with his treasured hammer guns for years thereafter, the hammerless gun in both sidelock and boxlock form steadily took over.

With hammers no longer cocked manually, there arose the need for some sort of internal safety mechanism. Safeties had been around for years, in the form of external sliding latches that blocked each hammer; now, the safety also moved inside the gun. It was not long before the safety on double guns took the form we know today: a piece of metal that blocks the sear and that is applied automatically when the barrels are dropped. The catch is in its natural home on the tang behind the top lever, where it can be pushed back and forth by the thumb of the shooting hand. Automatic safeties are standard on English double shotguns, but not on double rifles; however, an automatic safety can easily be disconnected by a gunmaker, to suit the shooter's preference. True to form, W. W. Greener adopted the boxlock as his own (being a good Birmingham boy), but developed his own safety, which operated the same way but incorporated the catch on the left panel, behind the frame. This could hardly be less convenient, and while they worked well and were beautifully made, such safeties remain a Greener affectation. As Greener was a rifle specialist and made many boxlock double rifles, it is not unusual to find such guns sporting this style of safety.

For bolting the barrels closed, Purdey's double underlug became the standard. The top lever as we know it today became possible when William Middleditch Scott invented his spindle, which connects the top lever to the sliding lugs and is powered by a spring. This was known as a "snap action," and it eventually relegated all other mechanisms to the scrap heap. The snap action worked even on double rifles (it is the standard method today), but the Jones

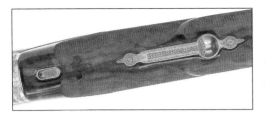

William Anson and John Deeley, inventors of the Anson & Deeley boxlock action, separately and together invented several other features that have become standard. The two most common methods of detaching a fore-end are the Deeley latch (shown here on a Heym rifle) and the Anson plunger, a spring-loaded button on the end of the fore-end. The Deeley latch is generally favored when a larger fore-end is used, but neither has an advantage as to strength. *RCMP Photo*

underlever remained popular for rifles long after the top lever came into use. Here is what Henry Holland had to say on the subject:

> *Different kinds of "action" are constantly being invented for double-barrelled rifles, but very few, if any, have the sterling qualities of the old double-grip lever, especially when used for rifles shooting heavy charges. No doubt snap-actions of various kinds are made which are sufficiently sound to stand the strain of the charges fired, especially if the "body" be long and deep, but none of them have the binding down power of the grip lever, which is really a kind of screw grip.*
>
> *Should there be a piece of cap or other obstruction between the action and the barrels, the grip lever will have sufficient power to force the action to close and allow the rifle to be fired; and the same thing applies when a very tight cartridge, or one with too thick a rim, requires to be forced home. Now, under the same circumstances, a rifle with a snap-action could not be closed at all, or, at all events, only with great difficulty and with unusual force, because all spring bolt systems require that the barrels should close up freely upon the action before the bolt can move into its proper position for fastening down the barrel.*

Those are Henry Holland's words, but they reflect Sir Samuel Baker's voice of experience from decades of hunting the most dangerous animals under the worst conditions, when reliability was everything.

Many of the largest black-powder cartridge rifles, such as the .577s and the 8- and 10-bore guns firing round lead balls, stuck with the Jones underlever as a positive, reliable, and silent means of opening and closing the breech, independent of breakable springs. With the camming feature that pulled barrels down into position, the Jones underlever afforded the shooter some extra leverage in seating slightly oversized cartridges or coping with powder fouling in the chamber. Even today, many double rifles remain equipped with the Jones under-lever. It is an extremely durable mechanism, and where it lacks the speed of the top lever in opening and reloading, it makes up for this deficiency in reliability. It is notable that a few years later, when W. J. Jeffery introduced the mammoth .600 Nitro Express, the majority of the firm's rifles in that caliber, even as late as 1929, were made with underlever actions.

* * *

Thus evolved the basic sidelock design that endures to this day. Other features and modifications came and went.

The Purdey sliding double underlug is very strong—more than strong enough on its own to handle the stresses of firing even the behemoth .700 H&H that was introduced in 1988. In 1870, however, this design was not fully understood and more than one gunmaker pursued the idea of the "third bite"— an additional bolt to augment the Purdey system. The most common approach was some form of rib extension that seats in the frame. Purdey developed its own hidden third bite, a metal extension located between the extractors, one that seats in a recess in the standing breech. It is an elegant addition to a rifle or shotgun, but is not needed for strength. Westley Richards pioneered the use of the "doll's head," a rib extension (shaped as its name suggests) that fits tightly into an opening in the frame. And P. Webley created the "Webley screw-grip treble bite," which uses a rib extension and an interrupted thread on the spindle to cam the barrels down into position.

The most widely accepted design of them all was William Wellington Greener's crossbolt. A flat steel rib extension fits into a slot in the standing breech. A round bolt inside the fences, operated by the top lever, moves at right angles to the bore and slides into a round hole in the rib extension, holding it firmly in position. This bolt holds the barrels down, while the walls of the slot hug the extension and prevent the barrels moving from side to side. Greener himself was the biggest promoter of his crossbolt, and there is no doubt it is strong: In fact, experiments have shown that it is sufficient by itself to hold an action closed, with no underlugs at all. The crossbolt became a standard feature on boxlocks made in Birmingham, and German gunmakers seized upon it with joyous cries. The Kersten fastener, a kind of double crossbolt found on Merkel over/unders, is really just an adaptation of the Greener concept.

Whether because it was redundant, or because it was a Birmingham development, London gunmakers such as Holland & Holland, Purdey, and Boss never took to the Greener crossbolt. For that matter, they never had much enthusiasm for the boxlock except as an economically priced alternative to their blue-blooded sidelocks, and this applied to shotguns as well as rifles. To a great extent, the age-old rivalry between working-class Birmingham and upscale

The Greener crossbolt, invented by W.W. Greener of Birmingham in the late 1800s, has become a standard item on all kinds of continental double guns, although in Britain it is generally not found on 'best' guns. It is shown here on a Merkel sidelock. While not necessary purely for strength, the Greener crossbolt has been proven to be amply strong on its own, without underlugs,  so it adds insurance as well as keeping the barrels from flexing side to side under recoil, a function usually performed by sideclips. This rifle has both, which, while not unusual, is the rifle equivalent of wearing a belt and braces.

Courtesy GSI

 The Purdey double underlug, invented by James Purdey & Sons during the tumultuous few decades of side-by-side development in the mid-1800s, has become the cornerstone of side-by-side design everywhere. Amply strong on their own for any double rifle, this has not stopped various makers (Purdey included) from seeking the ideal "third bite," of which the Greener crossbolt (also included on this Heym rifle) is an example.

RCMP Photo

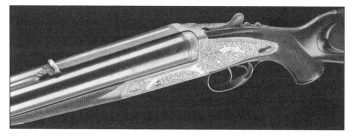

A Holland & Holland 10-bore Paradox gun, made around 1890. This gun is fitted with back-action locks. *Courtesy Holland & Holland*

London dictated the shape of rifles and shotguns that came from their respective makers. If you see an H&H or Purdey double rifle today, it will be a sidelock, while a Westley Richards will almost certainly be a boxlock.

* * *

The question of which action type is superior for double rifles has been asked for a hundred years with no clear answer emerging. From a purely functional point of view, neither action has indisputably demonstrated its superiority. Certain facts are, however, beyond question: One, vastly more boxlock double rifles were made than sidelocks, and two, sidelocks, both new and used, are far more expensive. The latter point leads to the question, why are so few boxlock double rifles being made today? The short answer is that building a best-quality boxlock is just as expensive as producing a "best" sidelock, so anyone with the money chooses the latter.

In the heyday of big-game hunting in Africa, India, and Asia, double rifles were made by scores of gunmakers, large and small, big names and unknowns. Companies such as the Army & Navy stores in London purchased rifles and shotguns from various companies and put their name on them. A used Army & Navy double rifle can be a prize indeed, because it may have been made by Westley Richards, Rigby, John Wilkes, Greener, or W. J. Jeffery. Puzzling out the origin of an Army & Navy from its configuration and action features is a lot of fun—not always possible, but always intriguing. The point is, most of these are boxlocks.

The Manton .470 that belongs to Derek Hurt is a quite plain boxlock rifle, but it is extremely well made, pushing a century old and still going strong. But then, so are many sidelock rifles.

While the argument goes back and forth, most authorities agree that an Anson & Deeley boxlock has the edge in overall strength, primarily because the stock, where it fastens to the frame, is thicker. Proponents of the sidelock insist that its frame is stronger because less metal is cut away to accommodate the sear and tumblers, but where strength really counts is in the action bar and the right angle where it meets the standing breech. This is where metal is cut away to accommodate the spring in a bar-action sidelock, which is why most are back-action locks. Still, even this area can be beefed up by adding a bolster.

Arguments abound in favor of both boxlocks and sidelocks, and since none has gained a real ascendancy, it is reasonable to assume that neither demonstrates any meaningful superiority. If one had, when it comes to rifles for dangerous game, the loser would have long since disappeared. And that has not happened.

For the buyer of a double rifle today, the choice between boxlock and sidelock is almost always determined by what is available and what that buyer can afford—not by any mechanical advantage of either. As with shotguns, however, one rule is set in stone: A good boxlock is better than a poor sidelock.

Nitro Express!

The .450 Cordite Express is the largest bore recommended. The energy developed by this powerful cartridge is so enormous that there is a difficulty in utilizing all of it to advantage in the killing of the animal. It is suitable for elephant, rhino, lion, tiger . . . Recoil considerable, but not too severe.

                                                              W. W. Greener, 1910

The cartridge that changed everything: Rigby's .450 Nitro Express 3¹/₄".

In 1898, John Rigby & Co. introduced the .450 Nitro Express and changed the hunting world. The .450 NE was not so much the beginning of a new era as the end of the old one—the culmination of a long quest in which all the threads finally came together. The .450 NE delivered a 480-grain jacketed bullet at 2,150 fps, ballistic performance unheard of at that time. And in the century-plus since that momentous event, nothing even remotely comparable has occurred. There has been refinement and tinkering—nothing more.

From today's vantage point, Rigby's development seems obvious to the point of being inevitable: The company simply took an existing black-powder cartridge that fired a 365-grain bullet at 1,700 fps, and put in a heavier bullet and smokeless powder. But this simple development had far-reaching consequences.

First, it rendered obsolete every big-game cartridge then in use for dangerous animals, as well as dooming all the huge, old muzzleloaders. It was followed very quickly by other cartridges converted from black powder to nitrocellulose (the "nitro" in nitro express), including the .500 NE in both its 3" and 3¹/₄" configurations. The old .577, which had been a standby since it was adapted from the original 24-bore muzzleloader configuration, became the .577 NE—an elephant cartridge extraordinaire. Sam Baker would have loved it! Going the other way, several forms of the .400 were created, including a .450 necked down.

It would seem that no other cartridges were needed, but commercial reality dictated otherwise. The London gun trade was fragmented, consisting of dozens of small and medium-size companies, and cartridge developments were, unless designated otherwise, proprietary. The effect was similar to the patent laws. Even where a cartridge was not proprietary, companies labored under a "not-invented-here" syndrome that demanded they introduce their own bigger, better, faster, heavier (or whatever) cartridge, available only in their own rifles (with ammunition available only from them, as well).

Technical difficulties also arose. The old black-powder cartridges used very thin brass, and the different pressure curve of smokeless powder caused some sticking problems with some cases, in some chambers. In 1902, the ammunition company Eley Brothers solved the problem by introducing a cartridge of their own—the .450 No. 2—which was longer than the .450 NE, with heavier walls and a very thick rim. The roomier case ensured lower pressures, while the heavier brass prevented overexpansion and sticking. The design was released to the trade, meaning that any gunmaker could chamber it. The cartridge was immediately adopted by many smaller riflemakers who could not afford to develop their own proprietary designs, which is why today the .450 No. 2 is synonymous with lesser names such as Army & Navy.

Holland & Holland developed a .450 of its own by taking the .500 NE 3¹/₄" and necking it down. It was called the 500/450. In physical size it fell between the other two .450s, but ballistically the three are virtually identical.

Things might have ended right there had politics not intruded.

From 1871 to 1888, the Martini-Henry was the standard-issue British Army rifle, as well as a popular civilian single-shot. It was chambered for the .577/.450, a black-powder cartridge. Although by 1905 the army had adopted the Lee-Enfield rifle with its .303 British cartridge, there were still tens of thousands of Martini-Henry rifles kicking around the colonies—all over Africa, India, and in lesser outposts like Burma and Ceylon. Not all of these possessions were happy in their status as part of the British Empire. In India and the Sudan, especially, there was unrest and the threat of insurrection. Fearful that all the Martini-Henry rifles could be turned against them, the British government banned the importation of .450-caliber rifles in those colonies.

In the heyday of British India, the double was the classic tiger rifle. The hunter is unidentified, but the rifle is a .375 Holland & Holland Royal. Such is fame.

Courtesy Westley Richards

The date usually given for this edict is 1907, although there is evidence that it took effect in some areas as early as 1905. Even today, there is no completely satisfactory explanation of exactly what happened or why. Obviously, a .450 No. 2 cartridge would not have fit in a .450 Martini. Were the authorities afraid rebels would pull the bullets from commercial ammunition and reload Martini cases? Far-fetched as it seems, that is the only explanation that is remotely plausible. Whatever the reason, .450s were effectively banned.

India was critical. It was the jewel in the British imperial crown and a major gun market, involving the wealthy rajahs as well as British officers and civil servants. No colony in Africa even approached India's importance: the Sudan was not a prime hunting destination, Kenya was in the very early stages of settlement, Tanganyika was still a German possession, and South Africa was almost denuded of really big game. But India was vital, so British rifle makers fell over themselves to design new cartridges that would be legal there.

Almost all began with the .500 NE case, either the long or short version. H&H took its existing 500/450 and necked it up to .465. Westley Richards took the .500 3" case and necked it down to .476. Eley took its .450 No. 2 and necked it up to .475. And, according to legend, Joseph Lang took the .500 3 1/4", necked it to .470, and produced the most famous of them all: the .470 Nitro Express. None of them was one whit better than the others ballistically, although later idiosyncracies in bullet type differentiated them in terms of performance. When Joseph Lang released his .470 to the trade, however, allowing everyone to chamber it, with ammunition freely available from Kynoch, its fortune was made. While Westley Richards chambered its .476 NE and Holland & Holland its 500/465, almost everyone else adopted the .470. Most significantly, John Rigby made the .470 its standard chambering rather than developing a successor to its own .450.

A few other cartridges came along. One example is the .475 NE, which is a straight-walled case similar to the .450 NE, but scaled up. There is evidence it was introduced around 1900, before the .450 ban, as a competitor to the .450, but exactly who originated it is unknown. Although it is an excellent cartridge— a 480-grain bullet; 2,175 fps; 5,040 ft. lbs.—the chambering is rare.

While most of the development was concentrated on cartridges heavier than .450, there were .400 calibers, as well. Some were original black-powder cartridges, others were converted from BP to NE. Still others were necked down from larger rounds. The most famous was the .450/400—as its designation implies, Rigby's great cartridge necked down. The most renowned devotee of the .400 was Jim Corbett, the hunter of man-eating tigers and leopards in India. Corbett used, at various times, a .500 Express (black powder), a .450/400 double rifle, and a .275 Rigby (7x57 Mauser) bolt action. The .400s were considered good lion cartridges, and probably the best all-around caliber, though most thought they were not quite enough for Cape buffalo or elephant.

Finally, there was the largest of the large: the .600 Nitro Express. This monster was a W. J. Jeffery development, introduced in 1901. William Jackman Jeffery was a London gunmaker who specialized in rifles, and his .600 was frankly intended to be the last word in elephant cartridges. The case was a new design, not based on any black-powder cartridge, and it hurled a 900-grain bullet at 1,950 fps. Rifles for the .600 were heavy—weighing up to sixteen pounds—and from the beginning they were the tool of the professional ivory hunter. Even then, such a weapon was not an everyday rifle; it was carried by a gunbearer and saved for the most dire of circumstances: wounded animals and thick brush. Given the .600's legendary status, it is surprising that so few were ever manufactured: According to H&H, who has added them up, barely a hundred were made, by all makers in all configurations.

Ironically, the .600 overshadowed the .577 NE, even though the .577 was older, had longer lineage, and was made by more companies in much greater numbers. The .577 fired a 750-grain bullet at 2,050 fps and was renowned for its penetration. Both rifles and ammunition for the .577 were lighter than for the .600, and it was more practical in every way. But for the man who wanted the ultimate, the .600 was it.

By 1910, the double-rifle nitro-express lineup was set for years to come and could be grouped generally as follows: The .400 was an all-around rifle, good for

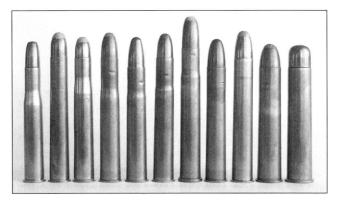

Major players of the nitro-express era, from left: 450/400 Jeffery (3"), .450 NE, 500/450, 500/465, .476 NE, .470 NE, .475 No. 2, .500 NE 3", .500 NE 3¹/₂", .577 NE, .600 NE.

Major cartridges introduced for Mauser 98 magazine rifles, in order of appearance: .404 Jeffery (1909), .416 Rigby (1911), .505 Gibbs (1911), .375 H&H (1912), .500 Jeffery (circa 1925).

lions and the occasional bigger game. The .450-470 class dominated and was good for everything up to elephant in almost any situation. The .500 NE, both 3" and 3¹/₄", had a small but devoted following, and was a serious cut above the .470. The .577 and .600 were emergency rifles carried by ivory hunters, for critical situations where their everyday .450 was deemed not quite enough.

As new cartridges were developed, new bullet designs also emerged. The conflict of the 1880s, between Baker and the heavy, solid-lead-bullet crowd on the one side, and devotees of light, fast, hollow-point bullets on the other, did not end with the demise of the black-powder cartridges. There was a long period of trial and error in which various bullet designs were tested in the nitro-express cartridges, including hollow points and a number of variations thereon, such as copper-capped bullets. Some worked; many did not.

* * *

The same year the .450 NE arrived, 1898, saw the beginning of a parallel series of developments around a completely different type of rifle: the Mauser 98 bolt action. The Mauser was a magazine rifle, originally a military design, that was the final step in an evolution begun by Paul Mauser many years (and a dozen models) earlier. The 98, adopted by the German army, was the *ne plus ultra* of Mauser's line. It was never refined further. It is the opinion of many gunsmiths and gunmakers even today that no further refinement was possible. The Model 98 was the epitome of the magazine rifle.

The Mauser 98 did not immediately take the hunting world by storm, for a variety of reasons. One was that cartridges comparable to the .450 NE simply did not exist for it (the 98 was originally chambered for the military 8x57, and only later were larger cartridges developed). What's more, it was considerably more difficult to design and adapt a cartridge for the 98 than for a double rifle. Magazine limitations were a problem, as were bolt-face size, feeding, and extraction. Still, German gunmakers began to build hunting rifles on the 98 action almost immediately, and they designed some very large cartridges for it.

John Rigby & Co. became the London representative for Mauser and introduced cartridges of its own. Several other British gunmakers did likewise, and so a smaller but no less lethal line of rimless magazine-rifle cartridges saw the light of day. These included the .404 Jeffery (1909), .425 Westley Richards (1909), .416 Rigby (1911), .505 Gibbs (1911), and .500 Jeffery (exact date unknown).

The most famous and successful of all, however, was Holland & Holland's .375 Belted Rimless Magnum, introduced in 1912. Firing a 300-grain bullet at 2,550 fps, the .375 H&H quickly established itself as perhaps the greatest hunting cartridge of all time.

The nitro-express double-rifle cartridges are rimmed, while all of the magazine-rifle cartridges are rimless; the belted .375 H&H is the lone exception. At least two of the rimless cartridges have rebated rims (a rim diameter smaller than the base diameter), which sometimes causes feeding problems and always feeds controversy.

In terms of dangerous-game cartridges, that was it for almost fifty years. No other development of any real significance occurred until 1956, when Winchester introduced its .458 Winchester Magnum, a straight-walled, belted case whose ballistic performance, on paper, was intended to duplicate the oldest of them all—Rigby's original .450 Nitro Express. While its career has not been without controversy, the .458 is a fine cartridge when loaded to its potential.

Section II

DOUBLE RIFLES

The Great English Double

I have a number of friends in the Nairobi cemetery who put their faith in magazine rifles. I have relied on a Holland & Holland .500 double barrel fitted with 24-inch barrels and weighing 10 pounds, 5 ounces. If it had failed even once, I would not now be writing these notes.

J. A. Hunter

The British firearms industry has always been fragmented, composed mostly of companies that are quite small by modern industrial standards. Makers of double rifles especially have been low-volume, high-quality shops, with Holland & Holland probably the largest of the group.

Historically, some companies were noted for their shotguns while others were rifle specialists, although at one time or another almost everyone made almost everything. A man who was a Purdey client for shotguns would naturally go to Purdey when he wanted to order a rifle, whether it was a single-shot stalking rifle for Scotland or a .500-bore elephant stopper for a sojourn in Kenya.

Relatively few firms made their name in rifles, and even fewer were noted as either innovators or inventors of rifles and cartridges. In double rifles, the major names were (and are) Holland & Holland, John Rigby, and Westley Richards. W. J. Jeffery was prominent until its absorption by H&H. In magazine rifles (i.e., Mauser bolt actions), the big names were Rigby, H&H, George Gibbs of Bristol, Westley Richards, and Jeffery.

James Purdey & Sons, and Boss & Co. both made rifles of extraordinary quality, but neither became dominant in rifles. In part this was because they catered to the very wealthy. Rigby, Westley Richards, H&H, Jeffery, and Gibbs were names you found on working rifles in the hands of professional hunters as well as those of their moneyed clients.

Holland & Holland

Holland & Holland has been in business in London since 1837 at a variety of addresses in or around Mayfair in the West End. As previously noted, its founder, Harris Holland, was a tobacconist who entered the gun business largely by accident. His guns were engraved "H. Holland." Later, he brought his nephew Henry into the firm, and H&H was born. It has been a fixture in the London trade ever since.

The firm's close relationship with Sir Samuel Baker, from 1860 to his death in 1893, was a tremendous benefit. Their joint development of the .577 Express has already been mentioned, as well as innovations such as the over-the-comb top strap. But H&H acquired more than Baker's hunting experience and knowledge of firearms. Sir Samuel White Baker was a national hero and an eminent Victorian, and being known as his gunmaker gave H&H great prestige. He helped the firm become the force in rifles that it has been for the last 150 years.

If H&H is almost always placed behind James Purdey when shotguns are discussed, it can rightly claim to have been the largest, most innovative, and influential of all the British custom rifle makers. Over the years, the company has manufactured sidelock double rifles and boxlock doubles (although not many). Its Mauser bolt actions are legendary, and H&H designed and still makes its own quick-detachable scope mount, similar in concept to the German claw mount.

Holland & Holland has one other claim to fame that should not be dismissed: Its sidelock pattern has become the standard for shotguns and rifles around the world. At one time, there were many different sidelock designs in use, including the Beesley (used by Purdey), the Boss, and the Woodward, to name the three most famous. Today, the vast majority of sidelock makers on the continent (Spain, France, and Belgium), as well as various resurrected London names, such as Churchill, use a mechanism that is described as "H&H-type," including the optional self-opener. This is a testament to the simplicity and sound design of the H&H action.

J. A. Hunter, one of the most prominent Kenya professionals of the twentieth century, used many different rifles during his career, eventually settling on the .500 Nitro Express as the best for all-around game-control work that involved elephants, Cape buffalo, and rhinos. In his best-selling book *Hunter* (1952) he stated flatly, "In my opinion Holland & Holland are the best in rifle makers. My .500 has never let me down." Tony Henley, another East African professional from the generation that followed Hunter, finished up his career using a well-worn H&H 500/465. Tony did not agree with "J. A." on everything, but he agreed about Holland & Holland.

The 500/465 was H&H's greatest double-rifle cartridge development, but the company also introduced the 500/450. In recent years, the company designed and built the first rifle chambered for the behemoth (there is no other word!) .700 H&H. This cartridge, which fires a 1,000-grain bullet at 2,000 fps, was a special project for a California rifle collector, Bill Feldstein, in

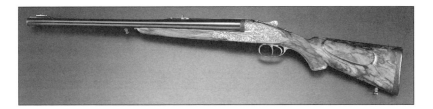

A .700 H&H Royal sidelock double rifle.
Courtesy Holland & Holland

Holland & Holland *Royal de Luxe*, with engraving celebrating the great age of African hunting.
Courtesy Holland & Holland

Right: The new H&H round-action .500 NE is almost austere in its simplicity. *Courtesy Holland & Holland*

collaboration with Jim Bell of BELL brass fame. At last count, H&H had made, or had in progress, two dozen .700s at more than £100,000 apiece (approximately $180,000).

Roger Mitchell, retired chairman of H&H, told me in 1993 that the .700 was good only "for driven mammoths," and that certainly sums up its capabilities. It is overpowered for any game on earth, and it would take a very strong man to carry and use the nineteen-pound rifle. Ammunition costs about $100 a round from H&H, although A-Square will supply it for just $65 a shot. It is not included in this book in any serious way because it does not qualify as a working dangerous-game rifle, no matter what H&H says.

By far, Holland's greatest achievement in rifles was the .375 H&H. It is the finest all-around hunting cartridge of all time, usable on any animal up to elephants; for many years, it was the standard cartridge in Alaska among big-game guides in brown-bear country. Every serious rifle maker has chambered it at one time or another, and it is a standard chambering for most major companies even today, as it approaches its hundredth birthday. The ammunition is the most widely available of any dangerous-game round.

As well, the .375's belted case (which may or may not have been an H&H invention, but the firm is credited with it) has been the basis of more wildcat cartridges, especially big-bores, than any other. The belted version has a brother, the .375 Flanged, which is the same cartridge with a rim, intended for use in double rifles and single-shots. It is loaded to slightly lower pressures and velocities than the belted round, but the differences are so slight as to be meaningless. For a handloader who likes working with cast bullets, the .375 Flanged in a light rifle is delightful. The only reason it is not more popular is that the belted version can be chambered in doubles and single-shots just as easily, and the ready availability of ammunition in the belted configuration is an overwhelming advantage. Although the .375 Flanged is still manufactured, it is not common.

H&H used the belted case as the basis for a whole series of smaller cartridges. The .300 H&H is still around and has a strong following; the high-velocity .244 H&H is all but dead, while the .275 H&H, a twin of the later 7mm Remington Magnum, died because it was a half-century ahead of its time.

In 2000, after years of urging, H&H decided to add two major dangerous-game rounds to its lineup. One is a .400, the other a .465, and both are based on the belted case.

* * *

H&H's efforts to stay up to date go beyond cartridges. Its double-rifle models have varied over the years, and at one time there were two distinct lines—the Royal and the Dominion. Although both rifles and shotguns bore both names, construction was different. Royal shotguns were bar-action, while Dominion shotguns were back-action. In a bar-action lock, the mainspring is forward of the tumbler, along the arm of the lock that is inletted into the bar of the action. In a back-action lock, the mainspring is behind the tumbler.

While there is no functional difference for shotguns, the distinction is important for rifles. Double rifles are almost always back-action, in order to remove as little metal as possible from the bar. Dominion rifles were out-and-out back-actions, but the Royal has varied. The early Royals were semi bar-action: they looked like a bar-action, but the spring was actually behind the tumbler. Since the introduction of the bolstered action in the late 1920s, however, they have been fully back-action. Either way, the Royal has always been an ultra-deluxe rifle.

Although Dominion rifles and shotguns were not intended to be economy models of their deluxe brethren, that is how they were (and are) generally perceived. Dominion-grade firearms seen today are decidedly more subdued, which leads to the conclusion that they were economy models. It must be remembered, however, that they are all older guns, built in an era when decoration was kept to a minimum, even on the Royal.

Throughout the 1990s, as the market for double rifles became hot and then hotter, prices for both new and used rifles skyrocketed. The price of a new H&H Royal was beyond the reach of any but the wealthy, and delivery times were measured in years. This was true of H&H shotguns, as well. Aware that the lengthy waiting time was costing them sales, especially in the vital U.S. market, H&H set out to design a genuine economy-model sidelock rifle and shotgun. It came to be known as the round-action and was initially available in a 12-bore shotgun and a .500 Nitro Express rifle. The price was pegged at about $50,000 for the rifle—less than half the price of a Royal—and delivery times were projected at six to nine months. The plan was to produce the round-actions to a stage of partial completion where they would be kept in readiness for a buyer and then finished to the client's specifications forthwith.

At this writing, the project is still not fully operational, but I have had the opportunity to shoot both the shotgun (in 2002) and the rifle (2004) at the H&H shooting ground near London. At $50,000, the double rifle is hardly in the price range of the average professional hunter, which is unfortunate because H&H has produced a gun that really is a "working rifle"—and I use that term only in the most admiring way. While they have attempted to reduce the cost by such seemingly minor changes as designing a safety catch that can be machined without hand labor, these modifications have not cheapened the rifle. It is made with minimal engraving on the locks, which are case-colored; the walnut stock is nice but not extravagant; subtle and expensive touches, such as a tang that extends down the pistol grip to the grip cap, have been eliminated.

For $50,000 the client gets a simplified, stripped-down double rifle, ready for action. In case you are wondering how much action the new rifle can take, the .500 NE I tested at the shooting ground has, at this writing, had more than 1,000 rounds fired through it and is still as tight as a drum.

Whether the round-action rifle will succeed remains to be seen. It is now in production, according to Steve Denny at H&H. I, for one, certainly hope it does because, at the risk of offending my friends at H&H, I prefer it to the Royal. The reason is, I like working rifles, not ornaments, and too many new doubles—while completely functional—are exactly that.

The H&H Royal, the standard by which every other double rifle is judged today, is both expensive and ornate. Granted, the client determines the extent of engraving and gold inlay, and —to a degree—the level of walnut used, but even in its most basic form the Royal hardly qualifies as a "working" rifle. That is not to say that it is not superbly functional, because it is, but the Royal is simply out of reach for the average professional hunter. Steve Denny points out that at the Safari Club International show every year, professional hunters all stop at the H&H display and drool over the Royal, insist they would love to have one, and, he says, a few even order one. "The Royal is the benchmark for double rifles," Steve says. "It is that simple."

Needless to say, any used double rifle bearing the H&H name commands a premium price, whether it is a black-powder hammer gun or a modern side-lock. As a general rule, the premium is justified if for no other reason than the buyer then has the option of shipping the rifle to H&H for anything from a simple cleaning to a complete refurbishment.

Holland & Holland, it should be pointed out, has a completely equipped factory in Harrow Road, where its rifles are produced from the ground up. Barrel regulation and testing are done by Steve Cranston at the shooting ground outside London, which is managed by Steve Denny. And, of course, there is the gunshop and headquarters in Bruton Street, off Berkeley Square. In other words, H&H has absolute control over every aspect of its rifle production.

W. J. Jeffery

W. J. Jeffery is included as an active name because it has recently been res-urrected. The original company was taken over by Holland & Holland in 1960; for a while after that a few guns and rifles were made with the Jeffery name, but it gradually disappeared. In 2000, Paul Roberts (former owner of John Rigby & Company) acquired rights to the name and began making Jeffery double rifles. At the time of this writing, he had about a half-dozen rifles in progress. Since Roberts is one of the most knowledgeable double-rifle men in the world, the new Jeffery rifles should be extremely good.

William Jackman Jeffery entered the gun business in the mid-nine-teenth century. Boothroyd's *Directory of British Gunmakers* lists no fewer than thirteen gunmakers named Jeffery, most located in Dorset and Surrey, but W. J. was a London man. Among his claims to fame (and there are many), Jeffery has easily the most misspelled surname in the gun business, but per-haps that is understandable since there were also gunmakers in England

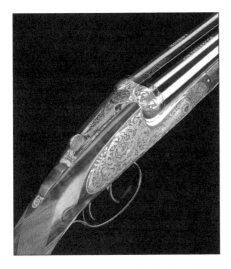

A new W.J. Jeffery sidelock double rifle in 9.3x74R. This is a popular caliber in Europe for red stag and driven boar, but it also makes an excellent leopard rifle. The Jeffery sidelock is available in all calibers.
Courtesy W.J. Jeffery

A new W.J. Jeffery boxlock in .500 NE.
Courtesy W.J. Jeffery

named Jeffries (1), Jefferies (2), and Jeffrey (1).

From the beginning, rifles were W.J. Jeffery's passion and he was a prolific innovator. At the age of twenty-eight he obtained his first patent, for a device to inspect gun bores; this was followed in 1886 with a patent for a vernier and wind-gauge sight adjuster. He went into business first with a partner named Davies and in 1889 set up as W. J. Jeffery & Company. Over the next thirty years, the company had multiple premises in and around Mayfair. In the years immediately following the Boer War (1899–1902), rifle shooting was a passion in England, with clubs springing up all over. The big annual meet was Bisley, where teams from across the empire met to determine the best rifle shots out to 1,000 yards. By 1910, Jeffery had won prizes at the Bisley meetings, and the name was established.

The firm was best known for its vast range of double rifles, dominated by the magnificent .600 Nitro Express, which was introduced in 1901. However, like most London makers, Jeffery made some of everything, and the name may be found on boxlock and sidelock shotguns in grades from good to great, single-shot rifles, double rifles (both boxlock and sidelock), and bolt actions. The company began building rifles on the Mauser 98 almost as soon as it became available, but over the years used various bolt actions; after 1945, Jeffery even made .404s on Enfield P-14 actions.

Jeffery's interest in sights for rifles led to several notable developments. In 1900, W. J. obtained a patent for a "graticule" (English for "reticle") for telescopic sights, one that consisted of a vertical post rather than the popular crosshair. The firm's last patent, according to Boothroyd, was for an aperture sight that attached to the breech bolt of a Mauser rifle. The range of innovations and patents illustrates just how important W. J. Jeffery was to the English rifle trade.

The company's lasting claim to fame, however, is the cartridges it introduced over the years. As an overall lineup, it shades even H&H. The name Jeffery is associated with calibers from the diminutive .225 Rook up to the .600, with great cartridges in virtually every category. The .333 Jeffery, in both rimless and rimmed versions, enjoyed a fine reputation even in Africa. The .400 Jeffery, a rimmed nitro-express cartridge firing a 400-grain bullet, was considered the best all-around cartridge for Africa until the .375 H&H came along. The .404 Jeffery was and is a fine magazine-rifle cartridge for all sizes of dangerous game. Actually a .423 (bullet diameter), the .404 was for many years the .416 Rigby's major rival in its class.

The .600 Nitro Express speaks for itself. For years it was the king of cartridges, and it is still the patriarch of the ultra-bore clan. An interesting note: The Jeffery design for a .600 double rifle was almost always (never say "always" in the English gun trade) an underlever.

The .475 No. 2 (Jeffery) and the .500 Jeffery were not actually W. J. Jeffery developments, but the company did adopt them, it made them popular, and the name lives on. The .500 Jeffery is enjoying a somewhat perplexing but genuine renewed lease on life in the year 2005; Empire Rifles reports that this caliber is its most popular custom chambering. On paper, the .500 Jeffery outpaces the .505 Gibbs (albeit at higher pressures). It was originally a development of Schuler in Germany, where it was known as the 12.5 x 70mm Schuler. Only a very few were made by the original Jeffery company—perhaps twenty-five rifles altogether—but it certainly established a reputation. The .475 No. 2 (Jeffery) is a .475 No. 2 with a slightly heavier and larger-diameter bullet, at a slightly lower muzzle velocity. No one has ever offered even a remotely plausible explanation for its development. The desire just to be different appears to be the most likely reason, and it has caused rifle owners fits ever since as they try to match the right ammunition to the right rifle.

* * *

William Jackman Jeffery died in 1909, but the business carried on—first under his brother Charles and later a nephew, Pierce. The first world war provided an immediate boost in the form of military contracts for sniper rifles and related equipment, but that was followed by the inevitable hangover of reduced civilian business. Through the 1920s and '30s, Jeffery closed showrooms, moved premises, and finally ended up at Golden Square in Soho. The second world war was no kinder, leaving England with a disintegrating empire and Jeffery with even fewer clients. Still, the firm hung on. In 1955, Jeffery relocated to Pall Mall, and its catalog that year offered a sidelock rifle, three A&D boxlocks, and the P-14-actioned bolt rifle in three different calibers, including .404.

In 1960, Jeffery was saved from extinction by H&H. Technically, the two firms "shared premises," but in reality Jeffery was living on the kindness of relatives; although rifles and shotguns were still made with the Jeffery name, there were fewer and fewer each year, and eventually the name became moribund.

In 2000, an investor purchased the Jeffery name and records from H&H, and Paul Roberts once again began producing rifles marked "W. J. Jeffery" at his shop in London, J. Roberts & Son (Gunmakers) Ltd. The firm's rifles are offered in boxlock or sidelock, in .470 NE, .475 No. 2 (Jeffery), and .500 NE, among others. As well, Roberts makes bolt-action rifles built on original Mauser actions, the Czech Brno action, and recent-manufacture Mausers.

John Rigby & Co.

John Rigby is the oldest gunmaker in the English-speaking world, with a long, checkered, and distinguished history. Its symbol—addorsed (back to back) Rs—has graced generations of the finest shotguns and rifles.

The company was founded in Dublin in 1735, originally as a maker of duelling pistols. Rigby opened a shop in London in 1801 and sold off its Dublin operation in the 1890s. For the next hundred years, John Rigby & Company was a London gunmaker.

Although noted for double rifles and superb single-shots, Rigby was forward looking. In the early 1900s, it became the London agent for Mauser, importing Mauser 98 actions. As well as supplying them to other gunmakers, Rigby adopted the bolt action as its own, making complete rifles of outstanding quality and introducing its own proprietary cartridges. According to legend, Mauser began producing its large magnum action at Rigby's request.

Rigby's first major cartridge introduction was the .450 Nitro Express in 1898, but even that has been eclipsed by the big bolt cartridge it unleashed in 1911: the .416 Rigby. This is one of the finest big-game cartridges ever developed. The huge case requires a genuine magnum Mauser action. Ammunition, which was available only from Rigby, was loaded with bullets jacketed in soft

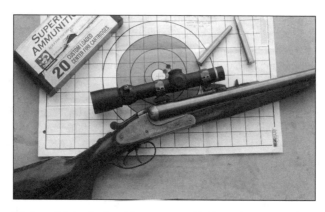

A new Rigby sidelock double in .400 Jeffery (.450/400 3"). Craig Boddington: "The .400 Jeffery 3" is one of the double rifle cartridges that deserves a revival. It has plenty of power for buffalo and such, but much less recoil than the .450-plus cartridges. It's ideal for hunters who want to use a double rifle but are unlikely to do a lot of elephant hunting – although it is certainly minimally adequate for elephant." *Photo by Craig Boddington*

steel; their outstanding performance on Cape buffalo and elephant, and the performance of the soft-nosed bullet on lions, became legendary. Today's love affair with the .416 caliber (there are a half-dozen cartridges of that diameter extant) all began with the .416 Rigby. As well, its case has been the foundation for any number of wildcat and proprietary cartridges of both larger and smaller caliber.

Robert Ruark's professional hunter, Harry Selby, had a battered .416 Rigby that was his favorite lion rifle, and both Jim Corbett and W. D. M. Bell used Rigby .275s, the British adaptation of the Mauser 7x57. Rigby's other major entry in the small-caliber stakes was the .350 in both rimmed and rimless form; today, both are moribund. The .416 Rigby, however, is alive, well, and getting livelier. In the mid-1990s, Paul Roberts (who then owned Rigby) took the .416 case, necked it up, and the .450 Rigby was born. A couple of years later, Roberts sold the company to an American group headed by Geoff Miller, and the operation was moved to Paso Robles, California. There, it continues to make rifles primarily.

Traditionally, Rigby made both sidelock and boxlock double rifles. After the aforementioned .450 ban, it adopted the .470 NE as its standard chambering, but also offered .577 NE. Rigby sidelocks have a distinctive scalloped shape that makes them instantly recognizable. Since moving to California, Rigby double rifles, both boxlock and sidelock, have been built on Merkel frames imported from Germany.

Westley Richards

Westley Richards of Birmingham is Holland & Holland's main rival in English rifle making today. The company was founded by William Westley Richards in 1812 and quickly rose to prominence. Geoffrey Boothroyd, a connoisseur of such nuances, says that although Westley Richards was in Birmingham, it was not a typical Birmingham shop. Its factory was some distance from the traditional "gun quarter," and from the beginning it operated much more like a bespoke London gunmaker. This requires some explanation.

Birmingham is England's "second city" of gunmaking. It has its own proof house, which is newer than London's. The London gunmakers are aristocratic, while Birmingham has always catered more to the common crowd—colonials and such. Birmingham supplied military muskets and rifles, trade guns for the colonies, and inexpensive rifles and shotguns that were sold by hardware merchants and blacksmiths. This does not mean that Birmingham guns were not good. Some were every bit as fine as a London gun, and famous Birmingham names include William Powell, W. W. Greener, and W&C Scott. P. Webley was a Birmingham company, as were BSA (Birmingham Small Arms) and Parker-Hale.

From the beginning, however, Birmingham made its guns differently than London. Instead of having all work done in-house, different operations were carried out by specialty shops, with one small company concentrating on barrels, another on locks, another on blacking (bluing), and so on. On any given day, the gun quarter of Birmingham was alive with shop boys hurrying hither and yon, delivering parts, taking partly finished guns out for work, and bringing finished parts back.

Westley Richards, located at some distance from the gun quarter, operated more like a London firm, with most operations carried out in its own shop and its products made to order rather than mass produced. Under the circumstances, then, it is ironic that Westley Richards made the greatest single contribution to the mass production of side-by-side guns: In 1875, two of its employees, William Anson and John Deeley, patented their design for a "boxlock" action—a break-open side-by-side double, without hammers, that revolutionized the gun business. To this day, the boxlock is a Westley Richards specialty.

In 1815, the company opened a retail outlet in London, in the center of London's "gun quarter," Mayfair. The shop on Bond Street, under the direction of William Bishop (the "Bishop of Bond Street"), predated even H&H in the neighborhood. All through the 1800s Westley Richards was an innovative company, and its specialty was rifles. Geoffrey Boothroyd says that between 1858 and 1866, patents were taken out for drop-down barrels, sliding barrels, top-lever and doll's-head extensions, patent rifle sights, and an early breechloader. In 1872, the company introduced a bolt-action design and a sliding breechblock, and this was followed a few years later by a locking system for a drop-down barrel gun. It was in the midst of this inventive frenzy that Anson and Deeley launched their A&D boxlock, which revolutionized not only shotguns and rifles, but the very way in which guns were made and marketed around the world.

It is worth noting again that over the next 125 years far more double rifles were built on boxlock actions than on sidelocks. By far, most of the working double rifles in the hands of game wardens, ivory hunters, and professional hunters in Africa and India were Birmingham boxlocks, not aristocratic London sidelocks (although London certainly dominated the trade with Indian maharajahs and, later, the oil sheikhs and Russian communist commissars).

Notes Geoffrey Boothroyd: "Westley Richards still builds the finest boxlock guns and when you place your order, you are given the serial number(s) of your gun and you can follow its progress through the factory."

* * *

When .450-caliber cartridges were banned in 1907, the company designed the .476 Westley Richards to take its place. It was quite similar to others of its ilk, except that it was based on the .500 3" case rather than the 3¹/4". This makes the .476 somewhat more compact than the .470 or 500/465, but also raises pressures slightly. Its standard load was a 520-grain bullet, which led some to believe it is actually a .500 (it's not—the caliber is .476), but it was certainly effective. Elmer Keith was a great admirer of Westley Richards rifles and at one time owned five of them, including a .476.

The company's large-bore bolt-action cartridge, the .425 Westley Richards, was less successful. It is a rebated-rim cartridge, which always gives rise to misgivings, but its main drawback was the rifle itself. For years, the company insisted on putting a twenty-eight-inch barrel on its bolt actions, which is much too long for a dangerous-game rifle. The .425 Westley Richards never achieved the popularity of the .416 Rigby, .404 Jeffery, or .375 H&H. The company's small-bore entry, the .318, became very popular in Africa but is almost unknown in America in spite of Robert Ruark's promoting it during one of his Anglophile periods.

In 1998, Westley Richards ventured once more into cartridge design with two calibers based on the immense .700 H&H case: the .500 Rafiki and 700/577 Nitro Express. (*Rafiki*, by the way, is Swahili for "friend.") The .500 fires a 570-grain bullet (2,420 fps, 7,500 ft. lbs.) while the 700/577 launches a 900-grain bullet (2,300 fps, 10,280 ft. lbs.) Obviously, these cartridges are only usable, if that is the word, in a double rifle or single-shot, and exactly what either was supposed to achieve is hard to imagine, aside from getting Westley

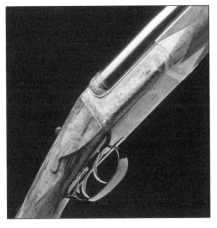

The classic A&D boxlock double rifle – austere, functional, and deadly. This model is used by several African professional hunters, including Richard Newgass and Peter Holbrow. Simon Clode, of Westley Richards, intended this rifle to be as economical as possible, although at a starting price of £23,000, it is still expensive by anyone's standards. It has a doll's head third fastener and replaceable hinge pin, and is completely hand-made at the Westley Richards factory in Birmingham. "It is a proper old-style hunting rifle!" says Clode.

Courtesy Westley Richards

Robin Hurt with his client, Sheikh Sultan bin Jassim Al Thani and a big, old Cape buffalo. The rifle is a Westley Richards droplock .500 NE 3", made in 2000.   *Courtesy Westley Richards*

Richards some ink. Ballistically, the Rafiki does not equal the .500 A-Square, which is an efficient cartridge suitable for a bolt action, while the 700/577 about equals A-Square's .577 Tyrannosaur (although it fires a heavier bullet). These cartridges fall into the same category as the .700 H&H—ballistic curiosities, not dangerous-game rifles.

Today, Westley Richards survives handily and appears to be thriving, with a new factory and showroom in Birmingham and an outlet in the United States. The company makes new rifles and shotguns, sells used firearms, and also has a line of branded ammunition.

Westley Richards will build a sidelock double rifle, a traditional A&D double rifle, or its own specialty, the A&D "droplock" boxlock, with self-contained lock mechanisms that are detachable through a hinged floorplate. Westley Richards droplock rifles are prized like fine sidelocks and priced accordingly.

Unlike most other companies, Westley Richards never objected to putting a single trigger on a double rifle, a feature Elmer Keith prized mightily. Even J. A. Hunter, who favored big guns with two barrels and two triggers, liked it. "I have used their rifles so fitted," he wrote, "with complete satisfaction."

Naturally, Westley Richards also makes bolt-action rifles based on Mauser-type actions. Robin Hurt has one in .425 WR, and has this to say about it: "Simon Clode [of Westley Richards] had this rifle built for me. It is the most beautiful rifle with the smoothest action I have ever used. It is also extremely accurate and when I test-fired it in Birmingham at the WR range, three shots were all in the bull at 50 yards, all touching. The nice thing about the .425 Westley Richards is that it has the power of the .416 Rigby but with much milder recoil."

Such a reduction in felt recoil is the result of a properly designed stock—a business Westley Richards has learned well over the last (almost) 200 years.

William Evans

I have had a soft spot for William Evans ever since 1971 when, as a broke and starving would-be foreign correspondent, I lurked outside the firm's shop on St. James's Street in London, lusting after the wonderful artifacts on display.

William Evans, the founder, worked for both Purdey and H&H before setting up his own business in 1883. From 1900 on the showroom was located in Pall Mall; in 1944, it was struck by a German bomb and relocated to St. James's Street, where it remains to this day. Evans was not a prolific inventor like W. J. Jeffery, but he owned at least one patent, a single-trigger design. A newspaper advertisement from the early 1900s promotes rifles and shotguns. The company offered doubles up to .600 Nitro Express, as well as all kinds of magazine rifles, for which telescopic sights were "a specialty." The company had a large shooting ground outside London and a royal warrant from the Duke of Connaught.

Today, the company is reduced in size from what it was, although it still occupies its charming premises at 67A St. James's Street. Its rifles and shotguns are all made in the trade. As of 2005, its double rifles are sidelocks, ranging in price from £55,000 (in calibers up to .500 NE) and £65,000 for a .577 or .600 NE. William Evans even offers larger double rifles, with prices available upon request.

A William Evans .500 NE 3" from between the two world wars, considered by many to be the golden age of the British nitro-express double. This is one of two William Evans double rifles (the other is a .470 NE) owned and used regularly by professional hunter Robin Hurt.

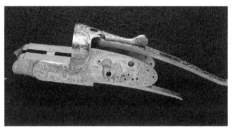

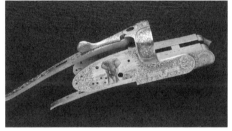

Above & below: William Evans sidelock ejector frame, in the white.

Professional hunter Robin Hurt with his William Evans .500 NE 3", an excellent example of the ideal working double as perceived by the English trade.

A final note: Robin Hurt owns two William Evans double rifles, a .470 NE and a .500 NE; his .500, especially, is a lovely old beast. "A lot of the double rifles used by professional hunters in Africa are made by William Evans," Robin told me. "Both my .500 and my .470 are Evans guns, both were made between the two world wars, and both operate perfectly to this day. William Evans, without a doubt, is one of the finest makers of double rifles even to this day."

Britain Past and Present

The demands of many generations of great hunters have thus influenced the British gun trade, until today their best products stand out alone as the absolute tops in weapons for all dangerous game.

Elmer Keith
Gun Digest, *1952*

Products of the English gun trade in the late 19th and early 20th century: From left, a Westley Richards 12-bore droplock, .470 J&W Tolley hammer rifle, Westley Richards 20-bore Ovundo, Holland & Holland .375, John Rigby .470, and H&H 500/465. The pistols are early Westley Richards flint guns, and the cased gun is a Westley Richards 64-bore (.410) single-shot percussion rifle.

Courtesy Westley Richards

In 1900 there were literally thousands of gunmakers in Britain—or at least, firms that referred to themselves as gunmakers. At one end of the scale stood Birmingham Small Arms (BSA), W. W. Greener, Vickers, and Webley & Scott, with large factories in Birmingham producing firearms by the thousand. At the other end were hardware merchants or blacksmiths in small villages, who ordered guns from Birmingham with their name engraved on the barrel and frame. Today it is possible to find well-made, well-balanced boxlock shotguns with full-coverage engraving, good barrels, and excellent balance, bearing the name of some long-lost Twickenham tinsmith.

In between lay some fine, genuine gunmakers, usually small shops with a handful of craftsmen, often handed down from father to son. Many of these names survive on guns that are still traded: William Rochester Pape (Newcastle), George Coster (Glasgow), and James Erskine (Newton Stewart), to name three.

Over the course of the twentieth century, with two major wars and many lesser ones, the Great Depression, and the disintegration of the British Empire, the number of gunmakers—real and so-called—dwindled steadily. Major names, so numerous in London in 1910, were reduced steadily by death, bankruptcy, and consolidation. Lancaster, Churchill, Atkin, Lang, Grant, Jeffery, Woodward, Watson Brothers—all merged or were taken over, and the names disappeared or became hyphenated. In the 1990s, with the dramatic reincarnation of interest in English doubles, many craftsmen who apprenticed with H&H or Purdey and became highly skilled at their trade went into business for themselves, resurrecting names from the past that still carried some cachet.

Among the reincarnated are E. J. Churchill; Watson Brothers; Atkin, Grant & Lang; Charles Hellis; W. W. Greener; and Cogswell & Harrison. Others, like William Evans and Boss & Company, continued in business throughout but found renewed life in the prosperous '90s. Generalizations are dangerous, but it is safe to say that most of these companies specialize in shotguns, since rifles are highly technical, very tricky, and extremely expensive. Also, they are regulated by law in a way that shotguns are not. A few of these resurrected companies say they will build a rifle; of those that do, almost all would take the order and have it made "in the trade"—that is, by employing specialist out-workers to do highly skilled operations like regulating the barrels.

Another generalization: All of these rifles will be expensive, virtually all will be sidelocks, and almost none will be what could be called a "working double." As the European Union has become more and more integrated economically, and trade barriers have largely disappeared, the way in which these rifles are made has changed dramatically. In Spain, for example, the fine gunmakers have embarked on rifle making as well, but because Spain no longer has rifle-barrel capability, they buy barrels from Austria.

At one time, some of the actions in English double rifles began life as forgings from a small company in the Netherlands that produced what could best be called "kits." These consisted of frames, locks, and barrels from which a skilled gunmaker could produce a double rifle. No longer can one boast of having "the finest English steel" in his big-name London gun. It might be Dutch steel, Spanish steel,

German or Austrian steel. It is all, one should add, perfectly good steel.

In the double-rifle business, the most critical of all skills is the barrel regulator, and barrel regulators who can work with big rifles in Britain today are very, very few. There is Steve Cranston at H&H and Paul Roberts at Jeffery; Bill Blacker is an independent barrel specialist who works in the trade and whose skills are available to all, but he is also in great demand. Westley Richards, of course, has a regulator. But beyond that, the list dwindles rapidly.

Not to be unduly critical of any of the resurrected companies, but what you see is not always what you get. The advent of the Internet, the website, and the digital camera have transformed business, and the gun trade is no exception. Any individual can acquire the name of a long-gone gunmaker, hire a talented website designer, take some photos of nice old guns, and conjure up a price list. The entire company may consist of that and little more. Any orders taken are farmed out into the trade, where the guns are made by independent craftsmen.

There is nothing wrong with this system; in many respects, it is the best way to keep all of these wonderful old gunmaking skills alive. My only caution to anyone looking for a double rifle with which to go hunting animals that bite, gore, stomp, and claw would be that great, great care be taken to ensure that the gunmaker who takes the money knows what he is doing. When you deal with H&H (as a company) or Paul Roberts (as a gunmaker) you can have absolute confidence. With some of the lesser-known companies, references should be checked very carefully.

Herewith is a list of some other English companies still (or back) in business.

E. J. Churchill

The firm of E.J. Churchill is alive and well in High Wycombe, outside London, owned by Sir Edward Dashwood and Mark Osborne. The name was resurrected in the 1990s after lying dormant for some years.

As with so many other English gunmakers, the firm's history is long and tangled, with some claims to fame. The original company, founded in 1891 by E. J. Churchill, was later taken over by his nephew Robert. Robert Churchill became famous in his own right as an author, shooting instructor, and ballistics expert testifying in criminal cases. His most notable achievement was popularizing (for a time) shotguns with short barrels. Churchill's XXV was a gun with twenty-five-inch barrels that Churchill insisted, with a showman's flair, was better than any long-barrelled gun. It ignited a debate that lasted over many a whiskey for many a year. Longer barrels eventually won out.

Robert Churchill died in 1958, and in 1971, E .J. Churchill amalgamated with Atkin, Grant & Lang to become Churchill, Atkin, Grant & Lang. That company "ceased to trade" in 1980, although both major elements were later resurrected.

Between 1980 and 1996 there ensued a legal entanglement worthy of Dickens, regarding the Churchill name and who had rights to what. In 1989, Mark Osborne and Sir Edward Dashwood opened a shooting ground at West Wycombe, and in 1995 they gained rights to the Churchill name. The first new shotgun appeared in 1998—No. 10,000—and I had the honor of breaking the first clay with it when it was still in the white. Later that year I killed the first bird with it (a mallard). It was an absolutely gorgeous gun.

At the time, Churchill's director of gunmaking was Steve Denny. He was also director of the West Wycombe Shooting Ground and guided the establishment of the gunmaking operation, with the workshops located on the Dashwood estate in the nearby town of High Wycombe. Sir Edward, by the way, is descended from one of the founders of the notorious Hellfire Club, and Churchill has a proprietary line of cartridges that includes the "Hellfire" high-pheasant round.

Steve Denny was determined to set E. J. Churchill apart from other London gunmakers. Knowing Americans' infatuation with beautiful walnut, Steve pulled out all the stops to corner a supply of the most spectacular Turkish blanks he could find. Having been sworn to secrecy, I cannot give details on exactly how Steve beat everyone else to the best blanks when they arrived in the United Kingdom, but I can say it involved night flights from small airports, frantic dashes by car, and more than a few dashes of single malt. Denny's efforts paid off, and the first Churchill shotguns were easily the most beautiful guns on display at various exhibitions from the Game Fair in England to the Safari Club in Reno.

As its head gunmaker, Churchill hired Lee Butler, who learned the trade at Westley Richards in Birmingham. Lee's first love is rifles, and shortly after 2000 the company produced its first big double: a .500 NE. As of 2005, Churchill is offering sidelock double rifles at a starting price of £55,000 (about $97,400 U.S.). Would that I had £55,000. . . .

Cogswell & Harrison

Cogswell & Harrison as it now exists claims to be the "oldest London gunmaker," tracing its antecedents to 1770, when Benjamin Cogswell started in business as a pawnbroker. This led first to the trading of guns, then to their manufacture. Edward Harrison came into the business in 1837, and the current name was adopted around 1860. Over the next hundred years, the principals of the company were both ambitious and inventive, getting into other businesses in addition to inventing and patenting gun parts and mechanisms. Some of these patents related to rifles, including different target sights.

Another Harrison, Edgar, invented a trap to throw glass balls, and later one for clay pigeons, and the firm organized trap-shooting competitions at their shooting ground outside London. Not content with the gun business, Cogswell & Harrison ventured into bicycles, fishing equipment, and even tennis rackets.

According to Geoffrey Boothroyd, the company began making double rifles in a wide variety of calibers around 1893—just before the advent of the nitro express—and these became very popular in Africa and India. Cogswell & Harrison survived two world wars and the depression, but by 1957, along with many other smaller London firms, it was falling on hard times. It was taken over by Interarmco, which later absorbed Churchill and Boswell. After 1963, rights to the Cogswell name changed hands several times, and the company was finally liquidated in 1982. Ten years later, it was purchased by a group of investors headed by M.J.E. Cooley. Alan Crewe (formerly of Purdey's) became director of gunmaking, and its operation was set up in Maidens Green, Berks. Since then, the company has acquired the rights to Harrison & Hussey, and to William Moore & Grey.

Cogswell & Harrison rifles are not uncommon on the used-gun market, and given the firm's checkered history it is not surprising that it went through periods when quality was not what it might have been. This is not peculiar to Cogswell & Harrison, by any means; every gunmaker in business for that long, with so many changes in personnel and ownership, is bound to have had off periods. This does not mean their rifles trade at a discount, but they do not command a premium, as H&H rifles do.

Today, Cogswell & Harrison's website states that the company will make double rifles in calibers up to .600 NE. These, it says, are normally built on the Beesley action with its integral self-opener (the same as that used by Purdey), although C&H will build a rifle on other actions, including boxlocks, if the client wishes.

A letter to Cogswell & Harrison requesting information and photographs of newly built rifles elicited this reply from Michael Cooley:

> We have not built double rifles in recent years although we would do so if a customer required it. The material I have therefore is more historical . . . .

That is an honest answer and one that is appreciated. Repeated requests to other companies received no reply or acknowledgement whatsoever.

W. W. Greener

Greener is one of the great names of British gunmaking. There has been a Greener somewhere in the trade since William Greener set up in business in Newcastle in 1829, after apprenticing with John Manton in London. He later relocated to Birmingham. His son, William Wellington Greener, came into the business and surpassed even his father in writing books and invent-

A 16-bore double rifle by W.W. Greener of Birmingham. In the years prior to the development of smokeless powder and the nitro-express cartridges, hunters of dangerous game relied on heavy lead balls flung from oversized bores. A 16-bore fires (theoretically) a one-ounce sphere of lead (437.5 grains), which is small compared to the mammoth 4-bore and 8-bore elephant guns. By today's standards, such a projectile would be marginal for anything more than a white-tailed deer. In the late 1800s, these guns were often used to hunt the large antelope and even, on occasion, the big cats. Greener was a major manufacturer of all types of guns and rifles.   *Courtesy Graham N. Greener*

ing firearm mechanisms.

W. W. Greener has several claims to fame, but the best-known are *The Gun and its Development*, which has gone through a dozen printings since it was first published in 1881, and the Greener crossbolt, a "third bite" involving a round sliding bolt that locks into a rib extension in the receiver. The Greener crossbolt became almost a trademark of all the Birmingham A&D boxlocks that were turned out in the tens of thousands for the lower-end English trade as well as for the colonies. It has been used in shotguns and rifles of all kinds for more than a century and is a fixture of the business today, particularly in Germany. The famous Kersten fastener used on Merkel O/U guns is merely a variation on the Greener.

W. W. was a vastly opinionated man as well as a knowledgeable and talented gunmaker. He was a fierce "Brummy," as natives of Birmingham are known, and when the A&D boxlock was invented in 1875, he took it to his bosom and made it his own. Well, not quite. Greener began marketing an action called the "Facile Princeps," which so resembled the Anson & Deeley that, in 1880, Westley Richards sued for patent infringement. Greener won the case and went on to show that a boxlock could be every bit as good a "best" gun as any sidelock. By 1923, Greener claimed that its factory in Birmingham was the largest maker of sporting arms in the world.

Greener loved rifles, especially single-shot target rifles, and he produced thousands of Martini-Henry rifles for target shooting and hunting, from .22 RF on up. After W. W. Greener's death in 1921, the company was managed by his descendants until 1965, when it was finally sold to Webley & Scott. Eventually, all were acquired by another company, which sold the W&C Scott name to

Farquharson falling-block rifle by George Gibbs of Bristol, fitted with a modern scope. This rifle has the very rare "Selous" reinforced grip. While undoubtedly strong,

the steel plate became very hot in the tropical heat, which did not make the rifle any more comfortable to shoot. Gibbs specialized in rifles, and was the originator of the .505 Gibbs cartridge. *Courtesy Holland & Holland*

Holland & Holland, while the Greener name returned to Graham Greener, great-grandson of W.W., and author of the company history.

The current firm of W. W. Greener is run by Graham Greener, and it has a small operation near Birmingham. The company offers to make double rifles in either sidelock or W. W.'s own Facile Princeps boxlock action. Current production is listed as .375 H&H rifles, but the company says it can make larger calibers as well. Greener even has a falling-block single-shot in the offing.

According to Mr. Greener, the company has completed one rifle and has three more under construction, as of September 2005.

* * *

This is not a complete list of British companies purporting to build double rifles. According to a reliable source, David Mackay Brown, Watson Brothers, and Medwell & Perrett, a small independent company that performs out-source machining, have all made at least one rifle. James Purdey & Sons still makes one or two double rifles a year.

The money involved, for the average individual, is immense. Most companies list starting prices at £55,000; at today's exchange rate, that is $90,000, give or take a few cents. Before starting work, most companies demand a third or even half up front, with more as the rifle progresses. The final price paid is the list price on the rifle at that time—not what it was at the time the gun was ordered, which might be as much as two or three years earlier. Hence, a potential buyer should insist on a written contract spelling out all the provisions regarding the final price of the rifle and how it will be affected by the exchange rate.

The Continental Divide

The old Boche knew about rifles.
Major H. C. Maydon (late 12th Lancers)
Big Game of Africa, *1935*

London may be the birthplace of the big double rifle, but continental Europe is the home of small-caliber doubles for all kinds of hunting. Both side-by-side and over/under rifles have been made in Germany, Austria, Italy, Belgium, France, and Spain for centuries. In some countries, the double rifle is an art form, a tool for gentlemanly hunting, an object almost of reverence.

With due deference to the European heritage of the double, however, a hunter in search of a stopping rifle needs to tread carefully when shopping on the continent.

There are, and have been for many years, reputable companies making fine rifles in .375 H&H and larger. In recent years, as the market for double rifles in the United States has become white hot, an endless stream of individuals and companies has entered the business in an attempt to cash in. Any one- or two-man shop that makes double shotguns now believes it can build a double rifle—all the way up to .600 NE—with the snap of a finger. The task is not that simple. Making a rifle is different than building a shotgun, and making a big rifle is vastly different than manufacturing a small rifle. Constructing a flawless mechanism that will continue to function under the worst conditions, while taking a battering from its own recoil, is a skill the London gunmakers have developed over a long period. It is not acquired overnight.

This is an area where there are more bad examples than good, but to choose one at random, I just visited an Italian gunmaker's website and was greeted by a photograph of a nice-looking side-by-side rifle with a scope. The scope is so poorly mounted it would be unlikely to survive more than a couple of shots. The rings are installed close together, both forward of the turret, with the rear three-quarters of the scope hanging out over the action like a crane. The eyepiece is in line with the comb of the stock. Pity the eye of the man who pulls the trigger. This does not appear to be a large-caliber rifle, but it would not want to be.

Any attempt to sort out which gunmaker is legitimate and which is not by actually visiting, talking to the company, and handling its products would be an undertaking of impossible proportions, the major reason being that the situation changes almost from hour to hour. One day you hear that an old name has gone out of business; the next day you hear that they are back in business. Then you find out that the firm is under the management of some lawyer working for the bank; meanwhile, the website sits pristinely advertising wares that may or may not exist—or have ever existed—except in a kind of digital smoke and mirrors.

Many European companies make over/under double rifles. This is a completely separate field that has little to do with dangerous game. Such rifles are almost never made in any caliber larger than 9.3 x 74R, which puts them right on the edge in our terms. For driven boar and red stag in the mountains, they are wonderful rifles, and they might be good for leopard, as well, if the hunter insisted. Technically, over/unders just do not lend themselves to big cartridges. The barrels have to drop too far when reloading, for example, and the ability to feed more cartridges into a big double quickly during an emergency is important. In 1993, Boss & Co. built an over/under .470, using its famous action. The asking price for the rifle was astronomical—about $200,000 in today's terms—and several years after I first saw this gun, it was still in the white. I believe Boss sold it eventually, but has not attempted another. Over/unders are not a serious factor in the market for dangerous-game doubles.

The European double-rifle market of today is more confusing than it has been since 1945. There are few suggestions I can offer, except to remind you that a big rifle in a heavy-recoiling caliber is a vastly different animal than a 7 x 65 for shooting roe deer. And, I suggest that you deal only with the most reputable of importers.

Germany

Germany has an established gunmaking tradition that goes back 500 years, and the first proof system originated there. The town of Suhl is the ancient center of gunmaking in Germany. After 1945, Suhl found itself behind the Iron Curtain, but many gunmakers escaped and established new businesses in the west. During the Cold War, imports from East Germany were slim or nonexistent, but with reunification the borders opened. Now guns from Suhl are plentiful.

Germany makes a range of double rifles, from the absolute best to be seen anywhere, to guns that are relatively inexpensive.

To begin with the best, Hartmann & Weiss of Hamburg is reputed to be the finest gunmaker in the world, bar none. Interestingly, Gerhard Hartmann himself insists that Britain's Peter Nelson is the finest gunmaker in the world. Nelson makes both shotguns and double rifles, while Hartmann & Weiss make both of those, as well as extraordinary magazine rifles on Mauser-type actions.

The finest Merkel side-lock, which retails for about $30,000 (2005). It is ornately engraved, with gold inlay. The octagonal barrels are a Merkel feature available on a number of models.   *Courtesy GSI*

A Merkel boxlock, thoroughly typical of its type: Sideclips, Greener crossbolt, and a substantial bolster to strengthen the action at the intersection of action flat and standing breech. At $11,795 (2005), this rifle has been

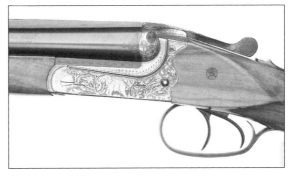

called "the only bargain to be had in a double rifle."   *Courtesy GSI*

Aside from mutual admiration, Hartmann & Weiss and Peter Nelson are alike in that their total output is spoken for years in advance, and the chances of any of their rifles ending up in the field, actually killing game, are remote at best. While superbly functional, their firearms are not "working" guns.

Probably the best-known German gunmaking company of all time is Merkel, which stayed in Suhl after 1945. Merkel is famous for its over/under action with a Blitz trigger-plate lock and Kersten fastener, but it also manufactures a complete line of rifles and shotguns, side-by-sides, over/unders, and single-shots. Merkel makes actions and barrelled actions available to the trade, and rifle makers around the world build guns on Merkel actions, both boxlock and sidelock.

After the reunification of Germany, as Merkel guns found their way into western markets, their prices were considerably lower than those of their competitors, prompting Geoff Miller of Rigby to call them "the only bargain" to be had in the double-rifle business. "At $9,000 for a big double, you can't beat it," Miller told me in 1999. At the time, Miller was importing Merkel actions on which to build the John Rigby rifles at his plant in Paso Robles, California. Merkel was able to deliver surprising quality at an astoundingly low price because wages in the former East Germany had still not caught up. This is changing steadily, of course.

Today, Merkel firearms of all types are imported by GSI of Trussville, Alabama. Several types of double rifle are available, including sidelocks and boxlocks. At the low end is a boxlock, in several calibers from .375 H&H to .500 NE, for about $11,000. Given the gyrations of the euro over the past three years, that is a remarkably low price.

At the high end, there is a sidelock rifle, available only in .470 NE, for $26,000. At first glance that looks like a steal, but consider this: It is not a custom rifle, and there are few options in terms of barrel length, stock dimensions, and so on. As well, GSI was unable to rein in Merkel's Teutonic propensities, so the rifle comes with 23.5-inch octagonal (!) barrels and with extractors rather than ejectors. The great thing about ejectors is that they can be disconnected if you prefer extractors, but the reverse is not true.

From here, the boxlock looks like a bargain—a good working double rifle at a price any serious hunter can afford.

* * *

The second major German name is Heym. Now known as *Heym Waffenfabrik GmbH*, the company has been around since 1865 and has undergone several transformations from a small, family-owned firm to a public corporation.

Heym was founded by Friedrich Wilhelm Heym in 1865, in Suhl. His products were the usual German mixture of shotguns, rifles, and combination guns, and his initial export market was the Russia of the Czars. In 1891, Heym patented the first hammerless "drilling" (three-barrel gun). The company survived both world wars, but in 1945, Rolf and August Heym fled East Germany and reestablished themselves in Ostheim, in Lower Franconia. Times were tough in the sporting-gun business, but being skilled gunmakers they were capable of producing a range of precision products. For a time, Heym's new factory produced everything from slide rules to cuckoo clocks— ironic when you recall Jack O'Connor's acerbic comment about German guns resembling cuckoo clocks. But Heym did what it had to do and gradually moved back into gunmaking.

Heym established itself as a fine rifle maker in the 1980s, and in 1985 it made the third rifle in the Safari Club's "Big Five" series, a double in .375 H&H. Then came another highlight: In 1991, Heym came to the SCI conven-

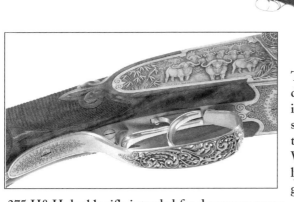

This Heym sidelock double rifle was No. 3 in the SCI "Big Five" series, dedicated to the Cape buffalo. While extraordinarily ornate, it is still a good example of a .375 H&H double rifle intended for dangerous game.   *RCMP Photo*

The Heym SCI "Big Five" No. 3 Cape buffalo rifle, in .375 H&H — a masterpiece of the gunmaker's art. Like most German double rifles, it uses both a Greener crossbolt and sideclips.   *RCMP Photo*

tion with the first-ever bolt-action .600 NE. The company did it to show that it could be done and came away from the convention, somewhat bemused, with orders for about a dozen more at $10,000 apiece.

During this time, American rifle authority Tom Turpin was a consultant to the Heyms, advising them on the U.S. market and the products needed to establish themselves here. American riflemen have a puzzling relationship with German tastes in rifles. Much of American gunmaking tradition has German roots, with the German gunmakers who settled in Pennsylvania and created the *schuetzen* rifles of the nineteenth century. Oddly enough, except for the *schuetzen* rifles, the Teutonic penchant for turning firearms into totem poles evinced itself more in American shotguns (witness some of the higher-grade L. C. Smiths and Ithacas) than in rifles, which tended to the plainly elegant. O'Connor's comment about cuckoo clocks was right on the money, though, and

The second set of locks for the Heym SCI "Big Five" No. 3 rifle illustrates several features often found on 'best' double rifles. It was not uncommon for a rifle destined for India or Africa to have two sets of locks. Gunmakers were few and England was distant; a hunter in the field could replace a damaged lock easily (one serious advantage of sidelocks over boxlocks, the Westley Richards droplock being an exception). The latch in the center is the spare screw to attach the locks. Gold plating was often applied to internal parts to prevent rust in humid climates.   *RCMP Photo*

some of the weird and wonderful contraptions that German gunmakers dream up to hang on rifles must be seen to be believed.

When it comes to dangerous-game rifles especially, Americans do not dig weird: They want traditional, austere, businesslike English styling. Tom's main task during his years with Heym was to convince the company that it could sell big rifles in America, but only if it made them look like English guns. To a great extent, the strategy worked. The SCI rifle was magnificent, and Heym was well on its way to becoming a force in the American rifle market. Unfortunately, the firm then moved into other areas—a straight-pull bolt action, for example—and overstepped itself financially. In 1997, the company filed for bankruptcy. The following year, it was reorganized and is now a public company. The reorganized Heym is concentrating on the emerging hunting markets of eastern Europe.

Today, Heym makes some serious rifles for dangerous game—both bolt action and double. The company's bolt action is the "Heym Express Magnum Big Bore," available in a vast range of calibers from .375 H&H to .600 NE, including the .378 Weatherby and .577 NE, as well as all the standard English rimless cartridges. The rifle is built on a magnum Mauser action produced in Germany.

Heym also makes a very stylish break-action single-shot. The largest available caliber is 9.3 x 74R, which perhaps qualifies it (barely) as a dangerous-game rifle. Mainly, it is a traditional stalking rifle for those who prefer a larger caliber for red stag.

Heym's big double rifle is the real star of the show. The firm now makes eight different types of double rifle, both boxlocks and sidelocks. A couple are more properly combination guns, and two models offer paired barrels in different calibers (for example, the right barrel is 9.3 x 74R, while the left barrel is 7 x 65). I started to count the calibers offered and gave up. Suffice to say, you can buy a Heym double rifle in dozens of chamberings, from .22 Hornet to .600 NE.

Being a German firm, with all the positives (and negatives) that implies, Heym will torment you with demands for your preferences, like a waiter asking what you want for salad dressing, then countering your answer with another six options. Heym, with its myriad offerings of rifle types and features, threatens to drive you mad, although it will certainly keep you off the streets as you go through the catalog, price list, and order form.

* * *

Krieghoff is another German name that dates back to the early twentieth century. The Krieghoffs were among the gunmakers who fled Suhl in 1945 and reestablished themselves in Ulm. The company made its name in shotguns—especially trap guns—but also makes a range of rifles, both single-shot and an innovative double rifle called the Classic.

The Classic and its big brother, the Big Five, were introduced in 1996, and the author had the privilege of shooting the prototype .470. Because the Krieghoff Classic evokes mixed reactions, both extremely good and extremely bad, it would be best to begin by describing how it works. And here, we shall confine ourselves to the Big Five, which is made in dangerous-game calibers (.375 Flanged, .375 H&H, 500/416, .470 NE, and .500 NE).

The Big Five has the lines of a classic London double, although Krieghoff has begun using a *schnabel* fore end that rather spoils the effect. It is a boxlock-type rifle but does not incorporate an Anson & Deeley action. Therein lies the big difference. Where one would expect to see the safety catch on the upper tang, there is what appears to be an oversized safety catch with a high ridge. This is the cocking lever. The rifle is carried uncocked; when the shooter is ready to fire, he pushes the lever forward, cocking both tumblers. The rifle is then ready to shoot. To return the Krieghoff to a "safe" position, you push the lever forward a fraction of an inch and release it; the tumblers return to the "rest" position and the rifle is uncocked.

This system is common in Europe but rare in America. Some hunters, especially professional hunters, dislike it violently. In the event of an unexpected charge—a Cape buffalo boiling out of the bush at short range—it is more difficult to push the cocking lever forward than it would be merely to snick off a safety catch. This issue is more than theoretical: In 2004, two men were killed—one in Tanzania, one in Kenya—by Cape buffalo that came out of the bushes in exactly that way. Neither man had reason to suspect a buffalo was even there. Of course, if you were going in after a known, wounded animal, the rifle would already be cocked. But then you would be carrying a rifle cocked and off-safe, which is highly unrecommended.

My opinion? If the Krieghoff is the only side-by-side you will own, of any description, then learn the system and stick with it. If you are accustomed to a side-by-side, either rifle or shotgun, with a traditional safety then I would avoid the Krieghoff.

That aside, the rifle is very well made, well thought-out, and certainly affordable. When it was introduced, a Classic could be had for $6,000 and the Big Five for $9,000. The latter is more expensive now, but still affordable in big-double terms.

Originally, the rifle had a single trigger set by inertia—that is, the trigger for the second barrel was set by the recoil of the first. This is such a bad idea on a dangerous-game rifle that it hardly bears thinking about. When I was testing the first Krieghoff .470, I asked if it had an inertia trigger. No, I was told, it does not. So, says I, if there is a misfire, you can still fire the second barrel? "*Zere vill be no misfire,*" they snarled, in Teutonic. So what happened? The first barrel misfired, and the trigger dangled there like a loose banana. My Teutonic hosts gulped, and shortly thereafter it was announced that the Big Five would be available with double triggers only. What an excellent idea.

That rifle also had a stock so poorly designed it was almost unshootable—a high, sharp comb that made using the iron sights virtually impossible. That was also redesigned. And, while the Classic has a system of reregulating the barrels with a movable block, held in place with a set screw, this system is not available on the Big Five, which I believe is a good thing.

One Krieghoff option that I really question is sideplates. Throughout this book, we have dealt with boxlocks and sidelocks, and have largely ignored the sideplate rifle so beloved among continental gunmakers. This is as good a spot as any to deal with them.

A sideplate rifle is merely a boxlock with false sidelock-type plates attached. This makes the rifle look like a sidelock and also affords the engraver a large canvas on which to work. Mechanically, however, sideplates contribute nothing. In fact, they weaken the rifle. The argument has raged for 125 years as to which is stronger, the boxlock or the sidelock. Boxlock advocates point to the fact that less wood is cut away from the stock to accommodate the locks; sidelock advocates point to the fact that there is more steel in the center of the frame, since it is not hollowed out to accommodate the locks.

Sideplate rifles give you the worst of both worlds. The receiver is hollowed out, but more metal is cut away on the sides to fit the plates, and wood is removed from the stock for the same reason. Sideplate guns are usually more expensive, and all you get for the extra money is a tarted-up boxlock.

But the bottom line on the Krieghoff Big Five is that, in my opinion, it is a very well-made rifle at an unbelievably low price. If you can live with the cocking mechanism—and I, for one, could learn to—I do not believe you will find a bigger bargain anywhere.

Austria

Austria is listed next only because it shares a gunmaking tradition with Germany and exhibits many of the same traits and tastes that are the hallmark of the Teutonic gunmaker. The center of the Austrian gun trade is the small town of Ferlach, in the mountains on the border with Slovakia. Ferlach has an ancient tradition, a highly respected gunmaking school, and a trade that consists of many small companies. The level of craftsmanship in Ferlach is second to none. At one time, the name Franz Sodia was well-known in the United States, much like Spain's AyA. It was the largest company in Ferlach, but went under in the early 1990s. What remains are tiny companies—shops with a half-dozen employees at most, producing a few dozen guns a year.

While some Austrian gunmakers are rifle specialists, and many are devoted hunters of chamois and roe deer, very few have African experience and even fewer are serious hunters of dangerous game. There is no quarreling with the quality of rifles made in Ferlach, but whether they are good candidates for dangerous game is another question altogether.

In 1995, at the Safari Club International convention, I visited an Austrian gunmaker's booth where there was a magnificent side-by-side .470 NE on display. Beside it was a framed reprint of a magazine article that talked at length about this gunmaker's hunting experience and described how, ornate as his rifles are, they are "made for real hunting." I looked over the gun. It was gorgeous— an express rifle in the most austere English style. The stock was exhibition-grade walnut with a glossy oil finish. I asked if it was going back to Austria to be completed. "No, no, it is ready now," the maker assured me proudly. "I expect to sell it here, and the buyer could take it to Africa next week." The only problem was, there was no checkering on either the grip or fore end. I mentioned this. The maker was aghast. "No, no! You cannot checker it—you would not see the grain of the wood!"

Therein lies my problem with many of the products of Ferlach. They are always beautifully made and often ingenious in their design, but the region's gunmakers do not have the English heritage of making rifles for people going to dangerous places, and it shows. Checkering is not decoration, affectation, or an optional extra; it is there to give sweaty hands a firm grip on a big rifle.

On a visit to Ferlach in 1997, I saw a prototype double rifle touted as having a much stronger fastening system than the English double underlugs. Over the breech opening of the barrels was a sheet of steel that fitted onto the standing breech. A retractable bolt locked into this and pulled it down. That was fine, except the sheet of steel hampered the shooter's ability to load the rifle or clear a jam. It was in the way—not good in a rifle for bad animals—and solved a non-existent problem, since double underlugs are more than amply strong.

The gunmakers of Ferlach are wonderful people, the food is fantastic, the scenery gorgeous, and the craftsmanship second to none, but if I were going to have a dangerous-game rifle built there I would rent a room at the local hotel and oversee every step of the rifle's construction to ensure that I received a working gun and not some masterpiece of the gunmaker's art that would be worthy of a museum but might get me killed.

Belgium

Since 1900, Belgium has been the major European producer of rifles in the English style, just as the nation's gunmakers turned out shotguns that emulated those of Holland & Holland. The Belgian gunmaking area is Liège, home of Fabrique Nationale (FN) and forever associated by Americans with the name of John M. Browning and the nearby town of Herstal.

Like Suhl and Ferlach, Liège has a long tradition of small shops and hand craftsmanship, and it has produced many fine double guns. Being close to Britain, with strong ties to the English, the Belgians naturally made guns and rifles that closely followed the English style. The best-known Belgian producer of double rifles was probably Francotte, now defunct, with Lebeau-Courally regarded as the closest thing to a Belgian Purdey. While its products are still advertised, whether Lebeau is really still in business is questionable. Its U.S. importer is William Larkin Moore, and David Moore assures me that Lebeau-Courally is still making guns and rifles, but only a tiny number compared with former years. It is also keeping busy doing custom work for Browning.

In the 1980s and '90s, Marcel Thys made an attempt to crack the American double-rifle market, but that firm, too, is now gone.

Aside from Lebeau-Courally, the only Belgian company still building fine side-by-side rifles in the English style is Dumoulin. Ernest Dumoulin founded his company more than fifty years ago and today builds double rifles, shotguns, and bolt-action rifles. Dumoulin guns are imported by the Empire Rifle Company of New Hampshire, which, itself, makes custom rifles on new Mauser 98 actions. The relationship between Empire and Dumoulin is part importer/exporter, part partnership. Dumoulin does work on Empire rifles, such as engraving, as well as providing some of the barreled actions for smaller calibers. This is an important distinction. Over the years, like many continental gunmakers, Dumoulin has had various importers in the United States, and the experience has not always been happy. Having a U.S. agent that is more like part

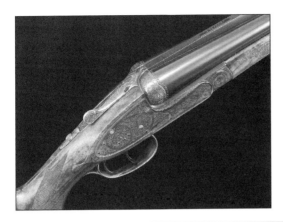

Lebeau-Courally .470
Nitro Express sidelock.
*Courtesy
William Larkin Moore*

of the company benefits both parties. Particularly, it will help any client who goes to George Sandmann at Empire to order a double rifle from Dumoulin.

The company offers both sidelocks and boxlocks, in .375 H&H, .470, and .500 NE. The lowest priced boxlock in a big caliber lists at $23,500—more than reasonable in today's world, given the value of the euro. It has a Greener cross-bolt and the austere appearance of a working London double rifle (hence its appearance on our cover). From there, as usual, the sky is the limit, including sidelock rifles, fully engraved, inlaid, with matching accoutrements. Sidelocks start at about $45,000. There is also a (ugh!) sideplate model.

Mechanically, the only distinction a Dumoulin offers is a proprietary system of soldering the chopper-lump barrels, which the company insists delivers gilt-edged accuracy. The firm's rifles are regulated by the Belgian proof house in Liège, which is interesting. Beyond that, they offer the direct involvement of Ernest Dumoulin himself; he works every day in the shop, and the tradition of Belgian craftsmanship takes a back seat to no one on the continent.

Dumoulin bolt-action rifles are available in calibers up to .505 Gibbs, and many are built on original FN Mauser actions. Now that is mouth-watering.

France

Chapuis Armes of France makes more double rifles than any other European company. Its production, according to David Moore, is close to five hundred rifles a year, in all calibers and configurations.

Chapuis Armes was founded by Jean Chapuis in the 1920s and is now run by his son, René. The company has a big, modern factory with a large complement of CNC machinery, as well as a staff of fifty gunmakers. Over the years, Chapuis rifles have been imported by various American companies; today,

William Larkin Moore handles Chapuis, and David Moore is very enthusiastic about the quality of Chapuis rifles, for the price.

"There are lower-priced double rifles available," he told me, "But the main thing you need to look for is the way they are 'regulated.' Chapuis rifles are tested by firing the gun and adjusting the barrels; others, the cheaper ones, are regulated by laser. It is not the same."

Barrel regulation is an art, a science, a craft, and just a little bit of alchemy. When you walk into a shop where barrels are being regulated—Steve Cranston's place at the H&H shooting ground, for example—you are greeted by an odd smell of hot solder and burning wax, and weird tangles of wires and wedges that hold the barrels together. When the process is complete, the rifle will put its bullets, from both barrels, into a small spot at whatever distance, with whatever ammunition the buyer has stipulated.

When barrels are regulated with lasers, the process is essentially the same as bore-sighting a rifle with a collimator: A spud with a laser is inserted into each muzzle and the barrels are adjusted until the spots are in the right relation to each other at whatever range; at this point the barrels are soldered together. Traditional barrel regulation requires a skilled man and a shooting range next to a properly equipped shop; laser regulation merely requires a vise, a wall, and a soldering iron. Whether the rifle will actually shoot any particular type of ammunition well is purely chance. "This is why shot-regulated rifles are more expensive," David Moore said, "But it is a far superior system."

Chapuis offers different models, both boxlock and sideplate; its big calibers are limited to .375 H&H, .416 Rigby, and .470 NE.

Spain

In 1987, while researching a magazine article, I travelled to the Basque Country of Spain for the first time and visited the remaining small gunmakers there. Since then, I have returned a dozen times and written at least two dozen articles about the place, as well as a book on the Spanish gunmakers. I am more familiar with the gunmaking industry in Spain than that of anywhere else on the continent.

Spain's tradition of gunmaking goes back to the 1500s, during which time the Basques have made every type of firearm imaginable. The tradition of fine-gunmaking—double shotguns in the English style—dates from the 1880s, when Victor Sarasqueta went into business. Later came Ignacio Ugartechea, AyA, and the other prominent names of today. As far back as the 1920s, Sarasqueta and Ugartechea made what were called "express rifles," doubles in calibers up to .600 NE. By the 1960s, only Sarasqueta was still licensed to make them, and that company went under in 1981.

By 1987, the express-rifle business in Spain was dead. A year later, however-er, I saw a prototype side-by-side double rifle being built by Armas Garbi (a 9.3 x 74R), and within a year or two it seemed that everyone was getting into it. A decade later, rifles were being made by Pedro Arrizabalaga, Arrieta, and Grulla Armas, as well as Armas Garbi.

At first, all said they intended to make sidelock rifles no larger than 9.3 x 74R, which is very popular for hunting red stag and wild boar in Europe. The reason was simple: they did not feel they had the special skills required to make a hard-recoiling rifle that would stand up to hunting in Africa. This approach was straightforward and honest. By 1999, however, Arrieta had produced at least two big rifles, a .470 and a .500. They were both sidelocks, and both were as beautifully made as one would expect from Arrieta. The makers were cagey about saying where the parts came from, although they admitted that the bar-rels were imported from Austria because Spain no longer has a company that produces rifle barrels of this type. Some frames were of Spanish origin, others Austrian. Given the nature of globalized sourcing, it is pointless to worry about the origin of steel anyway.

Armas Garbi stuck to its limit of 9.3 x 74R, but José Luis Usobiaga at Grulla Armas was preparing to make an express rifle in the largest calibers. For most Spanish gunmakers, the upper limit was .500 NE. I have seen and han-dled rifles from all of these companies, and all were mouth-watering. The Grulla E-95 rifle, especially, is a masterpiece and, with an original retail price of $20,000, it was a steal. Since then, the appreciation of the euro has driven up the price, but it is still a fraction of the cost of a new English double.

Pedro Arrizabalaga enjoys an advantage over the other Basque companies when it comes to rifles because of its long association with Paul Roberts in London. Paul's family company, J. Roberts & Son, has long been the London agent for Arrizabalaga, and when Paul owned Rigby, he sold guns marked Rigby-Arrizabalaga. In 1993, David Winks, the former director of H&H, told me that Paul Roberts was the best barrel regulator in the world and was overall one of the best double-rifle makers in existence. So having him as a mentor when you begin to make double rifles is a huge plus. Paul Roberts would not allow Arrizabalaga to put a foot wrong.

Having never owned, hunted with, or shot a really big Spanish double, I cannot offer first-hand experience as to how they perform. Nor do I know any-one who has owned or hunted with one of these rifles.

That said, no one in the business has a higher regard for the Basque gun-makers than I do, and I can point to several Sarasqueta and Ugartechea double rifles that were made many years ago, in .475 No. 2 and .450 NE, that are still working and still hunting. So the Basques are not newcomers to the game. Still, if I were offered the opportunity to hunt Cape buffalo with a .500 from Arrieta or Grulla I would insist on receiving the rifle at least a year ahead of time and would fire at least five hundred full-power shots through it before taking it on safari. But then, I would do exactly that with any double rifle from any company in the world. It is a good rule to follow.

Italy

In some ways, Italy is the most difficult of the European countries to gauge. It has a fine-shotgun industry that rivals, and in some ways exceeds, that of Britain, especially in over/unders. The country has one huge gunmaking company—Beretta, the oldest industrial concern in the western world—and many smaller ones.

Over the years, several different Italian gunmakers have advertised double rifles, and some of these have even been imported to the United States. Perugini-Visini is one such firm. Abbiatico & Salvinelli, which sprang to prominence in the 1980s with some absolutely spectacular guns and put Italian *bulino* engraving on the map, today makes double rifles. These are imported by William Larkin Moore.

Anyone thinking of an Italian-made double rifle should consult David Moore, because the acquisition process is truly a labyrinth. Having come to terms with the arcane Spanish trade, I have no desire to embark on the same tortuous path with the Italians and would defer to David's much greater knowledge. However, the reservations expressed about the Spanish double rifles apply equally to the Italian.

The exception is Beretta. The members of the Beretta family are serious hunters and insist that the company's rifles be top-notch. They build an over/under double rifle in .458 Winchester and have built side-by-side doubles as well. All are custom products.

Buying New and Used

Choose one by any of the best makers and buy it second hand. You will get it for £20 or £30 if you look long enough.

Major H.C. Maydon

There are various ways in which one can purchase a double rifle. One can order a new one from a reputable British gunmaker, usually by dealing directly with the company. Holland & Holland, for example, exhibits regularly at the Safari Club International convention and has a retail outlet in New York City.

If one wishes to buy a European double rifle, the situation becomes more complicated. Generally, one would need to deal through an importer in the United States, a firm that would take the money, place the order, and look after delivery.

Finally, one can buy a used rifle from any number of fine-gun dealers scattered across the country. Champlin Arms of Enid, Oklahoma, is the preeminent dealer in used double rifles, George Caswell having been at the game since long before it became fashionable. No one in the country knows more about double rifles, of all makes and nationalities, than George Caswell.

For the buyer who is wealthy enough to go to Holland & Holland to order a bespoke rifle, little remains but to wish him the best. The people at H&H are the finest in the business. No one makes a better double rifle, no one knows more about making them than Russell Wilkin, and no company has more experience or is better equipped to ensure that you get the finest rifle your money can buy.

Other English companies are also in that select group. Westley Richards is H&H's only rival in terms of the number of rifles produced, and it has an outlet in the U.S. as well. After Westley Richards comes the reconstituted W. J. Jeffery under Paul Roberts. The fact that Roberts is associated with the company is, to me, assurance enough. Finally, professional hunter Robin Hurt speaks very highly of William Evans, which still produces double rifles in small numbers, and Robin's endorsement is good enough for me.

Beyond those four, the view becomes murky, and anyone wishing to order a rifle from a newly resurrected old British name will probably want to go through an importer in the United States. It is possible to fly to London, visit an establishment, order the rifle, and import it yourself, but only a tiny number of Americans actually follow that route.

Which brings us to the question of importers. There are two names I would recommend without hesitation: Griffin & Howe of New Jersey and William Larkin Moore of Phoenix, Arizona. There may be other reputable importers—in fact, I'm sure there are—but these are the people I know. Griffin & Howe has been in business since the 1920s, in and around New York, and while the company has changed hands several times, it remains the northeast's preeminent gunshop. Paul Chapman has been with the company since birth, it seems, has survived several changes in ownership, and is an extremely knowledgeable rifle man. Griffin & Howe has been importing Purdeys from London for decades and has been bringing in Arrietas from Spain for at least fifteen years. It is a firm that can be trusted.

William Larkin Moore began dealing in fine doubles in the dark days of 1973 and has built his business into the west-coast counterpart to Griffin & Howe. Bill himself is now semiretired, and the company is run by his son David. The Moores—father and son—know more about the continental European fine-gun trade than anyone in America. WLM imports only great names—Abbiatico & Salvinelli, Piotti, Pedro Arrizabalaga, Armas Garbi, Chapuis, Lebeau-Courally. As well, Moore deals in high-end used double rifles. If I were contemplating the purchase of a European double and did not know where to begin, my first call would be to David Moore.

* * *

Both Griffin & Howe and William Larkin Moore import new double rifles. George Caswell at Champlin Arms deals only in used double rifles. A visit to his booth at the Safari Club show is a revelation in the breadth and depth of the double-rifle trade over the past hundred years. At any given time, George is likely to have a black-powder hammer gun with Damascus barrels or a stubby .577 made for an Arabian dwarf or the most elegant of sidelock stalking rifles originally given to a Scottish laird by his grateful monarch. You never know what you will see.

Alas, the days of finding a bargain in a double rifle are long gone.

Four years ago, at the SCI convention, a potential buyer approached Russell Wilkin at the H&H booth and asked what he had available in a used .470 for $20,000. The answer: Nothing. "If you find any," Russell said as the man departed, "Please let me know. I'd love to get some for stock." Shortly thereafter, H&H received Tony Henley's old .500/.465 Royal to sell, and the asking price was more than $50,000. It did not sell immediately, but it certainly did sell.

Since this is a book about dangerous-game rifles, we will stick to used doubles in sufficiently good condition, and sufficiently large caliber, to be used for

Derek Hurt's Manton .470 NE, a rifle that is probably 75 years old and still working daily in Tanzania's Great Rift Valley. This is a typical—and typically fine—working boxlock double rifle from the Age of Empire. Such rifles are in great demand, increasingly scarce, and relentlessly expensive.

actual hunting. Unfortunately, this is the precise area where the shortage has become most acute and the prices the most outrageous. I would venture to say that it is impossible to find a used and usable dangerous-game double today for less than $10,000. If I did find one, I would be very suspicious and want to wring it out thoroughly before venturing into the lion's lair.

If I were to go looking for a working double for the big stuff, I would start with two rules. First, I would confine myself to boxlocks. This is partly because there were many more boxlock double rifles made than sidelocks, and partly because most sidelocks were built by big London names. Second, I would put out of my mind any thought of finding one with a name like H&H or Rigby— or, for that matter, W. J. Jeffery, Westley Richards, or W. W. Greener. Those makers have appeared in too many books by people like J. A. Hunter and John Taylor, and they now command a serious premium.

Lesser-known names likely to deliver better value include Army & Navy and Manton of Calcutta. Army & Navy, particularly, is a dark horse. The Army & Navy Stores was a company that outfitted army officers and colonial civil servants departing for far shores; it bought rifles and shotguns from all kinds of suppliers, and while the A&N name may appear on the barrels, the rifle might have been made by anyone—including Westley Richards, Jeffery, and Webley. John Wilkes, a small but very fine London name, made many rifles and shotguns for Army & Navy, and you can hardly do better than a Wilkes. The only thing one can say for sure about an Army & Navy rifle is that it is likely to be good. The company had high standards.

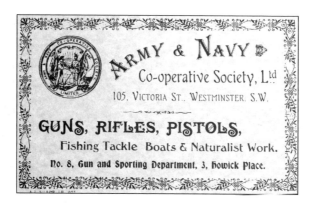

The Army & Navy Co-operative Society sold all kinds of firearms under its own label, including fine double rifles that might have been made by any of the prominent names—Webley, John Wilkes, Westley Richards, or Joseph Lang, for example. Army & Navy is one of the best 'dark horse' names in used doubles.

Other names to look for include Alex Henry, Henry Atkin, Isaac Hollis, Joseph Lang, Charles Boswell, Charles Lancaster, Daniel Fraser, Thomas Mortimer, Rodda & Co., Webley, Scott, E. M. Reilly, and Vickers. Just when you think you have mentioned everyone of note, another name pops into your mind and you reach for Boothroyd's *Directory of British Gunmakers.* Anyone searching for a British double rifle should own a copy.

* * *

When buying a used double rifle from a professional dealer, one needs to ask certain questions, and get some guarantees. The most important is the cartridge. Is ammunition available, and more important, is the rifle regulated to shoot current commercial ammunition?

Some dangerous-game calibers carry their own premium. The .470 NE is by far the most popular, and a .470 might cost 20 percent more than the same rifle chambered for one of the original .450 cartridges. The .500 NE has come roaring back in the last ten years, and it is now a standard chambering in new doubles. Naturally, older .500s (either 3" or 3 1/4") command full price. Cartridges that might work the other way include the .450 No. 2, the .475 NE, and any of the .400s. Personally, I feel a good rifle in an obscure caliber is a better deal than a ramshackle .470, but much depends on whether you are a handloader and how much trouble you are willing to take to get cartridges.

Ammunition today is far less of a problem than it was in the 1970s. With Kynamco and Westley Richards offering commercial ammunition loaded with

Woodleigh bullets and duplicating the original Kynoch ballistics, there are few calibers that are relegated to the wall for lack of ammunition to shoot. A-Square also offers many of the old nitro-express calibers, and if you handload, brass and bullets are freely available. All of this has a direct bearing on whether that exquisite Henry Atkin .450/.400 is a good deal for you, or not.

With a dangerous-game rifle, it is difficult to tell exactly what you have until you have fired it several dozen times, and most dealers will not allow you to do that much testing before deciding on a purchase. Nor can one blame them. What you can do, however, is get some form of written guarantee, not necessarily of performance, but what they are prepared to do to correct any situation. This is a rather murky area. If you are dealing with George Caswell at Champlin, you are already ahead of the game: George has a fully equipped shop in Enid, and his gunmaker, J. J. Perodeau, is a skilled Belgian craftsman. If Perodeau can't make it right, no one can.

Similarly, Griffin & Howe and William Larkin Moore have the connections and the facilities to ensure that any used rifle they sell works to begin with and stays working.

Section III

BOLT ACTIONS

The Mauser 98

The most widely used, the most widely copied, and in many ways the best bolt-action in the world, is the Model 98 Mauser.

Jack O'Connor

The Mauser 98 is the greatest bolt action—and probably the greatest rifle of any kind—ever invented. For dangerous game it has no serious rival in terms of the numbers used or its reputation among enthusiasts. The only credible pretenders to the Mauser's title are sons of the Mauser like the Winchester Model 70 and the Enfield P-17. For the largest cartridges from the .505 Gibbs on down, the 98 is king.

Since it was adopted by the German Army in 1898, the Mauser 98 has set the standard for strength, durability, and reliability. It is capable of fine, and even outstanding, accuracy. Some early bench-rest rifles were built on Mauser actions, and they performed quite well.

Almost from the beginning, the Mauserwerke in Oberndorf produced sporting rifles and actions. John Rigby became the London agent for Mauser and made a specialty of Mauser-actioned magazine rifles for such cartridges as the .416 Rigby. Other makers followed suit, including George Gibbs (he of the .505), W. J. Jeffery (the .404 and .500 Jeffery), Westley Richards (the .425), and of course, Holland & Holland (the .375 H&H). Mauser made actions in different sizes, and its magnum version—introduced at Rigby's behest—was the mainstay of the English big-rifle trade for years thereafter (allowing for minor interruptions, such as world wars).

The so-called double square-bridge Mauser became legendary. We say "so-called" because an action has but one bridge, but that is the accepted terminology. Original magnum Mauser actions now change hands for $5,000 or more. When supplies of commercial Mausers dried up, there was (and is) a seemingly unending supply of military actions salvaged from government warehouses around the world. Because of military contracts, many other German munitions companies, such as Ludwig Loewe and DWM, produced Mauser rifles as well; inevitably production spilled over into other countries and other companies.

In Belgium, Fabrique Nationale d'Armes de Guerre (FN) produced military and later civilian rifles of outstanding quality. So did the Czech arms factory at Brno. In Spain, the government arsenal at Santa Barbara produced excellent rifles and actions that were later made into sporting rifles by Parker-Hale, and in Yugoslavia, Zastava produced the Mark X, a civilian-market 98 that for some years was the only civilian Mauser available. France was never a big rifle maker, but it had one claim to fame: the Brevex magnum Mauser. After Oberndorf stopped production of its magnum action, the Brevex was the only civilian action that could accommodate seriously large cartridges. Like the original from Oberndorf, Brevex actions today are rare and expensive.

* * *

What makes the Mauser 98 so desirable? Why is it so much better than other bolt-action rifles that came along at the same time, such as the British Lee-Enfield or the American Springfield?

Back in 1918, when all three rifles were engaged on the Western Front, there was a saying that the Germans were armed with a hunting rifle, the Americans with a target rifle, and the British with a battle rifle. Without going into all the reasons for this glib assessment, it is essentially true. The British Lee-Enfield was a battle rifle: fast operating, with interchangeable, ten-round magazines, hardy and dependable. The Springfield was long and cumbersome, but notably accurate. The Mauser 98 did not load as quickly as the Lee-Enfield, but it was handier than the Springfield and also very accurate.

The 98 was the final product of a long evolution that saw Paul Mauser design, market, and build several models before reaching perfection. Once the 98 went into production, he made no further changes. From a hunting point of view, the 98's virtues are strength, durability, and reliability. Fill the action with mud, and it will still operate. The twin locking lugs that rotate into raceways in the rear of the barrel make an enormously strong joint, so much so that the third lug, on the underside of the bolt near the rear, is really superfluous. But it's there, and it gives comfort in times of pressure.

Unlike its predecessors, the 98 cocks on opening. As the bolt handle is lifted, the striker is cammed back over the sear. When the bolt is closed, the only resistance is from the cartridge being pushed up and out of the magazine. There is a three-position safety that locks striker and bolt, or locks the striker in place even while the bolt is being operated. No more positive safety has ever been developed for a bolt-action rifle. The trigger mechanism is simplicity itself—a couple of moving parts and a spring. Because the safety interacts directly with the striker, not merely by blocking the trigger, it is much safer and allows the trigger to be simpler.

Paul Mauser put a great deal of effort into designing the magazine box to accommodate the original 8mm rimless military cartridge, molding the sides of the box and the follower in order to hold the cartridges at the correct angle for dependable feeding. Even today, it is not really understood by backyard rifle mechanics that you cannot simply rebarrel a bolt action to a new caliber and expect the different-shaped cartridges to feed properly. Length, width, depth, follower shape, the angle of the rails and the shape of their edges all play a part in making a rifle feed and chamber its cartridges smoothly. In a hard-recoiling rifle, the effect of repeated shots on the cartridges held in the magazine must also be taken into account. With the Mauser 98, in the hands of a gunsmith that knows what he is doing, all of this is eminently possible.

The same cannot be said of the other two rifles mentioned above. To the best of my knowledge, no one has ever effectively rechambered or rebarreled a Lee-Enfield to another cartridge, except maybe a wildcat derived from the original .303 British. Springfields were certainly altered, but most gunsmiths limited themselves to the .30-06 and offspring like the .270 Winchester. For larger cartridges, it was easier to alter a Mauser 98, actions were freely available, and the buyer would have a superior rifle in the end.

Paul Mauser also perfected the claw extractor. The bolt rotates within the extractor's collar, so the extractor moves forward and back, but is otherwise stationary. As the bolt moves forward, the bottom edge of the bolt face pushes the cartridge forward. The rim rises out of the magazine into position behind the extractor, which grips it firmly and guides the cartridge into the chamber. The cartridge never pops up out of the magazine, the way it does with a "push feed" bolt action like the Weatherby Mark V or the Remington 700.

The "controlled-feed" claw extractor has achieved iconic status among hunters of dangerous game. The system's great advantage is not that it extracts cartridges any better than the smaller spring-loaded mechanism found on the 700, nor even that it makes feeding any more dependable, although it does both. The 98's real advantage is that it allows a cartridge to be fed into the magazine more slowly and quietly, and this can be a major concern when in the presence of game. Push-feed bolt actions function well, but the bolt needs to be operated smartly for them to work at their best, and that is a noisy operation. Whether controlled feed is as desirable as its proponents would have you believe is a matter of opinion, but it is certainly perceived as essential on a blue-chip dangerous-game rifle.

Military Mausers became the mainstay of the custom-rifle business in Europe and the United States. No one has any real idea of how many Mauser rifles were manufactured between 1898 and 1943; millions, certainly, and maybe tens of millions. This does not even count the models from before the 98, such as the Swedish 94 and 96, and the Spanish 93. The Lee-Enfield was the firearm of the British Empire, and the Springfield the rifle for America, but the Mauser 98 became the military rifle of the world. Exporting rifles on military contracts became a major industry for Germany, with dozens of companies involved. Rifles were sent to Argentina, Mexico, Chile, and Siam, among other places; Ludwig Olson's book *Mauser Bolt Rifles* lists a bewildering number of variations.

As stockpiles of such rifles are discovered and released to the surplus market, they are snapped up by gunmakers (and in some cases, hoarded by them). A few even gain some cachet in custom-rifle circles. The Mexican Mauser was highly prized for mountain rifles because the action was slightly shorter and lighter; the Argentine Mauser of 1909 is prized because of the quality of the steel and overall workmanship. Because there were so many models, made by dozens of different companies in a score of military calibers, it is not surprising that some were favored by gunmakers, while others were less desirable or even unusable because of some idiosyncrasy. Some manufacturers began with softer steel, which was easier to work, and then case-hardened the actions. This makes them difficult to alter—to drill and tap for scope mounts for example—because they may have a glass-hard skin. Others, made from high-carbon tool steel, can be relatively easy for a gunmaker to remodel into a sporting rifle.

The one trait all the original Mauser 98s had in common, it is safe to say, was German workmanship. While a dozen different companies might have had different ideas on the very best way to do something, and the client-countries might have had odd demands, there is no arguing with the quality of the rifles produced under these military contracts. Those made before 1914 are especially fine.

The same is not true of the various commercial Mausers (those made at Oberndorf being the obvious exception). Some are exceptional, such as the FN Supreme; of course, FN was founded by Ludwig Loewe, the famous German company, expressly to manufacture Mausers, so they should be good.

Almost always, the military Mausers were preferred to the Zastava Mark X, because at times it was so sloppily made, with uneven polishing, that it was impossible for a gunmaker to mask the imperfections. The Spanish Santa Barbara was good, and the Belgian FN Supreme was superb. The fabled Brevex, while desirable because of its large size, was made of chrome-vanadium steel that was so difficult to work with, it gave gunsmiths fits. The Brno was widely respected, and after the supply of commercial Mausers dried up, many London gunmakers such as John Rigby used Brno actions for their big bolt rifles.

* * *

Over the past quarter-century, a number of small companies and individuals have attempted to bring back the Mauser 98. After all, with demand so intense, it would seem logical for supply to rise to meet the demand. And, with prices so high, the cost of production for a good action would not seem to be an obstacle. To a certain extent, all of this is true. Most early attempts to make a commercial Mauser action came to grief for one reason and another. In the 1960s, gunsmith and wildcatter P. O. Ackley tried to market a 98 with his name on it, an action made in Japan. According to Frank de Haas (*Bolt Action Rifles*),

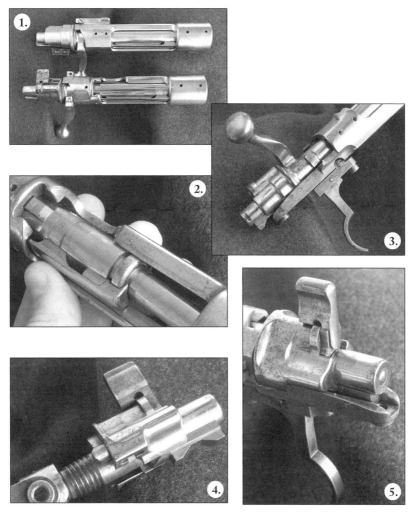

A military Mauser 98 (bottom) by DWM (1) and a commercial Santa Barbara. The thumb-notch, three-position safety, and stripper-clip guide grooves are all eliminated. A cartridge in place with its rim under the claw extractor (2). Note the integral guide rail in the bolt (beneath the bridge). This feature is usually eliminated on commercial designs, but contributes greatly to a bolt that does not bind. The 98 trigger (3) is uncomplicated because the safety is in the shroud. Note the safety lug, forward of the bolt handle. With the safety in the upright position (4), the bolt is easily disassembled with no tools. The three-position safety (5) physically holds the striker away from the sear.

only about a hundred and fifty were made before the Japanese manufacturer went bankrupt and the project died. In the 1980s, a company called Royal Arms tried to market a Mauser 98 made in South Korea. It never got beyond the advertising stage. A couple of gunsmiths in the United States wanted to hand-make Mauser actions for the trade. They went nowhere.

The problem everyone encountered was the cost of production. The Mauser 98, excellent design though it is, is intricate, with many machine cuts. A machinist does not simply throw a piece of round bar stock on a lathe and emerge an hour later with the basic receiver and bolt. The 98 has flat surfaces, milled surfaces, holes that are bored and tapped, and raceways that are broached.

The bolt is assembled like a Chinese puzzle, with a minimum of extraneous fastening devices that would require tools for disassembly—tools that might be lost in field-stripping. The 98 was, after all, a military rifle. The only tool needed to strip one in a muddy trench is a military 8mm cartridge. The price of this, however, is a number of intricate milled parts that are expensive to make and fit. It takes time, skill, and the right equipment. The Royal Arms actions from Korea were projected to cost thousands of dollars; as it turned out, even that was not enough to get them into production.

As the Mauser spread, commercial manufacturers made actual 98s, some good, some poor. Others made modified Mausers, and some of the modifications were sound. For example, a military Mauser has a milled slot in the bridge for stripper clips and a half-moon-shaped cut in the left receiver raceway for the thumb as it presses the rounds down into the magazine. Neither is necessary on a civilian rifle and, in fact, the thumb slot was criticized as "weakening" the action. Eliminating both features simplified manufacture, saved money, gave the action a clean appearance, and made it stronger.

The original safety was an obstacle, especially as rifle scopes became popular. A common solution was to replace the original shroud with a simpler one and install a side-safety catch that blocked the trigger. This modification is found on Zastavas, Santa Barbaras, and FN Supremes. It replaces a superb three-position system with a marginally acceptable two-position one.

Some method had to be found to open the floorplate other than using an 8mm military cartridge with a spitzer bullet. A movable catch was the answer, and the factory at Oberndorf introduced one with a knurled release in the front of the trigger bow.

At one point, FN replaced the entire bottom metal with a trigger guard and floorplate that were made of either plastic or pot metal, painted shiny black with gold inlay. This appeared on the Browning High Power rifles of the 1960s, which were otherwise gorgeous.

Not surprisingly, gunmakers introduced many actions that were based on the Mauser design but departed from it in enough significant ways that they were recognized as a new product. Sako rifles from Finland were always referred to as "modified Mauser" designs. They had dual opposing locking lugs, a one-piece floorplate, and the general appearance of a Mauser, but departed from it radically in the trigger, safety, and shroud.

Birmingham Small Arms (BSA) in England made rifles that were also modified Mauser 98s—very poorly made, too, in the union-addled '50s. Various importers in the United States, such as Herter's, imported actions from different sources, including BSA, and marketed them here. The quality was so-so.

Then, one by one, the mass-production commercial Mausers disappeared until only the Zastava from Yugoslavia was left. Brno still made Mausers in Czechoslovakia, but they could not be imported; then, in the '90s, with the Brno available, the Zastava disappeared because of sanctions against Serbia. Throughout this whole period, custom gunmakers intent on building a fine custom rifle preferred to start with a good, solid military Mauser 98 rather than one of the commercial actions. The problem with many of the latter was the difficulty in undoing the so-called improvements; overall, a Ludwig Loewe 98 from 1910 has better underlying quality, with no ham-handed alterations or ill-advised cheapening to modify. With a military action, the initial outlay was cheaper and the final product was exactly what was wanted, without compromise.

Even the question of action size was not insurmountable. Military Mausers came in slightly different sizes; some, like the Mexican Mauser, which is touted as being shorter and hence—as already noted—highly desirable for a light mountain rifle, is actually only a fraction of an inch shorter than the standard model. Other famous actions, like the German 33/40 intended for mountain troops, commanded a premium price.

When magnum actions from the Mauserwerke at Oberndorf were not available, a skilled gunsmith could make his own long action by taking two standard actions, cutting them in two, and welding the pieces back together. The trick was to start with two identical actions, from the same maker, and preferably with serial numbers that were reasonably close. They were cut in such a way that each action yielded a short piece and a long piece; by welding the long front to the long rear, the maker then had a magnum-length action; welding the leftover short pieces together gave him a miniature Mauser as well. The bolt also needed lengthening and this, I am told, was actually considerably more difficult. The whole operation is much easier to write about than to accomplish, but it was not uncommon.

* * *

The Mauser 98 also spawned military imitations. England and the United States each recognized the superiority of the Mauser to, respectively, the Lee-Enfield and the Krag, but they wanted to make their own rifles. Accordingly, the United States designed the famous Springfield rifle, which was a Mauser in everything but name.

Jack O'Connor:

It was designed at the Springfield Arsenal by crossing the Mauser with the Krag. Various departures were made from Mauser design, and in every instance the designers laid an egg. If these departures were made as an improvement, they failed. If they were made with the worthy notion of avoiding royalty payments to Paul von Mauser, they also failed, since Mauser put the bite on Uncle Sam for a royalty payment of one dollar for every rifle manufactured for many years.

What were these failures? A two-piece striker that was prone to break, compared to the stronger, one-piece striker in the Mauser; a safety lug that did little; and the absence of gas-escape ports. The Springfield safety imitated that in the Mauser, but was more complicated, with more parts.

The desire to avoid paying royalties to Mauser for patent infringement was the cause of many inferior features found in other actions, as well. To avoid copying a good Mauser feature, like cocking-on-opening, a designer would use an inferior cock-on-closing feature, like that found in the Enfield P-14 and P-17.

The Enfield was Britain's attempt to upgrade in the years before 1914. The action is a Mauser 98 with some changes, including the cocking mechanism, the bolt shroud, and the safety. It was originally intended to use a 7mm cartridge. When war loomed in 1913, the project was delayed; Britain gave large contracts to Remington, Winchester, and Eddystone to produce the rifle in .303 British, in order to avoid logistics problems during a war. Winchester went to great lengths to adapt the magazine, designed for a rimless 7mm, to feed the rimmed .303. When the United States entered the war in 1917, faced with a shortage of rifles, Remington spearheaded an effort to convert the .303 P-14 to the .30-06 P-17, and hundreds of thousands of rifles were produced by all three companies to supplement the Springfield.

The Enfield P-17 action is many things, but graceful is not one of them. It is huge—far larger than required for any of the above cartridges. It has a deep box magazine that gives the rifle a pot-bellied appearance. The bolt handle is dog-leg shaped, and the rear sight is protected by unsightly steel "ears" on the bridge. The bolt-release spring is so stiff that it requires two hands to operate. But—and this is a big but—it is both large and extremely strong. In the hands of a good gunsmith, it can be turned into a fine custom rifle in any caliber up to A-Square's mammoth .577 Tyrannosaur, a cartridge that dwarfs even the .505 Gibbs.

There's an interesting fact about the Enfield: It was designed to allow the extractor to snap over a cartridge if one is simply dropped in front of the bolt and slammed into the chamber. You do not need to put the cartridge in the magazine and feed it from there, as you do with a Mauser 98. In a dangerous-

A Remington-made Enfield P-17, moderately sporterized. The unsightly ears have been milled off to a square bridge, and drilled and tapped. The rifle is cocked, with the safety on. The safety is very positive and secure: It cams the striker back from the sear and holds it solidly in place. Note how the stem of the bolt serves as a safety lug, locking into a notch in the receiver. The P-17 is large and strong; while not pretty, it is an excellent foundation for a dangerous-game rifle.

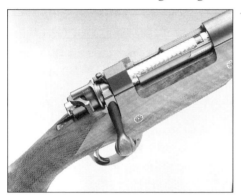

The ultimate in custom rifles, built on a military Mauser 98 action by the David Miller Co. This is a .458 Winchester. Although heavily modified, functionally the 98 action remains essentially as it was issued to the military. Actions manufactured in the early 1900s are so well made and well designed, and manufactured from such high quality steel, that in the right hands they can be turned into a masterpiece.

Photo by Ron Dehn

game rifle, this can be a lifesaver. Most custom rifles are altered to incorporate this feature, but the P-17 already has it.

For many years, the Enfield was the automatic choice for anyone wanting a .416 Rigby, and Jack O'Connor was one famous user of such a rifle. Customized, with the ears milled off the bridge, the bolt handle replaced, the magazine shortened, and converted to cock on opening, it becomes a very attractive and slick custom rifle. After the second world war, W. J. Jeffery in London made custom rifles on converted P-14 actions, and even today, A-Square's Hannibal rifles are all built on military-surplus P-17 actions.

In 1918, with the war over, the U.S. government promptly cancelled its contracts with Remington, Winchester, and Eddystone. At the end, Remington was producing some four thousand rifles a day; looking over its factories full of machinery, the racks of barrels and bins full of parts, the company decided to

Holland & Holland, in .375 H&H, built on a military Mauser 98 action. A fine example of turning a military action into a functional work of art. This rifle was built to be a working rifle, with a new bolt shroud and Model 70-style wing safety, Oberndorf floorplate release, an island rear sight (rather than the more elaborate quarter rib), and no provision for a riflescope.

Courtesy Holland & Holland

turn all these erstwhile P-17s into civilian rifles. The result was the Remington Model 30, introduced in 1921. It was available only in .30-06. A few years later it was replaced by the Model 30S, which was replaced in turn by the Model 720 in 1941. Looking at the 720, you can still see the Enfield heritage, although by that stage Remington had incorporated many of the usual alterations, such as converting the action to cock on opening. Because of the war, relatively few Remington 720s were manufactured; Frank de Haas described it as "the Cadillac of Enfields," and Philip Sharpe wrote that the 720 was the strongest rifle ever made in the United States. In 1948, when Remington returned to full civilian production, it was with an entirely new bolt-action rifle—the Model 721. It was a total redesign and the beginning of a new era.

* * *

After 1918, America's Springfield rifle went a completely different route. With the end of hostilities, hundreds of thousands of rifles were released to the public through the Director of Civilian Marksmanship. To a great degree, the Springfield introduced the American hunter, a lever-action devotee, to the virtues of the bolt action. Many were sporterized, and the Springfield provided the basis for companies like Griffin & Howe to create a whole new custom-rifle market. Theodore Roosevelt used one in Africa in 1909, and Ernest Hemingway took a sporterized Springfield to Africa in 1933. Although some were chambered in cartridges as large as the .375 H&H, the action was not as adaptable as the 98. Since superb surplus 98s were available for a song, that is what most makers used. As fine civilian rifles like the Remington Model 30 and the Winchester Model 54 (and later the Model 70) came along, the Springfield was eclipsed. Eventually, the old soldier just faded away.

The Modern Mauser

The greatest of the great has to be the Model 98 Mauser. The momentum of its functional excellence will easily carry it to the end of this century and beyond.

Jim Carmichel, 1986

The era of the commercial Mauser action, made by the Mauserwerke in Oberndorf, ended in the 1930s. Since then, the Mauser company has made several different models of rifle, but none based on its founder's masterpiece. What a genuine Mauser-made 98, with its distinctive banner on the action ring, might be worth today is anyone's guess. Thousands, at least—and it is a continuing puzzle as to why the Mauser company has never tried to turn this opportunity into commercial reality. Others have, with considerably less to gain.

There is a waiting market for Mauser actions of all types, in the short (*kurz*) configuration and in the standard length, but mostly in the magnum action for dangerous-game rifles. In the 1980s, an SCI member donated five original magnum Mauser actions to the organization, and they were made into rifles and auctioned. At the time, the estimated value of those actions was $5,000 apiece; it would be much higher now.

There is a thriving market in Mauser actions, not only original Oberndorfs but FN Supremes, the top military actions, and commercial actions that can be worked over and polished up. The market is companies like H&H and Jeffery in London, Hartmann & Weiss in Hamburg, and individual rifle makers in the United States. It is a point of pride with these prominent names that they can offer "genuine Mauser" actions. In some cases, such as H&H, a supply of actions was squirreled away in the days when they were freely available (a magnificent piece of foresight).

Among hunters and rifle lovers, there is a continuing interest in rifles with real Mauser actions—not modified Mausers or Mauser derivatives or "mostly Mauser" actions with corners cut to save money. Nor even, for that matter, actions that have legitimate improvements. A real market still exists for genuine 98s.

This has not been lost on individual gunsmiths and gunmaking companies. The only solid attempt to emulate the magnum Mauser was the French Brevex, which lasted but a few years (and the Brevex actions are worth far more today than when they were new). Since the demise of the Brevex, there have been several attempts to do it again. Gunsmith Parker Ackley attempted to have Mauser actions made in Japan; a company called Royal Arms tried to have one made in Korea. All foundered for one reason or another, usually economic.

If an authentic Mauser action can retail for $5,000, however, economies of scale become considerably less important, and a few gunsmiths have produced actions, one at a time, one machine cut at a time, in small shops. This requires equipment and skill beyond the resources of all but a handful of gunsmiths. However, with the advent of CNC machinery, the small-scale, high-dollar manufacture of rifle actions becomes not only possible, but economically viable.

In Europe, Reimer Johanssen began making Mauser actions in the 1990s and selling them to rifle makers and gunsmiths. In the United States, Granite Mountain Arms of Arizona began making a magnum Mauser in 1998. A Granite Mountain action sells, in the white, for about $3,000 (2005).

Of course, the Granite Mountain action is not a "pure" Mauser. It uses different (and allegedly better) steel than the original magnum Mauser, and it is made specifically to accommodate the mammoth cartridges that are popular today, calibers such as the .416 Rigby and .505 Gibbs. Its dimensions are different, and there are some minor modifications to eliminate wobble in the bolt (when it is pulled back fully) and so on.

* * *

The average consumer is more interested in being able to buy a finished rifle than an action in the white, and few can afford a full-blown custom rifle such as those built on the Granite Mountain. In 2002, George Sandmann and his partners formed a company called Empire Rifles, with the goal of building genuine custom and semi-custom Mauser-actioned rifles.

Empire formed an alliance with Dumoulin–Herstal of Belgium (Empire is Dumoulin's North American importer) and put together a network of craftsmen to build its rifles. For smaller cartridges, Empire used actions made in Italy and refined in Belgium; for magnum rifles, Sandmann used the Granite Mountain. Then, in 2005, Sandmann contracted for the first Empire Mausers, made to his exact specifications.

"There were some minor changes I wanted, from the Granite Mountain," he told me. "Also, the base price of a Granite Mountain was forcing our finished rifles prices higher than I wanted them to be. By making our own action, we are able to keep our prices down."

The initial run of Empire actions was finished in the summer of 2005. The very first of these was chambered for the .495 A-Square and turned into the rifle that graces the cover of this book.

Although Empire Rifles offers any caliber imaginable, most interest from

A new .500 Jeffery, by W.J. Jeffery of London. The action is a magnum Mauser, by Ritterbusch. The takedown feature is optional, and most rifles in this caliber are solid frame. Other options on Jeffery bolt actions include grade of wood, type of safety, engraving, and all dimensions.   *Courtesy W.J. Jeffery & Co.*

The quintessential Mauser: This *East Africa* rifle, from the Empire Rifle Co., incorporates every feature expected on a dangerous-game rifle. Built on a magnum Mauser 98 action, this .500 Jeffery has a quarter rib with folding leaf sights, barrel-band sling swivel, Oberndorf floorplate release, Model 70-style three-position wing safety, and riflescope in a detachable claw mount. Empire now manufactures its own Mauser actions.   *Courtesy Empire Rifle Co.*

the firm's customers has been dangerous-game rifles, and the cartridge in which there is the most interest is that beast from the past, the .500 Jeffery. This is understandable because the Mauser 98 is the particular darling of the elephant-hunting crowd. Those interested in accuracy or ultralight weight or maximum velocity go elsewhere; those who want absolute reliability combined with maximum power look first to the Mauser 98. And many will not look anywhere else.

Sandmann's goal in creating Empire Rifles was not just to have one more custom-rifle maker. There are many such, and they are all good (or they would not still be in business). Beyond that, his ambition was not unlike that of Don Allen in the 1980s, when he founded Dakota Arms, and that was to make a rifle the way he felt it should be made, at a price the average serious rifle lover could afford.

The Empire Rifle Company is putting a genuine, Mauser-actioned dangerous-game rifle—a serious, traditional stopping rifle—within the financial reach of anyone who can afford to hunt big bears in Alaska, elephants in Botswana, or Cape buffalo in the Rift Valley. And, Empire is helping to keep the Mauser 98 and the Mauser mystique alive.

Mauser's Rivals

In many respects the 98 Mauser is superior to any of the modified Mauser-type actions that followed it.

Jack O'Connor

After 1945, efforts to design new actions to replace the Mauser 98 really began in earnest. Manufacturers would have you believe it was a pious desire on their part to make rifles safer and more accurate, but the real driving force was to reduce manufacturing costs. This was part of a larger trend that afflicted gun-making in every country, with every type of firearm, for fifty years. Since the 1890s—the high-water mark of craftsmanship—standards in gunmaking declined steadily everywhere there was mass production. Consider, for example, the lever-action Savage 99, which was manufactured throughout this period: An 1899 made in 1910 is far better finished, with greater attention to detail, than one made in 1925; the 1925 rifle is better than one from 1940; and a 99 from 1965 does not bear thinking of.

As we have seen, the Mauser 98 action was expensive to produce and had features that were perceived as faults. Also, the design was fifty years old. Manufacturers learned during the war that equipment could be thrown together cheaply and still work. Why not rifle actions as well? Also, this was an age that worshipped the new and purely functional. Up to 1948, Remington had been manufacturing sporting rifles based on the Enfield, which was itself based on the Mauser and incorporated many of its features and manufacturing drawbacks. So Remington set out to design a completely new mechanism. The result was the Model 721.

The 721 did away with the claw extractor and used a bolt turned on a lathe, with a bolt face surrounded by a rim that completely enclosed the head of the cartridge. The extractor was a small, spring-loaded claw that snapped over the rim. The ejector was a spring-loaded plunger on the opposite side of the bolt face. The bolt itself extended a fraction of an inch past the twin locking lugs, and this extension was enclosed by the receiver—hence the "three rings of steel" claim. The 721 received rave reviews from virtually everyone. General Julian S. Hatcher hailed it as "the strongest rifle in the world" and told of a torture test that pitted the 721 against a Springfield, a Mauser 98, and an Enfield P-17. The

721 outlasted them all; its rivals failed in the order listed.

The 721 was undoubtedly strong. It was also very accurate. And it was homely. Every authority who reviewed the rifle and loved it for its strength and accuracy also commented on its cheaper aspects: The trigger guard was a stamping more suited to a kid's .22, and the floorplate was not even hinged. The receiver was round, so it could be turned inexpensively on a lathe rather than milled with a flat surface, and users soon found that a round receiver will split a stock if the guard screw is tightened too far. Instead of an integral recoil lug, either milled into the receiver or brazed on afterward, the 721 had a separate piece of flat steel that was held in place by the shoulder of the barrel when it was screwed into the receiver. This approach is common today. In 1948, it was anathema.

The cookie-cutter mentality of mass production, stamping out cheap but serviceable goods, had finally and irrevocably come to the firearms world. General Hatcher, Phil Sharpe, Frank de Haas, and others who saw rifles and shotguns as artifacts of craftsmanship, lovingly created by skilled and devoted men, were horrified. Even so, they could hardly argue with the facts: A Remington 721, demonstrably accurate and stronger than any of its competitors, could be had (according to the 1955 *Gun Digest*) for $80.35, compared to $120.95 for a Winchester Model 70, the "rifleman's rifle."

Not every rifle maker followed Remington's path, of course. In Europe, while many companies did try to cut corners to reduce the cost of making a Mauser 98 (including, ultimately, FN), others tried to design actions that were genuinely better. Out of all these conflicting trends emerged a few actions that did make an impact on the world of dangerous-game rifles, where saving pennies counted considerably less than saving lives.

Remington 700

In 1962, Remington killed the 721 and replaced it with the Model 700, which has been the mainstay of the company's high-powered rifle line ever since.

The 700 is the 721 turned into a lady: The trigger guard was milled, and the rifle was given a hinged floorplate. Ironically, the new milled trigger guard had the same shape as that in the original Enfield P-17—a distinctive form it retains to this day—and the 700 stock was more elegant. The 700 has never shaken that "mass produced" look, but there is no arguing with either its strength or its accuracy. Over the course of forty-some years, it has killed a great deal of game all over the world, including the biggest game in Africa.

For years the Remington 700 was the unchallenged accuracy king. The U.S. Army adopted it as their specialist sniper rifle, and custom gunmakers from Kenny Jarrett on down used the 700 as the basis for super-accurate "bean-field" rifles. Recently, small-production specialty actions have come along to nip at its heels, and word is that the machinery on which the 700 is built is on its last legs, with a resulting drastic slip in quality. Jarrett told me in 2003 that he would no longer build a rifle on a Model 700 because the new actions are so ramshackle. Be that as it may, it is still in production and is still chambered in a wide variety of cartridges.

As a dangerous-game rifle, the Model 700 is perfectly adequate. It has never been the basis of any truly fine custom rifles, even though it dominated the "customized" or "rebuilt" market of rifles in the $2,500 range. Every gunsmith who fancied himself a gunmaker and wanted to offer guaranteed accuracy could do so with reworked 700s, but very few of those rifles were chambered for really big cartridges. From the Remington factory, chamberings in serious dangerous-game cartridges have been relatively few. For years, the 700 "Safari" was available in .375 H&H and .458 Winchester. Starting in 1989, the .416 Remington chambering was added. The "Safari" has always been available only from Remington's custom shop, not as an off-the-shelf 700.

The 700 has had no real impact on the professional-hunter market and relatively little on clients hunting the biggest African game. Where it has had an influence is on other rifles and actions. The concept of reducing costs by making the major parts (bolt and receiver) lathe-turned cylinders has spread throughout the industry. Even Dakota, which swam against the tide with its lovely original Model 76, later introduced a lower-priced model, the 97, with a cylindrical receiver. The 700's "three rings of steel" bolt face has been emulated all over the place.

Schultz & Larsen

About the same time Remington was coming out with the 721, Philip B. Sharpe and the Danish firm of Schultz & Larsen were combining in a project that ultimately failed, but had a lasting impact in several areas.

Phil Sharpe was many things, all of them genuine: Rifle expert, ballistician, author, and captain in the U.S. Army. During the 1930s he was an experimenter and wildcatter, and he is given much of the credit for development of the .357 Magnum cartridge. In the late '30s he wrote two magnificent books—*The Rifle in America* and *The Complete Guide to Handloading*. Both are huge, running to eight hundred and seven hundred pages respectively, and went through several editions each, growing with every revision. The mass of detail is daunting even to look at. Although these books are both almost fifty years old, the material they contain is still valid and valuable—to say nothing of fascinating.

During the second world war, Sharpe was a captain in the army ordnance department and spent his time in Europe poking around secret German arms installations. When he came home, he bought some property in Maine and built a "gunbug's paradise" with a house, shooting range, and ballistics laboratory. During his time in Europe, Captain Sharpe came to know personally many of the influential men in the European arms industry, including Niels Larsen of Schultz & Larsen, a Danish manufacturer of fine target rifles (and later free pistols). As well, Sharpe came across a secret experimental French 7mm machine-gun round that gave him an idea for the project he hoped would give him immortality: A factory 7mm magnum cartridge—the 7 x 61 Sharpe & Hart. Richard Hart was a colleague who helped in the development and became a business partner, but Phil Sharpe was the driving force behind the cartridge.

Two influential men became interested in the project: Niels Larsen, and Amund Enger, president of Norma Projektilfabrik, the Swedish ammunition company. The important aspect of this from our point of view is the action the Danish firm developed to house Sharpe's cartridge. The Schultz & Larson Model 54J (54 for the year of its introduction, "J" for *jaeger*, or hunter) was a massively long and heavy action with four rear locking lugs instead of two larger ones at the front. This allowed the receiver to remain a solid steel tube enclosing the chamber, with no raceways. The four lugs afforded a remarkably low bolt-lift (all to the good) and the action was as slick and smooth as Danish craftsmanship could make it. The magazine box was an in-line, rather than staggered, column, which gave the rifle a distinctly deep-bellied look. The magazine could be loaded only through the floorplate. If its appearance was strange to American eyes, there was no denying its virtues: Schultz & Larsen knew how to make accurate rifles, and this one was accurate. It was also enormously strong.

Phil Sharpe and Richard Hart formed a company to import the rifles, which were chambered only in the 7x61 S&H; Norma made the ammunition and shipped it in boxes labelled *Sharpe & Hart Associates*.

At the time, American Roy Weatherby had just returned from his first safari in Africa and had designed his huge .378 Weatherby cartridge. Up until this time, Weatherby rifles had been built mainly on FN Supreme Mauser actions, but the .378 was too bulky. The Schultz & Larsen, on the other hand, was perfect, and early .378s were built on the new Danish action. When Weatherby later designed his Mark V, in the late 1950s, some of the concepts it embodied were borrowed from the Schultz & Larsen; if you compare illustrations of the Mark V rifle with the later Schultz & Larsen Model 65 (in *Gun Digests* of the time) there is an unmistakable resemblance in styling. The Schultz & Larsen was the more expensive of the two.

In the final edition of *The Rifle in America* (1958), Sharpe devotes a chapter to the 7x61 project, explaining in obsessive detail the work that went into development of both cartridge and rifle. He claims that the cartridge took five years to develop and cost him more than $10,000. Although it began life as an experimental French military round, the final design was a shortened, reshaped .300 H&H case. It is hard to see where $10,000 and five years went, but this is not really unusual. Ned Roberts referred to "many years of development" for his .257 Roberts, a necked down 7x57. Today, a wildcat can be conjured up in an evening, with head-stamped brass in production a week later.

In spite of all this, Sharpe's baby went, essentially, nowhere. Frank de Haas concluded, with some regret, that it ended as a failure for a number of reasons, not least of which was Sharpe's obsessive testing and retesting to reprove points that were already proven. But mainly, the 7x61 never delivered the phenomenal ballistic performance claimed (a 160-grain bullet at 3,100 fps), although it was a fine cartridge (and a handsome one, for that matter). Recently, it has made a reappearance as the 7x61 Super.

The Schultz & Larsen rifle was redesigned as the Model 60, which was then followed by the 65 and 68DL (the numbers all denoting the year of introduction). The odd appearance of the 54J gave way to the distinctly racy lines of the 65. As a gun-struck teenager I lusted after one mightily and even had a Norma promotional sheet for the 7x61 Sharpe & Hart taped to my bedroom wall. In 1990, I saw one of the two Schultz & Larsens it has ever been my privilege to handle. It was a Model 60 (not as seductive as the 65), and the price was out of my range. It certainly was slick, but it was unnecessarily heavy and no thing of beauty; regretfully, I handed it back. The second Schultz & Larsen was an original .378 Weatherby. It had a deep fore end that was also narrow, a shotgun-style bow trigger guard, and a stock of blonde wood that would gag a goat. The barrel was long and the rifle extremely heavy. I handed it back with absolutely no regrets.

Frank de Haas handled only one Schultz & Larsen rifle and while he admired some aspects of it (the workmanship was superb), he disliked one vital element: It was very difficult to load. With a scope, holding it upside down to put cartridges into the magazine was awkward. The receiver had an opening in the side through which it could be loaded as a single shot, but the opening was tight and stuffing a cartridge through it was tricky. In the case of the .378— intended for dangerous-game—this is a damning fault.

Granted, Phil Sharpe did not intend the Schultz & Larsen, whose design he oversaw, as a dangerous-game rifle. But he did intend it to "correct" what he saw as failings of the Mauser 98. The S&L's rear lug lock-up "strengthened" the receiver, and allowed the bolt face to be completely enclosed. It also provided a lower bolt lift and shorter bolt travel. It was an action that moved in the direction Sharpe saw the shooting world going: to higher velocities and ever-higher pressures, with extreme accuracy being the ultimate demand.

Exactly what happened afterward is a matter of some mystery. Philip B.

Sharpe died in 1961, some say as an alcoholic and by his own hand. If so, he joins the ranks of gun writers who ended it with a bullet—an outcome that is almost an occupational hazard. Details are hard to obtain, and harder to confirm. Sharpe's business venture died with him. Schultz & Larsen struggled on in the U.S. market for another decade, offering its Model 68DL through a new agent in a wide range of calibers, but finally the company retreated to Europe. Today, the firm still builds very fine and stylish hunting rifles, but does not even have an American importer.

The year after Phil Sharpe's untimely death, Remington introduced the 7mm Remington Magnum in its new 700 rifle and put paid to virtually every other 7mm magnum, wildcat or factory.

It was for Philip B. Sharpe, as de Haas notes, a very sad end both to an extremely productive life, and a venture that could have resulted in an excellent rifle and cartridge if circumstances had been different.

Weatherby Mark V

Across the continent, in California, times and tastes were running in a different direction. With the introduction of his massive .378, Roy Weatherby needed a larger action than the FN Mausers he had been using. As already noted, he turned first to Schultz & Larsen; when the even larger .460 was introduced, it was built on the Brevex magnum Mauser action. None of these solutions really suited Weatherby, however. He wanted an action that would not only be the strongest and safest available, but the most stylish and streamlined as well.

According to Tom Gresham, in his book *Weatherby*, Roy was concerned at reports of blown primers and ruptured case heads resulting from overly ambitious handloaders. Normal actions would stand up to 70,000 copper units of pressure (cup); Weatherby wanted one that would withstand 200,000 cup.

Weatherby and his chief engineer, Fred Jennie, sketched an action and ordered a prototype. It was unlike anything seen up until that time. Even fifty years later, the Weatherby Mark V looks modern, efficient, and attractive. The bolt has no locking lugs in the Mauser sense. Instead, it has nine small lugs, in three rows, on the head of the bolt, set up as an interrupted thread. When the bolt is closed, the nine lugs lock into corresponding threads in the receiver ring. The lugs are machined into the bolt after the bolt itself is turned, so the body is the same diameter as the lugs. The bolt moves slickly and smoothly, with none of the wobble found on Mausers.

As in the Schultz & Larsen action, the bolt lift is short (54 degrees) because the lugs do not have to be turned far to disengage. Also like the S&L, there are three gas vent holes visible on the side of the bolt when it is closed, and the bolt is fluted. The bolt shroud is smooth and rounded, and gives the action the look of a tango dancer with slicked-back hair. It is pure Hollywood. The safety is a rocker on the side of the shroud that blocks the striker and locks the bolt shut.

For sheer size, the Mark V is almost in a class by itself. It is massive enough to handle the .460 Weatherby, which really makes it oversized for the smaller .257 Weatherby class, but there is no arguing with either its strength or safety. As well, for the first ten years, the Mark V barreled actions were made by J. P. Sauer in Germany, and the workmanship and finishing were superb. The author had a Sauer-made .300 Weatherby that was as slick as they come. By 1970, with costs in Europe skyrocketing, Weatherby moved production to the Howa factory in Japan, which is where it stayed until 1994. From there, manufacturing was moved first to Maine (1994), then to Minnesota (1999). As with virtually every other firearm, over the years the standard of finishing of Weatherby actions, especially internal finishing, has declined. A Howa-made action is not nearly as smooth as a Sauer, and the first American-made actions from the mid-90s were not as smooth as the Howa. Of course, none of this affects strength or safety.

The Weatherby Mark V can also be superbly accurate, delivering almost benchrest-quality groups. I once had a Howa-made .257 Weatherby that consistently printed five-shot, half-inch groups with factory ammunition.

As fine as the Mark V undoubtedly is, it has never had much impact on the dangerous-game market aside from its use by movie stars on safari. There are many reasons for this, not least of which is the visceral dislike of professional hunters for both Weatherby rifles and the whole high-velocity concept. In thirty-five years of traveling to Africa, I have seen exactly one professional hunter who used a Weatherby rifle (a large Spaniard with a .460). Prejudice aside, the Mark V lacks a couple of vital elements. The two-position safety does not allow the bolt to be cycled, and the rifle unloaded, with the safety on. In the larger calibers, it has only a two-round magazine capacity, making it a three-shot rifle at most, and loading the big cartridges through the spring-steel magazine lips is tricky. Naturally, being a "push feed," it has neither a claw extractor nor controlled-round feeding.

Also, the Mark V is not as easy to disassemble as a Mauser 98 for cleaning and maintenance, and there are several small parts that are easily lost. The first time I dismantled the bolt of a Mark V, the retainer ball bearing that aligns the striker popped out and, as ball bearings will do, rolled far and fast. In the wilds of Africa that would put the rifle out of commission.

The Mark V's stock has been an object of both adoration and ridicule for its "California" styling, its exaggerated Monte Carlo comb, flat-bottomed fore end, white-line spacers, and exotic inlays. Personally, I always found that the Weatherby stock, while a little outlandish for my taste, felt really good. It was

The author with an Alaska brown bear and a .300 Weatherby. This rifle is an amazingly slick Sauer-made action from 1969. The Mark V's push-feed action made no difference in this instance. The author did learn, however, that when in bear country, be loaded for bear, not deer. Luckily (!), the third 150-grain Nosler broke his neck.

A .416 Weatherby and a 43-inch Cape buffalo in Tanzania in 1990 – the author's only one-shot kill on this durable beast. This is the one (and only) time he has used a muzzle brake when hunting. Never again.

not blocky or awkward like some modern stocks that seem designed for something other than the human hand and shoulder. In his book, Tom Gresham points out that Roy Weatherby paid great attention to his stock design, and every aspect of it was carefully thought out. He wanted a stock that would come to the shoulder naturally and point where the shooter looked, like a fine shotgun. The fore end, triangular in cross-section, provides an excellent hold for the leading hand, for control under recoil. If its appearance is no longer to my taste, functionally it is still excellent.

Having said all that, I have hunted with Weatherby rifles from Alaska to Botswana, including several outings that involved dangerous game. In Alaska in 1988, I was armed with a .300 Weatherby when a brown bear came boiling out of the bush, and that slick Sauer bolt worked like silk as I fired three of the fastest shots of my life. I have also hunted Cape buffalo, twice, with a .416 Weatherby. It is a very fine cartridge, but the Mark V floorplate had an alarming tendency to pop open (a matchstick and some tape solved that, temporarily), and it was all too easy to have a cartridge jam solid if it was misaligned as I attempted to charge the magazine.

Finally, there is the question of barrel length. At one time, the Mark V was available with either a very whippy twenty-four-inch barrel or a thicker twenty-six-inch barrel. The big rifles (.378 to .460) now come only with a twenty-six-inch barrel and a removable two-inch muzzle brake. There is no combination of those components that adds up to a really good dangerous-game rifle. With the brake on, the report is ear-splitting and the barrel is far too long; without the brake, the gun is still awkward—not the kind of rifle I would want in my hands going into dense brush.

Fine as it is in many ways, the Mark V is not a major player among dangerous-game rifles—at least, not for those who carry them for a living.

Winchester Model 70

After the first world war, Winchester also introduced a bolt-action rifle, but did so with some reluctance. For a half-century, the company's mainstay had been the lever action—a design with which it will forever be associated—and there was some resistance to offering a "military" rifle.

Like Remington, Winchester had extensive experience producing the Enfield P-17. Unlike Remington, however, Winchester took its time and drew upon other designs before introducing the Model 54 in 1925. The 54 was greeted with almost universal admiration. It incorporated features of the Mauser 98 and the Springfield, along with some innovations. The 54 was available only in smaller calibers, it was on the market for eleven years, and only fifty thousand were manufactured. In 1936, Winchester pulled the 54

The author in 1993 with PH Duff Gifford and the Mount Longido Cape buffalo that took a bullet through both lungs and, ten minutes later, came out fighting. The last shot, fired from the hip at four feet, hit the bull just below the boss. The bullet went right through the skull, destroyed two vertebrae, and deflected into the chest. Retained weight was 404.7 grains—81 percent. The rifle is a post-64 Model 70, .458 Winchester handloaded with 500-grain Trophy Bonded Bear Claws.

Jack Carter with his Cape buffalo, on safari in Tanzania with Robin Hurt in 1990. The rifle is a .450 Ackley, custom-built on a pre-64 Model 70.

and replaced it with the rifle that became the definitive American bolt action: the Winchester Model 70.

The 70 came to be known as the "rifleman's rifle," a nickname that is richly deserved, because this is one of the finest bolt-action rifles ever produced in just about every way. Design, workmanship, materials—all were top-notch. During the brief life of the 54, Winchester paid careful attention to comments and suggestions, and these were reflected in the final design of the Model 70. The safety, which had been a vertical wing, became a horizontal, three-position wing safety, moving from front to back. It is without question the finest safety ever designed. The stamped-steel trigger guard of the 54 was replaced with a graceful, milled-steel guard.

Essentially, the Model 70 remained a Mauser 98 derivative, with some modifications that are serious improvements. Today, rifles built on original Mauser 98 actions routinely incorporate some of these features, notably the wing safety.

The introduction of the Model 70 brought another milestone: for the first time, an American-made rifle was available in .375 H&H, as well as .300 H&H. The latter cartridge had established itself on the American scene in 1935, when Ben Comfort shot one to win the 1,000-yard Wimbledon Cup match at Camp Perry. Alaska guides who regularly dealt with brown bears and grizzlies immediately seized upon the .375, and within a decade or two it was being noted that there was higher per-capita ownership of the .375 H&H in Alaska than anywhere else in America.

Winchester did not make the Model 70 in a magnum-size action. It fitted the two long H&H rounds by trimming steel internally from the standard .30-06 action. In later years, when early Model 70s became the darling of the custom-rifle industry, most gunmakers preferred to start out with a .30-06 action rather than a .375, because it allowed them to remove steel where they wanted to and not have to live with Winchester's overzealous trimming.

As a dangerous-game rifle, the Model 70 hit a peak in 1956, with the introduction of the .458 Winchester. Instantly, it became *the* factory rifle for heavy game. The Model 70 was highly prized in Africa among professional hunters, and soon it was a common back-up rifle among the vast majority who could not afford a British double.

No one has ever offered a completely satisfactory explanation for why Winchester chose to design the .458 with such a short case. Granted, it was the age of the "short magnum"—short as opposed to the long .375 H&H. Two other Winchester cartridges introduced about the same time, the .264 and .338, were merely the .458 necked down. Neither the .264 nor the .338 case was too short for its bore, but the .458 undoubtedly was, and this is not merely hindsight; engineers at the Olin-Winchester ammunition plant knew they were being forced to compress powder unmercifully and even then were not attaining published velocities. So why did Winchester insist on a short .458 instead of something more closely resembling the later .458 Lott? Probably, no one will ever have a full answer, since Winchester records do not reveal it and the principals are no longer with us. One suggestion is that they had thousands of .30-06-length actions they wanted to use up; more probably, they looked at the amount of steel that was trimmed to make the .375 work, gulped when they realized that even more steel would need to be removed for a long .458, thereby weakening the action further, and decided to go with a short cartridge and more steel, rather than the reverse.

* * *

Corporately, all was not well with Winchester Repeating Arms. In the early 1960s, it was running into headwinds on several fronts. In 1962, Remington introduced its 700 with great fanfare. How much this took away sales from the Model 70 is difficult to say, but the following year Winchester undertook drastic measures. The machinery on which the Model 70 was built was reaching the end of its useful life; rifles coming off the line were displaying the usual hallmarks of tired machinery, in the form of lax tolerances and poor fitting. Faced with replacing the machinery, Winchester decided it was time to "update" the Model 70. This legendary decision—almost always condemned as a blunder — was understandable in retrospect.

One other factor often mentioned is the fact that Winchester brought in a new team of top management from the Ford Motor Company, and these people had a profound influence on Winchester's whole approach to rifle making. The venerated Model 70 was not only redesigned, but the aesthetics of the rifle were also hopelessly compromised. In a word, the gun looked cheap. The most important internal change was a switch from a full-length claw extractor to a plunger-style ejector similar to that of the Remington 700. The Model 70 ceased to be a controlled-feed action. As for its appearance, the monstrosity was "dressed up" with jewelling on the bolt, a band of knurling on the bolt knob, and white-line spacers on the stock. It looked like a small-town tart on Saturday night.

The reviews were almost universally negative. Even objective tests proving the new Model 70 to be stronger and more accurate than the old one had little effect. From that point, there was a steadily increasing demand for "pre-64" Model 70s; by the 1980s, dealing in pre-64s had become a cottage industry. There were gun dealers who did little else. It should be pointed out that "pre-64" is something of a misnomer. Jack O'Connor insisted it really should be "pre-63," and today most gunsmiths needing an action on which to build a custom rifle look for something made even before that—preferably in 1960 or '61. They avoid actions that were produced near the end, when the failings of the production equipment were becoming painfully obvious.

Winchester tried to sell the post-64 Model 70 with a glitzy, expensive advertising campaign starring East African professional hunter David Ommanney, but it did little good. With the arrival of the boys from Ford, and the demise of the pre-64 action, Winchester set itself on a downward spiral that culminated in several flirtations with Chapter 11, a management-leveraged buy-out, and eventually the reconstituting of the company as United States Repeating Arms and its absorption by the huge, European-owned arms conglomerate that also owns FN and Browning.

That final step was a boon for U.S. Repeating Arms, because suddenly there was money for new equipment. The late 1980s saw the arrival of computer-aided design and manufacturing (CAD/CAM) and computer numerically controlled (CNC) machines. Suddenly it was possible to reprogram production lines to produce small runs of special models. USRAC looked at the demand for pre-64 Model 70s and the success of the Dakota 76, and the company realized there was a market that could be tapped. They did a limited run of "post-93 pre-64s"—essentially a return to the original Model 70, with a few refinements—to test the market. This first run, priced at double that of a standard Model 70, sold out quickly. Within a few years, the new action had completely displaced the unloved post-64 throughout the line, with the post-64 still used only in the least-expensive models.

The change has certainly enhanced the image of the Model 70, and there is no doubt in my mind that the new post-93 is mechanically as good as the pre-64. That said, the pre-64 has attained a cult status, a chic, that will probably never be dispelled. Top-notch custom makers like David Miller still prefer the old one, but anyone looking for a good, working dangerous-game rifle is just as well off—and maybe better off—starting with a post-93 action.

How does the Model 70 compare with the Mauser 98? No one loved the Model 70 more than Jack O'Connor. When asked that very question, he said "The Model 70 is one of the two best bolt actions in the world."

Dakota 76

Don Allen was a top custom stock maker and Pete Grisel an outstanding metalsmith in the 1970s, when the pre-64 cult really began to gather steam. Why not, they asked, produce a whole new action based on the pre-64 Model 70, one that would be made of the finest steel, and incorporate some of the custom changes that had become commonplace?

The resulting action was the Dakota 76. Allen set up a company called Dakota Arms, located in Sturgis, South Dakota, and began production of

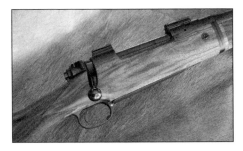

The Dakota 76 magnum-size action, here in the Traveler (takedown) configuration so popular in Europe. This rifle is a .458 Lott, but the action will accommodate much larger cartridges like the .450 Dakota and .505 Gibbs. It has a drop-box magazine (although not pronounced) with an Oberndorf-style floorplate release. The Dakota is undoubtedly one of the best and most stylish of the actions that have challenged the supremacy of the Mauser 98.

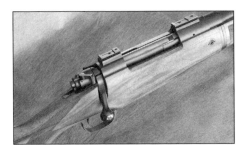

The Dakota magnum action from a different angle. The Mauser influence is obvious. Note the double shoulder on the Talley scope-mount bases to prevent the scope moving forward or back under recoil. If rail-type bases are used, such shoulders are essential–especially to keep the scope from flying off to the rear.

Subtle differences: The elegant Dakota bolt release, the catch that releases the shroud, the three-position wing safety.

actions, barrelled actions, and complete rifles. In the late 1980s, when a Zastava Mark X Mauser 98 action was available from Brownell's for about $300, the Dakota 76 cost $1,200. A decent pre-64 changed hands for about $400, so the Dakota was certainly priced at the high end.

While one would expect that the 76 would be greeted with joyous cries by the cognoscenti, such was not really the case, for a variety of reasons. First, however, let's take a look at the action.

The Dakota 76 can best be described as a hybrid of the pre-64 Model 70 and a commercial Mauser 98. It has the claw extractor and controlled feed; it has a stylish shroud with a beautifully designed wing safety. The bolt stop is unique; on all the Model 70s, the bolt stop is a rather cheap affair; Dakota replaced it with a small, hinged bar on the upper left part of the bridge. The 70's two-part trigger guard and floorplate are replaced by a Mauser-style one-piece guard. The action is made from 4140 steel, the finest available for the purpose.

Today, the action is available in three lengths. The magnum version can handle any cartridge on the market, including the .416 Rigby and .505 Gibbs. (Dakota's own line of proprietary cartridges includes a .450 based on the Rigby case.) So why is the Dakota not more popular among custom gunmakers? As D'Arcy Echols explained to me in 1990, it cost then about $2,000 to get to a basic, modified action suitable for building a custom rifle. It did not matter if you started with a $1,200 Dakota and added $800 in gunsmithing, or a $200 military Mauser 98 and added $1,800. The total always ended up about the same.

"The advantage of starting with the Mauser is that you can fashion every little detail exactly the way you, and the client, want it," D'Arcy said. "You are not stuck with someone else's idea of what a bolt stop should be or with the shape of the bolt handle."

Since 1990, Dakota Arms has grown to be America's foremost semi-custom maker of fine bolt-action rifles. The company will build you a completely bespoke rifle, or you can buy one ready-made off the shelf at a few higher-end dealers across the country. Don Allen, being a stockmaker, prized good walnut and was not only an expert in stock woods; he was also an astute trader who amassed a remarkable stockpile of walnut blanks in his Sturgis warehouse.

In 1997, Dakota introduced a modification of the 76 called the Model 97, a cheaper version of their established action. Its main difference is a receiver with a rounded bottom rather than a flat, milled bottom, which allows it to be made much more cheaply. The 97 has not exactly taken the world by storm, and I know of no one who has used it as the basis for a custom dangerous-game rifle.

Dakota did not stop with conventional bolt actions. One variation is a model called the Traveler, which is a takedown similar to rifles made in Europe. The receiver ring is a split sleeve that receives the barrel, and the breech-end of the barrel contains the lug raceways. So, when the barrel is slid into the sleeve and the bolt is closed, the bolt actually locks the barrel in place. The sleeve is tightened using a large Allen key, but when the rifle is fired, the only thing that counts is having the bolt closed. Of course, if you neglect to tighten the sleeve, the barrel could slide out as the bolt is being cycled—not exactly desirable in the middle of an elephant charge.

Another (admittedly niggling) complaint is that it actually takes a bit of practice to fit and remove the barrel. You may wonder what there is to learn about an Allen key. Well, pay attention.

The fore end is in two pieces, with the forward piece fastened to the barrel. At the breech end, it is equipped with a steel plate and a lug that fits into the corresponding plate on the action-side stock, aligning the pieces exactly. There are two Allen screws on the stock beneath the sleeve. One of these—on the right, as you look along the barrel—tightens the sleeve. The other one loosens the sleeve by pushing the two pieces apart, to make the barrel easier to remove. If the one on the left is screwed tightly while the other is loose, it will hold the sleeve in its spread position (this is such a small distance it is not readily noticeable), and while both screws feel tight, the barrel is actually floating inside the sleeve waiting to come off in your hand if the bolt is opened. As I say, this is tricky business. One must assemble the rifle with both screws backed out, then tighten the right screw until the barrel is gripped solidly; only then should you snug up the screw on the left to keep it from loitering there, waiting to fall out. If you take a Traveler to Africa, my only advice is to assemble it yourself, and once it is together, leave it together.

One advantage of having such a rifle is that, within reason, you can have multiple barrels for different cartridges, and if you fix it with detachable scope mounts, you can have interchangeable scopes, as well.

The Traveler is a beautifully made rifle of a type that appeals to Europeans, but it is also likely to gain fans in the United States as air travel becomes more difficult, the regulations grow more outlandish, and the appeal increases of a firearm that is not instantly recognizable as such to baggage handlers.

Finally, Dakota has branched out from bolt actions and now makes an extremely fine single-shot (the Model 10), which can be had in any cartridge, including the largest. Dakota has even made a double rifle. Only a couple have been completed; the first, a .500 NE, felt good to me and was certainly well made. It was built on a boxlock action with a pleasing round frame. Whether it can establish itself in the highly specialized and undeniably quirky world of double rifles remains to be seen.

Ruger 77

The last major American action of this era is an unsung hero —the Ruger 77.

From a standing start in 1949, Bill Ruger built Sturm, Ruger & Co. into the largest American firearms company—bigger than Winchester, Remington, or Smith & Wesson—and did so on the very simple basis of knowing what American shooters want and giving it to them.

William Batterman Ruger was a gun lover, pure and simple. He liked finely made firearms and also firearms that were purely functional and delivered the goods without fanfare or fine engraving. He had an instinct for what shooters liked, wanted, and were willing to pay for. Although the company's first product was a semiauto .22 pistol, Ruger's major triumphs came with seemingly anachronistic products that appealed to shooters' good taste. When Colt decided the single-action revolver was dead, Ruger countered with the Blackhawk and make a killing. When everyone else was looking for firepower, Ruger introduced his single-shot No. 1. Forty years later, the No. 1 is an institution on the American shooting scene.

In 1968, Ruger introduced the Model 77 bolt-action rifle, and almost forty years later I can still remember the rave reviews. With the controversy raging over Winchester's bowdlerized Model 70, Ruger's 77 was a breath of fresh air. It had a lovely stock of the style now known as American classic, designed by Lenard Brownell, one of the best stockers of the day. There were no white-line spacers, no garish fore-end tips, no machine turning or jewelling. The rifle had a full-length claw extractor, which gave it an instant Mauser 98 look, but the homage to Mauser was more than skin deep. Frank de Haas described it as a "modified Mauser." The 77 has a different trigger, bolt stop, and safety, and integral scope bases on the receiver, which are now common but certainly were not in 1968.

Mechanically, the 77 broke ground by using investment castings for the receiver, bolt, and bolt handle. Ruger overcame American resistance to the idea of a "casting" in any firearm, not just with the 77 but also the No. 1. Without getting into a long treatise on metallurgy, investment or "lost wax" casting is a method of producing very exact castings made of excellent alloys. The resulting parts require very little further machining and polishing, and are a far, far cry from the days of "cast iron." Still, the prejudice lingered, and it took the firearms genius of Bill Ruger to overcome it.

The safety on the original 77 was on the tang, and it moved forward and back exactly like a shotgun safety. The floorplate release was a lever with a striated projection in the front of the trigger guard, just like that of the Oberndorf Mauser. Overall, the Ruger 77 had a pleasing appearance reminiscent of the pre-64 Model 70. It was a rifle you could lean against a wall, and then just stand back and admire the lines.

The original 77 was available in just one action length, but additional lengths were added gradually. In 1971, a longer version was introduced and almost immediately became available in .458 Winchester, which remained a standard chambering for decades. It was, however, merely a variation on the standard rifle.

Ruger had a bigger idea in mind, and in 1989 the company introduced the model that redefined the American dangerous-game rifle: The M-77 Mk. II Magnum. It was available in .375 H&H and—unbelievably—.416 Rigby! The beast had a lovely stock of Circassian walnut and a three-position safety on the shroud to replace the shotgun-style catch. It had a barrel-band front sight and a quarter rib with three folding leaf "express" sights. This rifle off the shelf was pure Robert Ruark. As with the Blackhawk and the No. 1 years before, Bill Ruger had determined what such a rifle should be and what Americans wanted. Then he built it for them.

This news was greeted with disbelief. Why, the pundits asked, would Ruger make a bolt action in a caliber that was moribund at best? Yet again, though, Bill Ruger had tapped a deep-seated desire in the American shooter. The average guy might not be able to go to Africa, but he could now afford a .416 Rigby and do a little more than daydream.

With this move, Ruger singlehandedly resurrected the .416 Rigby cartridge. With a popular, highly respected company producing an affordable rifle, it provided impetus for brass manufacturers and ammunition makers to produce Rigby cases. Not long afterward, the No. 1 was also made available in .416 Rigby, which gave it added momentum.

The M-77 Mk. II Magnum is a serious rifle. In 1990, its price tag was $1,500—almost three times the cost of a 77 in .458 Winchester and approaching the price of the Dakota 76. The action is massive and strong, and accuracy is more than adequate. A recent modification has been to move the front sling swivel onto a barrel band—another hallmark of the classic express rifle. Today, the 77 Magnum is also available in .458 Lott, and remarkably, the suggested price is still less than $2,000. For dangerous game on a budget, this is about as good a deal as it is possible to get.

Since its introduction, the Ruger 77 has established a reputation in several different ways. For one, there is no question about its durability and reliability. The Ruger 77 in .338 Winchester has largely displaced the Model 70 .375 H&H as the standard bear-guide rifle in Alaska. Partly this is due to one Anchorage gun dealer who brought in these guns by the carload and sold them for a couple of hundred dollars apiece; many guides of my acquaintance would use a rifle for a couple of years, not worry about the salt spray as long as it worked, and then scrap it and buy another. Cost was certainly an advantage, but bear guides do not try to save money at the expense of reliability. The rifle's success in Alaska added, however, to the Ruger's somewhat "bargain-basement" image.

Excellent as it is mechanically, the 77 has never established itself as an action on which to base a fine custom rifle, but right now, the Magnum in .458 Lott or .416 Rigby is as good an off-the-shelf dangerous-game rifle as you will find anywhere in the world, at a remarkably low price.

A-Square Hannibal

The A-Square Hannibal is the P-17 Enfield, sporterized, customized, honed, and polished—but an Enfield P-17 nonetheless. Just by its existence, it reinforces the worth of the basic Mauser 98 action.

When Art Alphin formed the A-Square Company in 1979, its one goal was to make dangerous-game rifles. Although it has branched out since, offering rifles in smaller calibers, that is still the company's *raison d'être*. Alphin was designing big cartridges like the .500 A-Square, and he needed a big, strong, reliable Mauser action on which to build them. P-17 rifles were freely available at low cost, many still packed in Cosmoline from government warehouses. For years, gunmakers had been using the P-17 as the basis for .416 Rigbys and .505 Gibbs's. It was perfect for Alphin's purpose.

Although designed originally for the .303 British cartridge, the action is much larger than it needs to be and offers a gunsmith the opportunity to remove metal where he needs to and leave metal where he wants to. This is an advantage over such actions as the FN Supreme and Winchester Model 70 made for the .375 H&H, because the metal has already been milled away—and, in the opinion of some, in the wrong places.

The P-17 is made of good steel. The receiver and bolt are machined from $3^{1}/_{2}$ percent nickel-steel forgings. One fault that has been isolated is the existence, in a few actions, of hairline cracks in the receiver ring. For some reason, this fault has been attributed to Eddystone-made actions rather than those from Winchester or Remington, making the latter more desirable and expensive. Actually, it occurs in any of the three, and then only rarely. Exactly why has never been determined. The usual explanation is faulty heat treating, but Frank de Haas, a gunsmith as well as writer, says that since the problem occurs most often in actions from which the original barrel has been removed, the stress of the modification may be at fault. Be that as it may, A-Square is careful to ensure that all the actions it uses for its rifles are free of hairline cracks.

The company takes P-17 actions, mills the military sight base off the bridge, shapes the bridge for scope mounts, straightens the floorplate to get rid of the belly, polishes the entire action inside and out, and then reblues it with a pleasing matte finish. From 1979 until 1999, the rifles were left with the cock-on-closing feature of the original.

Alphin designed his "Coil-Chek" stock to reduce felt recoil as much as possible. This stock does reduce recoil, but for his own inscrutable reasons Alphin refused to checker them. His explanation was that the vicious recoil of the larger cartridges would strip the skin off your hand if the stock was checkered. That makes no sense to me, and since the stocks are generously proportioned and hard to really hold onto, I would prefer some checkering.

The other feature to which I object is cock-on-closing. It is easy to alter a P-17 to cock on opening, and since most bolt actions have that feature, I believe it is a poor idea to have something that feels strange on your dangerous-game rifle. In 1999, A-Square changed the Hannibal to cock-on-opening.

As it comes from A-Square's shop, the Hannibal is a very smooth custom rifle, every bit as good as a converted P-17 from one of the top shops of the past. The firm's gunmakers do an excellent job, the Hannibal is available in all the best large-bore cartridges, and it is surprisingly inexpensive. There are few better values in a dangerous-game rifle anywhere.

Ed Brown's New Rifle

Since 1960, there have been a dozen or more attempts by small companies, especially in the United States, to launch a custom-made action to compete with those of the large firms. The only one that can really be called a success is the Dakota. Other attempts include the Champlin, the Texas Magnum, and the Mathieu. Some were modified Mausers; a few, like the Texas Magnum, utilized the benefits of a three-lug bolt. Recently, Kenny Jarrett introduced an action of his own design on which to build his super-accurate beanfield rifles. Although Jarrett offers his gun in some larger calibers, it is essentially a custom proposition focused on high velocity and long-range accuracy.

Since the advent of the Remington 700, the Weatherby Mark V, and the post-64 Model 70, all within a few years of each other, the concept of controlled feed has come roaring back, and not just for heavy-caliber rifles. This feature may not contribute to accuracy, but it certainly provides reliability and a level of confidence not found in the various "push feed" actions.

Along this line, one development that is worth noting is a new action by Ed Brown, the Missouri pistolsmith and rifle maker. Brown is noted for producing some of the finest Model 1911 pistols in the world, and his first ventures into rifle making were based on the Remington 700-type action, heavily modified with all the parts manufactured in his own factory.

Wanting to add a dangerous-game rifle to his line, Brown recognized the importance of controlled feed and redesigned his action to incorporate a method that works without the traditional full-length claw extractor. As the cartridge is pushed forward, up and out of the magazine, the rim slides into the slotted bolt-face rim and is held firmly as it chambers. Unlike a traditional stationary claw, when Brown's bolt is closed the bolt face rotates around the cartridge and supports it underneath. The large, claw-shaped extractor is actually part of the bolt-face rim.

Ed Brown's forte is highly accurate rifles at affordable prices. His actions are functional, his stocks composite rather than wood. But the actions are as

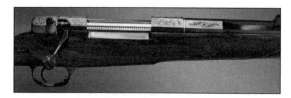

The Champlin action was the basis for the second custom rifle in Safari Club's "Big Five" series. The Champlin, made by Champlin Arms of Enid, Oklahoma, was one of several post-war attempts to produce a magnum-sized action comparable to the Brevex. Ultimately, they never established a place for themselves, while the Mauser 98 sails on, gaining admirers all the time. The Champlin was well-made, very strong, and provided the basis for a fair number of dangerous-game rifles; they still appear (and command good prices) on used-gun lists of high-end dealers. *SCI Photo*

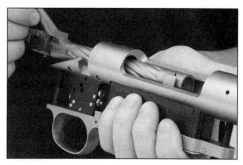

Ed Brown's new Model 704 controlled-feed action. Brown has taken a completely new approach to controlled feed, eliminating the full-length extractor and building the feature into the bolt face instead. He feels his design combines the best features of the Remington 700 (renowned for its accuracy) and the Mauser 98 (renowned for its reliability).

smooth as his CNC machinery and hand-fitting can produce. At this writing, only a prototype of Brown's controlled-feed action exists. It will be interesting to see if those who demand this feature in dangerous-game rifles will accept a new design.

Europe Today

European gunmakers are nothing if not inventive, and while there are dozens of companies making rifles, and many designing new actions, nothing has been forthcoming to rival the Mauser 98. For that matter, not a single new European bolt action has established itself as even a credible alternative.

In the Czech Republic, the firm of Ceska Zbrojovka a.s. Uhersky Brod (CZUB or simply CZ) is the heir to the Brno mantle. What used to be Brno Mauser actions are now CZ actions. The big number is the CZ 550, a massive, square-bridge number that has many Mauser 98 attributes. One unfortunate aspect of this action is a safety the company describes as "positive two-position" instead of the Mauser-type three-position design. As of this writing, the rifle is available in a wide variety of dangerous-game cartridges: .404 Jeffery, .416 Rigby, .458 Winchester, .458 Lott, .505 Gibbs. The rifles are imported by CZ-USA and sell at prices competitive with makers such as Ruger.

* * *

After 1945, the Mauser company was resurrected, but it shunned the 98 (explain that one to me!) in favor of a succession of somewhat weird designs, mostly involving straight-pull bolts. Some were outright failures; others went nowhere. None made any impact in big-bore terms.

Steyr Mannlicher of Austria is another inventive company of venerable origins and a maker of some extremely slick bolt actions. Again, none have made any impact in larger calibers.

In Italy, the only major manufacturer of bolt actions is Beretta. In past years, they have marketed rifles based on Sako-type actions and, briefly, on the Dakota 97.

Sauer & Sohn lays claim to the title of Germany's oldest gunmaker, having been founded in 1751. Until 1969, Sauer manufactured the Weatherby Mark V barrelled actions. Today, Sauer makes rifles based on a unique action that is absolutely buttery in its operation, but the largest caliber available is 9.3x62—hardly a dangerous-game caliber.

Also in Germany are Heym and Hartmann & Weiss, two firms that are covered elsewhere in this book. Both make bolt-action rifles based on new-manufacture Mauser 98 actions from Johanssen.

In Belgium, only Dumoulin and (perhaps) Lebeau-Courally are still with us. Dumoulin buys newly manufactured Mauser 98 actions in Italy and finishes them in Liège. In the future, their larger-caliber actions will come from Empire Rifles in New Hampshire.

A Question of Strength

The military Mauser 98 depends more on its design for strength than on special steels or heat treatments.

Frank de Haas
Bolt Action Rifles

Since its introduction, the Mauser 98 has been renowned for its strength, but that has not stopped critics from suggesting that it is not strong enough or that another, even stronger, action would be preferable for building a heavy rifle.

There are several aspects to this question.

First, the Mauser 98 is the safest and strongest of all the Mauser designs, mainly because of its third locking lug, located on the underside of the bolt at the rear, which rotates into a milled recess in the bottom of the receiver. In theory, should the dual lugs shear off, the third lug would keep the bolt from flying out of the receiver and killing the shooter. For this reason alone, authorities recommend that anyone wanting to convert a military rifle to a high-intensity cartridge such as the .257 Weatherby start with a 98, not with one of the "weaker" Swedish 94/96 or Spanish 93/95 Mausers. Fair enough.

Probably in an attempt to avoid infringing on a patent, designers of the Enfield P-14 eschewed the 98's third lug and turned the root of the bolt handle into a safety lug instead. It locks into a notch in the receiver.

Criticism of the 98's strength centers on the fact that a substantial amount of steel must be milled away in the receiver ring to accommodate the locking lugs. As well, the raceways along which the lugs travel are milled out, eliminating more steel. Even the thumb notch in the left raceway, found on military rifles, supposedly weakens the action. A related complaint is that the bolt face of the 98 does not enclose the head of the cartridge, thereby leaving it vulnerable to rupture, with the resultant escaping gases endangering life and limb for the shooter and bystanders. This is the basis of Remington's "three rings of steel" marketing claim for the Model 700.

Most such claims come from companies with a new action that is supposedly superior to the 98. Let us look at the actual strength of the 98 action—where it lies and where it does not. Most of these points apply equally to Mauser derivatives like the Enfield, Springfield, and Winchester Model 70.

The strength of the Mauser: This early (1896 Swedish) Mauser, without the vaunted third safety lug of the '98, finally gave in under the pressure of a vastly overcharged cartridge. A slab of wood is blown off the stock, the wrist is badly cracked, the extractor blown clean off, and the bolt stop severely damaged. The floorplate was blown off and the steel magazine box bulged. This action is destroyed, but the locking lugs held. The bolt was finally opened by pounding with a mallet.

This Enfield P-17 gave in under the extreme pressure of an over-charged cartridge. It suffered damage similar to the 1896 Mauser, but not so severe. There was no damage to the stock at all. The extractor is badly damaged but still in place (note collar curled over the action rail), and the bolt stop is jammed. The floorplate blew off, but there is no damage to the magazine. As with the 1896, the locking lugs held firmly and there is no evidence the Enfield's third "lug," the bolt stem, was called upon to do anything.

* * *

After 1945, when the troops came home and the gun business started to roar once again, there was a great deal written about the direction of rifles and cartridges in the space age. Many authorities (Roy Weatherby and Philip B. Sharpe spring to mind) wrote blithely about velocities climbing to the 5,000- to 6,000-fps range and about pressures that one day would routinely approach 100,000 psi. It was an age in which wildcatters were in love with high velocity, and making bullets fly faster was the goal of every rifle and cartridge maker.

Under these circumstances, with talk of sky-high pressures, concerns about action strength and potential cartridge ruptures were understandable but, in the case of dangerous-game rifles, they were largely misplaced. Most big cartridges do not generate anything close to those pressures. But that was the tenor of the times. Since then, we have learned that, for dangerous game, high-pressure, high-velocity loads are not the answer. Therefore, the case for a "stronger" action largely goes out the window.

Then we come to the actual strength of the action itself.

In the 1980s, gunmakers began building rifles that were substantially lighter than normal and, naturally, this trend turned into a race to see who could produce the lightest rifle. One can reduce poundage in various ways, but since most of a rifle's weight is concentrated in the action, that is the place to start. Makers began "Swiss cheesing" actions, removing metal wherever it was not needed—slimming this, trimming that. Melvin Forbes, at Ultra Light Arms in West Virginia, was one of the first of this crowd and became the best known. Forbes started in business lightening factory-built Remington 700s but eventually gravitated to making his own actions from scratch. Forbes discovered that in terms of strength, the only thing that really mattered was the locking lugs and the receiver ring. Everything behind counted for little—the receiver could be made of papier mâché and the bolt out of balsa wood, as long as the lugs were steel and turned down into solid, machined steel grooves.

Forbes's rifles were light as a feather and solid as a rock. Some of the tests he carried out with cartridges fired behind bullets already lodged in the bore would turn your hair white, but his actions never let go. Why? Because they had a strong lock-up between the lugs and receiver.

As for the raceways, they do not make the receiver weaker. They certainly make it less rigid, which is a concern for seekers after great accuracy, but this is not an issue for the average hunter. And even so, glass bedding can solve the rigidity problem. For the same reason, the thumb notch in the 98 may render a military action unsuitable to become a benchrest rifle, but so what?

In 2000, I embarked on a test of two rifles to see exactly what would cause them to come apart. The guinea pigs were an Enfield P-17 that I had owned for thirty-five years and a Swedish Mauser 96, made by Carl Gustav of superb Swedish steel. With the rifles in a vise and a long cord to pull the triggers, I fed them a diet of increasingly high-pressure cartridges. There were three goals. Since any fool can destroy a rifle by stuffing a cartridge full of Bullseye and pulling the trigger, I wanted to determine if it was possible for a handloader using a "legitimate" powder to accidentally blow up a rifle. Second, I wanted to see how the progressive effects of higher pressure manifested themselves as the psi mounted into the stratosphere. Third, I wanted to compare the performance of the supposedly weaker Swedish Mauser, without a third lug, to that of the Enfield, which has one.

Ultimately, both rifles were destroyed—the Swedish Mauser in a slightly more spectacular manner than the Enfield—but both hung on far beyond my expectations. Pressure signs manifested themselves in the form of cratered primers, bolts that were progressively more difficult to open, and finally vapor-ized cartridges, splintered stocks, and bulged actions.

As I neared the end of the test, the bolts had to be pounded open with a hammer. In fact, I began to fear that the bolts would seize solid before the actions let go. Finally, the Swede blew a foot-long piece of kindling off the side of the stock, the action bulged, and the extractor tried to make its escape—but the lugs held like granite.

The destruction of the Enfield was slightly less lurid, with no stock splin-tering, but the overall result was the same: The lugs held firm. A faint smell of brimstone hung over my test area, and I would not have wanted to be holding either rifle when they were fired the last few times, but I would not have been injured—at least, not by flying bolts with their lugs sheared off.

That is typical of Mauser-type actions when confronted by high pressures, whether as a result of an imprudent load or the effects of the African sun: Instead of going to pieces, the lugs seize in place like a Rottweiler's teeth.

SINGLE-SHOTS AND OTHER PLAYERS

Single-Shot Rifles

I have never shot so well since the days of the single nor made so good a bag. When you have only one shot you aim to kill. Of course, I would rather have two barrels for dangerous game, but the axiom is the same. It all hinges on the one and only maxim for big game shooting, "it is the first shot that counts."

Major H.C. Maydon

The single-shot rifle has a long and honorable history in the field of dangerous-game hunting. In the black-powder muzzleloader era, the only weapons suitable for use on dangerous game were single-shots, because bores were so large and projectiles so heavy. Anything more than one barrel was impossible.

Before the self-contained cartridge revolutionized firearms, ivory hunters used 4- and 2-bore muzzleloaders, monsters that fired lead balls weighing up to eight ounces. The weapons themselves weighed as much as twenty-five pounds and were carried by teams of gunbearers. Even with such heft, recoil was excessive, fearsome, legendary. Sir Samuel White Baker's famous gun "Baby," made by Holland & Holland, weighed twenty-two pounds and fired a five-ounce projectile. Sir Samuel reported that when he fired the beast, the recoil "spun me around like a top—it was difficult to say which was staggered the most severely, the elephant or myself." To back up "Baby," Baker also carried a pair of 10-bore double rifles made by E. M. Reilly of Oxford Street.

This is a particularly apt example, because in one account of elephant hunting in *The Nile Tributaries of Abyssinia*, Baker tells of shooting an elephant with the huge single-shot and being almost as stunned by the recoil as the elephant was by the bullet. Baker and the elephant recovered their senses about the same time, with the elephant coming for Baker as Baker reached for one of the Reillys. He waited until the last possible second and then shot for the brain, putting the elephant down for good. No matter how big, a single-shot still offered just one shot.

Even after the advent of the self-contained cartridge and breech-loading rifle, however, many old-time hunters clung to the muzzleloading single-shot as the only weapon really suitable for the big stuff. The very first cartridges were quite anemic—rimfires in .32 and .44 caliber, barely suitable for a small antelope—and it took many years for rifle mechanisms to evolve to the point where they could withstand the pressures of truly high-power cartridges. As they did so, however, big-game calibers developed along with them until, by the 1890s, there were finally some rounds that were adequate for charging elephants or wounded Cape buffalo in thick bush.

Several trends were at work simultaneously. Bores were becoming smaller, projectiles lighter, and velocities higher. In 1898, Rigby introduced the .450 Nitro Express and the quantum leap in power, coinciding with a drastic reduction in the size and weight of the cartridge, essentially spelled the end of the single-shot rifle for dangerous game because the existing actions were too light. In a seven-pound single-shot rifle, the .500 NE would deliver unbearable recoil. The gun needed to be heavier to absorb the recoil, and the easiest way to make a single-shot heavier was to use a larger frame and add a second barrel. The double rifle, and later the magazine rifle, ended the single-shot as a serious force.

There were exceptions, of course. Not everyone could afford an expensive bespoke rifle from the best gunmakers, and there was a large market for cheaper weapons. Birmingham gunmakers continued to build rifles on the proven Martini-Henry action, and these were shipped to the colonies by the crate. Generally, however, they were chambered for cartridges such as the .500 BP Express, which was a fine round for lion and a favorite in India for tigers, but was not adequate for thick-skinned game in Africa. As well, older hunters were skeptical about new developments. Many professionals clung to the tried-and-true, and a small market persisted for single-shot rifles well into the twentieth century.

Weight was one consideration. Strength was another. Although dozens of single-shots were designed in the half-century between the advent of the cartridge rifle and the emergence of the nitro express, few were strong enough to handle the constant pounding of the big cartridges.

The one action that emerged as the unchallenged king of single-shots for nitro-express rounds was the Farquharson, and its direct descendant, the Ruger No. 1, is the modern-day champion. The Martini-Henry occupied its own place, mostly as the basis for mass-produced trade rifles. The break-action single-shot, so popular in Europe and Scotland for stalking rifles, was simply too light for the heavy calibers. None of the famous American single-shots—the Sharps, for example, or the Browning designs—ever played a role in Africa. They were adequately strong for American black-powder buffalo cartridges, but even the largest of these barely matched the ballistic performance of the .500 BP Express and were simply never a factor.

* * *

After 1898, single-shots gradually fell by the wayside. If a hunter could not afford a full-blown London double rifle, he could certainly find the money for

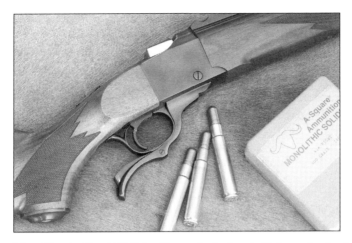

Ruger No. 1 Tropical in .416 Rigby. Ruger single-handedly brought the single-shot rifle back to life with the No. 1, and later did the same for the .416 Rigby cartridge. The Tropical model owes a great deal to the old Alex. Henry rifle for style and elegance. It is also strong, accurate, dependable, quick-handling, and a pleasure to shoot.

a bolt action in a serious caliber, and the single-shot had very little reason to exist. An exception to this rule was highly specialized, limited-use cartridges like the massive .600 NE. A double rifle in .600 weighed about sixteen pounds; a single-shot could be made somewhat lighter and considerably cheaper, yet it could still give an ivory hunter a heavy thumper for those anxious moments. According to H&H (which owned the W. J. Jeffery name and records), Jeffery made twenty-four single-shot rifles in .600 NE. A few were built on Anson & Deeley break-actions, but most used a Farquharson falling block, and all were made in the very early 1900s.

John Taylor had a high regard for "single loading" rifles, but even by 1948, when he wrote *African Rifles and Cartridges*, single-shots were not common:

> The old Farquharson falling-block single-loader, which was so popular in days gone by before it was superseded by the Mauser, is rarely seen now. It was a splendid action, one of the very best that has ever been designed; strong, simple, silent and reliable. Its one weak point was the extractor. . . .

As Taylor went on to explain, the weak extractor could leave the hunter unarmed if a case stuck in the chamber because of pitting or excessive pressure. Under the African sun, in African conditions, pitted chambers and blazing heat were more common than not. Still, Taylor said more than once that he felt magazine rifles should be banned or at least limited in their capacity, and that if hunters used single-shots they would be more likely to make every shot count. And, once accustomed to working the action, they would not be unduly hampered by having to reload each time.

Except for Baker and "Baby," which is easily the most famous single-shot ever used in Africa, Frederick Courteney Selous is probably the most notable devotee of single-shots. According to Taylor, he used a .450 black-powder falling block made by George Gibbs, then a similar rifle from H&H chambered for the .303 British, and finally another H&H in the obsolete .400/.375 cartridge. But Selous is not a particularly good example to use, just as W. D. M. Bell's choice of a 6.5mm for elephants is not proof that this caliber is a good one for the big stuff. Selous certainly hunted elephants, but he was not noted as an elephant hunter, so his use of single-shots does not automatically make them good for the purpose. Selous is widely admired as the greatest of all African hunters, for his ethics and standard of conduct as well as his pure hunting ability; in his hands, a single-shot was used as a surgeon uses a scalpel.

Taylor's sentiments about single-shots making better hunters have been echoed ever since, and he may well have been right—when it came to amateurs. For professional hunters, either those hunting on control or guiding visiting sportsmen, the single-shot rifle is simply not adequate. Once a professional hunter is called upon to step in, the situation usually calls for more than one carefully placed shot, which is why, to a man, they carry either big bolt actions or even bigger doubles.

* * *

Since John Taylor's day there has been a renewed interest in hunting with single-shot rifles, especially with the Ruger No. 1. The Ruger was introduced in 1967, and to say that it swam against the tide vastly understates the situation. Much of the shooting world was simply bewildered. A single-shot? In 1967? Is he mad?

Well, Bill Ruger was—yet again—far from mad. A dedicated collector of rifles as well as a manufacturing genius, Ruger loved all the old single-shots, both European and American, and he believed there was a well of affection for them among other hunters, too. At the time, there was no high-quality, new, single-shot rifle or action available, so Ruger set out to correct that situation. Although the No. 1 is most commonly compared to the Farquharson, Ruger said he tried to emulate the Alexander Henry single-shot, which is considerably more graceful. In the end, the No. 1 outwardly resembled the Farquharson with its underlever, but it is a far prettier and more elegant rifle.

The No. 1 action is an investment casting of top-quality alloy steel, and while Bill Ruger wanted the No. 1 to have all the elegance of a traditional falling

The classic Farquharson: This rifle was made by W.J. Jeffery and shipped to Lyon & Lyon in Calcutta in 1903. It is chambered for Jeffery's great 450/400 3". The rifle was restored by a consortium of craftsmen: stock by Al Lind, metalwork by Roger Ferrell, engraving by Robert Evans. The rifle is owned by Sid Johnson. *Photo by Mustafa Bilal*

Sid Johnson with his classic Farquharson 450/400 3" and a 43-inch Tanzanian Cape buffalo, taken in 2005.

---

block, he was also determined to correct some of the problems that had dogged those actions for a century. In particular, his designers came up with an extractor/ejector that is considerably stronger than the Farquharson. The ejector can be deactivated if a shooter prefers not to fling his hulls across the county, and it works equally well with rimmed, rimless, and belted cartridges.

Originally, the No. 1 was to be named "The Victorian." What happened to that idea, we don't know. When the gun went on the shelves in 1967, it was called the No. 1.

Almost from the beginning, the rifle was offered in big calibers. The No. 1 Tropical was introduced in 1968, chambered for the .375 H&H and .458 Winchester. It is still available, forty years later, as "The Tropical." It has a lovely Lenard Brownell stock of ultra-classic form—no Monte Carlo, no cheekpiece—and the fore end is in the Alexander Henry style, with a racy, angled groove. The rifle has a quarter-rib on a heavy, twenty-four-inch barrel; a sling swivel on a barrel band; and a barrel-band ramp front sight. In 1989, Ruger added the .416 Rigby to the calibers available in the Tropical, and the company has since expanded the list to include the .458 Lott and .405 Winchester.

The No. 1 is immensely strong, very accurate, and dependable, with a modern mechanism employing coil springs. As well, the No. 1 may be the most stylish production rifle in American history. From the beginning, Ruger's production standards for this gun were high, and the polish, bluing, stock finish, and quality of walnut have all been far better than one would expect on anything except a custom rifle. In the modern age of stainless steel and laminate stocks, the No. 1 has kept pace, appealing to tastes that would appear to be completely contradictory. In short, it is an ultra-traditional rifle in ultra-modern dress.

The only other production single-shot rifle that merits mention here is the Dakota Model 10. It was introduced in 1990 specifically to compete with the Ruger No. 1 and is generally a more compact and delicate action. Like the No. 1, it is an under-lever falling block, and while it is available in just about any cartridge one could name, the vast majority have been produced in smaller cartridges, and in a "mountain rifle" configuration: light in weight, with a short barrel. In fact, weight could well be the factor that determines what could, or could not, be done with the Model 10. Certainly, one could hang a very heavy barrel on it and that would have two advantages: It would make the rifle easier to shoot accurately and make recoil at least tolerable. My Ruger No. 1 .416 Rigby has the heaviest barrel of any hunting rifle I own, and I shudder to think how it would kick with a standard-profile barrel. The same approach could be used with a Model 10, but it seems out of place—like trying to turn an Arabian into a cavalry steed.

Various independent gunsmiths have produced single-shot actions over the years. Wilbur Hauck was one of the first, in the 1960s, and Martin Hagn followed suit in the 1980s. Single-shot rifles are very popular in Europe, in a "stalking rifle" configuration that is not unlike the American mountain rifle. Beginning in the 1980s, there has been a renaissance of interest in the old American single-shots, with small companies going into production to build the Sharps, Ballard, Winchester High Wall, and other, more obscure, names. Browning, ever the sharp marketer, realized there was a market for single-shots and brought out, usually as limited editions, reproductions of some of John M.'s best designs. While these rifles are interesting, shoot very well, and are eminently usable for hunting, most are simply not up to the task of hunting elephant or Cape buffalo. A few have been taken to Africa, and some African animals have fallen to them—including a Cape buffalo or two—but these have been stunts, pure and simple, to prove that it could be done.

Although it has a long history as a dangerous-game rifle, the single-shot today hardly qualifies. No professional hunter in his right mind would use one, because his job is to keep his client alive and a single-shot just does not have adequate firepower in a bad situation. And only a client who is mad about single-shots is likely to take one to Africa, unless the motivation is to revel in emulating Frederick Courteney Selous. Still, when you think of it, there are worse motives.

Big-Bore Lever Actions

Lever action rifles are intended for short- to medium-range shooting in heavy cover.

Bob Hagel

The lever-action rifle is peculiarly American. With the tiniest of exceptions, only Americans make them, and only Americans shoot them.

The earliest successful repeating rifles in America were lever actions, and Winchester, Marlin, and Savage all made their reputations primarily with lever-action rifles. As cartridges became more powerful, lever actions were redesigned, strengthened, and improved to accommodate them. In terms of power, the lever action reached its zenith in 1895, with the introduction of the Winchester Model 95. The 95 is a heavy action with a box magazine that allows the use of longer cartridges and more aerodynamic bullets, but this makes the rifle very awkward to carry comfortably. Where the Winchester 86 was so smooth it was almost fluid, the 95 clanks and clunks and feels like a not particularly happy machine.

Still, the 95 was powerful. Chambered for the .30-06 and .405 Winchester, among others, the 95 was adequate for everything from big bears in Alaska to lions in Africa. Theodore Roosevelt took a 95 on safari with him and pronounced the .405 Winchester his favorite lion cartridge. The factory load is a 300-grain bullet at 2,200 fps, with muzzle energy of 3,220 ft. lbs. This makes it, ballistically, about like a light .375 H&H—certainly adequate for lion provided it is loaded with good bullets. Unlike most American cartridges designed for lever actions, the powerful .405—with its straight, rimmed case—gained some recognition elsewhere in the world. A few double rifles were chambered for it, and Kynoch even made ammunition in this caliber.

But John Taylor was lukewarm on the .405 lever-action Winchester:

This rifle's caliber compels it to be included in this group [of large medium bores] *tho* [sic] *it does not otherwise deserve to be. . . .*

It got a great boost after the ex-president, the late Theodore Roosevelt, was known to have preferred it for his lion shooting. But nobody thought to ask, to what did he prefer it? If he preferred it to his .30-06, that would be quite understandable.

Taylor's jaundiced view was based on hard fact. While he agreed that the .405 was perfectly capable of killing lions, he said, "the sectional density was none too good, with the result that it lacked penetration on all the larger species." The standard bullet in the big British .400s weighed 400 grains; the .405's bullet was only 300 grains; so, Taylor's reservations make perfect sense. It seems that many Winchester 95s made their way to Africa, but most ended up gracing farmers' gun cabinets, not the hands of professional hunters.

The .405 was the most powerful cartridge used in lever actions up to that time and the only one that was even noticed in Africa, but others—like the .45-70 and .45-90 (in the Winchester 86) and even some of the lesser Model 95 chamberings (like the .38-72)—were fine for American game. Where these rifles really made an impression was in Alaska, and until the advent of the Winchester Model 70 made the .375 H&H the Alaskans' favorite cartridge, most bear hunters used big lever actions. While no one kept score, I expect the bears held their own in face-to-face encounters in the alders.

Allen Hasselborg, the famous Alaska bear hunter who was savaged and left for dead by a gigantic bear on Chichagof Island in 1918, was using a lever-action rifle. After his first shot dropped the bear, Hasselborg put down the rifle and reached for his knife, only to turn and find the bear on top of him. Later, apparently, the rifle made a useful crutch when Hasselborg struggled back to shore where his boat was anchored. No one would blame the rifle, of course, but it shows that cartridges in the .33 Winchester class will kill a bear most of the time, but it is the *rest* of the time that is worrisome.

A few Alaska bear hunters were known to favor big British doubles, but the salt spray and endless rain of the Alaska coast does them no good. Anyway, how many Alaska guides could afford one? It speaks well of the American lever action that it continues to operate in such climes. In one of his early articles about Hasselborg, Frank Hibben mentions the rusted old lever action the old man still carried with him everywhere, often using it as a staff when crossing treacherous waters. As long as you keep pouring oil in and working the action every so often, the lever action will endure a lot.

* * *

There is only one modern lever-action rifle that can be considered a real dangerous-game rifle, and then only for use in Alaska. The Marlin 336, one of the best, strongest, and simplest of the lever designs, has been available for many years in some large calibers. In 1965, Marlin introduced the .444 Marlin cartridge, which is merely a lengthened .44 Magnum, and chambered it in a rifle called the Marlin 444, which was a strengthened version of the 336. Unfortunately, the only bullets available for the 444 (at least in factory ammunition) were the thin-jacketed .44s intended for use in handguns. At the .444's

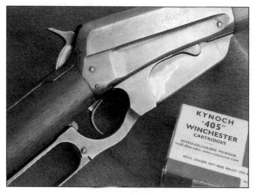

The Winchester 95 was a favorite rifle of Theodore Roosevelt, and after publication of his book *African Game Trails*, gained a modest following in Africa. Its most powerful cartridge, the .405 Winchester, was also chambered in some continental double rifles, and Kynoch loaded soft-point ammunition for it. The .405 was considered an adequate lion cartridge, but not suitable for buffalo or elephant.

higher velocities, the bullets did not hold up. Many who initially pronounced it "the ideal moose rifle" later had reason to recant. Handloaders could buy good, heavy-for-caliber bullets from Barnes during that period, and loaded with a Barnes 300-grain roundnose the .444 was a serious proposition, even for big bears.

In spite of the ammunition problem, the 444 sold well. When it was introduced, gun writers were almost as horrified as they would be a couple of years later, when Bill Ruger unveiled the No. 1. The .444 Marlin was a rimmed, straight case, throwing a heavy, large-caliber bullet. Everyone hated it except the American hunter, who bought the rifle steadily. Although redesigned in 1972, the 444 has been available ever since. Obviously, in a world of small-caliber, high-velocity belted magnums, there was still a place for a rimmed, straight case in a lever-action rifle.

Realizing it was on to something, in 1972 Marlin used the 444 action as the basis for a new rifle designated the Model 1895, in honor of a famous rifle that the company had discontinued many years earlier. It was chambered in the venerable (or obsolescent and archaic, depending on your point of view) .45-70 Government. For Marlin, it was a stroke of genius. It not only tapped into hunters' residual love of big-bore lever guns, it also brought back a really serious bear rifle. On paper, the .45-70 is less powerful than the .444, but its larger, heavier bullets hold together better and pack more wallop overall. As with most cartridges of its vintage that have survived into the modern era, the .45-70 is plagued by the fact that, over the years, it has been chambered in some very weak rifles. Ammunition makers, adhering to SAAMI specifications for the cartridge, have to keep this in mind. As a result, there is a great divide between

Richard Venola with a black bear taken in Alaska in 2005. The rifle is a Marlin 1895M Guide Gun with an 18.5-inch barrel, chambered in .450 Marlin. Ammunition used was a new Hornady round, using a 325-grain bullet with a soft polymer spitzer tip, safe for use in tubular magazines. Even with this light-for-caliber bullet, recoil was fearsome.

what is available in a factory box and what a serious handloader can put together for a modern rifle. In the .45-70, a 400-grain bullet at 2,000 fps is not out of the question, and that combination delivers 3,200 ft. lbs. of energy.

In 2000, delighted with the reception of its big-bore levers but dismayed at some of the questionable loading practices taking place with .45-70 ammunition, Marlin took the next logical step with a cartridge it hoped would be taken very seriously among Alaska hunters, both guides and visiting sportsmen. The .450 Marlin is a shortened .458 Winchester belted case designed to work readily through the 444 action. It fires a 350-grain bullet at 2,100 fps—comparable to a souped-up .45-70, but without the complications. It is chambered in the 1895M, a lever-action with an 18.5-inch barrel that weighs a mere seven pounds. With its short barrel and light weight, recoil is brutal. But, for a fast-action defense weapon in thick alders, it would be very hard to beat. A lever action practically works itself under recoil, and the 1895M has no shortage of that! In an effort to counter the recoil, the rifle now comes with a ported barrel. As someone who values the ability to listen to *The Lark Ascending*, the thought of having a ported muzzle that close to my ears is more frightening than the kick, but maybe I would feel differently if I were sharing a thicket with a brown bear.

Today's cartridges for big-bore lever rifles, from left: .444 Marlin, .45-70, .450 Marlin.

* * *

Although Marlin pioneered the modern big-bore lever movement, its success did not go unnoticed, and several other companies moved quickly to emulate it. Browning and Winchester countered with some production and limited-run rifles in the old, big calibers.

In 1995, Winchester brought back the Model 95 in Roosevelt's favorite .405 Winchester. This sparked a mild renaissance of interest in the .405 (the Ruger No. 1 is now available so chambered), and for the first time in sixty years you can buy factory .405 ammunition. Anyone with a deep desire to follow in Teddy Roosevelt's footsteps and take one to Africa can now do so. But, anyone thus inclined should pay attention to John Taylor:

> *The .405 Winchester is perfectly capable of killing lions; but an experienced man would prefer something more powerful if it came to stopping a charge.*

> *Holland & Holland supplied at least two of their .500/.450-bore nitro express rifles to the Roosevelt expedition. Roosevelt had the late R. J. Cunninghame as his professional; and it's a positive certainty that Cunninghame would have had some such weapon handy when Roosevelt was shooting-up his lions with the Winchester.*

* * *

With good bullets and hot loads, the .444 Marlin, .45-70, and .405 Winchester would all be adequate for lions and leopards. In fact, the 1895M might make an excellent weapon for wounded leopards in thick brush, but that is the extent of their application as dangerous-game rifles in modern-day Africa. The big-bore lever action was always a rifle for the alder thickets of coastal Alaska, and that is where it should remain.

Section V

CARTRIDGES AND BULLETS

The Perfect Cartridge

The .375 H&H is undoubtedly one of the deadliest weapons in existence.

John Taylor, 1948

Holland & Holland's masterpiece, the great .375 Belted Rimless Magnum (aka .375 H&H).

There is no such thing as the perfect cartridge. Not yet and probably not ever. What we have are good, and sometimes great, calibers for specific purposes.

What makes a good dangerous-game cartridge? What sets apart an acknowledged top performer such as the .375 H&H from the also-rans? The answer is not power, because power in a cartridge is easily obtained. Nor is it accuracy, because accuracy in a dangerous-game rifle, while certainly desirable to a point, is never (or never should be) the deciding factor in choosing a weapon.

Over the past hundred years, scores of cartridges have been introduced by gunmakers all over the world, to say nothing of hundreds of wildcats dreamed up by American experimenters and gunsmiths looking for the ideal combination of power and accuracy. Most of these creations have flared briefly and died; some have hung onto the outer fringes, gathering a few adherents but never achieving great popularity. In every case, there was a solid reason for success or failure.

There is more to designing a successful dangerous-game cartridge than simply putting a heavy bullet in a big case. It must fit comfortably into its intended rifle action and function in that action in every aspect—from feeding, chambering, and firing, through extraction and reloading. And, that cartridge must perform flawlessly every time.

* * *

The .375 H&H is an excellent example. It was introduced by Holland's in 1912 for use primarily in bolt-action rifles and has been a top seller ever since, from Alaska to Zimbabwe. It is offered in bolt actions, doubles, and single-shot rifles.

The .375 H&H is both accurate and versatile, but beyond that it offers the paramount virtue in a dangerous-game cartridge: It is absolutely reliable. Case-sticking is unheard of, and in a bolt-action magazine rifle the cartridges feed like butter, whether loaded with spitzer or solid, round-nose bullets. The .375 H&H owes a great deal to the heritage of black-powder cartridges, which were just fading from sight when it was introduced. It has a long, roomy case with a pronounced body taper and a tiny shoulder. The shoulder would be a problem if the cartridge headspaced on it, but that is not what happens; the .375 H&H headspaces on the belt, thereby combining the advantages of a rimless cartridge in a magazine rifle (no danger of rims getting behind one another and jamming the bolt) with a rim for positive headspacing.

The .375's distinctive belted case has been the foundation for any number of spin-off cartridges, such as the Weatherby line and the original Winchester and Remington belted magnums. Many shooters believe the "belt" on a belted cartridge is there to increase strength at the base of the case, but it is not. It is there to provide positive headspace, and by so doing, to provide some other advantages, as well.

Headspace is the distance between the bolt face (or the standing breech, in the case of a double) and a point in the chamber where the brass of the cartridge case meets an immovable chunk of steel. In the case of a rimmed cartridge, it is the rim itself, while a rimless cartridge headspaces on its shoulder. Obviously, if a cartridge headspaces on its shoulder, then it not only needs a distinct shoulder, it also needs to fit the chamber fairly snugly. If there is too much headspace, the striker blow can push the cartridge deeper into the chamber, resulting in a misfire instead of detonating the primer.

A belted case headspaces on the front edge of its belt. Not only is this easily measured and adjusted, it also allows the body of the cartridge to be slightly undersized in the chamber. According to some authorities, this was a consideration when H&H was designing its .375. The gunmaker wanted enough room that the cartridge would chamber and fire even if there was some dirt in the chamber (or on the cartridge) and so that the chance of cases sticking would be reduced.

Another criticism of belted cartridges is that they do not feed as quietly or as smoothly as a rimless cartridge. Never have I noticed such a thing, and it strikes me as grasping at straws on the part of those who would sell rimless cartridges over belted ones. For years, belts were all the rage; now it is rimless designs that get the nod. At some point, the pendulum will begin to swing back. If significant differences exist—and I, for one, do not believe it—they are measurable only in units so tiny as to be meaningless in terms of a dangerous-game rifle.

In a Mauser-type box magazine, the cartridges lie in a staggered column. The bolt pushes them forward as the follower spring pushes upward. The nose of the bullet encounters the feed ramp and is guided toward the chamber. The rails of the magazine must hold the cartridge in place and keep it from springing out prematurely, but they must still allow it to glide smoothly forward and be released at the final instant to enter the chamber. When Paul Mauser designed his original Model 98, the box magazine was meticulously tailored to the 8mm Mauser cartridge. The action was the exact width and length to allow the cartridges to be loaded easily into the magazine, stay stable under recoil without damaging either bullet tips or the front of the magazine box, and chamber effortlessly. Taking a 98 and rebarreling it to another cartridge, either larger or smaller, requires equally skillful modification of the magazine, the follower, the rails, and the feed ramp, to ensure that the action functions properly.

In the case of the .375 H&H, the taper of the case allows the cartridges to lie in the magazine angled slightly inward toward the feed ramp, and the belt even increases this advantage slightly. This makes the cartridges chamber almost on their own. If a case is blown out so its walls are almost parallel, the feed ramp must be widened to catch the bullet and guide the cartridge. Otherwise it may simply jam or, if excessive force is required, the cartridge may jump out of the magazine. This problem is exacerbated with the use of blunt bullets—either round-nose softs or solids, which are standard with large-bore dangerous-game rifles. As well, obviously, the fatter the case the farther off center is the nose of the bullet and, therefore, the more difficult to guide out of the magazine and into the chamber. A long, slim, tapered case always feeds more easily than a short, fat and parallel one and is therefore immensely preferable.

The .375's taper also works to the shooter's advantage in the chamber, because the cartridge fits like a cone rather than a cylinder. If the case walls are close to parallel (they can never be absolutely parallel), they may grip the chamber walls excessively if pressures are high. In contrast, a tapered cartridge fits like a cone and can easily be sprung free.

The .375 itself has been "improved" by any number of experimenters, and if velocity were the only criterion, then the qualifier would not be misplaced. But remember, we are talking about rifles for dangerous game; in ballistics, improvement in one area always costs you something in another. In the case of the .375, an improvement in velocity can mean a loss of reliability. Because of its pronounced taper, there is a great deal of scope for experimenters to blow out the .375 H&H case to increase powder capacity. Unfortunately, modifying the case in this manner reduces taper to a minimum. As I have already said, this taper is vital to the cartridge's reliable feeding, and it also ensures that case-sticking in the chamber is almost unknown.

In 1990, for the first time, I witnessed the adverse effect of "improving" the .375 H&H. Robin Hurt owned a rifle chambered for the .375 Weatherby, a blown-out H&H. We had been out in a vehicle all day in the sizzling sun, had a breakdown, and needed to fire a signal shot. Robin touched off one round. Weatherby ammunition is always loaded to maximum, and the bolt in the rifle jammed absolutely solid. When we finally reached camp, we had to soak the action in cold water, then pound the bolt handle with a mallet to get it open. That is a lesson I have never forgotten.

Such incidents never occur with the .375 H&H, nor with any of the big British nitro-express cases that were derived from original black-powder rounds. All of them have large capacities, low pressures, and distinct tapers.

* * *

There are good cartridges with rims, without rims, and with belts. The presence or absence of any of these features does not determine whether a cartridge is good or bad. In recent years, there has been a backlash against belted cartridges by some who insist they are not as accurate as rimless ones. I have never seen a discernible difference, and some of my rifles for belted cartridges (notably the .257 Weatherby) have been among my very best long-range performers. With a dangerous-game rifle such a minimal loss of accuracy is not an important factor, and the demonstrable advantages of a belt (as seen with the .375 H&H) far outweigh any theoretical disadvantage.

Although there are good cartridges of all configurations, cartridge and action should be matched, because some work well together and some do not. Rimmed cartridges and magazine rifles, for example, are not a good fit. The danger is that the rim of the top cartridge will inadvertently be loaded behind the rim of the one beneath, and the spring pressure—combined with the push of the bolt—will jam the rifle as solid as a cement block. This was a serious problem for soldiers using the rimmed .303 cartridge in their Lee-Enfield rifles through two world wars, and the British went to great lengths to design stripper clips and magazines to prevent it. Today, there is no good reason to chamber a bolt action for a rimmed cartridge—and every good reason not to.

Double rifles, on the other hand, can accommodate any of the above, but were designed originally for rimmed cartridges and, as a general rule, function better when rims are used. Extractors and ejectors for rimmed cartridges are simpler than those for rimless or belted designs. Although many double rifles have been made for the .375 H&H, its rimmed version (the .375 Flanged) was developed purely for use in double rifles. It never achieved anything like the popularity of the belted version, however, even for double rifles and single shots.

A slightly arcane point about doubles and rimless rounds: The standard approach is to incorporate a spring-loaded détente in the extractor at right angles to the extractor groove; as the cartridge is chambered, the body depresses the détente, which then springs up into the groove. When the cartridge is ejected, the force of the ejector spring throws the case out over the resistance of the détente. Many hunters like to disable their ejectors and have only extractors, either for silent operation or to save the cartridge cases. In an emergency, the rifle is simply opened, tipped up, and the empty cases drop out. This cannot be done with rimless cases because the détente holds them in place, and they must be physically plucked out against spring pressure. Doing this little operation with a Cape buffalo bearing down on you is not easy. One more good argument for rims!

Then there is the rebated rim. This is a rimless design in which the head of the cartridge is smaller in diameter than the body forward of the extraction groove. This allows the use of larger cases with smaller bolt faces. Two examples are the .425 Westley Richards and the .500 Jeffery. With a rebated rim, the potential difficulty lies in feeding. There is less rim for the bolt face to engage, and it may ride right over the cartridge, camming it back down into the magazine. This occurs most commonly with the last cartridge in the magazine, the one that is often the most vital in a tight situation. Persuading rebated-rim cartridges to feed reliably depends on getting the spring pressure exactly right— strong enough to push the last cartridge solidly up against the rail, but not so forceful that the cartridges want to vault out of the magazine when the bolt is drawn back. Getting the right spring pressure can give a rifle maker fits, to say nothing of his client. A rebated rim is best avoided on a dangerous-game rifle.

The question of taper has been largely dealt with, but a couple of points remain.

Black-powder cartridges were huge because large dollops of powder were required to get even minimal velocities. Smokeless powder occupies considerably less space while generating much higher pressures, so in fact as well as theory, a smokeless round can be much smaller than one for black powder. A prime example exists in the handgun world: The .38 Special was originally a black-powder cartridge, but smokeless loads occupy just a fraction of its roomy case. The 9mm Parabellum has a much smaller case because it was designed specifically for smokeless, yet it equals or exceeds the .38 Special in power. It is a more efficient cartridge, but it also operates at higher pressures.

Because the nitro-express cartridges were almost all derived from existing black-powder rounds, they are large, roomy, and tapered. Black powder burns differently from smokeless, and so pronounced tapers were required to prevent case sticking; this design feature was carried over into cartridges like the .470 Nitro Express, where it paid off in the form of ultra-reliable extraction. These cases simply do not stick in the chambers, and this is especially important with a double rifle. A bolt action has serious camming power to loosen a tight case; a double rifle's extractors do not.

This devotion to tapered, roomy cases continued with the design of cartridges specifically intended for magazine rifles, calibers such as the .416 Rigby and .505 Gibbs. Both are mammoth, although neither has a really pronounced taper.

American rifle and cartridge designers had neither the long experience with the double rifles of their British counterparts, nor with large, dangerous animals, and so American dangerous-game cartridges have tended to ignore these lessons. They are higher intensity ("more efficient," their designers would have us believe), smaller in capacity, and characterized by much higher pressures. The advantage of this approach is smaller cartridge cases and, hence, greater magazine capacity—six shots rather than four, in some instances. Usually the cases are blown out to maximize powder capacity, with the feeding problems and possibility of sticky extraction that result.

The .458 Winchester as it was originally designed is a particularly egregious example of vital characteristics in a cartridge being sacrificed to very questionable virtues. It was deliberately made short enough to work through a .30-06-length action rather than one long enough for a .375 H&H. Why? I have read many different explanations but never one that made much sense and certainly never one that justified it. Be that as it may, the case was short. To get decent velocity, Winchester packed in as much ball powder as possible, then compressed it mercilessly. The heat of the African sun, combined with the constant pressure on the powder, often caused it to solidify into a cake, with attendant ignition problems.

In the 1960s, such a cartridge malfunctioned in Jack Lott's rifle, and Lott was severely injured by a Cape buffalo as a result. This led to his designing the .458 Lott—essentially a .458 Winchester lengthened by three-tenths of an inch. A .458 Lott delivers the velocity originally claimed by Winchester (and then some), with a heavy bullet and no pressure problems. It should be noted that Winchester originally claimed 2,150 fps with a 510-grain bullet, but chronograph tests showed a muzzle velocity closer to 1,900 fps. Jack Lott carried out extensive tests on Winchester factory ammunition. In one of those tests, he witnessed the bullet come out of the muzzle at such low velocity it hit the ground before it reached the hundred-yard target.

So why did Winchester go this route in designing the .458? Longer actions existed; Winchester itself made them, for the .375 H&H. The company's reasoning will remain forever a puzzle. Perhaps it was simply arrogance—the belief

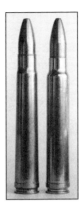

.375 H&H and an "improved" version. Note the difference between the pronounced body taper of the original and the almost parallel sides of the blown-out, so-called improved version. Resulting increased case capacity allows higher velocity, but brings the danger of case-sticking because of higher pressures and almost parallel sides.

Four head types, left to right: Rimmed, belted, rimless and rebated rim.

The difference between the "high efficiency" American cartridge (.458 Winchester, left) and the roomy, low-pressure British nitro-express cartridge (.450 NE 3¹/₄"). Both can propel a 500-grain bullet at 2150 fps, but do so with radically different pressure curves.

that the firm could make a cartridge more "efficient" than those oversized British rounds. Many writers accepted that explanation and even propounded the idea, because ever since, articles have been published condemning "banana-length" and "inefficient" nitro-express cartridges.

Mainly because of advances in gunpowder technology, factory .458 Winchester ammunition now approaches the ballistic performance claimed in 1956, and it is a decent dangerous-game round. It feeds readily with no extraction problems because, although pressures are high, the case is tapered. For a man on a limited budget, it is a hard cartridge to beat, but the .458 took almost a half-century to live up to Winchester's claims.

This brings up another point. For years, handloaders claimed they could get proper performance with the .458 Winchester, and they did—but with compressed powder and high pressures. Handloaders (almost all of them American) share one unfortunate trait: They try to squeeze the last drop of performance out of a cartridge in the form of either improved accuracy (a laudable goal), or the absolute maximum velocity (questionable). There is a tribal tendency to buy a .308 Winchester and try to turn it into a .30-06, or a .30-06 and force it to (almost) equal a .300 Magnum.

With a rifle for dangerous game, where a jam can be fatal, it is far better to buy a larger cartridge and then deliberately load it down slightly, thereby ensuring there are no pressure or extraction problems. This is the same principle as buying a motor with more power than you really need, then running it below maximum and putting no strain on it. The work gets done easily, and the motor lasts forever.

* * *

Having dealt with rims, belts, tapers, and case capacity, what is left? The answer is caliber and bullet weight.

In its standard heavy load, the .375 H&H fires a 300-grain bullet. The standard .416 bullet is 400 grains, and the .458 is 500 grains. These are nice round numbers that serve well to make a point. First, the heavier the bullet, the greater the penetration. On elephants and Cape buffalo, penetration is vital, and you should use the heaviest bullet practicable. Second, the larger the caliber, the easier it is to attain the desired velocity with a given bullet weight. Most shooters have difficulty believing it, but you can get .416 Rigby velocities from a 400-grain bullet in a .458 Lott case with no effort at all—and the Lott is a considerably smaller case. This is because the base of the bullet has greater area on which to exert pressure. The velocity is the same, but the working pressure is less. Similarly, a .458 Lott with a 300-grain bullet will run rings around the .375 H&H with a bullet of the same weight. Obviously other factors enter into it, such as bullet construction.

Ah, you say, but a .416 400-grain bullet has better sectional density and hence better downrange performance and greater penetration. True in both cases, but with a dangerous-game rifle you are rarely concerned with having a flat trajectory beyond 250 yards, and that is when the difference in downrange performance appears. As for penetration, tests in expansion boxes show the advantage of the smaller caliber in the same bullet weight to be minimal unless the caliber differential is extreme (a 300-grain .375 versus a 300-grain .458, for instance). The most stark example I can think of is the difference between a .416 Remington (a high-intensity cartridge with very little taper) and the .458 Lott. The Lott with a 400-grain bullet will do anything the Remington will do out to any range at which you might want to shoot such a bullet, and it will do so at lower pressures and with no case-sticking problems at all. Why anyone would buy a .416 Remington when the Lott is available is beyond me, but that is what makes horse races.

Another difference that is harder to quantify is the impact of a larger-diameter bullet with its greater surface area. The .500 Nitro Express fires a bullet that is only 70 grains heavier (570 versus 500) than that of a .458, at roughly the same velocity (2,150 fps) yet it is conceded to have considerably greater shocking power. Some of this is the 14 percent increase in bullet weight, but there is also an increase in striking surface of almost 20 percent.

It is possible to load a .458 with a 600-grain bullet and duplicate the ballistics of a .500 NE, but there are complications. First, a 600-grain .458 is a long bullet—too long for any cases except those of large-capacity, like the .460 Weatherby or .450 Rigby. In the .458 Lott, such a bullet cuts into powder capacity too much to be practical. Mammoth cases require oversize actions; if you are willing to carry a huge rifle, why not go to a cartridge like the .505 Gibbs or the more modern .495 A-Square? You get the same weight bullet and velocity with greater striking area at lower pressures—gains all the way around.

At some point, the law of diminishing returns kicks in, bringing with it such factors as rifle weight, recoil, weight of ammunition, and so on, but between .375 and the practical upper limit of .577 lie many different possibilities. For a stopping rifle, especially, bigger and heavier are undoubtedly better. As caliber and bullet weight increase, however, range and versatility decrease. For a professional hunter who needs a back-up stopping rifle, such concerns do not matter. For a one-rifle sport hunter, on the other hand, having long-range capability and the option of using lighter bullets for smaller game are important, which is why you find professional hunters favoring the .500 NE and sport hunters the .375 H&H.

* * *

Since 1990, there have been many developments in the world of ammunition. Brass for older cartridges has become freely available once again. Bullet makers have made great strides, and literally dozens of fine dangerous-game bullets are now available, both softs and solids, in every diameter imaginable. If you cannot find the bullet you want, the technology exists for you to buy equipment and make your own. Wildcatting, once the preserve of gunsmiths and other specialists, is now so widespread that the average rifleman, if he so desires, can not only design his own cartridge and have a rifle made, but he can also even name his creation the *.525 MbogoStomper* and have brass manufactured with the appropriate head stamp.

The bible of ammunition, *Cartridges of the World*, is now in its tenth edition and fortieth year of publication. The section on wildcat cartridges in the first edition (1965) was a mere fifteen pages long and included only one cartridge (the .475 Atkinson & Marquart) that would qualify for inclusion here. By contrast, the tenth edition (2003) has ninety pages of wildcat and proprietary cartridges, and at least thirty of them would qualify as appropriate for dangerous game. It is impossible to cover all of these in depth, nor is it necessary. Most wildcats have virtues in the eye of their creator and no one else, and they never achieve any recognition beyond (in a few cases) making the pages of *Cartridges of the World* because they are sufficiently original or offer some feature that is noteworthy. Only a very, very few achieve anything like standard status with custom-rifle makers, much less become factory chamberings or have factory ammunition available.

The following chapters look at the prevailing dangerous-game cartridges, mostly factory but some wildcat, divided according to common usage. Some cartridges, like the .375 H&H, are chambered in all types of rifles; since this caliber was intended for bolt actions and that is by far its most common application, it is included in the section for magazine-rifle cartridges.

Today's Cartridge Makers

The owner of a big rifle today has less difficulty finding brass, bullets, and high-quality loaded ammunition than ever before. Even in the halcyon days before the second world war, there was only one ammunition maker in Great Britain. Today there are (almost) two, as well as companies in Europe, Australia, and the United States that are involved in making components or finished ammunition for dangerous game. Even some of the larger companies have entered the business, with Federal Cartridge pioneering the production of the .470 Nitro Express, .416 Rigby, and .458 Lott.

If anything—and this is heresy—we may have too many people getting into the ammunition game. It seems that now anyone can buy some machinery and set up shop in his garage, making bullets and brass. Small-scale bullet making is an industry as old as the hills, and not much harm can come of it, but brass is something else again. Ruptured, split, and separated cases are no laughing matter, and all of these can occur with a hull that may look perfect to the eye but be work-hardened, improperly annealed, or drawn incorrectly.

Components and handloading are a completely separate subject from factory ammunition, although there is a certain amount of crossover, since some small brass manufacturers now supply larger ammunition companies. Any brass obtained from a company like Kynamco or A-Square (which makes its own) is likely to be safe and trouble free.

Kynamco

Kynoch is one of the truly legendary names in hunting and shooting, having been around in Britain, supplying the British Empire, since 1840, when the firm made paper cartridges. Beginning in 1918, a series of amalgamations turned five explosives companies into one, with a series of name changes that culminated, in 1926, in the creation of Imperial Chemical Industries (ICI). Since 1918, rifle ammunition had all been stamped "Kynoch," and ICI continued to call its product Kynoch and pack it in the distinctive yellow-and-red Kynoch boxes. In 1962, ICI announced that after 1963 it would discontinue production of almost all the nitro-express cartridges. The British gun industry was in the doldrums at the time, and the outlook for African hunting was gloomy. Holland & Holland wisely bought up the remaining supplies of all cartridges for which it chambered rifles and was thus able to keep itself and its clients supplied for years afterward.

After India achieved independence in 1947, there began a steady exodus of double rifles and single-shots, mostly to Australia. Shooting big doubles became a common pastime there. This gave rise to Australian brass (from Bertram) and bullets (from Woodleigh) for all the big cartridges. Woodleigh bullets are modeled ballistically on the old Kynoch bullets, which allows the production of ammunition that duplicates the loads for which older rifles were regulated; they also happen to be among the finest premium game bullets made anywhere. A happy combination!

My experience with Bertram brass has been mixed. Some has been good, some not so good. This seems to be the experience of others, as well. Bertram has made brass under its own name, and it has also manufactured some with headstamps for companies like the Old Western Scrounger (OWS). This brass is imported by Huntington Die Specialties in a wide range of calibers.

In the United States, Jim Bell went into business in the early 1980s, producing brass under the name Brass Extrusion Laboratories, Ltd. (BELL). His company made basic brass for a variety of nitro-express calibers and the old Sharps cartridges. Bell was one of the participants in the development of the .700 H&H in 1988. He made brass until 2003, when he retired and sold out to a company in South Dakota. Whether that firm is actually producing anything is, at this writing, doubtful. But, where this would have been a disaster twenty years ago, today it is just the ebb and flow of commerce, because we now have several companies making brass and ammunition.

In Britain, Kynoch returned in 1990, reconstituted as Kynamco and marketing most of the old Kynoch loads. In 2000, it announced the opening of a new factory, with new loading laboratories, workshops, climate-controlled storage, and a 100-meter range for proofing and testing ammunition. Here, customers are allowed to test ammunition in their own rifles.

Kynamco offers a much wider range of calibers than A-Square, including many smaller, obscure rounds like the .400 Purdey for black powder. The company's ammunition is loaded mostly with Woodleigh bullets, although it uses others, as well. In the United States, Kynamco ammunition is imported by Tony Galazan in Connecticut.

David Little, the head of Kynamco, describes his company's method of production:

Our brass is made by various manufacturers in Europe and the USA. When we have a group of brass of the same head size we put it out to tender and it is made to our specification and gauges. If you have any dealings

Tradition and technology: Today's Kynamco is carrying on an ammunition-making tradition that goes back to Kynoch's roots in 1840, combined with a completely modern manufacturing and testing facility. The famous yellow-and-red Kynoch boxes have been a fixture in Africa for almost a century.

in this type of manufacturing you will appreciate that different brass groups have the same first, second, third, fourth, and fifth draw. We will then buy basic brass for that group and finish it ourselves, which would include final tapering, necking, trimming and headstamping.

When we set out, we very carefully fired and measured hundreds of original rounds of Kynoch ammunition. We also had the original ballistics and a lot of range information from the original factory. When we first started loading we also had double rifles that we begged and borrowed to test the product after manufacture. We now have fifteen years of data, and although every batch of ammunition is proofed and checked, we have found that as long as it groups as the original and performs to our specifications, in nine guns out of ten it will shoot well. However, double rifles do go out of regulation and have to be reregulated on occasion.

Since the beginning, fifteen years ago, we have used Royal Ordnance powders that are specially formulated for us. They are very similar to Reloder 15 but more bulky, so they fill the case. Even so we had to develop a wadding system for some calibers.

One huge improvement Kynamco has made over the original Kynoch ammunition is using Boxer rather than Berdan primers. During the years before BELL brass, reloaders who were lucky enough to corner a supply of Kynoch ammunition then had to contend with decapping and recapping Berdan-primed cases, a task that is always a joy. As well, the new brass lends itself to reloading, where the original Kynoch cases were never intended for reuse.

Westley Richards

Westley Richards is the other British company offering ammunition. It is available in a range of nitro-express calibers, loaded with Woodleigh bullets, manufactured by Wolfgang Romey of Germany. As well as the standard chamberings all the way up to .700 H&H, Westley Richards has ammunition for its two variations on the .700 case—the 700/577 and .500 Rafiki.

Wolfgang Romey is well known in the industry, and it is not unusual to find brass with his "WR" headstamp—coincidentally, the same initials as those of Westley Richards, and if that does not add to the confusion, I don't know what does. Romey also makes ammunition for Holland & Holland's two new belted-magnum cartridges.

A-Square

A-Square was founded by Art Alphin in 1979 to market his own cartridges and rifles, but the company manufactured many of the nitro-express calibers, as well. It now supplies brass, bullets, and loaded ammunition, but does so only for cartridges that the firm considers practical dangerous-game rounds. This is eminently reasonable, but owners of rifles in more obscure chamberings are out of luck.

The ammunition-making side of the company is located in Jeffersonville, Indiana. The rifle-making shop and pressure-testing facility is in Bedford, Kentucky.

After the financial turmoil of the late 1990s, A-Square is once again on track, producing excellent brass and bullets, and slowly building up its inventory of the complete product list, from 6.5-06 up to .700 H&H. Its products are currently available from MidwayUSA and Cabela's, as well as direct from A-Square.

Bringing A-Square back from the brink of collapse has been an admittedly slow process, and has involved more than merely an infusion of cash; rebuilding relationships with customers—both individual and corporate—has not been easy and the process is not complete yet.

A-Square has a team of dedicated individuals in Jeffersonville; they all seem determined to produce top-quality bullets, brass, and ammunition. Everyone I have spoken with in the plant is a hunter or shooter, and the products they are making today are the finest overall that I have seen in fifteen years of dealing with A-Square.

The credit for the turnaround must go to Jim Smith, who managed A-Square from 2002 until early 2006.

Stages to a finished brass case. With a rifle—especially one chambered for an obscure or obsolescent cartridge—brass is gold. Producing top-quality brass requires a knowledge of metallurgy and good equipment. Here are three stages in the production of a .458 Lott case, from blank, through rimmed and stamped, to trimmed and finished case almost ready to load. A-Square brass today is the finest the company has ever produced, and the equal of the best made anywhere.

A-Square .505 Gibbs brass, polished and ready to load.

Smokeless Cartridges for Double Rifles

In thick cover you can seldom pick your shot, and if a beast comes, various obstructions may prevent you getting off a shot until the animal is almost on you. It is then that you need a heavy bullet.

John Taylor
African Rifles and Cartridges

Smokeless cartridges originally intended for double rifles are, without exception, rimmed. Almost all have been around a century or more. While a few have been introduced in recent years to fill perceived gaps in the cartridge line-up, none have achieved anything approaching standard status. The most common new cartridge is a rimmed .416, of which at least two variations exist, but rifles manufactured in these chamberings total a few dozen at most.

The .375 Class

The .375 H&H and its rimmed twin, the .375 Flanged, are both dealt with in Chapter 16. This caliber's European counterpart is the 9.3x74R, a long, tapered cartridge with a slight shoulder. The standard load is a .365-inch, 286-grain bullet exiting the muzzle at 2,350 fps. It is slimmer, lighter, and slower than the .375s, but is still excellent for some purposes. European hunters love it for driven wild boar and red stag, and continental gunmakers have chambered it in double rifles (both side-by-side and over/under) and single-shots of all persuasions for about a century. Over the years, European sportsmen have taken everything in Africa with this cartridge, including elephant, but that does not make the 9.3x74R a good elephant load. While it would be a good caliber for leopards, it is marginal for lion and decidedly light for Cape buffalo.

For the man (or woman) who is determined to own a double rifle, the 9.3x74R is unique in that good rifles, both new and used, are freely available, as is fine factory ammunition. For this reason, it is a more practical choice than the .375 Flanged. Oddly enough, there is no European cartridge for doubles larger than the 9.3x74R (aside from a few obsolete obscurities), and nothing at all suitable for Africa's biggest game.

* * *

The .375 Flanged (left) and .375 H&H. Both are used in double rifles, and both are excellent. In recent years, more rifles have been chambered in the belted, rimless version because it works so well, and ammunition is freely available.

The .369 Nitro Express was introduced in 1922 by James Purdey & Sons for chambering in the company's own double rifles. The cartridge never achieved wide acceptance in the trade, and rifles chambered for it are limited almost exclusively to Purdeys, which guarantees that they are also expensive.

Ballistically, the .369 is similar to Holland's .375 Flanged, introduced a decade earlier. The original .369 fired a 270-grain bullet at 2,500 fps, achieving muzzle energy of 3,760 ft. lbs., which is fine for thin-skinned game; for dangerous game the .369 NE is marginal, especially since it is not available with 300-grain bullets or solids. A Purdey double rifle in this caliber would be a fine combination for leopard, wounded or otherwise. Modern factory ammunition for the .369 is available from Kynamco, loaded with a 270-grain Woodleigh bullet.

The .400s

Once upon a time, there was a black-powder cartridge called the .450/400. It was, as the name indicates, a .450 necked down—and what a neck! It was a full inch long, and—since the cartridge was formed from a typical black-powder case with thin brass—it tended to stick in the chamber. W. J. Jeffery solved this in 1902 by shortening the case and moving the shoulder forward, creating a typical nitro-express cartridge. So there now exists the .450/400 (3¹/4") and the .450/400 Jeffery (3"). They are similar but not interchangeable. Each fires a 400-grain bullet at about 2,150 fps.

The .450/400 is a great cartridge and immediately established itself in India. Jim Corbett, the hunter of man-eating tigers, switched from a .500 black-powder rifle to a .400 NE, and this double was the gun with which he hunted throughout his career. An interesting sidelight is *Cartridges of the World* noting that .450/400s tended to be heavier than necessary because gunmakers did not realize a rifle weighing less than ten pounds would be sufficient for such a rela-

The two .400s, in modern loads by A-Square with Dead Tough soft and Monolithic Solids: Left, the original .450/400 (3¹/₄"); right, the .450/400 Jeffery (3"). This was originally a black-powder cartridge. The radically different case configuration of the modernised Jeffery round was intended to overcome a tendency to case-sticking in the original, with its extremely long neck. Properly loaded, both are fine cartridges in a double rifle.

tively mild cartridge. Corbett refers several times to the weight of his .400, and in one account where he is surprised by a tiger, he is able to kill it because he is carrying his .275 Rigby bolt action instead. He was able to bring the .275 slowly to bear with one hand—something he could not have managed with the heavy double.

Until the arrival of the .375 H&H, the .400 was considered *the* all-around rifle. Elmer Keith owned several .400s and said it was his ideal weapon for the thick alders of coastal Alaska. As a stopping rifle for Cape buffalo and elephant, however, it is too light.

For many years, the .450/400 was the unloved child of the used double-rifle business. As opposed to a premium for the .470, there was a discount for the .400. In 1998 in England, I handled an exquisite Henry Atkin sidelock .450/400 whose asking price was $10,000. In a fit of uncharacteristic fiscal prudence, I did not mortgage everything to buy it; today, this rifle would change hands for at least twice that, maybe three times.

* * *

Other .400-caliber doubles have been few. In the mid-1990s, John Rigby & Co. was persuaded, for the first time in its history, to make a double rifle in .416 Rigby. Although there is no problem chambering a double for a rimless cartridge, this had never been done and Rigby always preferred to chamber rimmed cartridges.

In 1991, A-Square developed a cartridge called the .416 Rimmed, which was essentially a .416 Rigby with a rim, and with its case lengthened to reduce pressure. Although it was supposedly developed at the request of double-rifle makers on the continent, the .416 Rimmed went nowhere and A-Square makes neither ammunition nor brass for it at this time.

A Dumoulin Pionnier boxlock ejector double rifle in .470 Nitro Express and an Empire Rifles "Express" in .495 A-Square. *Photo by Mustafa Bilal*

This rifle is the author's vision of the ideal working bolt-action dangerous-game rifle. It is a .458 Lott, built on a Dakota action (.375 H&H-length, not the larger magnum) with a 22-inch E.R. Shaw barrel. Being purely a working rifle, it has a glass-bedded laminate stock for strength; being wood, the stock could be fitted exactly for length and cast. The barreled action is matte blued; there is a simple island rear blade sight, with a hooded barrel-band front sight and barrel-band sling swivel. The scope, a Leupold Vari-X III 1.5-5x20, is mounted in an EAW detachable swing mount. The rifle was built by Edwin von Atzigen, a master rifle maker. Loaded, with a sling, it weighs 10 1/2 pounds and handles like a fine shotgun.

A David Miller Classic .458 Winchester built on a Mauser 98 action. This was created from the ground up to be a dangerous-game rifle, with a reworked bolt shroud with wing safety, integral quarter-rib with adjustable rear sight designed and manufactured by David Miller, and a barrel-band sling swivel. Internally, it has been refashioned to operate flawlessly, as a dangerous-game rifle should. The Classic retails for about $40,000, and most of that investment is internal. While undoubtedly beautiful, the Classic is far from ornate.

Photo by Ron Dehn

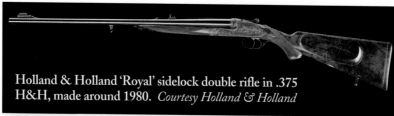

Holland & Holland 'Royal' sidelock double rifle in .375 H&H, made around 1980. *Courtesy Holland & Holland*

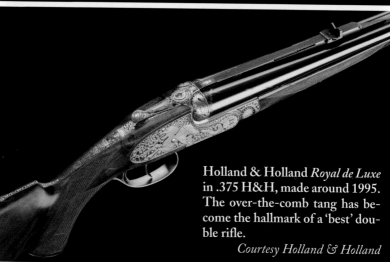

Holland & Holland *Royal de Luxe* in .375 H&H, made around 1995. The over-the-comb tang has become the hallmark of a 'best' double rifle.

Courtesy Holland & Holland

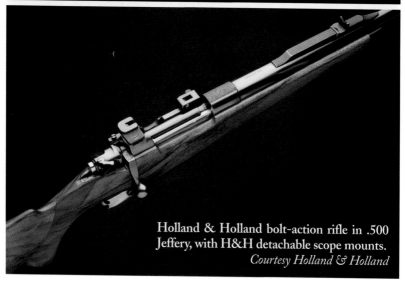

Holland & Holland bolt-action rifle in .500 Jeffery, with H&H detachable scope mounts.
Courtesy Holland & Holland

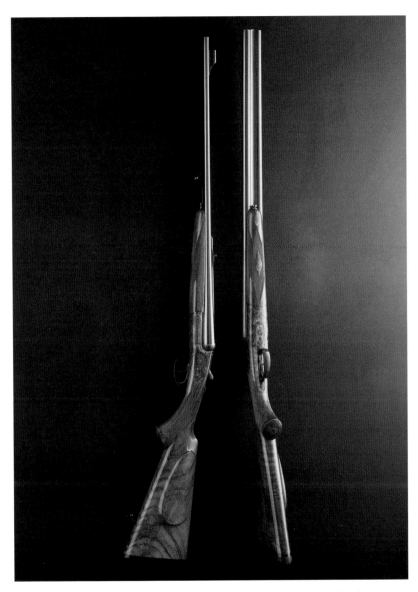

Two new Holland & Holland round-action rifles, in .300 H&H (left) and .500 NE. The new action is being used as the basis for double rifles large and small, as well as 12-bore shotguns. Many of the parts are interchangeable. Lean and stripped down, with embellishment kept to a minimum, the .500 is a fine working double rifle in the style of an earlier age. *Courtesy Holland & Holland*

John Rigby & Co. .500 Nitro Express 3" sidelock double rifle, newly manufactured (2000) in Paso Robles, California. This rifle is an uncompromising 'best' quality rifle, with exhibition-grade walnut, exquisite engraving, and a modicum of gold inlay. Rigby builds its double rifles, both sidelock and boxlock, on action blanks imported from Merkel in Germany. Geoff Miller, Rigby's proprietor, considers the Merkel actions to be among the strongest in the world. As with many German companies, Merkel is in love with the Greener crossbolt and sideclips. Note the distinctive Rigby scalloped sidelocks.

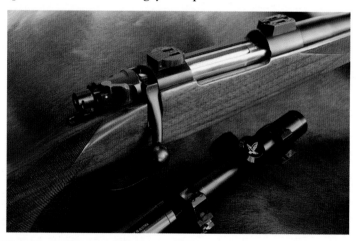

A .450 Ackley built on an FN Supreme Mauser action, with a three-position safety in a custom bolt shroud. The scope mount is the classic German claw, the most effective yet designed for a dangerous-game rifle. This rifle was made in the early 1990s by Siegfried Trillus, an Old World master gunmaker. It is stocked in black walnut from a tree he cut, sawed, and dried himself.

Manton & Co. .470 Nitro Express boxlock, and a recent John Rigby (California) .500 Nitro Express sidelock. *Terry Wieland Photo*

A new William Evans sidelock
ejector in .470 Nitro Express.
Courtesy William Evans

Westley Richards .500 NE 3"
droplock, made in 1997 for Jim
Kilday, who now manages the
Westley Richards shop in Boze-
man, Montana. Engraving by Peter
Spode. Delivered price in 1997 was
about $55,000; today (2005), the same
rifle would cost £44,000 ($77,000).
Courtesy Westley Richards

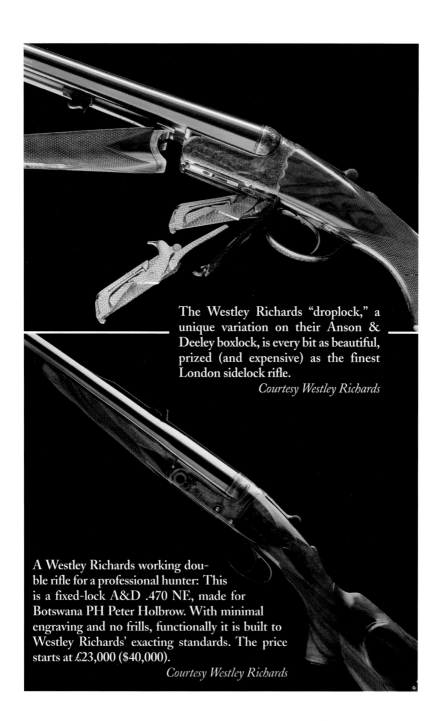

The Westley Richards "droplock," a unique variation on their Anson & Deeley boxlock, is every bit as beautiful, prized (and expensive) as the finest London sidelock rifle.

Courtesy Westley Richards

A Westley Richards working double rifle for a professional hunter: This is a fixed-lock A&D .470 NE, made for Botswana PH Peter Holbrow. With minimal engraving and no frills, functionally it is built to Westley Richards' exacting standards. The price starts at £23,000 ($40,000).

Courtesy Westley Richards

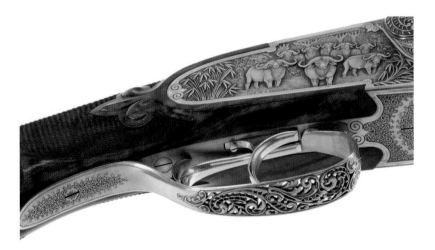

This Heym sidelock double rifle was No. 3 in the SCI "Big Five" series, dedicated to the Cape buffalo. While extraordinarily ornate, it is still a good example of a .375 H&H double rifle intended for dangerous game.   *RCMP Photo*

A lovely (!) Masailand Cape buffalo, taken in the famous Mto Wa Mbu district south of the Ngorongoro Crater, made famous by Robert Ruark, among others. "This is my best buffalo," Boddington says. It was taken with a Dakota rifle in .416 Rigby using 400-grain Hornady handloads. The professional hunter was Geoff Broom. *Photo courtesy of Craig Boddington*

Grulla Armas sidelocks for the E95 are back-action – that is, the mainspring is behind the tumbler. This allows more steel to be left in the frame where the bar extends forward. Combined with the bolster, this makes an extremely strong frame to withstand the stresses of recoil.

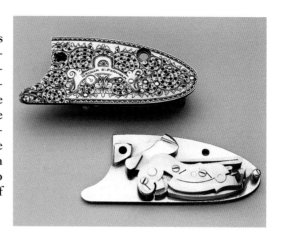

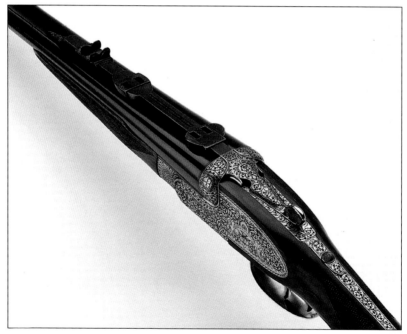

The Grulla Armas Model E95 sidelock double rifle in 9.3x74R is a good example of the rifles made by the great Basque gunmakers. The barrels originate in Austria (Böhler Rasant), as do the frame and locks. Note the discreet bolster and classic claw scope mount. This rifle has an over-the-comb tang and generally exhibits all the features of a best-quality double rifle. Grulla offers the E95 in calibers up to .500 NE. It retails (2005) at about $20,000.

Our Masai tracker, Lakina, loved to carry my John Rigby .500 Nitro Express.
Terry Wieland Photo

The first rifle in Safari Club's "Big Five" series of custom rifles is the "Elephant Gun," built by the David Miller Company of Tucson, Arizona. It is a .458 built on a military Mauser 98 action. While unusually ornate, it is functionally typical of the upper class of custom rifles based on Mauser actions. *SCI Photo*

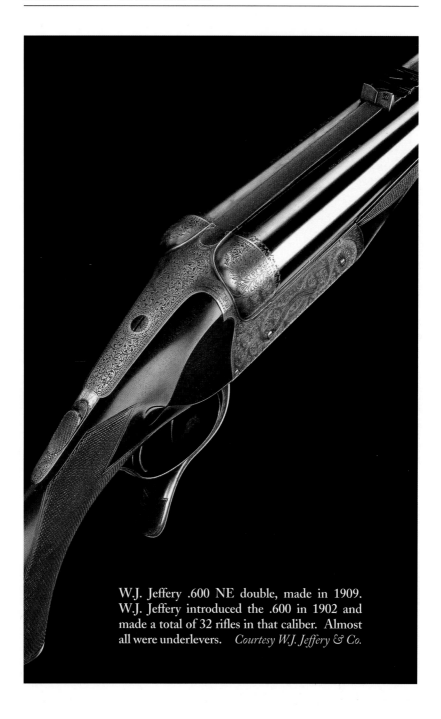

W.J. Jeffery .600 NE double, made in 1909. W.J. Jeffery introduced the .600 in 1902 and made a total of 32 rifles in that caliber. Almost all were underlevers. *Courtesy W.J. Jeffery & Co.*

The late, lamented .450s: From left, the original .450 Nitro Express, introduced by John Rigby, that revolutionized hunting. The 500/450 (center) is the .500 NE necked down. This was H&H's standard chambering in .450 to counter Rigby. Finally, a .475 No. 2, shown to indicate the difference in case size; the original .450 No. 2 was simply this cartridge with a smaller bullet.

In 2000, Krieghoff combined with Wolfgang Romey, the German ammunition maker, to develop a cartridge they call the .500/416 NE (3¹/₄"). It is the .500 NE case necked down. Reported ballistics are a 410-grain bullet at 2,330 fps. The chambering is offered in Krieghoff's Classic "Big Five" double rifle and in doubles by John Rigby in California.

Finally, there is the .405 Winchester, a straight, rimmed case whose ballistics do not quite reach those of the 9.3x74R (firing a 300-grain bullet at 2,200 fps). The .405 became a moderately popular caliber for European double rifles in the early 1900s, and Kynoch (among others) manufactured ammunition. Probably, it was in demand in Africa because, as already mentioned, a number of Winchester 95 lever rifles found their way there. Kynamco is once again loading for the .405, but it cannot be considered a dangerous-game cartridge.

The Big .450s

Rigby introduced the .450 NE in 1898. H&H matched Rigby with the .500/450, and Kynoch later introduced the .450 No. 2 in a longer, heavier case to provide the trade with a cartridge that would not suffer from the thin-brass problems of cartridges derived from black-powder rounds. In 1907, the entire caliber went into limbo when .450-diameter bullets were banned in India and the Sudan.

Although it is certainly possible to have any of the .450s built today, to the best of my knowledge no gunmaker offers any of them as standard. This is really unfortunate because they are wonderful cartridges, and there is a tremendous variety of bullets available—both cast lead and jacketed—for a handloader to play with.

The major players in the .470-class of cartridges: From left, Holland's 500/465, Westley Richards's .476 NE, the famous .470 NE, and the .475 No. 2. The .470 was introduced by Joseph Lang, adopted by John Rigby, and chambered by almost everyone; the .475 No. 2 was a "trade" cartridge developed by Eley Brothers to be chambered by anyone. Not shown is the .475 NE, a straight-taper cartridge similar in shape to both the .450 NE and .500 NE.

The .470 Class

This group includes all the cartridges introduced by British gunmakers to replace the .450s. Since the .500 NE already existed, all the replacement cartridges were around .475—roughly halfway between the .450 and .500. While the diameter is greater, bullet weights are about the same, generally allowing the .475s greater velocity, less pressure, or both.

In the group, there are at least four different bullet diameters, with standard weights ranging from 480 to 520 grains. Most of these cartridges are based on the .500 NE 3$^{1}/4''$ necked down, and all hurl their bullets at about 2,150 fps, producing some 5,000 ft. lbs. of muzzle energy. All have been used to take every dangerous game animal, under every conceivable condition; they have done so successfully and will again. Ballistically, there is absolutely nothing to choose among any of them. Logistically? That's another matter.

The .470 NE is the dominant nitro-express cartridge of all time. More gunmakers have chambered it than any other; ammunition is, and has been all along, the most widely distributed. There is a ".470 premium" affixed to any double rifle so chambered. There are several reasons for this, not least of which is that Robert Ruark used a .470 double. The scramble for Africa he set off in 1953 with *Horn of the Hunter* also cemented the .470 in the public imagination. But, Ruark was just one of many who sang the praises of the .470. John Taylor did likewise, as did J. A. Hunter.

Is it numerous because it's popular, or is it popular because it's numerous? Probably some of each. The .470 was developed by the well-known London firm of Joseph Lang around 1907, but instead of keeping it as a proprietary cartridge, the company released it to the trade. Anyone could chamber a rifle in it, and

A Zambezi Valley dagga boy, exactly 40 inches wide. Craig Boddington shot him at about 25 yards in heavy cover, with a "quick right-and-left" from a new Rigby double .470, firing 500-grain Swift A-Frames.

Courtesy of Craig Boddington

many did. Most prominent was John Rigby & Co. Instead of developing its own cartridge to replace the .450, Rigby adopted the .470. With that, its fortune was made. The .470 had momentum coming out of the gate and never lost it.

H&H countered with its .500/465, but that cartridge remained an H&H property; similarly, Westley Richards with the .476 NE. Kynoch necked up its .450 No. 2 to .475 and released it to the trade as the .475 No. 2, but it never matched the .470's popularity. The remaining member of the group, the almost forgotten .475 NE, was a nice, straight-taper cartridge that was never made in great numbers. One should also not forget the .475 No. 2 NE (Jeffery), which is another variation.

With everyone making .470s and users loving the cartridge, it is no wonder that when you say "nitro express" most people think ".470."

Today, ammunition is available for all the cartridges in this group, so availability of ammunition is not really an issue for anyone buying a rifle. If you want a .500/465, you will almost certainly be forced to pay the "H&H-premium," because only Holland's chambered it. The .500/465 is the smallest diameter bullet of the bunch, at .468, followed by the .470 and .476, the .475 and .475 No. 2 (.483) and the .475 No. 2 (Jeffery) at .488.

Westley Richards's .476 is shorter than the others, being based on the .500 NE 3" case rather than the 3¼" version. This gives it slightly higher chamber pressures. At 520 grains, its bullet is the heaviest of the bunch, and this has given rise to the misconception that it is actually a .500. How it could be, when it is the .500 necked down, is never explained. Be that as it may, the bullet is the same diameter as the .470. Elmer Keith loved the .476; for that matter, he loved Westley Richards rifles (and, as I have said, owned five of them).

The best chance of finding a relatively low-priced boxlock working rifle lies with the .475 No 2. There always seems to be a fair number around, including some from continental makers such as Victor Sarasqueta of Spain.

The .475 NE is a strangely anonymous case. No one knows who introduced it, and not many gunmakers chambered it. There are very few around and little mention of it in literature from the golden age. This does not make it any less a good cartridge, but there are pitfalls to owning one. According to *Cartridges of the World*, bullet diameter actually ranges from .474 to .483 inches, which indicates a lack of standardization. This is the reason A-Square refused to make it, but ammunition is available from both Kynamco and Westley Richards. Kynamco loads a 480-grain .483 bullet at 2,175 fps, while WR loads a 500-grain at 2,125 fps. Since Woodleigh offers several ".470" bullets in different diameters and weights, one would be advised to slug the bore of a rifle before ordering ammunition—or, better yet, have it slugged and sort out availability before you buy it.

In the event that nitro-express ammunition again becomes hard to find, the advantage will lie with the .470/.465/.476 trio, since all are based on the .500 case, with the same base dimensions. The last nitro-express cartridge to go will be the .470, and any of the four can be formed from it.

The .500 Nitro Express

The .500 Nitro Express is one fantastic cartridge—possibly the best ever designed for dangerous game. It has been around forever (its antecedents go far back into the black-powder days) and, while it has had its ups and down, it just keeps hanging on. In fact, the .500 NE has now hung on to the point where it is enjoying a renaissance. More and more rifle makers are offering the .500 as a standard chambering.

The odd thing is not the cartridge's current popularity but the lack of popularity it suffered throughout most of its career. Although the .500 case is the parent for the majority of nitro-express cartridges, the .500 itself was always in the shadows.

The .500 was originally derived from a 3¼" case called the .500 Black Powder Express. It fired a 340-grain bullet at 1,925 fps (2,800 ft. lbs. of muzzle energy) and was considered a fine cartridge for tigers in India, but not a rifle for elephants and rhinos in Africa. Jim Corbett used one early in his career, then traded it for a .450/400. With the arrival of smokeless powder, however, the .500

Finn Aagaard with Tony Henley's old H&H Royal 500/465 double. This was a working rifle in every best sense, and served Tony well for many years. He insisted it had significantly less recoil than a comparable .470, although the two cartridges are ballistically identical. Some years after Tony's death in 1994, the rifle was put up for sale by H&H and eventually sold for more than $50,000—an indication of both the continuing value of a good double, and the fascination they hold for both hunters and collectors.

---

was transformed. Two versions emerged—one with a 3" case, the other with a 3¹/4" case—and they are identified accordingly in cartridge nomenclature.

In the rush to replace the .450s in 1907, major makers introduced their own cartridges and promoted them relentlessly, but the .500 belonged to no one and was generally neglected. Most rifle makers offered it, but none really pushed it.

Ballistically, the smokeless .500 falls into a middle ground between the .470 class and the huge, elephant-stopping .577 and .600. At 2,150 fps, its 570-grain bullet delivers 5,850 ft. lbs. of energy. John Taylor gave the .500 a "knockout value" of 87.8, compared to 71.3 for the .470, and 126.7 for the .577. Everyone from J. A. Hunter to Craig Boddington agrees that the .500 delivers a significantly heavier blow than the .470. Midway in his fabled career, Hunter traded his .470 for a .500, and that is what he carried for the rest of his life.

Everyone made .500s, but no one made many. Demand for ammunition was modest, and in 1948 John Taylor warned that Kynoch was planning to discontinue it altogether. As it turned out, the .500 hung on until everything was discontinued in 1963.

Aside from its undisputed ballistic virtues, the .500 has another advantage: The majority of nitro-express cartridges, including the .470, are formed from it. In the course of making .470 brass, you start with a .500 case. This means brass will be obtainable as long as anyone makes a .470.

As mentioned earlier, there were two lengths of .500. The majority of rifles were made with three-inch chambers. George Caswell of Champlin Arms, the

The .500 trio, from left: the original .500 Black Powder Express, an original Kynoch .500 NE 3" loaded with a solid, and .500 NE 3¹/4". The black-powder cartridge fired a 340-grain bullet at about 1950 fps; the nitro-express loadings fire a 570-grain bullet at 2150 fps. In between, there is also a .500 Nitro for Black Powder, a low-pressure load with cordite powder for use in black-powder rifles.

largest U.S. dealer in used double rifles, says he sees about ten 3" .500s for every one 3¹/4". Short ammunition can be safely fired in a long chamber, but not the reverse. Ammunition once again is available for both, but 3" cartridges are much more common. Ironically, while the short case was more popular in and of itself, the long case was the basis for more variations. The .500/450, .500/465, and .470 NE are all based on the 3¹/4" case, while only the .476 NE is based on the 3" case.

There are several possible explanations for the resurgence in interest and demand for .500s. Boredom with the .470 is one; fascination with larger bores is another. If one is a handloader, the .500 offers much more variety, with all kinds of bullet molds available because of the big American .50-caliber buffalo cartridges. Finally, rifle makers need something new to sell. Why not the .500?

When Holland & Holland built the first of its new round-action double rifles, the gun was a .500 NE. When E. J. Churchill built its first new double, it was a .500. When Krieghoff introduced its Classic "Big Five" double in 1996, the .500 was a standard chambering. When Arrieta produced its first two big doubles in 1999, one was a .500.

Modern .500s are being built somewhat lighter than they used to be. One complaint about the older rifles was that they usually weighed about twelve pounds, when ten and a half would have been perfectly adequate. That has been remedied.

The .500 NE seems finally to be receiving the recognition it has long deserved, and given the logistical advantages of both case and bullet—to say nothing of the cartridge's ballistic capabilities—it should be with us for a long while. Professional hunters, whose job is to stop big animals at close quarters, are overjoyed. Even for the average big-game hunter, the .500 is now just as good a choice as the .470. As well, for the handloader, especially one who casts bullets, the .500 offers more than any other nitro-express cartridge, including the .450s.

* * *

Westley Richards offers a cartridge called the .500 Rafiki, which is a .700 H&H necked down to .500. It launches a 570-grain bullet at 2,420 fps, producing 7,500 ft. lbs. of muzzle energy. No one else makes this cartridge, and its existence is a puzzle. According to Lee Butler, late of Westley Richards and now with E. J. Churchill, Westley Richards created the cartridge just to show that it could and to generate some ink. Early reports indicated that there were pressure problems with the huge case, but Westley Richards now says it has ammunition being made "subject to availability."

My only question is, why? Similarly, there is a .700/577, which is the same deal but with a larger bullet. And still there is the same question: Why?

The .577 Nitro Express

There is tremendous, renewed interest in all the big-*big*-bore cartridges— anything a half-inch or larger.

Although it has been overshadowed by the .600 Nitro Express for more than a century, the .577 NE is an excellent cartridge with a long lineage. Its roots can be traced back to muzzleloaders whose load was determined by dividing a pound of lead into equal parts: twelve for a 12-bore, twenty for a 20-bore, and so on. The .577 equates almost exactly to a 24-bore, which was a popular shotgun size. The British military Enfield muzzleloader was a 24-bore, which

The .577 NE was derived, more or less directly, from the military .577 Snider (left), by way of a number of black-powder variations. Although it has existed in several lengths, the 3" case is now standard. Shown are an original Kynoch soft-nose, and a new German-made solid.

evolved into the Snider-Enfield cartridge rifle (in fact, many Enfields were converted). The Snider cartridge was derived from the existing Enfield bore, and all the civilian .577s sprouted from that stalk. For this reason, there are all kinds of different .577s around, from both the black-powder and smokeless days.

The first "modern" .577 was made by Holland & Holland for Sir Samuel Baker. Indian potentates had a particular fondness for this caliber in its varied forms, and many elaborate London doubles were made to order for them. When the time came to convert the .577 case to smokeless powder, different lengths were tried before the trade settled on the current standard 3".

Once finalized, however, the .577 Nitro Express was an impressive beast indeed: It launches a 750-grain bullet at 2,050 fps, for 7010 ft. lbs. at the muzzle. Penetration was astonishing: More than one account tells of a bullet going end to end on an elephant. As for smashing power, Tony Henley told me of shooting a Cape buffalo that came down a bank at him. The rifle doubled and threw Tony one way, the buffalo the other. At the time, Henley was hunting with one of Jimmy Sutherland's .577s.

There were far more .577s made than .600s (and very likely .500s), the majority of them boxlocks, so they are not uncommon. John Rigby made a specialty of the .577, and H&H also made a good number; at the other end of the trade, it was a favorite caliber in Birmingham. Almost any of the current rifle makers will build you a .577, and if you intend to hunt elephants a great deal, it would be an excellent choice. It is really overkill for anything else, except perhaps Cape buffalo.

With the .577, weight starts to become an issue. The average .577 rifle weighs about fourteen pounds, and that is a hefty amount to carry around hour after hour. When you have to lug your own big rifle for a while, you realize the practical value of a gunbearer—and it wasn't laziness on the part of white hunters. It was purely a matter of having the strength left to handle the rifle smartly when the critical time came.

Today, .577 ammunition is freely available. Compared to other calibers, there is even a fair variety of bullets. For practice, cast bullets are the cheapest and most plentiful, and because of the .577's black-powder heritage there is a wide range of molds.

The .600 Nitro Express

For almost a century, the fabled .600 NE was the benchmark for dangerous game—the most powerful sporting-rifle cartridge ever made. When its name was mentioned, strong men gulped and elephants ran for cover. Think of it: A bore six-tenths of an inch in diameter; a 900-grain bullet; *8,400 ft .lbs.* at the muzzle. Awe-inspiring, to be sure. The cartridge's reputation was wide-

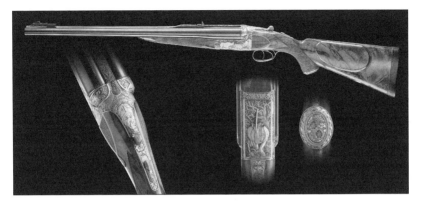

Westley Richards .600 NE droplock, made in 1996 for an American client. The rifle was engraved by Westley Richards engraver Peter Spode. Delivered price for this rifle at the time was $75,000; today (2005), such a rifle would cost £64,000 ($112,000).   *Courtesy Westley Richards*

spread and unchallenged, which is all the more impressive when you consider that barely a hundred .600 NE rifles were made, by all gunmakers combined, in all the years before 1980, and that a good number of those guns resided in the armories of Indian princelings, pristine and unfired.

The .600 was introduced by W. J. Jeffery in 1901. At least, he made the first rifles for it; the designer of the cartridge itself is lost in antiquity. In 1985, *The Shooting Field*, a history of Holland & Holland, traced the .600 from the beginning. At the time, H&H owned both the Jeffery name and records:

> *The first Jeffery .600 bore double rifle, No. 12175, was an "under snap" Anson & Deeley-action rifle, and weighed 15 lbs. 10 oz. It was finished in February 1902 and sold for £45.*

For those who take pride in London sidelocks and British steel, note that this gun was a boxlock and sported barrels of Krupp steel from Germany. The last Jeffery .600 double was sold in 1929; altogether, the company made only thirty-two doubles and twenty-four single-shots; most of the latter were built on Farquharson falling-block actions. H&H then traced the total number that might have been made: Westley Richards, three; John Wilkes, nine; Rigby never made a .600 (the company preferred the .577), but H&H and Purdey each built six. A couple were made in Belgium and at least one was completed in Spain, but H&H estimated that the total number of doubles came to no more than seventy-five. With Jeffery's singles, plus a few from P. Webley and others thrown in, the total came to about one hundred.

Kynoch records show that the first batch of cartridges was loaded in 1901; Eley Brothers also loaded it until 1918. In that year, all five British explosives companies amalgamated, calling themselves, initially, Explosives Trades Limited, then becoming Nobel Industries in November 1918. From that day on, all .600 ammunition produced was headstamped "Kynoch."

The early ammunition was loaded with 100 grains of Cordite or Axite and delivered 1,850 fps (6,840 ft. lbs.) Later loads were 110 grains (1,950 fps, 7,600 ft. lbs.) and 120 grains (2,050 fps, 8,400 ft. lbs.), the modern load that gave the cartridge its awesome reputation. Rifles were made and regulated for any one of the three and were so marked on the barrel. H&H states that the 110-grain load was the standard for the cartridge and insists that John Taylor is wrong when he says all Jeffery rifles were regulated for the 100-grain load.

The first Jeffery rifle weighed almost sixteen pounds, and that is considered normal for a .600. But H&H says that one Jeffery rifle—No. 12431, made in 1902—was regulated for the full 120-grain charge and weighed just 12¼ pounds! No one knows what became of the rifle—or its owner.

From the beginning (in spite of the fascination it held for maharajahs), the .600 was the tool of the professional ivory hunter. It was for use only in the most dire circumstances, and most .600 owners would also have something like a .450 for everyday hunting. It is not surprising, considering how few were actually made, that the .600 is not associated with any prominent hunter in the way that the .577 is associated with Samuel Baker or the .500 with J. A. Hunter.

One professional who owned a .600 was John Taylor. He admired it greatly, but in his book he writes at length about the rifle's weight, about the difficulty of carrying it for any length of time, about its suitability only for very specialized purposes, and about the need to have a .450-class rifle, as well. Having said all that, he accorded it a "knock-out value" of 150.4 and said that a solid head shot would knock out an elephant for up to thirty minutes, compared to twenty for the .577 and ten to fifteen for a .500 NE. Even Taylor was somewhat in awe of the big .600. He said that his Jeffery, which was regulated for the 100-grain charge of Cordite, had noticeably less recoil but no difference in killing power than heavier loadings. Taylor recommended that anyone ordering a .600 choose the lighter load. He also specifically recommended against its use by the sport hunter; it was the emergency tool of the professional, thought Taylor, and it should stay that way.

In 1970, believing that the days of African hunting were nearing their end, H&H built a rifle billed as "The Last .600 Bore." David Winks, the firm's famous barrel man and later director, made the barrels, Ken Hunt did the engraving, and the whole project took five years to complete. When it was done, the company called the last .600 "the finest double rifle H&H ever made." It was sold to an American collector, and a chapter in hunting history ended.

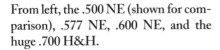

From left, the .500 NE (shown for comparison), .577 NE, .600 NE, and the huge .700 H&H.

As with many endings, however, there was yet a *dénoument*. In fact, there were several. In the 1980s, as interest in African hunting and big-bore rifles was rekindled, many potential buyers tried to convince H&H to make them a .600. Always, they were rebuffed, because the "Last .600" had been sold—at a very high price—on the premise there would never be another.

In one case, American Bill Feldstein said fine, then build me a .700, and that led to the creation of the biggest Holland & Holland rifle, which we will get to shortly. Meanwhile, demand kept building, and H&H realized there was a large potential market. The company approached the owner of the "Last .600" and asked him to name his price; reportedly, the cost of letting H&H out of the agreement was a new H&H shotgun for each of the man's children. Today, the company is back making .600 NE double rifles once again.

The .700 H&H

Although the cartridge is correctly called the .700 H&H (*not* the .700 NE), it was a joint project of Holland & Holland, Bill Feldstein, and Jim Bell, who made the brass. It reportedly cost Feldstein a quarter of a million dollars in development fees, and only after the cartridge was completed could he order the first .700 double for about £110,000.

The cartridge is a half-inch longer than a .600 and launches a 1,000-grain bullet at 2,000 fps, for 8,900 ft. lbs. of energy. As noted previously, the rifles weigh about nineteen pounds apiece—too heavy to carry and almost too heavy to shoot. Even so, the recoil gets your attention. You hold on tight, keep your weight on your front foot, prepare to roll with the punch, and pray you manage to hang on to the rifle; you would really hate to drop a $200,000 rifle in the gravel! Even with preparation, it rocks you and the muzzles end up pointing at the sky. The target looks as if a sparrow flew through it.

Although the .700 H&H rifles are beautifully made and fully functional, the .700 cannot be considered, by any definition, a practical dangerous-game rifle for either professional or amateur hunters.

Cartridges for Bolt Actions

I've this damned cannon.

Robert Wilson

It is rapidly approaching a full century since the first cartridge was designed specifically for hunting dangerous game with a bolt-action rifle. The gun was the Mauser 98, which appeared in the hands of the military in 1898 and in hunters' a couple of years later. At the time, Germany possessed what is now Tanganyika—then, as now, the greatest hunting country in Africa. The British held Kenya, immediately to the north, and safaris throughout East Africa were mounted from its capital, Nairobi. Almost immediately, bolt actions (magazine rifles) appeared in East Africa, and they have been a standard item of safari kit ever since.

British rifle makers specialized in doubles, but quickly saw the possibilities of magazine rifles. John Rigby seized upon the Mauser 98 (and became Mauser's representative in London), along with W. J. Jeffery, H&H, Westley Richards, and George Gibbs. The .404 Jeffery and .425 Westley Richards were introduced in 1909, and the .416 Rigby and .505 Gibbs in 1911. For its part, at Rigby's behest, the Mauserwerke in Oberndorf began producing the legendary (if misnamed) double square-bridge magnum action. This monster could accommodate cartridges up to the .505 Gibbs.

Except for the belted .375, they were rimless; however, all owed a debt to the nitro-express heritage. The cases were spacious, to keep pressures down, and generally had a distinct taper for ease of feeding and extraction. By today's standards their ballistic performance was not overwhelming, and a handloader could (and can) easily exceed factory velocity in any of them. However, the British had established a standard for elephants and Cape buffalo based on the original .450 Nitro Express: A 500-grain bullet at 2,150 fps. These cartridges were intended to match that, more or less. It is a standard that is equally valid today.

German gunmakers also developed large cartridges, but never to the extent of the British because there was not the same dedication to sport safaris in Tanganyika, even among the German upper class. However, the Germans did develop several cartridges that were, in terms of power, every bit the equal of the British. Their 9.3mm cartridges, of which there are several, have a bullet diameter of .365 and standard weight of 286 grains—comparable to the .375 H&H. They were fine rimless designs. Where German ammunition had a serious failing, however, was bullets. John Taylor noted repeatedly that German bullets had a lamentable tendency to break up and fail to penetrate. Since factory ammunition was all that was available and you took what you could get, this was extremely serious when it came to dangerous game. As well, there was an innate British colonial prejudice against German rifles simply because they were not British, and the term "cheap Continental magazine rifle" became pervasive. This does not in any way detract from either the quality of the Mauser 98 or many of the cartridges developed for it.

The largest of all was the 12.5x70mm Schuler, also known as the .500 Jeffery. No one knows whether it was introduced by Schuler or Jeffery, or even when. Rifles were available in the 1920s, and that is all that is known. Taylor noted that ammunition could be had only from Germany, which indicates that this caliber was Schuler's development. For many years it was the most powerful cartridge chambered in a magazine rifle, delivering ballistics that substantially exceed the legendary .500 Nitro Express. It is a "modern" cartridge in that it has a relatively small case (compared to the .505 Gibbs) and is loaded to high pressures.

Between the 9.3s and the 12.5, there were several other German cartridges that received mixed reviews fifty years ago but, when loaded with modern premium bullets, would undoubtedly be fine choices for dangerous game.

* * *

In 1948, reflecting on big rifles and cartridges in Britain and postwar Europe, John Taylor wrote:

> *Maybe the great American firms will turn out large bore stuff in days to come, and build rifles to handle it. There's an immense market awaiting the enterprising manufacturer who cares to cater for it. The demand for powerful rifles and ammunition is unprecedented; there was nothing like it after World War I. It is doubtful if the British will ever satisfy it; and Germany is out of the running for many a long day to come.*

Eight years later the first major American company entered the fray. In 1956, Winchester introduced the .458 Winchester Magnum as part of the original "short magnum" line that also included the .264 and .338. The .338 was an unqualified success, the .264 a qualified failure, and the .458 a bit of both, a ballistic failure but a commercial success. This is ironic when you consider how many times the opposite has occurred. Winchester advertised the .458 as delivering a 510-grain bullet at 2,130 fps, and if it had done so, it would have been fine. Unfortunately, as I have noted elsewhere, most tests showed velocities closer to 1,900 fps from a standard-length barrel, and some cartridges produced considerably less if the compressed powder caked and solidified.

By the time Winchester got around to its .458, wildcatters had already been busy. The only big British cartridge really familiar to Americans was the .505 Gibbs, partly because Abercrombie & Fitch imported a few rifles in this chambering and partly from Ernest Hemingway's reference to it in *The Short Happy Life of Francis Macomber*. Philip B. Sharpe covers the cartridge in his *Complete Guide to Handloading*—the only big British round so honored. Americans wanted an elephant cartridge that was adaptable to bolt actions such as the Winchester Model 70, and since this rifle was available in .375 H&H, that case was a logical place to start. Most big-bore wildcats intended for Africa were of .458-diameter and based on the full-length .375 H&H case, necked up and blown out. One early wildcat (circa 1950) was the .450 Watts, followed about ten years later by the .450 Ackley (designed by gunsmith Parker Ackley). They are ballistically identical and while the Watts predated the Ackley, the latter achieved some lasting fame and even quasi-proprietary status. It is loaded today by A-Square, and commercial brass is available. These two .450s will launch a 500-grain bullet at 2,400 fps (and sometimes more), so they offered a substantial edge over even the paper ballistics of the .458 Winchester.

Both cartridges have been largely eclipsed by a later development, the .458 Lott, and the differences make an interesting comparison of three cartridges that are ballistically the same yet quite different in approach. The Watts and Ackley were designed by gunsmiths in America; the Lott was designed by a big-game hunter who had been hammered by a Cape buffalo and barely survived. Jack Lott designed his cartridge as a reaction to the failure of the .458 Winchester. The .458 Lott is simply a .458 Winchester lengthened by three-tenths of an inch. The greater powder capacity allows it to deliver a genuine 2,150 fps with a 500-grain bullet; there is no powder compression nor any pressure problems. As well, it can be loaded considerably hotter if desired. It is a straight, tapered case with no shoulder—easy to feed and to extract.

The Watts, on the other hand, was the .375 H&H necked up, and that was that. It left a vestigial shoulder that accomplished nothing except giving the case a neck. Parker Ackley stated bluntly that his development was intended to maximize case capacity and minimize body taper. Although it is blown out to maximum, the .450 Ackley offers no significant increase in powder capacity or velocity over the Watts, but it is more difficult to feed and can stick if pressures are pushed. As well, the tiny shoulder creates potential problems with a compressed load; a little too much pressure when crimping can bulge the case ever so slightly—a change that is indiscernible to the naked eye but is enough to keep the cartridge from chambering. These minor quibbles do not make the Ackley any less a good cartridge, but when the Lott is available, there is not much justification for it.

Another great advantage of the Lott is that standard .458 Winchester ammunition can be used in an emergency. The same is true of the Watts. An identical claim has been made for the Ackley, but the substitution is not as straightforward. In an Ackley chamber the case blows out more, with velocity reduced and accuracy compromised; it is generally not recommended. With the Lott, shooting the standard Winchester round is exactly the same as shooting a 3" .500 NE in a 3¼" chamber or a .22 Short in a .22 LR chamber. The substitution works perfectly well with no problems at all. Since factory .458 Winchester ammunition is available all over the world, this advantage can hardly be exaggerated.

These are the differences between a cartridge designed by a hunter whose life may be on the line, and one designed by a gunsmith interested in maximum efficiency and paper ballistics. The ascendancy of the .458 Lott continues. It is now chambered in several factory rifles, and ammunition is available from both A-Square and Federal.

A similar situation took place in the 1970s and '80s, when interest in .416-caliber rifles was being rekindled. The .416 Rigby was moribund; factory ammunition and brass were extremely hard to come by, and such a bulky cartridge requires an oversized action. Hunters began looking for an alternative. Again, the .375 H&H case was the basis for most of the developments. In 1972, hunter/writer Robert Chatfield-Taylor necked down the .458 Winchester and called it the .416 Taylor. Shortly after, professional hunter George Hoffman created the .416 Hoffman on a blown-out .375 H&H case. These were the main players until 1988, when Remington capitalized on the interest with the .416 Remington, which is almost identical to the Hoffman. A year later, Weatherby introduced its own .416, a necked-up .378. The .416 Weatherby is a tremendous cartridge, generating substantially more velocity than the Remington.

With the advent of the .416 Remington, the Taylor and Hoffman wildcats virtually died. Oddly enough, however, the .416 Rigby made a strong comeback and is, today, more popular than ever. Given a choice, many have gone with the proven Rigby instead of the Remington, which is a high-intensity cartridge with potential extraction problems if pressures are pushed too far.

The .375s

The .375 H&H is not just the head of the .375 family, but of all cartridges with a belted case. When it was introduced in 1912, a companion cartridge, the .375 Flanged, was created as well. The flanged was rimmed and beltless, intended for double rifles and single-shots, and while it gained some popularity, its belted brother really left it in the dust. When gunmakers discovered that dou-

Three approaches to the .375, from left: .375 H&H, .375 Dakota, and the .378 Weatherby. The H&H is a slim, tapered cartridge that offers medium power, and almost foolproof feeding and extraction; the Dakota emphasizes compact size that can be fitted into a standard action; the Weatherby is a huge cartridge that emphasizes high velocity, but requires an oversized action and inflicts extreme recoil.

ble rifles could easily be chambered for the belted version, for which ammunition was more widely available, the flanged cartridge faded. (Ballistically, the .375 Flanged is remarkably similar to the German 9.3x74R, a tapered, bottlenecked, rimmed cartridge used in doubles and single-shots, especially O/U doubles, and favored for wild boar and red stag.)

As soon as the .375 H&H became available in the United States in the mid-1930s, wildcatters went to work on it. The most common alteration was simply to blow out the case to increase capacity and velocity. Roy Weatherby based an entire line of cartridges on this belted case, and among these was his original .375 Weatherby Magnum—a blown-out H&H with Weatherby's trademark double-radius shoulder. Weatherby increased velocity with the 300-grain bullet to 2,800 fps, compared to 2,550 fps for the H&H cartridge.

Then, in 1953, Weatherby designed a completely new .375 cartridge based on the larger .416 Rigby case, but with a belt added. The .378 Weatherby fired a 300-grain bullet at more than 2,900 fps. The sheer size of the .378 led to one notable development: Federal Cartridge designed its magnum primer, the F215, specifically to ignite slow-burning powder in the cavernous .378.

At the time, Weatherby believed that the .378 would spell the end of all other large-bore cartridges. To ensure its acceptance, the company deliberately killed off its own .375, and for a long period neither rifles nor factory ammunition were available for it. Many people (rifle writer Jon Sundra among them) believed that the .375 Weatherby was the optimum .375 design, and Sundra not only designed his own very similar cartridge (the .375 JRS), but also persuaded a number of rifle makers to offer it as a standard chambering. At least one ammunition manufacturer (A-Square) offers factory ammunition.

Other .375 cartridges have been introduced since that time, including the .375 Dakota (based on the .404 Jeffery) and the .375 A-Square (on a shortened .378 Weatherby case). All have been aimed toward higher velocities and greater range, rather than greater knockdown power close in. This really takes them out of the realm of dangerous-game cartridges, especially since the higher velocities are possible only with long barrels (twenty-five inches and up).

Here is what Art Alphin has to say:

> *Like all of the high-velocity .375s, the .375 A-Square would not be the primary choice for dangerous game at close range. In such a situation it is better to go to the larger bullet (.416 or above) than to higher and higher velocities.*

Therein lies the dilemma with .375 cartridges and the basic reason for the .378 Weatherby's mixed reputation. Undoubtedly it has made some spectacular kills during its fifty-year career, but I have yet to meet an African professional hunter who regards it with anything except suspicion. In 1990, Botswana-based Lionel Palmer told me about stalking a lion with a client who used a .378. The first bullet struck the big male on the shoulder at close range, and the animal leapt into the grass. There followed a hair-raising twenty four-hour chase; when the lion was finally put out of its misery, Palmer found that the first shot had created an enormous surface wound but had done no real structural damage. Palmer characterized the .378 as a "wounder" and insisted the fault lay with the velocity of the bullet. He may well have been right.

The .375 H&H has a reputation for excellent penetration, largely because its 300-grain bullet has good sectional density. As well, even in a soft point, at 2,550 fps, the striking velocity is not high enough to cause excessive expansion. The .378 jacks velocity up past 2,900 fps. A close shot and a soft bullet traveling at muzzle velocity could cause the bullet to practically disintegrate, inflicting a surface wound with little penetration.

A related problem is the recoil of the .378 Weatherby, which I find to be the worst of any factory cartridge. It is violent, sharp, and jarring, like a left hook from a middleweight contender, and many professional hunters tell of clients scared to death of their rifles.

In the right hands, the .378 Weatherby may be a fine long-range rifle, but it is not a good choice for dangerous game.

Many believed the original .375 Weatherby to be better overall than its replacement, the .378, and ballistically that may be true. However, the almost parallel sides of its case, combined with high pressures from its maximum loads, can create real problems with case sticking, especially in the heat of Africa.

Of all the .375s that have come along, the .375 Dakota is the only one that offers an advantage other than velocity over the original H&H. Based on the fatter .404 Jeffery case, it affords greater powder capacity yet is short enough to be chambered in a standard .30-06-length action. Whether that is a significant improvement is a matter of opinion. The last I heard, Dakota is still getting more orders for the .375 H&H than for its own .375.

The .375 Remington Ultra Magnum is in the same class ballistically as the .375 JRS, employing an oversized, rimless case. It, also, is more of a long-range cartridge than a dangerous-game caliber, although it is certainly capable of killing anything up to an elephant.

The .416s and Their Ilk

Forty-caliber cartridges were enormously popular all over the world in the late 1800s, for long-range target shooting as well as hunting. Once the bolt action arrived and proved its worth, it was natural for British rifle makers to develop .40-caliber cartridges for it.

John Rigby had the Mauser agency and, in 1911, developed the .416 Rigby, one of the finest big-game cartridges of all time. In fact, Frank Barnes (*Cartridges of the World*) calls it "probably the best magazine cartridge for big game ever offered." It employed a bulky rimless case with a small but sharp and distinct shoulder, and it fired a 410-grain bullet at 2,400 fps. Rigby augmented this fine ballistic performance with a bullet that became legendary in its own right—the steel-jacketed solid. The factory soft-nose was just as good, and the .416 became the lion cartridge *par excellence.*

W. J. Jeffery was another rifle specialist and had a long association with the rimmed .450/400, a superb double cartridge that was regarded, until the arrival of the .375 H&H, as the best all-around cartridge available. Jeffery wanted a magazine-rifle equivalent to the .450/400, and so the company created the .404 Jeffery (also known as the .404 Rimless NE). The .404 is a rimless case, slimmer than the Rigby, but utilizing a bullet of .423 inches rather than .416. There is no practical difference between the two in any way, except possibly bullet construc-tion, but I have never heard that the .404 failed in that regard. The .404 estab-lished a reputation for reliability and became the standard-issue rifle for several game departments, notably that of Tanganyika. Into the late 1980s, Parker-Hale made .404 Jeffery rifles on Mauser actions specifically for sale to game depart-ments. Combined with the steady demand for ammunition, this did much to keep the cartridge alive. At the same time, in a kind of reverse psychology, the .404 came to be thought of as a rather blue-collar "game scout" cartridge.

The third member of this triumvirate was Westley Richards's .425. Ballistically, the .425 is every bit as good as the other two, but it developed a dicey reputation for a couple of reasons. First, Westley Richards insisted on fitting its bolt-action rifles with twenty-eight-inch barrels, which made them very unwieldy. Second, the cartridge has a rebated rim, which can give feeding prob-lems; while this may be more theoretical than real, it caused concern. The .425 is an excellent example of how the British proprietary system can affect a cartridge's reputation through no fault of its own. John Taylor hated the long-barreled rifles ("fitting a stupidly long barrel on a magazine rifle of this caliber is certainly asking for trouble"), but he thought very highly of the cartridge ("undoubtedly one of the finest lion-stoppers in existence") and the bullet ("these capped bullets of Westley Richards are the best expanding bullets extant").

In Germany at this time, several gunmakers developed rimless cartridges for Mauser and Mannlicher rifles. The most popular in Africa was the 10.75x68 Mauser (bullet diameter: .424), which was introduced in the 1920s. It fired a 347-grain bullet at 2,200 fps. There was nothing wrong with the cartridge, but bullet performance was poor. Bullets tended to break up and not penetrate on dangerous game, and their users tended to not come home. In a modern rifle with good bullets, this is an excellent cartridge in the .375 H&H class.

In the United States, the .416 Rigby enjoyed a modest following into the 1950s but was available only in custom rifles. Ammunition from Kynoch was expensive and hard to get, and brass was impossible to make from another basic case. Supplies of .416 bullets were sporadic, although Fred Barnes did make them at various times. Jack O'Connor was one writer who liked the .416 Rigby and had a rifle built on an Enfield P-17 action. In 1953, things became slightly easier when Weatherby introduced its .378, because it was possible to remove the belt on a lathe and form .416 Rigby cases. It is an indication of the cartridge's reputation that hunters felt it worthwhile to go to all that trouble.

Interest in .416 cartridges really heated up in the 1980s. At the time, the .458 Winchester was the only readily available big-bore cartridge for magazine rifles, and its failings in factory form were widely apparent. The .416 Rigby was inconvenient, so several wildcatters created their own .416s.

In 1972, Robert Chatfield-Taylor took the .458 Winchester case, necked it down to .416, and called it the .416 Taylor. It did not quite duplicate the performance of the Rigby, but it came close, it was easy to make, and it could be chambered in a .30-06 action. A few years later, George Hoffman took the .375 H&H case, necked it up and blew it out, and called it the .416 Hoffman. This cartridge would match the .416 Rigby, but did so at higher pressures. When Art Alphin went into business with A-Square, he introduced factory ammunition for both the Taylor and the Hoffman, and made rifles chambered for them, as well.

In 1992, Alphin was commissioned by a client to develop the .400 Pondoro (named for John Taylor). Bullet diameter of this oddball is .409, which allows it to use everything from 210-grain slugs intended for the .41 Magnum handgun all the way up to A-Square's 400-grain Monolithic Solid. Alphin calls it the "most versatile big-game cartridge ever developed," and has played with the idea of offering ammunition that can be used on everything from prairie dogs to elephants. Although listed in the A-Square loading manual as the .400 Pondoro, a recent price list calls it the .400 A-Square DPM (for dual-purpose magnum). Confusing.

Craig Boddington with a Masailand lion. The rifle is an open-sighted Mauser action Dumoulin in .416 Rigby. Virtually from the day it was introduced, the .416 Rigby has been renowned as a lion cartridge *par excellence.*

Courtesy of Craig Boddington

In the late 1980s, some Los Angeles gun writers got together and created the .425 Express, a .300 Winchester Magnum shortened slightly and necked up to take a .423 bullet. Colonel Charles Askins then used it extensively while hunting Asiatic buffalo in Australia. The cartridge will fit a standard .30-06 action and offers ballistics identical to those of the .416 Rigby. This cartridge is also offered by A-Square.

Rumor had it that a major company would legitimize one or the other of the popular .416 wildcats, but as it turned out, Remington created its own .416 in 1988. It was the 8mm Remington necked up to .416 and is virtually identical to Hoffman's cartridge, although the two are not interchangeable. Its arrival spelled the end for the two wildcats, however. They offered nothing that could not be obtained with the Remington, at considerably lower cost.

A year later, Weatherby introduced its .416—essentially the .416 Rigby with a belt, loaded to significantly higher velocities. The Weatherby launches a 400-grain bullet at 2,700 fps—a 300 fps gain over both the Rigby and the Remington.

Meanwhile, just to make things truly interesting, in 1989, Sturm, Ruger & Company announced that it would offer its Model 77 bolt action and Number One single-shot rifle in .416 Rigby. This was followed by an announcement that Federal Cartridge would offer factory .416 Rigby ammunition. Suddenly, the .416 Rigby was back. With factory rifles and ammunition available for all three .40-caliber cartridges—the Rigby, Remington, and Weatherby—a potential buyer could make the choice based on purely ballistic considerations.

The major players in the .416 family, from left: the patriarch .416 Rigby, .404 Jeffery, .416 Remington, .416 Dakota, and .416 Weatherby.

Since that time, the Rigby has become extremely popular, the Remington has established itself fairly well (but not as well as one would have expected), and the .416 Weatherby remains a Weatherby property. What happened? Ballistically, the Weatherby cartridge is clearly the most powerful, but along with that performance goes severe recoil. To realize its potential, you need a twenty-six-inch barrel, which makes the rifle somewhat unwieldy; it also has a removable muzzle brake, which reduces recoil but makes the barrel just that much longer (twenty-eight inches), as well as producing nearly unbearable muzzle blast.

The Remington .416 matched the original Rigby ballistics, but did so at high pressures. It is a high-intensity cartridge that presents the same potential case-sticking problems as the .375 Weatherby. For the .416 Remington, SAAMI specifies a taper of twenty-two one-thousandths of an inch from base to shoulder, while the .375 Weatherby is eighteen one-thousandths. Perhaps the difference is enough, because I have never heard of a .416 Remington bolt jamming from high pressures.

In the mid-1990s, Dakota brought out its line of proprietary cartridges and included a .416 based on the .404 Jeffery case, blown out and necked down ever so slightly. With a case capacity about 15 percent greater than that of a standard belted magnum, the .416 Dakota can better the ballistics of the .416 Remington (firing a 400-grain bullet at 2,450 fps). Because it has a rimless case, it also offers the (largely theoretical) advantages of smoother feeding and potentially greater accuracy. It can be chambered in any rifle that will accept the .375 H&H. Its greatest advantage, to my mind, is that it can equal the .416 Remington, but with lower pressures, and can match the Rigby, but in a smaller action.

Cartridge fads come and go, and it would not surprise me if, in twenty years, the .416 Rigby is the only one still being offered. Remington now offers its .416 only through the firm's custom shop (although ammunition is still avail-

The author in Botswana with one of the first .416 Weatherby rifles taken on safari. Loaded with good bullets, such as the Trophy Bonded Bear Claw (used here), the .416 Weatherby is a tremendous cartridge for the largest game.

able), and the Weatherby cartridge has never been adopted by anyone else.

The most recent addition to the .416 stable is the brand-new .400 H&H Magnum, one of two new large-bore cartridges created by Holland & Holland. Devoted H&H users were demanding a cartridge with more punch than the .375, in a cartridge with a Holland & Holland headstamp. When your clients are as wealthy as H&H's undoubtedly are, it makes sense to cater to their whims, even if it means reinventing the wheel.

Russell Wilkin, Holland &Holland's technical director, approached the question in a very logical and measured way. Since the .375 generates muzzle energy of about 4,000 ft. lbs., and the company's venerable, rimmed .500/465 produces 6,000 ft. lbs., Wilkin decided to create two new cartridges rather than one. The larger of the two would be a belted, rimless .465, while the cartridge in between would be a .416 producing about 5,000 ft. lbs. of energy.

Wilkin and his team of rifle makers then thought the whole thing through with considerably more attention to detail than the average wildcatter would. Every aspect of cartridge design was considered, from feeding and chambering, to case sticking, pressures, velocity, and trajectory. Naturally, he began with the tested and proven belted .375 case. The result is two new cartridges that mesh beautifully with the .375, giving trajectories with factory loads that are all very similar out to 200 yards—the distance Wilkin and his colleagues determined to be the maximum for a dangerous-game rifle. Wilkin also adhered to the British principle of heavier bullets and moderate velocities, giving good penetration and knockdown power, but also being as comfortable to shoot as is possible in such a large rifle.

The new .400 H&H Magnum shoots a 400-grain .416 bullet at 2,400 fps. The case is tapered, with a gentle shoulder for optimum feeding. Rifle for rifle, you should get one more cartridge in the magazine than you would with a .416 Rigby.

Another way of looking at this project is that Russell Wilkin examined all the available .416s, then set out to incorporate each of their good qualities while eliminating the problems. The Rigby's bulk, the Remington's parallel sides, the rebated rim of the Westley Richards—all are eliminated. To date, no ammunition maker has announced it will manufacture .400 H&H Magnum ammunition, but if any do, it would be a fine choice for anyone wanting a .416. H&H offers its own ammunition, made by Wolfgang Romey.

The debate over whether the .416s are as good as—or better than—the various .458s has raged for years; proponents of the .416 point to its long-range superiority, but that only evinces itself beyond 250 yards, and even then is not a serious factor unless one is hunting eland or some similar large beast at long range. For typical dangerous-game rifle distances—from four feet to a hundred yards—the .416's 400-grain bullet is inferior to the .458's 500-grain bullet. Is it a life-threatening difference? Probably not. The .458s are, without exception, more versatile, but only because there is a much wider range of bullets available for them.

The Big .450s

The .458 in its many forms is one of the oldest calibers, dating back to muzzle-loading days. The 500-grain .458 at 2,150 fps has been the standard for dangerous-game rifles for more than a century. Any gun that will deliver that ballistic performance is good for anything up to elephant under almost any conditions. Some hunters have insisted on bigger rifles: ivory hunters liked the .577 and .600 NE when they were dealing with wounded bulls in a herd, in the worst thickets, but that was highly specialized work. Usually those specialists had a .450 or its equivalent for everyday elephant hunting. The first nitro express was a .450; the first American factory cartridge for dangerous game was a .458.

Today, a half-dozen .450s are available in factory rifles and ammunition, and sorting out which is best can be confusing. Essentially, they can be divided into two groups: those based on the .375 H&H case and those based on the .416 Rigby case. The .458 Winchester belongs to the first group, and the .460 Weatherby to the second. Some have written that Weatherby brought out the .460 in response to the .458 to one-up Winchester, but what actually happened is a little different.

In 1953, Roy Weatherby tried to promote his .378 as the ultimate dangerous-game cartridge, but ran into political difficulties. New regulations were

The big .450s, from left: .458 Winchester Magnum, .458 Lott, .450 Ackley, .460 Short A-Square, .450 Dakota, .460 Weatherby. The Ackley and Short A-Square are both factory-loaded with the two-diameter Dead Tough bullet.

introduced in the mid-'50s in east Africa, prohibiting the hunting of thick-skinned game such as elephant with anything less than a .40-caliber cartridge. Weatherby believed the change was aimed at him personally by hide-bound professional hunters who believed in big, slow bullets. But there was nothing he could do except make a bigger cartridge.

Since Winchester already had its .458, Weatherby settled on that diameter for his new round. He necked up his .378 and the resulting creation, the .460 Weatherby, fired a 500-grain bullet at 2,700 fps (8,095 ft. lbs. of energy). Current factory ballistics call for only (!) 2,600 fps, which reduces energy to 7,500 ft. lbs.—still a handful for the average shooter. Weatherby's stated purpose in introducing the .460 was to offer the most powerful commercial cartridge, and he succeeded. Even at its reduced level, the Weatherby cartridge still delivers numbers comparable to those of the .600 NE, so it has not exactly been emasculated.

The .460 Weatherby was touted to deliver both bullet weight *and* velocity—a devastating combination in the right hands. Unfortunately, men who could handle it (or even wanted to) were few and far between. In all my trips to Africa, I have seen exactly one professional hunter who used a .460 Weatherby, and he took a perverse pride in being a maverick. Undoubtedly, this lack of enthusiasm is due at least partly to the Weatherby Mark V rifle itself, which has never gained much favor among PHs. But it was certainly not because of either cost or availability; I have seen professionals go to much greater trouble and expense to get ammunition for a .500 NE or .577 than they would need to arm themselves with a .460.

For most amateurs, the .460 is just too much gun. The recoil, while not as alarming as that of the .378, is still bad. No sane man would go out and plink with one for an afternoon.

Even after the .460 thundered onto the scene, it was felt there was still room for a .458 that delivered a little more with a little less—more velocity than the .458 Winchester, that is, with less pressure. A roomier case, more powder, no powder compression, and maybe the option of using a 600-grain bullet. All of this can be done by a handloader with the .460 Weatherby, of course, but that does not answer the factory-ammunition question.

In 1995, while he still owned John Rigby & Co., Paul Roberts took the .416, necked it up, and called it the .450 Rigby. A year or two earlier, Don Allen at Dakota Arms had done exactly the same thing and called it the .450 Dakota. The Dakota is blown out slightly more than the Rigby, and because of some dimensional differences the two cartridges are not interchangeable, but I defy anyone to tell one from the other from five feet away. Ballistically, there are tiny differences, too. The Rigby fires a 480-grain bullet at 2,350 fps, the Dakota a 500-grain bullet at 2,450 fps; this gives the Dakota the slimmest of edges in muzzle energy, the Rigby a tad less recoil.

The important thing about both cartridges is that they were not designed to deliver maximum velocity at any cost, as the original .460 Weatherby was. Quite the opposite, in fact. They were deliberately fashioned to deliver the desired optimum velocity (2,400 fps, give or take) at lower pressures, with no powder-compression problems. And that is exactly what they do.

It is the considered opinion of many knowledgeable, experienced danger-ous-game hunters that there is a "magic" level of velocity with a heavy bullet, and that 2,400 fps is it. Art Alphin, founder of A-Square, expert ballistician, and widely experienced hunter of elephants and Cape buffalo, certainly believes that. I have no opinion one way or the other; I do know, however, that trying to achieve 2,400 fps with a 500-grain bullet in a case that is not large enough will cause compression problems, and actually achieving that velocity in any rifle can put it over the top in terms of recoil

While the .458 Lott, Ackley, Watts, and others of that ilk are all touted as being capable of 2,400 fps, I have never achieved it without having to compress powder more than I like. Occasionally, attempting to do it, I have bulged cases; sometimes I have had to seat the bullet twice before it stayed, and then it did so only with a heavy crimp. On the range, the difference between 2,250 fps and 2,400 fps, with a nine- or ten-pound rifle, is noticeable. It pushes what I call the recoil threshold (mine, at any rate) from tolerable to uncomfortable.

* * *

There are two distinct classes of .458 cartridge here—those based on the .375 belted case and those based on the .416 Rigby case—so let's compare them.

The Lott and its brethren fit nicely into a .375 H&H–sized action, with a twenty-two-inch barrel, and make for a handy rifle weighing nine-pounds-plus.

The Dakota–Rigby types require a magnum action with a deeper magazine—if you don't want to reduce capacity by one cartridge. To pursue higher velocities with more powder, a longer barrel is needed to burn it—twenty-four inches at least—and (as already noted) Weatherby fits its rifle with a twenty-six-inch barrel plus a two-inch-long muzzle brake. These rifles are at least a pound heavier and certainly longer and more unwieldy than average. The extra weight will dampen the extra recoil, however, so that works out.

As you can see, there is more to making the decision than simply choosing an extra 150 fps of muzzle velocity. The difference between the rifles themselves can be such that you should consider all the things you will want to do with it before deciding one way or the other.

In my opinion, the cartridge that best combines a host of virtues with economical cost, versatility, and convenience is the .458 Lott—simply a longer version of the .458 Winchester. As noted elsewhere, if for some reason a hunter runs out of Lott ammunition, he can always shoot the.458 Winchester cartridge, which is readily available almost anywhere.

These are not the only big .450s, but they are the main ones. A-Square designed some entries in the field, notably the .460 Short A-Square, which is based on a shortened .460 Weatherby. It delivers 2,400 fps with a 500-grain bullet and does so in a cartridge of the same length as the .458 Winchester. This means that it can be chambered in a .30-06-length action. Art Alphin designed the cartridge in 1977, and it has been offered in a factory loading by A-Square since the beginning.

Alphin is enthusiastic about the .460 Short's accuracy, ease of loading, and sheer power. Even with his pride of authorship, however, Alphin admits that the cartridge presents problems when you try to convert an existing rifle to it. It does not feed as easily as it might, and certainly not without major gunsmithing; also, most rifles (even those in .458 Winchester) are not built to withstand the pounding of such a cartridge. They need to be heavier to absorb the recoil, and they should be reinforced in various ways, as well. Alphin's conclusion: A rifle built from scratch as a .460 Short A-Square can be a superb dangerous-game gun, but it is not a cartridge that lends itself readily to converting an existing rifle.

Interestingly enough, Alphin describes the .460 Short A-Square as "the 6 PPC of dangerous-game rifles," which would make it the forerunner of the whole series of short and short-short magnums that have been sprung upon the world since the 1990s. Leaving everything else aside—the high pressures, the dubious velocities—it is hard to make those cartridges feed smoothly in the average rifle. Marketing people would have you believe otherwise, of course, but many custom rifle makers want nothing to do with any of them. Earlier, we discussed the preferability of longer, tapered cartridges in terms of ease of feeding. The .460 Short A-Square is a perfect example.

Finally, the one area where the .458 shines over every other big caliber:

Bullet selection. If you are a handloader, the sky's the limit. You can buy jacketed soft points from 250 grains to 600, solids from 400 to 600, and lead bullets ranging from 300 on up. Because this diameter has been used in rifles for 150 years, virtually every shape and size has been tried, and molds old and new can cast anything imaginable. If you do not want to cast bullets, small suppliers for Cowboy Action and black-powder silhouette shooting can probably take care of you.

If you have a yen to load your .458 Lott down to the .45-70 level and hunt whitetails, with 405-grain bullets at 1,600 fps, nothing could be easier (or more fun, for that matter). Or you can use 300-grain jacketed hollowpoints intended for the same .45-70. The Barnes X-bullet in its various incarnations has been available in 300-, 350-, 400-, 450-, and 500-grain versions. These are spitzer bullets with good ballistic coefficients, and they can be loaded hot enough to turn a Lott into a genuine 300-yard rifle for hunting eland in elephant country, where you are on foot, distances are long, and the inevitable elephants are apt to be touchy. Or, you can load a 350-grain softpoint (Hornady makes an excellent one) and use it for tracking leopards on foot where distances are measured in feet and you need maximum, instant destruction. For the non-handloader, there are custom ammunition companies that can supply any or all of the above.

No other caliber can make this claim. A direct benefit is, as new applications are found for your .458 Lott (or Ackley or Dakota), your use of the rifle increases, and your skill and comfort with it grow accordingly. If I could have but one rifle, it would probably be my Dakota-actioned, custom .458 Lott. There is literally nothing I couldn't hunt with it.

The .465, .470, and .475

Compared with the .450s, the class of cartridge immediately larger is small and scattered. This is probably due to the sheer excellence of the .458s as a group. There is not a huge amount to be gained by adding a few thousandths of an inch in diameter and a few grains of weight. One minor advantage is the ability to drive a bullet of the same weight at the same velocity, but at lower pressures. Just as it is easier to push a 400-grain .458 at 2,400 fps than a 400-grain .416, it is easier to push a 500-grain .475 at 2,400 fps than a 500-grain .458.

Among double-rifle cartridges, this whole class exists because of the 1907 ban on .450s in the Sudan and India. No such artificial encouragement came along to force gunmakers to do something different for modern magazine rifles, so they have largely stuck with the caliber generally perceived to be the best overall. There are, however, a few that are larger.

The second of the new Holland & Holland cartridges is the .465 H&H Magnum, adopted because .465 is associated historically with H&H and the company is familiar with it. The story of the evolution of the .400, as related above, applies equally to the .465 because it was developed, step by step, with the .400, although the smaller cartridge moved into production earlier.

The .465 H&H shoots a 480-grain bullet at 2,400 fps, for muzzle energy of 6,000 ft. lbs. This is a bona fide heavyweight cartridge that offers ballistic performance comparable to the .450 Ackley at its top loading. In fact, if the H&H cartridge resembles any other, it is the Ackley. It is the .375 H&H case necked up, with a slight, gradual shoulder. For the man who prides himself on shooting only H&H rifles, it certainly has something to offer. For the rest of mankind, including the 99 percent of hunters who are not independently wealthy and would rather spend $25,000 on a safari than on a rifle, I'm afraid this new H&H caliber is not a great choice.

Along the same lines ballistically is the unfortunately named .470 Capstick, developed by A-Square in the early 1990s and offered as factory ammunition. It is the .375 H&H case firing a .470 bullet and is dimensionally almost identical to the wildcat .475 Ackley, developed many years earlier.

The selection of bullets in either .465 (.468, actually) or .470 (.475) is quite limited, but it is unlikely anyone will want to use these on prairie dogs or whitetails. For their intended purposes, the bullet selection is more than adequate.

The .500s

In terms of performance on big, tough animals, the .500 Nitro Express was demonstrably better than anything in the .450-470 class of nitro-express cartridges. At 2,150 fps its 570-grain bullet delivered 5,850 ft. lbs. of energy, which was significant enough. As well, however, the larger surface area of the .500 bullet meant this greater force was delivered that much more quickly. It had more punch, and it was only natural that rifle makers would try to recreate this performance in cartridges for magazine rifles.

The first to arrive was the .505 Gibbs, in 1911—professional hunter Robert Wilson's "damned cannon" from Hemingway's *The Short Happy Life of Francis Macomber*.

George Gibbs was a noted rifle maker going back to the days of single-shot target rifles at Bisley and Creedmoor, and he was the builder of Samuel Baker's ground-breaking (and everything-else-breaking) huge-bore of 1840. For reasons unexplained, Gibbs chose to use a bullet slightly smaller than the .500 NE (.505 versus .510) and lighter (525 grains). Muzzle velocity was 2,300 fps, and muzzle energy was 6,190 ft. lbs. The cartridge was introduced in the same year as the .416 Rigby, and it resembles the Rigby only scaled up—longer and wider, with a small, sharp shoulder and a long neck to hold the bullet securely.

Aside from its undoubted prowess in the bush against elephants and Cape

.500s for magazine rifles, from left: .375 H&H (for comparison), .500 Jeffery, .505 Gibbs, .500 A-Square, .495 A-Square. The difference in size and shape, and the resulting requirements for action size and feeding characteristics, become obvious when the five cartridges are viewed side by side. In terms of power, there is nothing to choose, but in terms of pure cartridge design, the .495 A-Square is clearly superior.

buffalo, the .505 cemented its reputation on the basement shooting range of Abercrombie & Fitch and in the pages of Hemingway. It held the heavyweight crown for magazine rifles for a little over a decade, until the early 1920s, when W. J. Jeffery (or Schuler) introduced the .500 Jeffery (the 12.5x70 Schuler) and shaded the .505 on bullet diameter (.510), weight (535 grains), velocity (2,400 fps) and energy (6,800 ft. lbs.) That's not by much, granted, but it was enough to matter to those who wanted the biggest and the worstest. Until the .460 Weatherby arrived, the .500 Jeffery's 6,800 ft. lbs. at the muzzle was as big as you could buy. Of all the cartridges available, only the .600 NE was more powerful.

For all their reputation, relatively few rifles of either caliber were ever made. Estimates for the .500 Jeffery are around two dozen in total. No one has put a number to the .505, but it cannot have been many. A hundred? Two hundred? For this reason as much as any, there are very few published accounts of their use by hunters, certainly nothing to compare with the .500 NE. One noted user of the .500 Jeffery was the Rhodesian professional hunter Fletcher Jamieson, a friend of John Taylor who loaned him his rifle on occasion. Taylor loved it and said so in print. He never used the .505 Gibbs (or .505 Rimless Magnum, to be absolutely correct), but felt it would be every bit as good.

In fact, the .505 is better in some ways. It may have been shaded ballistically, but its chamber pressures are lower because its case is notably more roomy. As well, the .500 Jeffery has a rebated rim, which raises doubts about reliability of feeding. Combine high chamber pressures with questions about extraction, and you do not have a wonderful situation. While everyone writes about these potential problems, no one says they ever came to pass. Certainly Taylor had no difficulties, and you can be sure he would have said so!

Ammunition for the .505 Gibbs was loaded by Kynoch but supplied by George Gibbs in a plain brown box rather than the distinctive yellow and red. Ammunition for the .500 was available only from Germany.

No one saw the need for any other rimless .500s. In fact, very few saw the need for these two. They had the field to themselves until 1974, when Art Alphin decided that the world needed a .500 in a readily available case, designed to work with modern powders. Alphin took the .460 Weatherby, necked it up to .500, and the .500 A-Square was born. With a 600-grain bullet at 2,475 fps, it delivers muzzle energy of 8,180 ft. lbs. When Alphin formed the A-Square Company in 1979, he said the .500 A-Square was its reason for existence. A quarter-century later, this caliber is still in production: Rifles, ammunition, and brass.

Then Art Alphin did something odd. About two years later he rethought the concept and came out with another cartridge, also a .500 but slightly smaller. With Alphinesque logic, he called it the .495 A-Square. Also based on the .460 Weatherby case, the .495 is almost exactly a scaled-up .458 Lott. The basic case is larger, as is the bullet, but in between lies the same tapered, straight case with no shoulder. It has been shortened by a tenth of an inch to allow maximum overall length of 3.65", short enough to be adapted to existing actions. If Art had designed the .495 first, I suspect there would never have been a .500 A-Square.

The .495 A-Square is nothing short of brilliant—every bit as carefully thought out as Russell Wilkin's new .400 H&H. The .495 delivers a 570-grain bullet at 2,350 fps for 6,989 ft. lbs. There is nothing anyone would want to do on dangerous game that this cartridge cannot do. It does not deliver Art Alphin's "magic" velocity of 2,400 fps, but it has many other attributes. First, foremost, and last-most, it presents no feeding problems. As you increase bullet diameter and case size, cartridges become a tighter and tighter fit, and feeding becomes geometrically more difficult. Bullets are blunt and farther from the line of bore, the feed ramp has to somehow turn them inward more, yet the huge cases do not maneuver with abandon under the action rails. Like its smaller relatives, the .375 H&H and the .458 Lott, the .495 A-Square puts a straight case and pronounced taper to work, and the cartridges feed effortlessly.

Alphin points out that the .495 has a "ghost" shoulder—it tapers to a point about six-tenths of an inch from the mouth, and from there forward, the case sides are parallel. You can feel this more than see it, but it is true. This allows the use of two-die rather than three-die sets, eases sizing stress when reloading, and reduces the amount of belling required to start a bullet into the case. It also means that the bullet will be held firmly, with even tension, its whole length. Of the four big .500s mentioned, the .495 is the only one with no drawbacks due to size or shape. Quite the opposite.

For the record, the very first animal killed with Alphin's Monolithic Solid was an elephant in Rhodesia in 1977. The bullet was fired from a .495 A-Square.

When you reach cartridges this size, power is not the issue. They all have power. Nor is it bullets. The bullets are interchangeable, and you can have them loaded with whatever you want. What sets apart the really good cartridges are the qualities that make them easy to use and ultra-reliable. The .495 has these characteristics in spades, and it is unfortunate that this cartridge has been over-shadowed throughout its lifetime by the other three in the group.

There is one other advantage to Art's creation, and this will only become more important as time goes by: In the current campaign to reduce gun trafficking, various governments (including that of the U.S.) have targeted .50 caliber cartridges. The alleged goal is to keep .50 BMG cartridges, which are used in ultra-long-range sniper rifles, out of the hands of undesirables. As a result, any export permit for a .50 or .500 or anything like that runs into difficulties. The .495? No problem, sir. Have a nice trip. Good luck with your hunt.

Some cartridges are born lucky.

Throughout the 1990s, as hunters embraced bigger and bigger rifles, the .500s began enjoying a serious renaissance. As I write this, the .500 Jeffery is Empire Rifles' most popular large bore for its magnum Mauser 98. The Czech company CZ is offering the .505 Gibbs in an economical (although sound) rifle.

Oddly enough, throughout the 1980s and '90s, when A-Square was the angel that brought dozens of cartridges back from the dead and gave commercial life to more than a few wildcats, the .500 Jeffery was not among them. A-Square loads the .505, the .500 NE, and—of course—its own two. Why not the Jeffery?

"There are just too many variations in dimensions," Alphin says. "It was never standardized, so chambers are not uniform. We would like to make it, but what size should we make? Better to stay away from it."

Factory ammunition is, however, made by Kynoch, and brass is available from a number of sources.

* * *

In the world of magazine rifles, there is only one factory cartridge larger than the .500s: A-Square's .577 Tyrannosaur.

According to Art Alphin, he designed this round in 1993 at the request of some Zimbabwe professional hunters who wanted the biggest of the big for use against bad elephants in thick cover. Art offered his .500 A-Square. Not big enough, they said. Can't you make something heavier? Since Art owned his own munitions factory, of course he could—and did. Starting from a blank sheet of paper, he designed the largest rimless cartridge that could be made to fit into the Enfield actions in his Hannibal rifles. The Tyrannosaur launches a 750-grain bullet at 2,460 fps, for more than 10,000 ft. lbs. of energy. It is an awesome brute of a cartridge—more powerful on paper than even H&H's gargantuan .700.

Within a few months of finalizing the design, Alphin had orders for about two dozen rifles and today, twelve years later, A-Square tells me it has more .577 Tyrannosaur rifles in production than any other caliber.

A-Square's mammoth .577 Tyrannosaur, dwarfing two cartridges generally considered large, the .458 Winchester (left) and .460 Weatherby. The Tyrannosaur is as large as a cartridge can be and still fit any conventional sporting bolt action. It also represents the upper limit of usable power and recoil for any conceivable hunting situation.

The .577 Tyrannosaur is a tight fit in the A-Square Hannibal bolt action, built on the over-sized Enfield P-17 action. This is as large as a magazine-rifle cartridge can be, and still be even remotely practical.

Partly, this can be explained by the current mania for huge-bore cartridges. How many of these rifles will ever see anything more threatening than a range officer is open to question. A few have gone to Africa, they have killed game, and they have done so very effectively. There is no question about the cartridge's killing power, but whether it qualifies as a working dangerous-game rifle is something else entirely.

Jim Smith, who managed A-Square, says the first question anyone asks about the .577 is "What is the recoil like?" To find out—since neither of us had ever fired one—we took a Tyrannosaur to a range in Kentucky and let fly. Shooting it offhand, with a firm grip, each of us was rocked onto his back foot, but nothing was dislocated and (lurid Internet videos to the contrary) we were neither thrown across a room nor out a window. A quick second shot would be very difficult, though. Fitted with Art's Coil-Chek stock, the rifle itself weighed thirteen pounds,. The stock was so large, it was difficult to hold onto—shooting the gun was like fencing with a railroad tie—and I would hate to have to stalk a dangerous animal with the rifle at the ready. I can only assume that Art's Zimbabwe friends were husky lads, if they hunt with one of these things.

Another difficulty did show up: The rifle was supposedly ready to ship to the customer, but (not surprisingly) it would not feed. With a dangerous-game rifle, reliable feeding outstrips accuracy and sheer power by a long way. Since the .577 Tyrannosaur fits so tightly into the P-17 action and has a blunt, round nose, it is very difficult to coax the cartridge to feed. In the end, we did not feed rounds from the magazine at all but simply laid them in front of the bolt and closed it.

The lesson? Monster cartridges may be fun to talk about and take to the range, but in a working rifle they can create more problems than they solve.

From Lead to Jackets

A crushing blow that may be depended upon is what is required, and reliance cannot be placed upon the short, light bullets so much used. No doubt a good deal of game is killed with the light bullets, even up to and including tigers, etc.; but much has been lost . . . in consequence of the bullet breaking up too soon, causing only a flesh wound, and not having sufficient penetration to reach a vital part...

H.W.H
Big Game Shooting, Vol. II, *1894*

The above words were written by a contributor identified only as H. W. H., in *The Badminton Library* volumes on big-game shooting, published in 1894. The chapter is called "Notes on Rifles and Ammunition." The author was, undoubtedly, Henry William Holland.

At the time, express rifles were taking over from the huge muzzleloaders for almost everything, including elephants, tigers, lions, and Cape buffalo. But the way express rifles became "express" was through velocity, and high velocity was achieved by reducing bullet weight. Already, the debate was raging about whether a light bullet could be relied upon to kill a big, dangerous animal.

Holland's most famous client was Sir Samuel Baker, and H. W. H. relied heavily on Baker's experience in his careful essay on killing power:

For soft-skinned animals, Sir Samuel used solid pure lead bullets, and he always found them to deliver the whole power of the charge upon the animal, being generally forced into the shape of a mushroom, and found under the skin upon the opposite side of the beast.

Sir Samuel Baker had no doubts about what constituted a good game bullet, and one would think that in 110 years, hunters could have come to some agreement about how a bullet should perform. If they could, bullet makers would have a much easier time. As it is, there is disagreement even among knowledgeable hunters. Excellent performance to one is mediocre to another, or even outright failure. The difficulties facing a manufacturer of hunting bullets are many and varied—not least of which is the lack of definition of what a good bullet even is!

Dangerous-game bullets are divided into two types: Solids and softs.

A solid bullet is exactly what the name implies: A bullet intended not to deform in any way when it hits the animal. Although there are many different ways of constructing a solid, everyone agrees that ideal performance on its part is to penetrate in a straight line and remain so pristine it could be reloaded and shot again. That is straightforward.

The performance of a soft is more complex. Because such a bullet has a soft nose, it is expected to expand as it penetrates, forming a mushroom shape or sprouting claws (or petals) in a more or less controlled deformation. Too often, however, this deformation is accompanied by disintegration, which is most emphatically *not* desirable. The less weight a bullet sheds in the process of expansion the better, because the heavier it stays, the more it will penetrate. The challenge for bullet makers for the past century has been to control that deformation under a bewildering array of circumstances.

Now the discussion gets interesting. One professional hunter of great experience will insist that the bullet should come to a full stop inside the animal, nudged up against the skin on the far side, having expended all its energy inside the animal—the performance Sir Samuel Baker admired. Another will insist the bullet should go right through, leaving a gaping exit wound that will bleed freely and leave a good trail if one is necessary. This was Elmer Keith's position. It may not seem like much of a difference, but in fact it is. For a bullet to deliver one or the other level of performance consistently, under all conditions, on all types of game, requires quite different construction.

The words "consistently, under all conditions on all types of game" introduces a demand that is, frankly, unattainable. No bullet in history has done that, or ever will. Faced with the knowledge that perfection will never be reached, a bullet maker can only try to produce a projectile that will consistently deliver acceptable-to-superb performance under a wide range of conditions, *and never really fail.* A bullet that "never really fails, regardless of conditions" is better than a bullet that is great some of the time but occasionally fails completely. All too often, it will fail when you need it most.

The search for the perfect game bullet has been going on since black-powder days. And today, in many ways, we are almost there. Game bullets are better now than they have ever been. This is true of all kinds of bullets—for target-shooting, small game, varmints, and big game. Dangerous-game bullets, however, are in a class by themselves in terms of the demands that are made upon them and in the way we measure their performance.

Imagine a hunter going on safari with tags for lion, leopard, and Cape buffalo. He has one rifle—a .458 of some description. He may use it to shoot a leopard out of a tree at fifty yards, but also (maybe) to shoot a charging leopard at two feet—a 200-pound fury intent on clawing him a new profile. He will use the rifle to shoot a Cape buffalo in the shoulder broadside at seventy-five yards, but may have to plant a second bullet into the back end of the buffalo as it disappears into the bush, hoping that it will penetrate three or four feet of rock-solid animal. And if the hunter goes into the bush after the aforementioned buffalo, he may need his bullet to penetrate eight inches of skull at point-blank range. What about the lion? It's soft-skinned, perhaps, but not when you have to put a bullet into the bunched muscles of its chest at a distance of a few feet.

For more than a century, ammunition makers have been attempting to create a bullet that will cope with all these situations, expanding readily when velocity has decreased, yet not over-expanding when it strikes something at muzzle velocity; expanding into a broad mushroom shape even on soft flesh, yet not flying apart whether it strikes bone, paunch, or muscle. When you then take into account the fact that a modern .458 bullet may be loaded into a cartridge at anywhere from 1,900 to 2,700 fps of muzzle velocity, you can see how difficult the task is.

* * *

The transition from black powder to smokeless generated a revolution in both bullet design and composition. While good terminal performance was always the prime requirement of a big-game bullet, other factors came into play, dictating the way bullets were made.

Once rifling became common and it was accepted that a bullet should be elongated rather than round in order to get a good ballistic coefficient (a term not yet coined), gunmakers and designers came up with some truly weird and wonderful ideas for matching bullet to rifling. Muzzleloaders were infuriating: It was essential the bullet fit tightly so that expanding powder gas would push on the bullet rather than leak out around it. At the same time, the bullet had to fit loosely enough that it could easily be seated down the bore. The two demands proved incompatible.

Gunmakers tried octagonal bores with fitted bullets, as well as bullets with one or two protrusions that fit into corresponding grooves in the bore, and any number of different rifling configurations. All failed because of the same obstacle: Fouling. Black powder was so messy that bores became caked, and after a few shots it was impossible to pound the projectile down the tube.

The minié ball was a great stride forward. By the way, the term "ball" does not necessarily mean a round projectile; it is used to describe one solid projectile, as opposed to "shot," which is many small ones. As with so many things military, the term "ball" was used in military parlance to denote a cartridge loaded with a standard bullet long after that bullet ceased to be a ball. It is the root word of "bullet," and the term "ball powder" is derived from it, as well.

A minié "ball" was a pointed bullet with a large cavity in the base. For easy loading, it was substantially smaller than the diameter of the bore. When the gun was fired, expanding gas caused the skirt around the cavity to blow outward and hug the bore, providing a gas seal and gripping the rifling. The minié ball was an important advance because it utilized the principle of gas expanding a lead bullet to fit, but in military terms it was overtaken by events and was never widely used for either hunting or target shooting.

For these reasons, the answer was the tried-and-true wad or patch, as had been used with round balls for a century. Bullets were cast smaller than the bore, then wrapped in a small piece of paper, cloth, or leather. This fabric was compressible and would not only fill the gaps between bullet and rifling; it would also push the powder fouling ahead of it, down into the tube, where it would be expelled when the gun was fired. The patch also served to keep the lead bullet from rubbing against the bore and depositing lead fouling. This allowed hunters to use bullets made of more or less pure lead, which was soft enough to expand readily even at low velocities and was as cohesive as chewing gum. As a result, it stayed in one piece and penetrated.

The arrival of breech-loading rifles raised many of the same questions, but in different forms. While it was no longer necessary to worry about having to push the bullet down the rifled bore, a gas seal was still essential, and pure-lead bullets were still favored for their superb terminal performance on game.

For a period of about twenty years, the solution was the paper-patched bullet. A pure lead bullet was wrapped in a double thickness of paper, applied damp so it would shrink and hug the bullet as it dried. The bullet itself was close to bore diameter. The paper provided a buffer between the bullet and the lands, and also filled the rifling grooves to provide a gas seal. As it sped down the bore, the rifling sliced the paper and it fell away as the bullet exited the muzzle, leaving a pristine projectile spinning toward the target. The application of the patch was an art in itself, yet if you look at vintage cartridges with their original, factory, paper-patched bullets, they seem to be perfection. The ammunition factories employed women and girls to apply the patches, and their nimble fingers were capable of patching thousands of bullets a day—each one seemingly flawless. After the patch dried, it was lubricated with fat or grease that both lubricated its passage down the bore and helped make the cartridge resistant to moisture.

Black powder and pure lead were a match made in heaven. Riflemen quickly found that a pure lead bullet behaves like a minié ball even without a hollow base. Because black powder is an explosive rather than a progressive-burning propellant, the sudden expansion of gas acts to "bump" the base of a pure-lead bullet, expanding it like a plug to fill the bore snugly. Where the minié expands a few hundredths of an inch, a paper-patched lead bullet enlarges by only a few thousandths. But it is sufficient for the purpose.

The obvious question, then, is, why do you need the paper patch at all if the

For an all-too-brief period, the paper patch was king. It provided a gas seal for the bullet as well as preventing lead from fouling the rifling. It was used in both military cartridges (.450 Martini-Henry, left) and sporting cartridges such as the .450 No. 1 Express (center) and the .500 Black Powder Express. The paper patch allowed the use of pure lead bullets, which afforded superb terminal performance.

Stages of development: Clockwise from top, a .500 caliber 530-grain cast bullet with lubrication grooves packed with lubricant; Woodleigh WeldCore soft, a copper cup with a lead core, and the open end forming the expanding nose; lubricated cast .500 bullet with copper gas-check; cast .458-caliber 500-grain bullet; Woodleigh Solid, the reverse of the soft, with the open end of the copper cup forming the base of the bullet. Center is a light-weight cast hollow-point; such bullets were the basis of the "express" rifle.

bullet will expand to fill the rifling? The answer is lead fouling. Pure lead, under heat and friction, fouls the bore unmercifully, and each successive bullet will become highly inaccurate. Whether it was riflemen shooting at 600-yard targets at Creedmoor, or buffalo hunters shooting distant animals on the plains, such a loss of accuracy was unacceptable. The paper patch prevented this. As long as velocities were kept to reasonable levels—approximately 1,800 fps with black powder—the paper patch was king. It was, however, not terribly convenient, and such bullets and loaded ammunition had to be treated gently.

Paper-patched ammunition required careful packaging, and such packaging may have contributed to one of the worst defeats ever suffered by a modern army. At Isandlhwana, in South Africa, a large British force armed with Martini-Henry rifles was wiped out by the Zulus. One of the reasons given was the difficulty the Englishmen had in opening the ammunition crates: .450 Martini ammunition, with its paper patches, was packed in weatherproof, waxed-paper-lined tins, inside stout wooden crates fastened shut with screws. As the battle progressed, unable to crack open the crates, the troops simply ran out of ammunition and were overwhelmed. That aside, European armies used paper-patched ammunition for several decades and fought many a war, with complete satisfaction. And a good deal of the ammunition that was shipped to Africa for hunters and colonizers in the 1880s and '90s was loaded with paper-patched bullets.

Shooters were always looking for a better (or simpler) way, and another method was soon discovered, one that worked almost as well as paper patches and was far more convenient: lubricated bullets. Bullets were cast with lubrication grooves, which were then filled with concoctions of beeswax, grease, bear fat, deer tallow, or various other substances. To this day, no one knows exactly what happens in a rifle bore when a lubricated, cast bullet is fired. All we know is that it works. For a buffalo hunter casting bullets on the plains of the American West, it was far easier to fill some grooves with buffalo fat and to tuck the bullet into the case than it was to patch it with paper. The driving bands (the raised ribs between the lube grooves) filled the bore to the depths of the rifling, providing a good gas seal but without excessive friction.

Even the ultra-demanding target shooters of the day adopted the lubricated bullet in preference to paper-patched ones. Such rounds were just as accurate, they said, and considerably easier to handle. For paper targets, this may well have been true. It was quickly discovered, though, that pure lead did not work terribly well because, while lubrication would reduce lead fouling, it would not eliminate the problem. The answer was to harden the lead, usually by alloying it with tin and, later, antimony or zinc. Hardened lead certainly reduced bore fouling, but it drastically affected expansion of the bullet—and not for the better. In some cases, bullets were hardened to the point where they did not expand at all. This was not necessarily a bad thing, depending what you were hunting. In other cases, however, the bullets became brittle and shattered when they hit bone.

The real virtue of the pure-lead, paper-patched bullet then became apparent: its tenacious cohesion on impact, staying in one lump but deforming into a perfect mushroom as it penetrated.

As already noted, John "Pondoro" Taylor is renowned for two books about rifles and cartridges for African hunting, both written in the late 1940s and drawing on his extensive experience hunting elephants, Cape buffalo, and other big game in Tanganyika, Kenya, and Portuguese East Africa (Mozambique) throughout the 1930s. Taylor had the predictable biases of the day: He favored double rifles over bolt actions for all life-threatening work and generally preferred bullet weight to velocity. One underappreciated aspect of his written work is his serious attention to bullets and bullet performance. He was one of the first hunter-authors anywhere to really examine terminal ballistics. Taylor took the time (whenever possible) to dig bullets out of animals, see where they had gone, and determine how they performed. As a result, he was able to make judgments

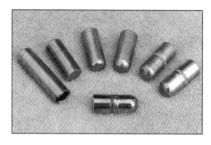

Copper and copper-alloy jackets replaced paper jackets for bullets to be used at nitro-express velocities. Shown are the components and stages of producing an A-Square Lion Load (made with pure lead and pure copper) and the bonded-core Dead Tough (made with solder and soft brass).

about those designs that worked and those that did not.

Toward the end of his life, having hunted everything, everywhere, using just about every rifle and cartridge combination then available, he wrote:

> *The solid soft lead bullet is undoubtedly the best and most satisfactory expanding bullet that has ever been designed. It invariably mushrooms perfectly and never breaks up. With the metal base that is essential for velocities of 2,000 f.s. (sic) and upwards to protect the naked base, these metal based soft lead bullets are splendid.*

As you will notice, there are two parts to that statement, and both are relevant. We will get to the question of metal (copper, brass or bronze) jackets in a later chapter. But back to pure lead.

Paul Matthews, an American who has shot, reloaded, and hunted with rifles since his childhood in Pennsylvania in the 1930s, is the modern guru of black-powder rifles and cast bullets. He says bluntly that the paper-patched pure lead bullet is "the most dependable expanding bullet ever devised by man." In 1991, Matthews even went so far as to write a book called *The Paper Jacket*. At the time, it seemed to me not only arcane but anachronistic to the point of irrelevance. Now, having spent considerable time studying various aspects of bullet performance, I believe that the modern hunter has much to learn about terminal ballistics from looking at how these wonderful old bullets performed, even if I stop short of advocating a return to the paper jacket in all applications.

As Matthews points out, had smokeless powder not come along in the 1890s and displaced black powder, the paper-patched bullet would have continued in use for many more years, and the technology would have progressed far beyond what it did. Instead, the advent of one technology cut short the use of another, and bullet development went in an entirely different direction. Only now, with the renewed interest in long-range black-powder rifles, have shooters returned to the study of pure lead bullets and paper patches, and taken the technology beyond the point it reached when it was summarily discarded.

Ever since, for more than a hundred years, bullet makers have been attempting to duplicate the terminal performance of those pure-lead paper-patched bullets, but with projectiles tough enough to withstand the much greater stresses placed on them by smokeless powder and its substantially higher velocities.

* * *

The .450 Nitro Express, introduced by John Rigby and Co. in 1898, fired a 480-grain bullet at 2,150 fps, performance that was astounding for the time and ushered in a whole new world of big-game hunting and rifles. All it really added, however, was a few hundred feet per second of muzzle velocity; the guns themselves did not change radically. Very quickly, gunmakers discovered that standard bullets could not handle the higher speeds.

In 1888, the British Army had adopted the famous .303 British cartridge; initially loaded with black powder, it was very soon switched to smokeless. The French Lebel (1886) was the first smokeless cartridge, and one army after another followed suit. Makers of hunting rifles absorbed the same lesson as had military ordnance officers: lead was not good enough, either pure or alloyed. While the military went to full-metal-jacketed bullets, civilian makers adopted copper-jacketed expanding bullets, as well as various forms of solid.

The first solids for hunting were little different than the military bullets. They were extruded from copper disks into cylindrical cups, pure lead cores were swaged in to give them weight, and the base was crimped over to prevent the lead flying out on impact. Because the paper patch had been replaced by a metal "patch," the term survives right up to the present, and the British often refer to a full-metal jacket as a "full-patch" bullet.

The first soft-nosed bullets were made essentially the same way, but were turned upside down: The open end with the exposed lead became the nose of the bullet, and the closed copper end became the base.

From there, bullet development scattered in a dozen directions. The concept of the hollow point was already well known, and some bullet makers tried that. Others varied the amount of exposed lead in the tip, depending on how slowly or quickly they wanted the bullet to expand. Still others took the hollow point and added a cap of harder metal (usually copper or brass) that would protect the nose of the bullet; on impact, this cap was driven into the lead, expanding it forcefully.

Some of these bullets worked very well; others did not. Under the British proprietary system, with ammunition for a particular rifle supplied only by that gun's maker, any credit that accrued went to the rifle and its manufacturer. Hence, the .416 Rigby with its jacket of soft steel became the byword for good performance. Westley Richards's "LT" bullet, especially loaded in the .425 WR, also established a fine reputation.

The Germans, usually so adept, failed miserably in the manufacture of bullets for dangerous game. While the Mauser 98 rifle established a good reputation, most of the metric cartridges for which it was chambered did not—almost always because the bullets over-expanded and disintegrated.

From 1898 until 1963, when Kynoch ceased production of nitro-express cartridges, its big bullets mostly consisted of pure lead inside pure (or almost pure) copper jackets. These jackets were thick and tough, and although bonding of the cores was unknown, the bullets stayed together because weights were high and velocities were low.

The Modern Expanding Bullet

If you wish the bullet to expand, use soft lead, but keep the metal solid. If you wish for great penetration, use hard solid metal, either 1/10 tin or 1/13 quicksilver.

Sir Samuel White Baker, 1890

This may well be the most important section of this entire book because, in the end, it is the bullet that comes out of the rifle that does the work on dangerous game. A fine double rifle may cost $50,000 and be an excellent firearm in every respect, but not do its job because of the failure of a ninety-five-cent bullet. Because bullets are disposable items, many hunters pay little attention to them. This is a mistake.

From the beginning, soft-nose (expanding) bullets presented far more challenges to bullet makers than solids did. First, there were the essentially conflicting demands: The bullet must expand, but not too much; it must hold together, but still expand; it must expand even at low velocity but not blow apart at high velocity. The final—and really least important—requirement was accuracy. A nitro-express bullet needed to be accurate out to 75 or 100 yards, and even then the definition of accuracy was liberal by today's standards. Especially in double rifles, with two barrels regulated to shoot to the same point of impact, the idea of an overall group better than four inches at 100 yards was as unlikely as it was unnecessary. The standards for single-shots, and later for bolt actions, were slightly tighter, but not much. Compared to the importance of designing and making a bullet that would keep the hunter alive in an elephant charge, printing small groups at a hundred yards did not even figure.

Lest anyone think that accuracy was not important to rifle makers in 1900, remember that this was the era of Creedmoor and Bisley, of long-range offhand matches, with rifle clubs springing up all over England. Many English rifle makers were major players in the competition world—Rigby, Jeffery, and Greener, especially—and they valued accuracy as much as any top competitor. However, keeping their clients alive was a higher priority with their big rifles, and these firms understood just where relative accuracy stood in the equation. It is a lesson that is lost on many of today's makers of bullets and rifles who claim to make equipment for dangerous game.

The British system of proprietary cartridges played a major role in the development of expanding bullets, but in one way it was an advantage: Bullet engineers at Kynoch and Eley knew exactly what cartridges their products would be loaded in and what velocities they would have to withstand. Cartridges were assembled accordingly and, for the most part, worked very well. But not always. Some cartridges were loaded with bullets that performed poorly, and the cartridge gained a bad reputation that spilled over to the rifle and even to the rifle maker himself.

From 1898 onward, there was a period of trial and error in which various bullet designs were tried and either proven or discarded. There were scattered instances of makers stubbornly staying with bullets that were inadequate, but not many. Almost from the beginning, the .416 Rigby gained a stellar reputation and a loyal following because of its bullets, which were jacketed in mild steel, and this example was noted by others.

Compare that situation with today: An independent bullet maker such as Hornady produces a range of large-caliber bullets for use on dangerous game. The company makes—and has made for years, when others did not—a 500-grain, .458 round-nose. The engineers at Hornady cannot know if that bullet is to be loaded into a vintage .450 NE, a .458 Winchester Magnum, or a .460 Weatherby. Muzzle velocity could range from 1,800 fps to 2,700 fps. With some of the outlandish wildcats now in existence, muzzle velocity could be even higher, and some of these rifles are actually taken hunting.

If that Hornady round-nose strikes a Cape buffalo skull at 2,700 fps, four feet from the muzzle, it needs to hold together; it if strikes a lion in the ribs at 2,000 fps at a range of seventy-five yards, it needs to expand. Those are tough demands—almost *impossible* demands—to make on a bullet.

* * *

It will not be lost on even the most casual observer that the big names in bullets today are not the big names in ammunition. The best dangerous-game bullets are produced by small, independent manufacturers and designers. When Federal loads premium dangerous-game ammunition, it uses bullets from Woodleigh and Trophy Bonded; Remington uses Swift A-Frames, and even Winchester has hooked up with Nosler. Various companies have loaded Barnes bullets. In my opinion, not a single dangerous-game bullet developed by a big ammunition maker is any better than merely adequate.

When Winchester introduced the .458 in 1956, it was loaded with a 500-grain soft point and a 510-grain solid, both of Winchester's manufacture. I have never tested any of this original ammunition, so I cannot say how the bullets performed. At the same time, I have never heard any real complaints about the bullets' terminal performance. Early users of the .458, with its many documented problems, were probably just happy to have the bullet go down range with enough velocity to hit something. Most failures with bullets occur when a weak-jacketed bullet flies apart at high velocity. It has been proven that reducing velocity will allow a heavy bullet to hold together and penetrate, so the .458's velocity problems may, ironically, have worked to its advantage by making the original bullets look better than they actually were.

As interest in African hunting grew among Americans in the 1960s and '70s, many went after dangerous game with either factory ammunition or hand-loads using readily available after-market bullets. The record of failures grew, and interest in designing a better bullet increased. Jack Lott's experience with the Cape buffalo and the .458 Winchester garnered considerable attention in the pages of *Guns & Ammo*, among other publications. Art Alphin, the founder of A-Square, became interested in designing both cartridges and bullets, and much of his research was done in the mid-1970s. Jack Carter, who designed the original Trophy Bonded Bear Claw, hunted in Africa in the 1970s, and it was the failure of a Hornady .458 500-grain bullet that inspired his outstanding design.

Bullet designers approached the problem from three directions. Since about 1950, the Nosler Partition had been the standard for premium hunting bullets in smaller calibers, and the idea of having a solid partition of copper jacket in the center of a bullet to keep it from disintegrating had been around since the RWS H-mantle. Logically, that was the starting point for, among others, the Swift A-Frame.

Others, like Jack Carter, took the near-legendary Bitterroot Bonded Bullet as an inspiration. Bitterroots had been around for years and Carter had used them in smaller calibers, but they were not made larger than .375 and supply was uncertain at best. So Carter set out to develop a large-caliber bonded bullet; since bonding technology was not readily available, even figuring a way of doing it was a challenge. Bill Steigers at Bitterroot was famously close-mouthed about his actual bonding process.

Art Alphin, at A-Square, put his military background to work in designing bullets that would both hold together and penetrate in a straight line, and the designs he came up with are worth almost a chapter in themselves. He called on the experience of the old black-powder competitors, using two-diameter bullets, along with a perfectly radiused nose (for dependable penetration) and a system of bonding the core to the bullet by, essentially, soldering them.

Finally, there is the Barnes approach. Since 1989, the Barnes X-Bullet has gained a following. Randy Brooks, who owns the company, eliminated the lead core altogether and used pure copper, reasoning that this would improve consistency and accuracy at the same time as eliminating the problem of bullets disintegrating. To an extent this has worked, but the design has not been without its problems and, ironically, it is consistency that has proven to be the greatest challenge.

Testing big, expanding bullets can be hard on the penetration box as well as on the bullet. Here, the impact on the soaked newsprint actually burst the box, which is made of heavy plywood held with screws. On the right, a .458 bullet is recovered from the newsprint. The soaked fibers provide a serious test of any bullet. The bullet's penetration can be followed page by page, if desired, allowing exact measurement and detailed study of the wound channel.

* * *

Now let's look at these bullet developments in greater detail.

Jack Carter was a retired IBM executive and lifelong hunter who set out on his bullet-making career when a 500-grain Hornady bullet performed poorly on a giant forest hog in Africa. He returned to Houston determined to develop a bonded-core bullet similar to the Bitterroot for the large-caliber, dangerous-game cartridges. Not being a metallurgist, he set out to learn as much as he could about what made bullets work and what made them fail.

Carter's first conclusion, and the most important in terms of bullet performance overall, was that alloys do not work as well as pure metals, whether you are dealing with lead or copper. This observation was not new: Since the days of unjacketed lead bullets, hunters knew that alloying lead with tin, antimony, or various others substances hardened lead but also made it brittle. They took this into account when casting bullets, whether they were designed with lubrication grooves or intended for paper jackets, and the end use determined how far they went in alloying the lead.

In many ways, a paper jacket was ideal because it allowed the use of pure lead, which expands readily but is, at the same time, as cohesive as chewing gum. It resists splitting, cracking, and breaking apart with the tenacity of warm taffy. Unfortunately, soft lead does not stand up well to high velocity and friction, and lead fouling in barrels becomes a serious problem very quickly. The paper jacket neatly solves this by keeping the lead from coming into contact with the bore; the paper engages the rifling, provides a gas seal, imparts spin, then drops away when the bullet exits the muzzle. These virtues of pure lead only hold true up to a certain level of velocity, after which the bullet tends to over-expand or "splatter." At high velocities (more than 2,000 fps) it needs a tough jacket to hold it together, as well as to engage the rifling.

For his jacket, Jack Carter decided on pure copper. Copper shares many of lead's virtues. It is tough, yet pliable and very cohesive. Unalloyed, it is heavy enough to be made into a bullet by itself, with no lead at all. Another valuable quality of copper is that it can be work hardened or, conversely, softened by annealing. Carter discovered that he could work his bullet jackets to exactly the hardness he wanted by swaging, and he employed this method in his later production.

Copper can be alloyed with tin to make bronze, or with zinc to make brass. Both of these metals are more brittle than pure copper and are less dense. Therefore, a 500-grain brass bullet will be longer than a 500-grain bullet of pure copper. This can become a factor. As well, bronze and brass tend to splinter, tear apart, and fly to pieces on impact. Often, the term "gilding metal" is applied to the copper-alloy jackets that are commonly used on expanding bullets. Loosely, gilding metal is a type of brass and since this book is not a treatise on metallurgy, I hope I am not offending any scientists by using these terms. For mass production, gilding metal is preferred by large companies because it is easy to work with. Pure copper gums up the machinery, which makes producing bullets with it more difficult and hence more expensive, which is one reason companies with an eye on unit cost and competitive pricing much prefer gilding metal.

But Jack Carter did not much care about such things. He was neither a lab man with a slide rule nor a bean counter with an adding machine. Carter was a hunter who went after Cape buffalo and lions and elephants, and he wanted a bullet that would perform to perfection every time. Carter did not care if a bullet cost two dollars or four dollars, and he knew his big-game hunting friends would not care either. If Jack built a better bullet, they would buy it. This philosophy served him well, and his creation—the Trophy Bonded Bear Claw—was one of the best premium game bullets ever made.

Carter ended up with three patents on various aspects of the Bear Claw, including his method of thermal bonding—remarkable for a retired executive with no background in metallurgy.

The real secret of his success was clear thinking. In bullet making, simplicity is the key to performance, and he realized that a marriage of pure lead to pure copper resulted in a bullet that was almost mystical in its yin-and-yang relationship. At lower velocities, the pure lead expanded and persuaded the copper jacket to open up; at higher velocities, the copper jacket held

"Safari life is very pleasant," as Teddy Roosevelt observed, and it was a life Jack Carter loved. On safari in Botswana in 1990, Jack tested—and proved—the value of his Trophy Bonded Bear Claws, a major influence in the revolution in bullet design that followed. Much of the credit for all the fine hunting bullets available today must go to Jack Carter.

High performance: This Trophy Bonded Bear Claw, a 500-grain .458 fired from a Winchester, penetrated completely through a Cape buffalo skull just below the boss, destroyed two vertebrae, and deflected down into the chest. It retains 81 percent of its weight, in spite of hitting the buffalo at four feet—virtual muzzle velocity. The Cape buffalo died instantly.

together and dissuaded the lead from expanding too far. The result was a bullet that set a new standard in mushroom shape and weight retention. Typically, an original Bear Claw would retain 90 to 98 percent of its original weight. Even under the most stressful circumstances, you could count on a Bear Claw to retain 75 to 80 percent, and that was performance that could only be termed phenomenal.

The development was a process of trial and error. Finn Aagaard, who had been Jack's professional hunter in Kenya on some early safaris, emigrated to the United States after the Kenya hunting ban in 1977, settled in Texas, and became a gun writer. Finn worked with Jack on some of the early testing, but he never allowed friendship to stand in the way of his telling the truth, and he noted that many of the early Bear Claws tended to over-expand and, as a result, not penetrate as much as they might. Carter fiddled with the jacket thickness until he achieved the right balance.

Around 1990, Carter conceived the idea of what he called the "solid shank" bullet. Made from pure copper rod, the rear half (approximately) was pure cop-

The Trophy Bonded Bear Claw solid shank (left, .358-caliber bullet) and the original design (.375-caliber bullet).

per, while the jacket extended forward into a cup that held the lead. In some weights, this bullet was formed into a semi-spitzer rather than a round nose. The solid copper shank worked much like the partition in the Nosler, stopping expansion absolutely, no matter what. Increasing copper content relative to lead made these bullets slightly longer, but not enough to become a problem.

Jack Carter eventually got his small company up and running, but doing so drained him financially. He was not a young man, and he was worried about his family should he die suddenly. The answer was to sell the company, which he did, while staying on as a consultant and manager. Later, the new owner licensed the Carter bullet to Federal Cartridge, which began making the smaller caliber Bear Claws in its own facility while Carter continued to manufacture the large calibers at his small plant in Houston. Later still, the whole business was acquired by Federal, which offered Bear Claws in its premium ammunition, along with Nosler Partitions. A series of amalgamations then left Federal part of the ATK defense conglomerate, along with the old Blount companies, including Speer Bullets. Speer began marketing Bear Claws as a premium hunting bullet for handloaders, which is where the situation stands today.

Jack Carter experienced a number of health problems during the 1990s, including a heart attack and lung cancer. In January 2001, he had a stroke at his home in Houston and died in the hospital two weeks later.

I met Jack Carter in 1988 and we hunted together for the first time the following year. On a trip to the Kenedy Ranch in south Texas to hunt nilgai and whitetails, we hauled Jack's bullet-testing apparatus along with us—an open trailer stacked full of Houston telephone directories and towed behind his huge Cadillac, with Jack in the passenger seat with the window down, chain smoking all the way. All we needed was a rocking chair strapped to the roof. Once at the ranch, we backed the trailer under a water tank to fill up and saturate the phone books—a twenty-four-hour process—while we went hunting. Every nilgai we shot, we then perforated with test bullets, carting the 600-pound carcasses intact back to the skinning shed, where we stripped to the waist and waded in to trace the wound channels and recover the remains.

That was my introduction to bullet testing—a fascination that has endured to this day.

In 1990, Jack, Finn, and I went to Africa, where we hunted in Tanzania and Botswana. The purpose was to test Jack's big bullets on Cape buffalo, and his new small-caliber Bear Claws (.243, .257, and 6.5mm) on everything else up to zebras and wildebeest. Jack did not think there was a serious market for high-priced premium bullets for small calibers, but being in love with the .257 Weatherby, I persuaded him to make me some bullets. This was how the 115-grain .257 Bear Claw came about, and since he was making those, he went ahead and did the .243 and 6.5mm, as well. Within a couple of years, the smaller calibers had become his biggest sellers.

An important attribute was their accuracy. Jack had teamed up with Jim Riley, a Detroit engineer who had a small handloading business, developing high-power, highly accurate loads for clients' rifles. Jim undertook all testing of Bear Claws, including calculating ballistic coefficients. For clients, he loaded Bear Claws exclusively, even though he would not, and did not, send a rifle back until it was capable of consistent groups under an inch at 100 yards. I mention this to show that a premium game bullet need not surrender accuracy to get terminal performance. The fact that, at the time, Jack's bullets were virtually hand-made ensured a degree of uniformity and consistency that is difficult to attain with mass production. It is also expensive.

Jack Carter proved, however, that serious hunters will pay for the bullets they want if they are assured of consistent, top-notch performance. He was a pioneer in many ways, but he was certainly not alone. Art Alphin (A-Square), Lee Reed (Swift), and Geoff McDonald (Woodleigh) all deserve credit for their work in creating premium dangerous-game bullets that were humane to the animals and kept hunters alive; as well, Bill Steigers at Bitterroot deserves credit for showing what bonding could do and inspiring Jack Carter, while Fred Barnes and his eponymous bullet company made heavy-for-caliber bullets that worked well under most circumstances. Randy Brooks, who later took over the company and developed the X-bullet, made a serious contribution in another direction.

Notably, every one of these men was either working on his own or in a small firm. Most were (and are) serious hunters of dangerous game. None worked for the big ammunition companies.

* * *

This section is not intended to be an endorsement of one type or brand of bullet over another. Nor can it be an exhaustive assessment of every bullet now available on the market. The past decade has seen the development of equipment that allows anyone with a little cash, a serious interest, and some space in his garage to become a bullet maker. The Internet permits anyone and everyone to market anything and everything. And so we find bullets of unknown name making all kinds of claims.

Bullet casting has been with us for centuries, but modern small-scale swaging equipment has added a whole new dimension. Jacketed bullets are available in such a wide range of types, sizes, and weights that it would be pointless even to try to list them, much less evaluate and report on them under all conditions.

As a hunter, I refuse to "test" a bullet on a game animal. I will not hunt with any bullet unless I am reasonably sure that it will perform. With a new dangerous-game bullet, that means extensive testing in expansion boxes to ensure that it will hold together and penetrate, as well as load development for velocity and acceptable accuracy, cartridge feeding in the rifle, and so on. To take an untested bullet into the field and shoot an animal with it, without having confidence that it will perform at least at an acceptable level, to me is unethical. Others may have no problem with it. I do.

As with most lessons, I learned this the hard way when, in 1993, an ammunition company introduced a new "premium" bullet with the usual dog-and-pony show at the SHOT Show and then handed me some of the ammunition to take to Africa. The company assured me it had been fully tested on the range; now they needed some reports from the field. Two boxes of ammunition arrived just as I departed, and I sighted in my rifle in South Africa. The bullets were 180-grain, the caliber .30-06; I was hunting nyala, but we were prepared to take something else if it crossed our path. The second day out, something did: a huge blue wildebeest that my guide, Kelly Davis, was sure would be close to a world record. Video cameras were relatively new, and Kelly was filming in order to make a promotional video, which is how we know exactly what happened next.

The wildebeest were in a line, facing us about 150 yards away, with the big one in the center. His long, long face was hanging, blocking his chest. Kelly advised me to plant a bullet in the middle of his face, which (we were sure) would go right through and into the chest. At the impact, the bull tossed his head into the air and bucked, and the whole herd departed. I never got a second shot. The blood trail was minimal. We tracked until dark and started out again early the next morning. A couple of times we caught up to him, enough to see the flesh wound in his chest. But I never got a shot, and eventually we lost him in the densely wooded ravines of Zululand.

When I returned home, I did what I should have done before leaving: I tested the wicked-looking black-and-silver ammunition, and found that the bullets broke up, squeezed lead out the back like toothpaste, bulged in the middle on impact, and exhibited various other undesirable traits. By coincidence, when the bullet was first announced at the SHOT show, I showed the schematics to Jack Carter, who took one look at the design and predicted how the bullets would perform. I should have taken heed and not used them in Africa, but we live and learn.

My report to Winchester did not sit well. I later learned that Craig Boddington took some of the new ammunition to Tanzania at the same time and had very unsatisfactory performance, as had some writers who hunted with it in Texas. Winchester redesigned the bullet—creating what became the Fail Safe—and inserted a steel cup in the rear to stiffen it and contain the lead. The bullet itself became very complicated, with many bits and pieces, none of which is conducive to accuracy. In August 2005—twelve years later—Winchester finally admitted that the Fail Safe was a failure and announced its replacement, the "Supreme Elite XP3," which combines a lead core bonded in the shank with a copper front end and a polymer tip. Now that the Fail Safe is on its way out, the company is no longer reluctant to condemn both its accuracy and terminal performance.

Since that day, I have never hunted with any new bullet that I have not tested myself, in advance. How? There are many ways of testing bullets, and not one of them is perfect. However, a good bullet-testing medium should do the following:

- Provide resistance to the bullet's forward travel
- Provide some fiber that tears at the bullet's claws
- Leave a permanent wound channel that reflects the actual expansion of the bullet
- Provide a measurement of penetration depth that is easy and exact
- The bullet should be recoverable
- The medium should be consistent for every shot, to provide a fair basis of comparison.

The method mentioned most frequently—and the one generally used by bullet makers, ammunition companies, and ballisticians—is ballistic gelatin. It comes in large blocks about the size of a car battery. It is easy to use, convenient, and looks relatively high-tech—in bullet-testing terms at least. For handgun bullets it is pretty good. For rifle bullets, especially heavy, dangerous-game bullets, testing in ballistic gelatin is so inadequate as to be useless (which does not prevent people from using it). First of all, the wound channel is misleading, at best, because the bullet sets up a shock wave that gives a wound channel several inches in diameter when the bullet is nowhere near that. Second, the gelatin is soft and provides no resistance similar to a bone. Nor is it fibrous, grabbing at the claws of the bullet as it expands. So the bullet gets a relatively easy passage. On the plus side, it is simple to measure depth of penetration, and bullet recovery is a breeze. In short, testing bullets in ballistic gelatin is, in my opinion, better than nothing—but not by much.

Another method, frequently used, is to shoot a bullet into a swimming pool or the equivalent. From the bullet maker's point of view, this technique is great because even the softest bullet comes out with a beautiful, seductive mushroom shape. However, there is no damaging resistance, so it proves nothing. Also, there is no wound channel and no way of judging penetration. The swimming-pool method is great for photographs, but it is completely, utterly, and totally useless from a performance point of view.

How about sand banks? Depending on whether the sand is wet or dry, it can provide reasonable resistance, but it is inconsistent, there is no wound channel, and penetration measurement is haphazard. The presence of any gravel whatsoever eliminates consistency.

Finally, we come to the method I use, the one I learned from Jack Carter. As noted in my tale of our Texas hunting trip, Jack obtained Houston telephone directories and soaked them in water. He then lined them up, compressed them, and shot into them. My method is a modification of that. I have plywood boxes four feet long, eighteen inches wide, and fifteen inches high. A standard broadsheet newspaper fits perfectly. I put newspapers into a water-filled container to soak for at least twenty-four hours; I then pack them into the box to whatever depth I need, compress them, and brace them at the rear with a sheet of thick plywood. For any .30-06 bullet, two feet is more than sufficient; for a 500-grain solid, four feet is not quite enough. That gives you some idea.

The soaked newsprint provides solid resistance, and the paper fibers become entangled in the petals of an expanding bullet; if there is any tendency for them to tear off, newsprint will do it. At the same time, this setup leaves a wound channel that can be inspected a page at a time, if so desired. When pieces fall off a bullet you can see exactly, to the millimeter, where it occurred. Depth of penetration is measured precisely, and the bullet is recovered with no difficulty.

The drawbacks of this method are that it is messy, time consuming, and requires extensive preparation in return for small but precious bits of information. When the box is set up with four feet of newspapers, it is good for five shots at the most, after which the packing must be replaced. You need to save a lot of newspapers in order to carry out thorough tests on even a half-dozen loads.

Also, there is nothing solid like a bone or really liquid like a paunch. As I said, the method is not perfect. If you want, though, you can put sheets of plywood in among the newspapers at different depths—or even water-filled plastic bags to see what happens when an expanding bullet strikes liquid. The system is nothing if not versatile. Over the years I have compared identical loads test-fired first into the boxes and then into a Cape buffalo. I have come to the conclusion that the boxes give a very good approximation of how a bullet will perform on even the biggest animal. The boxes are more gentle on the bullet than a buffalo's rib cage, as the accompanying photographs show, but overall they are the best method of bullet testing anyone has yet devised.

Even for solids, this method works well. If a solid has a tendency to veer off course, the boxes will show it, and inserting sheets of plywood into the mix will show if the bullet is prone to riveting.

Various bullet testers have attempted to simulate an animal by putting in actual bones—thighs and ribs from cattle, for example. The only problem with this is the lack of consistency. Two bullets shot into such a mix side by side will not necessarily encounter the same degree of resistance. It is useful to see how one bullet will behave upon striking bone, but not so useful in comparing one bullet to another.

Put to the Test: The Expanding Bullets

Just tell it straight and let me worry about the heat.
David C. Foster
Editor, Gray's Sporting Journal
1993

There are more fine dangerous-game bullets on the market today than ever before. Premium bullets are available in factory ammunition, handloaders can load rounds themselves, and non-handloaders can buy specialty ammunition from small, custom makers such as Superior Ammunition.

This chapter is intended as a guide, not as an exhaustive evaluation of every bullet type, caliber, and weight available. While considerable testing has been carried out, in penetration boxes and on game, and although I have discussed the merits of different bullets with other hunters and professionals in Africa, I do not pretend to have the firsthand knowledge of, for example, John Taylor when he wrote *African Rifles and Cartridges*.

In testing an expanding bullet for dangerous game, the first question that must be asked is, what constitutes good performance? Here's Elmer Keith's view:

> *Dangerous game is not really dangerous until it is in close proximity to the hunter, and when that is the case he doesn't need high velocity but rather a big caliber with a heavy bullet that will penetrate well and also deliver a heavy knockdown wallop.*

So, good performance in an expanding bullet for animals like Cape buffalo is, first and foremost, weight retention. The more weight a bullet retains, the deeper it penetrates.

But, it must also expand—readily at low velocities but not too much at high velocities. Finally, the resulting mushroom should be broad and even. Some bullets spread too wide, with long claws. While these may have a buzz-saw effect, they also tend to become entangled in sinew and tear off, or break when striking bone. Claws that fold over quickly stay attached. Some bullet makers tout the advantage of the "shrapnel effect" of claws flying off, but this is an attempt to turn a flaw into a virtue. When the claws break off, they do not fly through the animal in a different direction; invariably, they are found embedded in flesh very

.458 bullets recovered from bullet box. From left, Woodleigh, old Bear Claw, Hornady, new Bear Claw, Speer African Grand Slam, Barnes Triple-Shock X.

close to the wound channel, having flown nowhere. Claws flying loose do not weigh enough to penetrate in any meaningful way.

As of today, if I were planning to hunt Cape buffalo, I would probably choose Woodleigh WeldCore softs, backed up with Speer African Grand Slam Tungsten Core solids. When I asked Craig Boddington, who has as much expe rience with African dangerous game as anyone in North America, he said he would choose Swift A-Frames and "almost any" good solid—of which there are several. For lions, he said that any good "soft" soft would do just fine.

Larry Barnett, proprietor of Superior Ammunition, who loads every good bullet (and no bad ones) and gets regular reports back from his clients, told me that the two bullets he recommends are the Swift A-Frame and the Barnes Triple-Shock X-Bullet. He would use the Woodleigh for all nitro-express car-tridges, and he recommends the Swift over the Woodleigh in other calibers only because of price, not because of any difference in quality.

What follows are assessments of some bullets with which I have had personal experience—hunting, testing, or both. Some of the information comes from a series of tests carried out in the summer of 2004, which culmi-nated in a safari in Tanzania with Derek Hurt specifically for the purpose of bullet testing. It is no coincidence that I did this with Robin Hurt's compa-ny, since Jack Carter, Finn Aagaard, and I had hunted with Robin on a bul-let-testing safari in 1990. Other tests were conducted, at home and in Africa, from 1992 to 2001.

A-Square Dead Tough

Pride of place in this chapter goes to Colonel Arthur B. Alphin and the A-Square Company because Art deserves great credit for his work over a period of thirty years, designing cartridges, developing bullets, and perfect-ing his ammunition.

Art Alphin was a professional soldier and ballistician who spent time in Rhodesia in the 1970s, working with professional hunters on elephant-culling operations. It was there that he tested many of his theories, formed conclusions, and perfected what became the A-Square Dead Tough (bonded core, expanding) bullet, and his Monolithic solid. The term "monolithic" is now applied to any non-expanding bullet made of solid brass or bronze, but it originated with A-Square and is the company's copyrighted name.

The Dead Tough is a bonded bullet whose pure lead core is soldered into the jacket using flux and a blowtorch. Since solder is mostly lead anyway, simply heating it up is a brilliantly simple solution. The nose of the Dead Tough is a perfect radius and the bullet a two-diameter design; the slightly undersized front portion can extend into the rifled bore if necessary, allowing it to be seated out as far as the shooter wants (or the magazine can accommodate), without worrying about it encountering the rifling. This is a modernization of a technique used by target shooters in the late 1800s. The jacket is soft brass, which is annealed after the bullet is formed to ensure that it is not brittle.

Art also designed an expanding bullet called the Lion Load, which is an extremely soft bullet of pure lead in a very thin, pure-copper jacket. It is not bonded and is intended to expand explosively—literally to turn inside out on soft-skinned animals like lions or leopards.

Together with the Dead Tough and the Monolithic, the Lion Load is included in Alphin's "Triad" system of ammunition, in which all three bullets are guaranteed to shoot to the same point of impact. While I have not tested every caliber available, those I have worked with, including the .416 Rigby and .450 Ackley, do exactly as advertised at 100 yards, planting all the bullets into one group.

This is the only place in this book that you will find the Lion Load mentioned, and it is here only because it is part of the Triad. As a bullet for dangerous game, I believe it is a dreadful idea—an accident waiting to happen. The label on the box says it is "for use on cats or other thin-skinned game on frontal or broadside shots only." This is all very well, but no one can predict what will happen with animals that are wounded, and a lion that offers a broadside shot one moment is dashing into the bushes the next. At one point, it was suggested that a hunter using the Triad system fill his magazine and chamber according to the likely order in which situations would occur—that is, a Dead Tough in the chamber, another in the magazine, then a Lion Load and a Monolithic, or something along those lines. The theory was that you shoot the animal with the Dead Tough, shoot him again with the second DT, and if he charges you have the Lion Load. If, instead, he offers a departing shot, you eject the Lion Load, chamber the Monolithic, and shoot him lengthways.

Anyone who has ever hunted knows how completely unworkable such a scenario is. Even the age-old practice of loading softs on top and solids underneath is hard enough to keep straight without worrying about which type of soft you have in your chamber. It is not only unrealistic, it is complicated and just

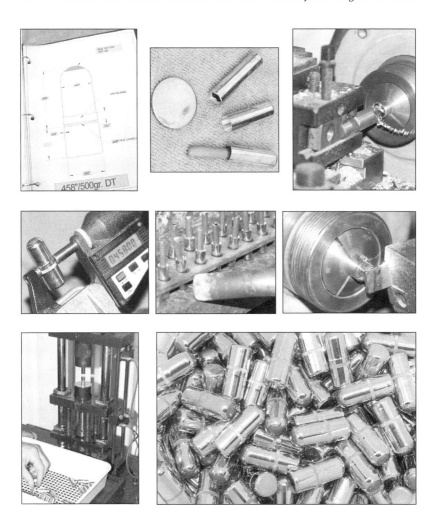

Stages of production of the A-Square Dead Tough. Art Alphin's brilliant design begins with a detailed blueprint for each caliber and weight. Note the dual-diameter design that allows the forward portion of the bullet to extend into the bore—a throwback to the sophisticated target-shooting techniques of the late 1800s. The Dead Tough begins with a brass 'coin' and a length of solder. The coin is extruded into a cup. The cup mouth is skived before the solder is placed in it. The fledgling bullet is heated with a blowtorch to melt the solder, which fills the cavity and bonds to the jacket. It is then trimmed, swaged, and polished. When complete, each Dead Tough bullet is a precision product – and as good a dangerous-game bullet as now exists.

asking for trouble. For the record, cartridges with the Lion Load are tinted red on the base for easy identification, and the Lion is copper, with more lead showing than the brass-jacketed Dead Tough, so there is little likelihood of confusing the two when loading. Expecting a gunbearer to keep them straight is another matter.

As a hunter, if I am using a soft, I want it to hold together and penetrate regardless of what the animal is doing. Give me that performance and let me worry about bullet placement, thank you very much. Over dinner one evening about ten years ago, I told Art Alphin exactly that, at which point he confided that the Lion Load was not the best idea he'd ever had and, if he had it to do over, would never have designed it. Unfortunately, the Lion Load is part of the Triad, which is the cornerstone of the A-Square ammunition line, and the company feels obligated to keep it.

Having said that, the Dead Tough is as good a premium expanding bullet as there is on the market today and has been since Alphin introduced it in the 1970s. Larry Barnett at Superior agrees that the DT is a fine bullet, but does not recommend it to his clients because in recent years it has not been readily available.

In 1997, A-Square became embroiled in a dispute with the Bureau of Alcohol, Tobacco, and Firearms (ATF) over ammunition exports, which effectively shut the company down for several years. Orders went unfilled, telephone calls were not returned, and its reputation deteriorated. In 2002, an outside investor, Jim Smith, came into the company as majority owner, with Alphin staying on as a consultant; in early 2006, Alphin bought out Smith's stake and resumed control. Since his arrival, Smith had been trying to return A-Square to a position in the market where it was producing and delivering good bullets and ammunition. This now appears to be the case, and A-Square products are available through MidwayUSA and Cabela's, as well as directly from the company.

In tests of Dead Tough bullets, they have consistently retained 90 percent of their weight, mushroomed well, and given excellent penetration. A-Square ammunition was given semi-official endorsement at one point by the Zimbabwe professional hunters' association, and both Art and his products are remembered in Zimbabwe with considerable respect and affection. These are gentlemen who hunt the worst animals under the worst conditions, and they trust A-Square ammunition.

On my last visit to A-Square, now located in Jeffersonville, Indiana, I met Bobby Rollins, the new bullet manager. Bobby is a man who is passionate about his work, and his goal is not only to make the best-performing bullets in the world, but also the prettiest. He wants bullets that are aesthetically as well as functionally perfect, and that is exactly the kind of dedication needed to make a really fine product.

A-Square's Triad in the .505 Gibbs: from left, the Lion Load, Dead Tough, and Monolithic Solid. In factory ammunition, it is guaranteed to shoot all three bullets to the same point of impact.

A-Square .505-caliber, 525-grain bullets, whole and sectioned, from left: Lion Load, Dead Tough, Monolithic Solid. Although the weight is the same, the bullets are different lengths. The Lion Load is the shortest because it is made from pure copper and lead; the Monolithic is the longest, because it is made of brass. Note the Lion Load's thin, soft walls compared to the Dead Tough.

A new 465-grain .458-caliber Dead Tough, with bullet recovered from penetration box. It expanded beautifully and retained 90 percent of its weight (420 grains).

A final note on A-Square: When Art formed the company in 1979, he did so to make bullets, brass, loaded ammunition, and rifles. The rifles are covered in the bolt-action section of this book. He loaded ammunition for many big nitro-express cartridges before brass was available from other sources and before Kynamco came back into the marketplace. In other words, his company kept alive many a cartridge and fine old double that was previously unusable for lack of ammunition. As well, he legitimized some first-rate wildcats, like the .450 Ackley, and was the first to offer factory .458 Lott loadings. Brass for older cartridges and wildcats is an extremely valuable commodity, and the brass being turned out today in Jeffersonville by A-Square is better than it has ever been.

Woodleigh

In terms of use, Australia today is the double-rifle capital of the world. After the partition of India in 1947 and the complete ban on hunting imposed in the 1960s, thousands of double rifles of every quality and caliber imaginable were gathered up and shipped Down Under. Something similar, although on a smaller scale, occurred with many of the rifles that became illegal in Kenya when hunting was banned there in 1977.

The Australians were more than ready to put the big guns to use because they had a plethora of Asiatic buffalo, the Cape buffalo's somewhat more mellow cousin, littering their northern landscape. Loading for the big rifles, hunting with them, using them in competition, and writing books about them became common among Australian shooters.

Ammunition requires brass and bullets. And, since double rifles are not easy to re-regulate, their loving owners wanted raw material that would duplicate as much as possible the performance of the original Kynoch loads.

Woodleigh was founded by Geoff McDonald in 1982 to do exactly that, and he developed the Woodleigh WeldCore soft and the Woodleigh solid. The solid is an excellent bullet with a steel cup surrounding the lead, beneath a copper jacket. The WeldCore is a bonded soft that is put together exactly as the name implies. Its jacket is a 90/10 (copper and zinc) alloy of gilding metal. Woodleighs are available in weird and wonderful calibers such as .483 and .488 for the two .475 No. 2 variations, as well as the nitro-express standards: the .470, .465, .577, and .600. In every case, where the bullet is made for a nitro-express cartridge, it duplicates the weight and conformation of the original Kynoch.

Kynamco, the new company in England run by David and Sue Little, manufactures and loads Kynoch ammunition (in its distinctive red and yellow boxes) and uses Woodleighs almost exclusively. Kynoch ammunition is imported to the United States by Tony Galazan's Connecticut Shotgun Manufacturing Company. Woodleigh bullets are imported from Australia by Huntington Die Specialties of California.

This is not to imply that Woodleighs are good only in double rifles. On the contrary, they are made in standard calibers like .416 and .458, and they are among the very best available anywhere for bolt-action rifles. There may be bullets as good as the Woodleigh, but there is none better as far as I can discover.

On my safari with Derek Hurt in 2004, I used a .458 Lott and a .500 NE. The actual hunting was done with Woodleigh bullets; test cartridges were loaded with other bullets to shoot into the buffalo after they were down. The accompanying chart gives the retained weight and penetration of all the bullets tested, but numbers do not tell the whole story. The first buffalo absorbed four shots from the .458 Lott at a range of 175 yards before he finally went to his

DANGEROUS GAME BULLET PERFORMANCE

Bullet	Orig. Wt.	Ret. Wt.	%	Penetration	Ret. Wt.	%
		EXPANSION BOX			CAPE BUFFALO	
.458 Lott						
Woodleigh .458	500	487	97	20"	394 to 496	79 to 99
Trophy Bonded .458 (old)	500	483	97	21	471	94
Trophy Bonded .458 (new)	500	417	83	25	357	71
Hornady .458	500	451	90	23	Not recovered	
Speer African Grand Slam .458	500	392	78	22	378	76
Barnes Triple-Shock X .458	450	449	99	24	393	79
.500 Nitro Express						
Woodleigh WeldCore	570	560	98	25	517 & 556	91 & 98
Huntington Hardened Lead .500	515	N/A		30-plus	Not recovered	
.416 Rigby						
Trophy Bonded (old)	400	396	99	23	(a) 276 to 383	69 to 96
Trophy Bonded (new)	400	391	98	23	(b) 247 to 379	62 to 95
Woodleigh WeldCore	400	400	100	21	N/A	N/A

(a) Bullets recovered from Cape Buffalo killed in Botswana in 1990 by Terry Wieland

(b) Bullets recovered from Cape Buffalo killed in Tanzania in 2004 by Robin Hurt's clients

.30-06				
Woodleigh WeldCore	165	155	94	14
Trophy Bonded (old)	165	159	96	14

This test was carried out solely to compare the performance of old-production Trophy Bonded Bear Claw with the Woodleigh WeldCore.

.500 NE 570-grain Woodleigh Weld-Core bullets—unfired, recovered from bullet box, and two recovered from Cape buffalo. Retained weight is 560, 517, and 555 grains (98, 91, and 97 percent) respectively. Superb performance.

500-grain Woodleigh WeldCores, fired from .458 Lott and recovered from Cape buffalo in Tanzania (2004). The badly mangled bullet (lower left) was the original killing shot that took out the near shoulder, top of the heart, lungs, a rib on each side, and smashed against the inside of the far shoulder, where it was recovered. The bullet (lower right) was also

a shoulder shot. The bullet (background right) smashed the hip and penetrated up into the chest cavity, toppling the buffalo. It still retained 469 grains (94 percent) and expanded into an excellent mushroom.

New Woodleigh 165-gr. and old-production Trophy Bonded Bear Claw, recovered from bullet box. The resemblance is uncanny. The Woodleigh retained 155 grains, the Bear Claw 159. Penetration was 14 inches each, from a .30-06.

reward. The first shot would have killed him in a few minutes, but with darkness approaching, thick bush nearby, and several hundred other buffalo milling around, Derek wanted to make sure. So I kept shooting until the animal's head went down for good. All four bullets were recovered, and their performance was exemplary.

Bullet #1 hit the shoulder, took out the top of the heart and lungs, and struck the far shoulder. Bullet #2 was recovered from the paunch, which it entered from the rear. Bullet #3 shattered the hip and toppled the buffalo, and was recovered from the chest cavity. Bullet #4 went into the shoulder beside #1 after the buffalo was down. The bullet that mangled the shoulder was deformed, but the other three were good mushrooms.

On the second buffalo, I used the .500 NE with 570-grain Woodleighs. At twenty-five yards, the first bullet duplicated the .458's performance on the other buffalo. And, like the first animal, this one would have been dead shortly, but we kept shooting as long as he was on his feet.

The accompanying photographs show the Woodleighs recovered from both buffalo, as well as those from my expansion box. As a group, you could not ask for better performance or prettier mushrooms. To my mind, the Woodleigh WeldCore is, today, a dangerous-game bullet against which others can be measured.

As the testing progressed, I was struck by the similarity in performance and appearance between today's Woodleigh WeldCores and the original Trophy Bonded Bear Claws. Out of curiosity, I loaded two bullets (165-grain .308) for my .30-06 and tested them in the bullet box. Each penetrated exactly fourteen inches, their retained weight was almost identical (159 grains for the Bear Claw, 155 for the Woodleigh), and their expanded shapes were remarkably similar.

Craig Boddington has a very high opinion of Woodleighs, but he offers one caution. With the proliferation of large-capacity cartridges, he told me, some hunters are loading Woodleighs to higher velocities than they are designed to withstand. The result is over-expansion. Woodleigh does not publish recommended velocity ranges for its bullets, but since they are designed for nitro-express cartridges, it is a fair conclusion that the big bullets (.416 and up) are intended for muzzle velocities up to about 2,500 fps.

Trophy Bonded–Old and New

Since being acquired by Federal Cartridge, the Trophy Bonded Bear Claw has changed. It is no longer the bullet that Jack Carter developed, either in its construction or performance. It was this change in the Bear Claw, which had become noticeable and cause for concern, that was largely responsible for the tests we undertook in 2004.

Carter's bullet was always both highly accurate and superb in its retained weight and expansion. The current bullet has suffered in all respects. In May 2004, Craig Boddington told me flatly, "The Bear Claw is not what it used to be." He said the bullets were now coming apart on impact. Larry Barnett at Superior Ammunition said much the same thing and added that bullets shipped in recent years were not as accurate as they had been.

Because I have experience with Bear Claws dating back to 1988 and a supply of original-production bullets in a range of calibers, I was able to do a test comparing old and new directly.

The old Trophy Bondeds matched the Woodleighs in both box and buffalo, and replicated the performance I witnessed on Cape buffalo in a .416

Weatherby (1990) and a .458 Winchester (1993). Put the old Bear Claw beside the Woodleigh, and they look like twins. For comparison, I have included a photo of some original .416 Bear Claws recovered from buffalo in 1990, and a .458 from a buffalo in 1993.

The new Trophy Bondeds, however, were disappointing. When Federal began making the bullets under license, they immediately changed one ingredient: Instead of using pure copper for the jacket, they switched to gilding metal. There were various reasons for this, the main one being that pure copper tends to gum up machinery; it is harder to work with, and therefore more expensive. Gilding metal, a copper alloyed with various levels of zinc or other metals, is easier to work with but is more brittle. Instead of holding together tenaciously, like chewing gum, it tends to rip apart under stress. I say "tends to" because that is not an absolute. Both A-Square and Woodleigh use gilding metal in their expanding bullets with excellent results. A-Square anneals theirs, Woodleigh does not; the only explanation I can offer is that one cannot simply substitute brass for copper and have it work, which is what Federal tried to do.

The new .458 Bear Claws broke up—a couple of claws snapped off—in both the expansion box and the Cape buffalo. As a result, weight was lost. Neither was so dreadful that I would not use the bullet, but it reduces the Bear Claw from excellent to average. Robin Hurt's experience with new Bear Claws in factory Federal .416 Rigby ammunition was comparable. Two of his recovered bullets had no claws at all. As the picture shows, they were reduced to slugs.

In a letter to me, Robin wrote:

"Enclosed are some .416 Bear Claws which I'm sure you'll agree give cause for concern. All the used bullets came out of buffalo bulls shot on safari with me recently in Maswa [Tanzania].

"I've never seen Bear Claws come apart before—and I'm now worried about recommending them to my clients!

"Can you please bring this to the attention of Federal Cartridge Company? [When we] tested the original Bear Claws in Kigozi–Moyowosi in 1990, they performed perfectly. I believe Federal should worry about this turn of events, and re-examine how their bullets are constructed."

I shot some of Robin's factory Federal ammunition into my expansion box; as well, I made up an original Bear Claw and a Woodleigh in identical .416 Rigby loads. The accompanying image shows the three bullets recovered from the box: the Woodleigh and old Bear Claw are almost identical, while the new Bear Claw has a distinctly different shape (although it held together admirably).

Also in 2004, Derek Hurt used factory Federal .470 Nitro Express ammu-

Original production (1990) Trophy Bonded Bear Claw 400-grain bullets recovered from a Cape buffalo in Botswana in 1990. These bullets were all fired from a .416 Weatherby at about 2650 fps muzzle velocity. The bullet in the foreground penetrated two feet of spinal vertebrae, accounting for the broken claw; it

still weighs 275 grains—69 percent retention. The others range from 355 to 383 grains—89 to 96 percent retention. Superb performance overall.

500-grain Trophy Bonded Bear Claw (old production) recovered from a Cape buffalo on Mount Longido (Tanzania) in 1993. This bullet went right through the bull's skull at muzzle velocity, penetrated the spine, destroyed two vertebrae, and deflected into the chest. It weighs 404 grains (81 percent retained weight), which is extraordinary performance.

500-grain Trophy Bonded Bear Claws, new and old. Foreground left: Old Bear Claw from buffalo; background left: old Bear Claw from box. Foreground right: New Bear Claw from buffalo; background right: New Bear Claw from box. The difference in performance of old versus new Bear Claws is obvious.

New-production 400-grain bullets, fired from a .416 Rigby and recovered from Cape buffalo by Robin Hurt in 2004. The performance does not even approach that of old Bear Claws recovered by the author from a Botswana buffalo in 1990.

Recovered from box, left to right: 400-gr. Woodleigh, 400-gr. old-production Bear Claw, 400-gr. new Bear Claw from Federal, all fired from a .416 Rigby. The difference between the old and new Bear Claw is striking.

New-production 500-grain Trophy Bonded Bear Claw, from factory Federal .470 Nitro Express ammunition, recovered from a wounded leopard by Derek Hurt in 2004. The mangled bullet weighs 388 grains (78 percent) which would be decent performance on buffalo, but very poor on a soft animal like a leopard. Now, Derek Hurt uses only solids on Cape buffalo.

nition on a wounded leopard at close range. The bullet was quite deformed—far more than one would expect on such a soft animal as a leopard.

As Robin requested, I did inform Federal and had a long discussion about performance with Larry Head, the company's chief bullet designer. According to Head, although the jacket was changed to gilding metal for production reasons, the core is still pure lead and the rest of the design is unchanged. He was very concerned to hear about the bullet's performance and is investigating what might be done to correct the problem.

The overall conclusion, however (pending a change at Federal), is that mass production of the Bear Claw has turned a superb bullet into one that is merely good.

Speer African Grand Slam

Speer Bullets have been a mainstay of the American hunting and handloading scene since the company was founded by Vernon Speer shortly after the second world war. Later, it became part of the Blount conglomerate, which was acquired by ATK. Speer now finds itself in a corporate stable with Federal.

The Speer African Grand Slam was introduced in the mid-1990s. It is heavy-jacketed and the core is bonded—exactly how, the company does not say. Overall, the Grand Slam is a fine bullet. In the test it retained its weight acceptably, penetrated well, and did not break up. Expansion was good in every case. Considering the price difference between the Grand Slam and other dangerous-game bullets, the Speer is a bargain (although, like parachutes, one should not look for bargains in dangerous-game bullets).

Hornady

Like Speer, Hornady was founded shortly after the second world war in the frenzy of shooting innovation that followed the troops' return home. Each company sought its own niche: Sierra became renowned for accuracy, Nosler for its Partition hunting bullet. Hornady made bullets that others did not, including a solid that was, for many years, the only one available in some calibers, and

500-grain .458 Speer African Grand Slam—new, recovered from box (394 gr., 79 percent), and from Cape buffalo (376 gr., 75 percent).

Hornady 500-grain soft point: new bullet, and bullet recovered from penetration box. The fired bullet weighs 451 grains for 90 percent weight retention. This is fine performance.

expanding bullets as large as .458. Roy Weatherby thought so highly of their accuracy that Hornadys have been standard in Weatherby ammunition from the beginning.

Hornady has one dubious distinction: It was the failure of a .458-caliber Hornady that inspired Jack Carter to develop the Trophy Bonded in the first place. Having said that, the Hornady as it is now made is hugely improved over what it was fifteen years ago.

Craig Boddington said I would be surprised at how well the newer Hornady performed, and he was right. The bullet turned in a creditable performance in the expansion box, holding together and retaining 90 percent of its weight. In Tanzania, the test bullet went right through the Cape buffalo, and we lost it in the hillside behind. This suggests that the bullet shed its petals, but it went through ribs on both sides—and the chest cavity in between—and that is decent performance, regardless. I would not hesitate to hunt with the Hornady as it is now made.

Since the testing was carried out, Hornady has introduced a large-caliber bonded-core bullet, which should make it that much better.

Barnes Triple-Shock X

The Barnes X-Bullet has now been around for more than fifteen years. It began as an intriguing concept—a pure copper bullet with no core—and has gained a good reputation in some circles. Eliminating the core does away with any core-separation problems. However, it means the manufacturer has to come up with a design that ensures the bullet will expand—but not over-expand—on impact, at any velocity.

As well, since copper is lighter than lead, a 500-grain X-Bullet is significantly longer than a 500-grain lead-and-copper bullet. In some cartridges with limited case capacity, such as the .458 Winchester, this is a serious concern.

Over the years, a number of problems arose with the X-Bullet. One was excessive cuprous fouling in barrels resulting from pure copper being pushed at high velocities. Barnes introduced its own bore solvent to counter that. Others testing the bullets found them to be brittle, with the claws breaking off instead of curling around and staying attached. At various times, in conversation with Barnes representatives over the years, reference was made to the "alloy" of the copper, but a recent explanation by Randy Brooks, owner of Barnes and developer of the X, is that the concern was partly the purity of the copper used and partly the degree of work-hardening required to make it expand properly.

Over the years, the method of making the X was modified to deal with one problem or another, and the bullet itself went through several incarnations, including the "XLC," which featured a dry film coating, and now the "triple-shock" configuration. This most recent change uses an old black-powder bullet approach: three driving bands on the shank of the bullet, these reduce bore contact and, hence, cut fouling and friction.

One less obvious concern with the X has been the bullet's longer length, greater bore contact, and the less compressible nature of copper versus lead. All of this can lead to higher pressures—or at least pressure differences—and various loading manuals now give separate loading data for X-bullets versus conventional designs. Getting exactly the right shape, combined with copper that is the right consistency and has the desirable metallurgical qualities, and then making the bullet with exactly the right degree of work hardening (or annealing, as the case may be) is quite a challenge. It has made the concept of a pure-copper bullet, while simple in principle, rather more complicated in the execution.

With the triple-shock design, Brooks now believes he has found the formula.

* * *

In 2001, I used some 400-grain X-bullets in a .450 Ackley on a greater kudu, and every single one performed poorly, with almost all the claws snapping off. These bullets were produced around 1996. When I told the people at Barnes about their performance, I was assured the "alloy" had since been changed to correct that problem. In my most recent test, I used the new Triple-Shock 450-grain bullet. While it performed excellently in the bullet box, the Cape buffalo was a sterner test, and two of the bullet's four claws snapped off.

Now here's the essence of the situation as I see it: As already mentioned, because copper is lighter than lead, an X-bullet is long for its weight. A 500-grain X-bullet is simply too long for the .458 Lott and similar cartridges (although it would be fine in the .460 Weatherby or .450 Dakota). This being the case, you have a choice of reducing the powder charge (and, hence, velocity) or severely compressing the powder or seating the bullet farther out. The last option may not

A 450-gr. Triple-Shock Barnes X—new bullet with one recovered from bullet box (left) and one from a Cape buffalo.

Three Barnes X 400-grain bullets, fired from a .450 Ackley and recovered from a greater kudu. These bullets were made around 1996, and used in 2001. The kudu was shot at close range, and velocity was undoubtedly a factor in the disintegration of the two bullets on the right.

The 500-grain .458 Barnes Triple-Shock X is substantially longer than a 500-grain Woodleigh in the same caliber. In order to make it fit through a magazine and feed properly, the bullet must be seated deeper, significantly reducing powder capacity.

be possible, depending on the action and magazine of the rifle you are using. If you reduce bullet weight to shorten the cartridge, you sacrifice penetration. Going to a 400-grain bullet, for example, negates much of the value of shooting a .458. These are not choices I relish when loading for dangerous game.

In this case, we used the 450-grain bullet, which of course is then fired at higher velocity. Higher velocity can cause excessive expansion, and greater stress tears claws off. It is not a complicated equation. A 500-grain Triple-Shock X-bullet, fired at lower velocity, would have greater impact than a 400 and hold together better. This, however, is where it becomes essential to match the bullet to the cartridge. The worst example of inadequate case capacity is the .458 Winchester. To use an X-Bullet, you would have to go to a 400-grain to get anything approaching adequate velocity, and a bullet of that weight negates much of the value of using a .458. In a .460 Weatherby, with so much case capacity, anything up to a 600-grain X-Bullet would be fine, with room to spare. In fact, using a heavier bullet and slowing it down might well improve terminal performance.

Because of the X-bullet's unique qualities, the matching of case, bullet weight, and velocity becomes critical to good terminal performance. If this is achieved, however, the Triple-Shock X gives fine performance. Larry Barnett at

Superior Ammunition reports that his clients have done very well with it, and he recommends it without reservation.

Hawk Bullets

The wide availability of swaging and casting equipment has allowed many small bullet makers to set up in business. Some cater to the black-powder market, others to target shooting, and a few to hunting. Of the latter, only a handful make bullets large enough to be considered for dangerous game.

Andy Hill, maker of Hawk bullets, takes a different approach than his larger competitors. He follows the proven formula of pure lead cores in pure copper jackets, but he does not bond the core in any way. Instead, he varies jacket thickness to control expansion. Five different thicknesses are available, from .025 inches to .060. In my penetration-box tests, Hawk bullets expand readily, but at higher velocities they may expand too much. In several instances, both core and jacket flattened out into broad cups more than twice the bullet's original diameter and were recovered nestled together like saucers. How they would perform in a real animal, with bones, sinews, liquid, and paunch—all of which tend to rip bullets apart and separate cores from jackets—is another question.

That said, since Hawks are available in a range of weights and jacket thicknesses, construction can be matched to velocity for optimum expansion.

Hill will supply bullets with or without a cannelure (groove) and will even position the cannelure to the buyer's specifications, which is very useful. Some rifles, especially newer guns with snug chambers, will not accommodate cartridges without the case mouth firmly crimped into a cannelure, which makes the location of the groove critical to overall cartridge length. If you are tempted to put your own cannelure on any bullet, you should use either a knurled cannelure or a pressed groove. Cutting a cannelure on a lathe leaves a ring of thin metal beneath it, which can seriously weaken the jacket and cause the bullet to break up as it expands.

Hawk bullets are made in a wide variety of hard-to-get diameters, such as .505, as well as heavier weights in common diameters and with different nose configurations.

Snake Oil and Pumpkin Balls

Unfortunately, the higher the velocity of the projectile, the more the bullet breaks up; consequently the short range at which [dangerous] *game is usually killed tells still more against* [light] *bullets for such sport.*

H. W. H.
(Henry William Holland)
Big Game Shooting, *1894*

The question of velocity and killing power has been touched on indirectly throughout this book, but such an important topic warrants a chapter of its own. Unfortunately, as soon as the words "velocity" and "bullet weight" are mentioned, one immediately is enmeshed in the morass of the Jack O'Connor–Elmer Keith controversy that dominated the big-game hunting world for the latter half of the twentieth century. Hunters already know which side they are on, so why read farther?

The purpose of this chapter, however, is not to take sides. There is considerable truth and common sense in the writings of both O'Connor and Keith, if one looks at them dispassionately. The real concern is the effect of high velocity on bullet performance and killing power. What constitutes optimum velocity in a dangerous-game rifle, and why?

* * *

In 1856, James Purdey & Sons of London pulled off a brilliant piece of marketing and inadvertently set in motion the controversy that has lasted to this day. Purdey took the word "express," which was synonymous with the ultra-fast trains then speeding across Britain, and applied it to the firm's new rifles, which delivered extraordinary velocity. It was the first time a gunmaker had deliberately tried to make its utilitarian product glamorous.

Initially, the rifles were muzzleloaders. Higher velocity was achieved by increasing the charge of black powder while decreasing bullet weight. Bullets were made lighter by giving them hollow points, which also made them expand more quickly; quick expansion, in turn, was encouraged by the higher velocity.

Standard calibers were .360, .400, .450, and .500—none of them suitable for dangerous game. Stag stalkers took the express rifles to Scotland and recorded some spectacular kills in the heather-covered hills. When muzzleloaders gave way to breech-loading cartridge rifles, the same principles were applied. Inevitably, some hunters took the light, high-velocity, hollow-point-loaded rifles to Africa and India and hunted seriously big game with them. Again, some recorded impressive kills, but others reported failures. Some did not live to report these failures, and investigators had to piece together what happened. It was the first manifestation of a phenomenon that repeats itself over and over and over again: Sometimes, high-velocity bullets deliver spectacularly, but for all the success, there are equally spectacular failures. When such a bullet failure occurs with a dangerous animal, the result can be fatal.

In Victorian England, with its fierce competition among rifle makers, bullet performance became an issue. In 1890, in *Wild Beasts and Their Ways,* Sir Samuel Baker came down solidly against hollow points. He insisted that even at lower velocities a solid lead bullet, because of its greater weight, always mushroomed beautifully, stayed in one piece, and penetrated to, and through, the vitals. Baker was no enemy of velocity; in fact, he had been a pioneer, boosting the velocities of big projectiles and making them truly deadly for the largest game. What he objected to was light bullets that expanded too rapidly, blew apart, and failed to penetrate:

> *The small-bore rifle has been universally adopted, but I cannot help thinking that, like many other fashions, it has been carried beyond the rules of common sense.*

> *The difference in the striking energy of a hollow bullet from that of a solid projectile is enormous, owing to the inequality in weight. The hollow bullet wounds mortally, but it does not always kill neatly.*

Baker described hollow-point bullets, recovered in post mortems, that virtually exploded within an inch of entering the animal's body, flying into bits, spraying lead in all directions, sometimes tearing apart lungs, liver and heart, but other times doing no immediate damage because they failed to penetrate.

> *Common sense will suggest that although such a bullet will kill, it is not the sort of weapon to stop a dangerous animal when in full charge.*

> *I could produce numerous instances where failures have occurred, and I know sportsmen of long experience who have given up the use of hollow bullets except against . . . small game.*

> *Personally, I should decline the company of any friend who wished to join me in pursuit of dangerous game if armed with such an inferior weapon.*

Baker believed the best rifle then available for the largest game was the .577 Express, loaded with a 650-grain hardened lead bullet, propelled at 1,650 fps by six drams of black powder. Even today, such a weapon would be formidable indeed.

After Baker's death, his friend Henry Holland carried on the fight. In 1894, in *Big Game Shooting,* he quoted Baker liberally:

> *For soft-skinned animals, Sir Samuel used solid, pure lead bullets, and he always found them to deliver the whole power of the charge upon the animal, being generally forced into the shape of a mushroom, and found under the skin upon the opposite side of the beast.*
>
> *A crushing blow that may be depended upon is what is required, and reliance cannot be placed upon the short, light bullets so much used. No doubt a good deal of game is killed with the light bullets, even up to and including tigers, etc., but much has been lost, and many accidents have taken place in consequence of the bullet breaking up too soon, causing only a flesh wound, and not having sufficient penetration to reach a vital part of the animal shot.*

By 1894, the debate between high-velocity, light-bullet proponents and those who preferred heavier projectiles was in full swing throughout the British Empire.

Then came smokeless powder and the age of the nitro-express cartridges. They launched bullets at more than 2,000 fps, demanding a whole new approach in jackets and bullet construction to withstand the extraordinary stresses. Almost immediately, a few intrepid gunmakers found they could reduce bullet diameter and weight, and boost velocities even farther—upward of 3,000 fps in some cases. When they tested these creations on game animals and scored a few spectacular kills, the cult of velocity was born.

* * *

In North America, history records a long line of inventors, promoters, and salesmen who tried to make their fortunes (and sometimes succeeded) on the backs of high-velocity cartridges. Arthur Savage, Sir Charles Ross, Charles Newton, and Roy Weatherby all rose up at various times to tout the supernatural killing power of high-velocity bullets. Starting in 1895, cartridges that benefited from this treatment include the .303 Savage, .22 Hi-Power, .250-3000, .280 Ross, .220 Swift, and, of course, all the Weatherby cartridges, starting around 1945. The era of the snake-oil salesman selling potions to yokels off the back of a brightly colored wagon had metamorphosed smoothly into brightly colored ads and outlandish claims in magazines.

At the time, small-bore smokeless cartridges were new. Hunters were accustomed to hunting with heavy, slow lead bullets from .40, .45, and .50 caliber rifles, and the idea that you could kill even a deer with a 170-grain bullet from a .30-30 was revolutionary. Hunters were conservative, and they took some convincing.

Arthur Savage set the tone when he hired hunters to roam the world with his new 1899 rifle and .303 Savage ammunition. They killed elk in Colorado, big bears in Alaska, and reportedly everything up to elephant in Africa. Savage followed this up with the .22 Hi-Power, a .228-diameter 70-grain bullet with a muzzle velocity of 2,800 fps. Reportedly, hunters killed tigers with it. The kills were described in breathless accounts and Wagnerian terms—"as if struck by lightning" seeming to be a favorite, although "poleaxed" also got a good workout.

In 1906, Sir Charles Ross introduced his straight-pull rifle and the powerful .280 Ross. Following Savage's example, Ross touted his creation as second only to the thunderbolts of Zeus. But, the Ross's reputation suffered a major blow in 1912 when George Grey, brother of the British statesman Lord Grey, shot a lion in Kenya with his .280 Ross. According to John Taylor's account, Grey fired five shots into the charging lion, "his five bullets blowing to atoms . . . without the slightest effect." The bullets did not kill the lion, the lion did kill Grey, and suddenly the "velocity kills" philosophy came under its first really severe scrutiny. Nothing gets attention like the bloody demise of an aristocrat.

Grey's death provided a vivid example that is used to this day as evidence of the erratic performance of high-velocity bullets and their lack of dependability in dire situations.

The other side of the coin was the irrefutable success of some equally high-profile hunters in using, if not high-velocity, then at least small-bore rifles for hunting big game. In Africa, by far the most famous was W.D.M. "Karamoja" Bell, who hunted elephants for ivory; reportedly, he dispatched 1,011 with small-bore rifles. Bell's favorite was a .275 Rigby (7x57) with solid bullets, but he also used a .303 British and occasionally a 6.5mm. Bell was a superb shot, a cool hunter, and a student of elephant anatomy. He knew exactly where to shoot to put a long, heavy bullet into the brain, and that was how he killed big tuskers.

If George Grey has become an icon to the anti-velocity crowd, Bell has become one among the small-bore folks. A fact that is generally ignored, however, is that Bell always had a large-bore rifle in reserve to deal with wounded animals.

In North America, Charles Sheldon hunted Alaska with a 6.5x54 and shot many brown bears and grizzlies, as well as sheep and moose. What Bell and Sheldon had in common, aside from hunting skill, was that they were using long, heavy bullets, not light, fast ones. A 175-grain 7mm bullet is long for caliber and has great sectional density—the ideal combination for deep penetration. Bell even went out of his way to point out that he used only solids.

But the world was into the age of speed, not just in cartridges but in airplanes, boats, motorcycles, and cars. When Savage produced its .250 and had a chance to market the first cartridge to break 3,000 fps, the company ignored designer Charles Newton's recommendation of a 100-grain bullet in favor of an

87-grain mosquito—purely to get the magic 3,000. They even incorporated it into the name—.250-3000—for marketing purposes. There then followed the ritual pursuit of the world's big game by hunters with the neat little .250s. They slew tigers in Asia and big game in Africa, and Savage's marketing department duly trumpeted this to the world.

It was about this time that metaphysics began to creep into the argument—suggestions that the bullet did not actually need to hit anything vital to kill. Gradually, the belief gained hold that there was something magical about sheer velocity. Exactly how this is supposed to work has never been satisfactorily explained. Much later the term "hydrostatic shock" gained some currency, the explanation being that the bullet, upon striking flesh, sent destructive shock waves through the animal's circulatory system, rupturing arteries and causing anatomical mayhem. No reputable authority that I know now espouses this theory, but it was bruited about in magazines and books for some considerable time.

Speed was the wonder of the age, and hunters who used high-velocity, small-bore rifles could claim to be glamorous, modern, cutting-edge; they could insist that "if you can shoot, you don't need a big-bore," with the obvious implication. High velocity was the way of the future; big, heavy bullets the baggage of the past. Just as the Bolsheviks appropriated the "river of history" to promote the inevitability of revolution, velocity fanatics pointed to the fact that since the dawn of firearms, bullets had become progressively lighter and speeds faster. The eight-bore elephant gun had given way to the .450 NE, and the .450 to the .375 H&H. Why should the .375 not bow in turn to (pick one) the .280 Ross, the .250-3000, or even (gulp!) the .22 Hi-Power?

Of course, carried to its ultimate conclusion, the absurdity of the argument is obvious. Eventually, the bullet would be a mere drop of lead, traveling at the speed of light—both impossibilities. The historical trend had to stop somewhere. The question was, where?

* * *

Toward the end of his life, Robert Churchill, the great English gunmaker, ballistics expert, and shooting instructor, said that, having expended 20,000 cartridges in tests over the years, he had amassed evidence to prove "just about anything." From George Grey's death onward, proponents on both sides of the velocity debate were busy amassing evidence to support their views. Both compiled very impressive dossiers to support their arguments, which proves there was a large element of truth on both sides.

With the advent of Roy Weatherby, however, the argument took a new twist. In 1951, having returned from a lengthy safari in Africa, Weatherby contributed to a two-part article in *Gun Digest* entitled "High Velocity vs. Heavy Bullets." It was one of the *Digest*'s early "pro and con" features. Weatherby's piece was called "Killing Power"; taking the opposite view was Elmer Keith, with "Pumpkin Rolling."

It is hard to imagine two men less alike. Roy Weatherby was Hollywood, glitz, glamour, salesmanship, the speed of the space age. Elmer Keith was a rough-hewn old cowboy who carried a sixgun, had watched men being hanged, and liked big old black-powder cartridges. A critical difference: Keith was a hunter and guide of great practical experience, while Weatherby was a wildcatter in love with velocity.

In later years, it was occasionally pointed out that Roy Weatherby had killed a Cape buffalo with his .257 Weatherby Magnum, but his defenders always insisted he had done it as an experiment, to prove a point, and never suggested that anyone else try it. The "Killing Power" article proves conclusively and absolutely otherwise. Weatherby returned from his safari where, he said, his group killed more than 150 head of game, and he began promoting high velocity with the zeal of an evangelist.

Undoubtedly, later in life, Weatherby thought better of some of the things he had written, because more than a few of his claims were patently absurd. He said large animals hit with light, fast bullets from his magnum rifles always died instantly, whereas animals hit solidly with .470s and .375 H&Hs would run off and be brought down only with a shot from a .257 or .270 Weatherby. This happened, according to Roy, not once, but over and over again. He claimed to have shot Cape buffalo (several, in fact) with an 87-grain bullet from his .257 and watched them drop instantly. And, he insisted, with a high-velocity bullet, you do not even need to aim for the vitals:

> "... it doesn't matter whether you shoot him in the ham, the ribs, the paunch, or the shoulder; you do not have to hit the heart, the lungs, or the spine, in order to kill when using a bullet that disintegrates inside his body."

Oh? In 1988, in Alaska, I shot an incoming brown bear at seventeen yards with a .300 Weatherby loaded with 150-grain Nosler Partitions. This was factory ammunition, with a muzzle velocity of 3,500 fps. The bullet hit the bear's shoulder blade and disintegrated. I never found a shard. As for the bear, the shot slowed him down, but what killed him was three more shots—two .338s and my second Nosler, which broke his neck. I was expecting a deer, not a bear, which is why I was using such light ammunition. Never again. But this experience is completely at odds with the Weatherby claim above.

As for Weatherby never suggesting that anyone else try his idiotic stunt, read this:

> "If you have never tried a high-velocity bullet, I recommend that you try a .25- caliber bullet traveling at 4,000 feet per second to shoot your next game animal, whether it be deer, moose, or African buffalo."

If there was a low point of the velocity debate, this was it. The claims were fatuous, the tone that of a snake-oil salesman in town to fleece the locals. Elmer Keith's companion article, by comparison, was a down-to-earth recounting of his experiences hunting big game under various conditions, using mainly a .45-70.

In fairness, the rhetoric of the anti-velocity crowd was no less vociferous at times, with some so-called experts claiming that the .270 Winchester was a barely adequate deer cartridge and that a mountain sheep shot with a 7x64 had absorbed a half-dozen shots in the vitals and still danced off merrily. These people made various other statements that only made them look ridiculous.

Eventually, the debate centered on two hunting writers—Elmer Keith and Jack O'Connor—with each supposedly espousing one view or the other, and everyone else taking sides. Nowhere that I have ever seen, however, did O'Connor suggest that velocity by itself could kill an animal or that you did not need to place your bullet carefully. In fact, a careful perusal of what O'Connor and Keith actually wrote over those years of rivalry shows they never really contradicted each other and, in fact, agreed on two basic points: One, if you hit an animal in the right place with almost anything it will go down, and two, you need to hit it in the right place. If you don't, it does not matter much what you hit it with. And if you hit it in *almost* the right place? That's when some extra bullet weight never hurts.

This is just common sense, and it would not matter much had the controversy not influenced the rifles and ammunition hunters took to Africa. It resulted in some animals being wounded unnecessarily, some narrow escapes (or non-escapes), and some disgusted professional hunters. By the 1980s, even mentioning the name "Weatherby" was enough to make PHs foam.

* * *

Most of the above relates to hunting with small-bore rifles, which is decidedly not the subject of this book. What does all this have to do with dangerous game?

Just this: Inevitably, the debate spilled over into the realm of big rifles for nasty critters. Some insisted that the day of the nitro-express cartridge was dead—that all you needed to hunt the big stuff was an 8mm Remington or .340 Weatherby, with a 200-grain bullet at 3,000 fps. Others, not so sanguine, suggested that lighter bullets, traveling at high speeds from the larger cartridges, killed more spectacularly than the old, slow, heavyweights.

In 1953, Roy Weatherby brought out his .378, which boosted the velocity of a 300-grain .375 bullet to 2,925 fps. He fully expected it to be the death knell for the big British cartridges. After all, where was the competition? The .458 Winchester was still on the drawing board, and the entire British gun industry was in the doldrums. If velocity was the way of the future, the .378 could not possibly lose.

Which brings us to the subject of velocity and its effect on a bullet's terminal performance. High-velocity bullets can and do kill spectacularly, yet they also fail and do so often enough to cause great distrust among professional hunters. Invariably, when the subject of high-velocity cartridges comes up, a PH will immediately start recounting anecdotes like Lionel Palmer's experience with the lion, the .378 Weatherby, and the surface wound. All complaints about high velocity boil down to one thing: premature, explosive bullet expansion, resulting in insufficient penetration and a wounded animal. That and that alone is how high-velocity bullets fail.

So what does this tell us?

There is a direct (if complex) relationship among bullet construction, velocity, and terminal performance. This relationship determines how a bullet will behave when it hits an animal. If a bullet is traveling too fast for its construction, it will expand too quickly or disintegrate, and penetrate a few inches at best. If a bullet is traveling too slowly, it will not expand enough and may fly right on through like a solid. In almost every situation, the latter is preferable to the former.

A hundred years ago, in the days of proprietary cartridges, when hunters accepted what they were given, life was much simpler for the companies that made bullets. They knew what cartridges their projectiles would be used in and what velocities they would have to withstand. Bullet makers designed their products accordingly. Some worked, some didn't. Those that did not were either discontinued, or hunters stopped buying them (and the rifles chambered for them). Today, a bullet maker faces much greater difficulties. A .458-diameter bullet may be loaded into a .45-70 and fired at 1,500 fps, or into a .460 Weatherby at 2,700 fps. When it strikes an animal, it may be a whitetail's rib cage or a Cape buffalo's shoulder. Or even that same Cape buffalo's skull at a range of four feet, at full muzzle velocity.

Obviously, no bullet can be designed to perform perfectly under so wide a range of conditions. All a bullet maker can do is make a projectile that performs acceptably under as wide a range of conditions as possible and to make shooters aware of what those conditions are. But there is no way that the manufacturer can prevent someone from buying a lightly clad bullet intended for the .45-70, at low velocity, and loading it to double that velocity in a .460 Weatherby, because it gives him 3,200 fps and he believes that velocity kills.

This is, admittedly, an extreme example.

There are two ways to increase velocity in handloading: Use more powder or lighter bullets. The latter option too often leads the hunter into using bullets that were intended for a completely different purpose, such as stuffing 130-grain varmint bullets into a .300 Weatherby. You will get spectacular velocity, but what that bullet will do to a deer at close range does not bear thinking of.

The same applies to dangerous-game rifles. The right bullet must be used and, more important, it must be loaded with the worst-case scenario in mind. If you are loading ammunition to hunt Cape buffalo, then it should be a bullet that will hold together and penetrate a buffalo skull even at full velocity. A bullet that will do that might not expand as readily out at 100 yards on a shoulder shot, but slight under-performance in that situation does not carry nearly the consequences of failing to stop a charge because your bullet disintegrated.

* * *

In 1990, during our bullet-testing safari in Tanzania and Botswana, Finn Aagaard told me bluntly, "Bullets kill by tissue destruction. They do not kill by shock." Finn, a former professional hunter who left Kenya after the hunting ban in 1977, was one of the most knowledgeable firearms writers of the period, especially when it came to big calibers and dangerous game. In Africa, he dug bullets out of animals to see how they performed; in America, he shot bullets into expansion boxes. He believed in bullets that expand, yet stay in one piece and penetrate.

Most other PHs think the same way, although there are two distinct schools of thought when it comes to bullet performance in the animal. One school wants the bullet to strike the animal, expand in a controlled manner as it decelerates, transfer all its energy to the animal while destroying vital tissue along the way, and come to rest under the skin on the far side. By contrast, the "full penetration" school wants the bullet to do all of the above, but continue right on through and out the other side, since an exit wound leaves a much better blood trail. Elmer Keith, by the way, was a member of this latter school.

Which is actually preferable, I do not know. I have experienced both and have generally been satisfied whichever way it went. I do know that pursuing full penetration is not a good idea if you are hunting animals in a herd. The last thing you want in most hunting situations is to have a bullet exit one animal and wound a second. This is eminently possible with Cape buffalo and is the main reason sport hunters should use an expanding bullet, only switching to solids if dealing with a wounded animal.

The one thing the two schools have in common is that they want penetration all the way through the vitals. At the same time, they want the bullet to expand and leave an ever-widening wound channel that will impart maximum shock and tissue destruction. To do this, the bullet must be soft enough to expand even at lower velocities, yet tough enough to hold together and not disintegrate, even at high velocities. There are many good, premium game bullets on the market today that will do this reliably.

When hunting dangerous game, you have to expect that at some point, you will need to shoot an animal at extremely close range, at muzzle velocity, so that becomes the upper limit. If your bullet performs well under those conditions, let the chips fall where they may in all other situations. It is impossible to allow for them all, so why try? Remember, however, that you can almost never go wrong with penetration, and as velocity drops and bullet expansion becomes less, you still get good penetration. Since your professional hunter will not allow you to take a first shot at a dangerous animal beyond about 150 yards, hitting one at seriously low velocity is highly unlikely anyway.

For the British, since 1898, the optimum muzzle velocity for a big bullet has been from 2,100 fps to 2,400, with the .375 H&H 300-grain bullet reaching 2,550. At dangerous-game ranges, striking velocity may be 200 fps below that, but no more.

Art Alphin, who had great experience culling elephant and Cape buffalo in Rhodesia in the 1970s (and later in Zimbabwe), said his professional-hunter friends insisted that 2,400 fps was the "magic" velocity for a big bullet. That velocity gives noticeably greater knockdown power, and many of Alphin's cartridges were designed with this velocity in mind. For my part, I have found that pushing a 500-grain bullet out of a .458 Lott at 2,400 fps certainly has greater impact at my end of the rifle, which is why I prefer to keep my loads down around 2,250 fps. Recoil is more comfortable, and the bullet still expands as much as anyone might like.

In an expansion box, a heavier bullet will sometimes not penetrate as far as a lighter one if it expands too quickly and resistance from the medium stops it sooner. Similarly, two identical bullets will perform quite differently because of varying velocity: A bullet fired into the box at a moderate velocity will hold together and penetrate; another bullet, 300 or 400 fps faster at impact, will overexpand and even disintegrate, and will always fail to penetrate as much as it should.

Let's go back to Lionel Palmer's client with the .378 Weatherby. I don't know what bullet was used except that it was a soft-nose. The lion was shot at close range. The high-velocity bullet struck the bunched muscles of the shoulder and overexpanded dramatically. In theory, if the lion had been farther away, the bullet might have stayed in one piece, penetrated, and killed the animal cleanly. That means, of course, that if the velocity had been lower, the bullet might have done the same thing close in. It is impossible to know at this late date, but this is conjecture that fits the facts.

Since this incident in the 1980s, many excellent premium game bullets have come onto the market. Virtually any factory ammunition you could name is now available with a fine premium bullet—Woodleigh, Barnes X, Swift A-Frame, Trophy Bonded Bear Claw, A-Square Dead Tough. These bullets are designed to perform well under any practical conditions, which means that even at high velocity (within reason) they will not come apart. Had George Grey been shooting Bear Claws in his .280 Ross in 1912, he might have survived the encounter with the lion. So the game has changed mightily because bullets have changed—and for the better. With a premium bullet today, sheer velocity is considerably less likely to cause a complete bullet failure.

Even so, for dangerous game one should use the heaviest bullet that is normal for the caliber: 300 grains in .375, 400 in .416, 500 in .458. By using a heavier bullet, you will automatically reduce velocity and the possibility of overexpansion. You will also guarantee maximum penetration.

Going the other way, seeking out lighter bullets because they can be loaded to higher velocities, is just asking for trouble, especially if you get into a bad situation at close quarters, with the bullet striking at muzzle velocity. It might drop the animal like a sack of cement. Then again, it might not. I prefer not to take the chance.

Solids–The Revered 'Full Patch'

A solid, or full-patch, bullet should be sufficiently strong to obviate any possibility of it being distorted, much less broken open, no matter how heavy or massive a bone it happens to strike, or no matter how close the range may be.
John Taylor, 1948

An interesting story appeared in *The American Rifleman* in 1956, told by a hunter named F. P. Williamson. He was in Africa with Kris Aschan, a well-known professional hunter. Williamson was armed with a .600 NE, Aschan with a .450 No. 2. They hunted lion, rhino, Cape buffalo, and elephant, and they were less than pleased with the performance of the solids in the .600. One solid, recovered from a buffalo, was found to have "riveted," or compressed, with the nose flattened.

When they got to elephant, things really broke down. Williamson put two shots behind the shoulder and another in the spine as the elephant made off. They caught up to the wounded animal and, from "a distance of ten feet," Williamson hit the elephant another *six times* with the .600, this time in the head. Seeing no effect, Aschan then took the .600 and fired a shot himself. Same result. Finally, Aschan put one bullet from his .450 No. 2 into the center of the group of .600 holes, and the elephant "died instantly."

An autopsy showed that all of the .600 solids had broken up on the bone protecting the brain. Not one had penetrated. As Finn Aagaard rather tersely observed, there was none of John Taylor's "knockout" effect. Not surprisingly, Williamson reported all this to Imperial Chemical Industries (ICI), which made Kynoch ammunition, and was told that post-war solids had been made with gilding metal jackets, rather than the pre-war steel jackets. During this period, both Elmer Keith and John Taylor warned about possible problems with Kynoch's post-1945 solids.

This story is interesting for two reasons. First, it shows that there is more to making a good solid bullet than one might think. And two, no matter how big the rifle, you have to have a good bullet.

* * *

Making a solid bullet would seem to be relatively simple, and in theory it is; in practice, however, there were several problems to overcome and some

— 244 —

Professional hunter Rory Muil and Craig Boddington with a cow elephant in Zimbabwe, brain-shot with a 400-grain Barnes Super Solid from a John Rigby .416. The cow was part of a crop-raiding herd that killed a villager a day earlier.
Courtesy of Craig Boddington

design questions to be answered. Although several good solid designs have been in use for almost a century—Rigby's legendary steel-jacketed solid being the most famous—it is only since the 1970s that first-rate solids have been available for virtually every cartridge.

The first question to be answered is what shape a solid should be.

Military bullets were originally round nosed, but they quickly evolved into the familiar spitzer for most cartridges, notably the German 8x57 (hence the Teutonic term). With its better ballistic coefficient (coefficient of form), the sharply pointed spitzer gave superior long-range performance because it encountered less air resistance. Velocity was retained better and trajectories were flatter. Almost from the beginning, however, there were questions about the solid spitzer's terminal ballistics. Pointed bullets had a tendency to veer off course when they encountered something solid, like bone, and all kinds of stories came out of various wars about miraculous survivals because of this.

Military bullets went in two directions: Almost all the 6.5mm cartridges (Swedish Mauser, Mannlicher, etc.) stayed with relatively heavy-for-caliber bullets with round tips; other governments adopted lighter-for-caliber spitzers. Hunters using these early military rifles in Africa confirmed that spitzer bullets veered off course when they encountered resistance, and all hunting solids quickly became round-nosed, or variations thereof.

Today, there are bullet designers and even some hunters who like the idea of a spitzer-type solid for hunting, and they point to military ammunition as evidence of this configuration's performance. This is not valid, because what the military demands of a bullet and what a hunter demands are two different things. Purely in terms of terminal performance, there is a vast difference. Prohibited by the Geneva Convention from using expanding bullets, various armies have experimented with spitzer solids that would tumble on impact, thereby inflicting a greater wound than a bullet that flies straight through. The bullet used in the .303 British Mk. VII, with its aluminum tip, was designed to do exactly that. In other words, the military may welcome the erratic performance of a spitzer solid; a hunter never does.

In hunting, long-range performance is simply not a factor in the use of solids. The two greatest uses of solids today are for elephant hunting (maximum range: fifty yards) and on charging Cape buffalo (ten feet and closing). Range is not even a tiny consideration. When you put your bullet in the right place, you want it to continue on into the vitals—the brain, the spine—and not go off on its own in some other direction.

As already noted, Walter Dalrymple Maitland Bell—"Karamoja" Bell—was one of the greatest elephant hunters of all time. He killed more than a thousand tuskers with small-bore rifles: the .275 Rigby (7x57), 6.5 Mannlicher, and .303 British. Bell accomplished this astounding feat by knowing exactly where on the elephant skull to aim to hit the brain. He was an excellent shot and he got in close. Bell insisted that no expanding bullet had ever "polluted" his rifle bore, so what he had to say about the performance of solids bears consideration. The solid that worked best—stayed true to its line and penetrated—was the long, heavy, round-nose.

During the early 1900s, as British gunmakers introduced one cartridge after another, various solid designs were tried. Some cartridges gained a good reputation, others fell by the wayside. Reputations were won and lost on bullet performance.

At the time, many cartridges were proprietary. For example, Holland & Holland introduced the .500/465 in its rifles. Ammunition was loaded to Holland's specifications by Eley Brothers or Kynoch (the two rifle-cartridge companies), and sold exclusively by H&H. Because of the proprietary system, cartridges were loaded with different bullets, depending on the whims and beliefs of the gunmaker. Some worked; some did not.

The .416 Rigby had a fabulous reputation from the beginning, and this was due in very large part to its bullets. It was a great cartridge, beautifully designed and loaded with some of the finest dangerous-game bullets (both softs and solids) ever made. John Taylor said, without qualification, that the 410-grain Rigby steel-jacketed solid was the finest on the market, bar none. He could not understand why every gunmaker did not load them. Possibly Taylor was slightly

A selection of solids, from left: .416-caliber Hornady, .458-caliber Woodleigh, .458 Speer Tungsten Core Solid, .458 Trophy Bonded Sledgehammer, .458 A-Square Monolithic. Note the variety of nose configurations. Also, the A-Square is 465 grains, yet it is considerably longer than the 500-grain Speer, with its heavier-than-lead tungsten core. The pronounced meplat on the Sledgehammer can create feeding difficulties in bolt-action rifles.

---

naïve, or he did not understand the patent laws; more likely, he had not seen in action the "not-invented-here" syndrome that affected British gunmakers from 1900 to the present, a syndrome that still affects the large American ammunition companies (although they are growing out of it in the face of irrefutable evidence and shifting market demands). Rigby might or might not have patented its steel-jacketed design, but regardless, no other gunmaker would admit its superiority by copying it, so some cartridges came from their vendors with good bullets, others were mediocre, and a few were outright dreadful.

Taylor has been criticized for being unduly scornful of "cheap Continental magazine rifles," meaning for the most part Mauser 98s. In many cases, Taylor's contempt was aimed at the cartridges for which they were chambered and the bullets with which they were loaded. The 10.75x68 Mauser and the 11.2x72 Schuler should both have been decent big-game cartridges, but both came to grief because their bullets tended to fly apart on impact.

* * *

Elephant hunters learned quickly that the best nose design for a solid bullet is a blunt radius. Taylor likened it to the letter "U." There is no better example of this design than the original Kynoch .600 Nitro Express. This cartridge had an unsurpassed reputation based on its effectiveness on elephant skulls at short range (the anecdote recounted above notwithstanding). As I've said elsewhere, Taylor gave the .600 a "knockout value" of 150.4 and said a shot that missed the brain would still render an elephant unconscious for up to thirty minutes.

By contrast, the .470 Nitro Express was—and is—loaded with a solid that is almost elliptical. It is a round-nosed bullet but features a long ogive that gives it almost a semi-pointed appearance. Taylor did not like that design at all. He said it was inferior to the solid loaded by H&H in its .500/465; as a result, he felt that the .500/465 had better knockdown power although ballistically the two cartridges are twins. According to Taylor, in several instances of using a .470

he was required to administer a second shot, and he attributed that to the design of the bullet. Whether this was a really serious criticism of the .470 is hard to say. It certainly had no long-term effect on the caliber's success, for it is far and away the most popular of all the nitro-express cartridges and many of its factory loads today mirror the design of the original Kynoch.

In ammunition for double rifles, gunmakers were free of any constraints regarding bullet design, but with magazine rifles, it was not so easy. The cartridges had to feed reliably from the magazine into the chamber. This was an added consideration that influenced bullet design—and continues to do so. Generally speaking, the makers of ammunition and rifles concluded that a solid with a round nose not only gave excellent terminal performance on game, but it also fed reliably. Hence, that became the standard solid-bullet configuration for about seventy-five years.

* * *

As for construction, it quickly became apparent that making a reliable solid was not so simple as extruding a copper cup and filling it with lead. On hitting something really hard like a Cape buffalo horn boss, such bullets would still deform in a number of ways. Sometimes, for reasons that are a mystery, the bullets would bend into an "L" shape; other times, the lead core would squeeze out of the base like toothpaste from a tube, or the nose would flatten (the aforementioned "riveting"). There is no telling how many solids did the job in spite of being deformed, with the hunter none the wiser. That's because with the animal down and dead, the bullet was never recovered and examined, or—more likely—because the bullet went right through and blew out the far side.

Enough mishaps occurred that bullet makers redesigned the solid, thickening the copper over the nose considerably or switching to jackets of copper alloyed with tin (making bronze) or zinc (making brass). This helped reduce the problem of riveting, and increasing the bullets' hardness overall certainly did not hurt. Thickening the walls of the jacket helped eliminate splitting and the tendency of the bullets to be squashed flat. As well, putting a thick, heavy fold of jacket over the base reduced lead extrusion.

Rigby, of course, had bullets jacketed in soft steel from the beginning, and before 1939, Kynoch made steel-jacketed solids up to .600 in diameter. These jackets were usually given a copper or brass wash to reduce wear on the bore, and so are not instantly recognizable as steel.

Modern Solids

After 1950, the hunting world changed. Where before, one ammunition maker (Kynoch) had been producing most of the elephant cartridges, now the

The distinctive bluff-nosed solid of the .600 Nitro Express (right) compared with a new Woodleigh solid in a .500 NE. The Woodleigh duplicates the traditional solid loaded by Kynoch in most nitro-express cartridges (except for the .600) in years gone by. The flattened-radius of the .600 was considered one of its strong points in hunting elephants.

American companies got involved. The late 1940s saw the birth of the small, independent bullet makers—Hornady, Sierra, Speer, Nosler—with products aimed at handloaders who demanded better performance in the way of accuracy or terminal ballistics. Barnes had been around since the 1930s, specializing in bullets that were heavier-for-caliber than others and also supplying solids in large calibers.

As more and more Americans hunted Africa, interest in handloading dangerous-game cartridges increased, and so did concerns about bullet performance.

In the mid-1970s, Art Alphin started experimenting with different forms of both solids and softs, as well as designing several new cartridges. Alphin developed a solid he named the "Monolithic"—a trademark that has since become as generic as kleenex or aspirin, much to Art's chagrin. It is now used to denote any solid made from a homogenous material rather than being pieced together with copper and lead. A-Square's Monolithic solid is machined from a solid piece of naval bronze. There is no danger of losing its core, because there is no core. The Monolithic has a two-diameter design that hearkens all the way back to black-powder target days, when a bullet would be bore diameter forward and groove diameter toward the rear.

Since naval bronze is lighter than lead, a solid made entirely of this metal is considerably longer than a conventional solid of the same weight. (The Monolithic, strictly speaking, is "naval brass," but since this is not a metallurgy class, we will stick with the usual term.) This being the case, either the bullet must protrude into the bore, or be seated deeper in the case, thereby reducing powder capacity.

The Monolithic solid may be the most significant development in solid bullets in almost a century. With its perfectly round nose, it penetrates in a straight line upon impact and feeds well from a magazine. It can be shot into anything short of a granite wall and retain its shape. Monolithics have been recovered from dead animals, reloaded, and used to shoot another animal. Since Alphin's development, other companies have begun making naval-bronze solids, but none are as scientific or as carefully thought out as the A-Square Monolithic.

The A-Square Monolithic solid in .700, .577 and .416. The Monolithic is one of the best solids on the market today. The perfectly radiused nose reduces feeding difficulties; however, its solid naval-bronze construction has been blamed for problems in some double rifles.

That said, the Monolithic has not been universally welcomed. When A-Square began producing ammunition for the nitro-express cartridges in the mid-1980s, some owners of old double rifles complained that the bullets were damaging their barrels. The tubes on a double rifle have much thinner walls than the barrel of a bolt action, and there was considerable variation in bore diameters in the early days. Being softer, a standard copper-and-lead solid will allow itself to be squeezed down if it encounters a slightly undersized bore. The Monolithic, being harder, will not. No less a figure than David Winks, former manager of the Holland & Holland factory and a director of the company, insisted to me in 1993 that he had seen barrels that had been deformed by firing Monolithics. He said the rifling was pushed through the walls—"imprinted"—so that, if you looked down the exterior surface of the barrel at a shallow angle, you could actually see the rifling reflected in the bluing.

At the time, Art Alphin vigorously denied that such a thing did, or could, occur, and the controversy was never finally resolved. I have never seen evidence of it myself, but I am not about to doubt the word of David Winks. If I owned an old double, I would have the bores slugged before I fired any modern solid through it, Monolithic or otherwise. A buyer of a new double rifle should get the opinion of the maker and abide by it.

* * *

Other bullet makers took different approaches to solids.

While a round nose is generally favored, there is evidence that a meplat (a flattened area on the nose) helps the bullet maintain a straight course on impact. Such designs have been around since at least 1860, and many of the old cast bullets for both hunting and target shooting have round noses with distinct meplats. For years, handgun shooters have used designs called, variously, semi-wadcutter or flat-nosed, for hunting and self-defense. Tests have shown that such bullets impart greater shock than contentional round-nosed solids in cartridges like the .45 ACP and 9mm Parabellum. The edge of the meplat "bites" when it strikes something solid, like bone, at a sharp angle, and chews its way through rather than deflecting.

With that in mind, Jack Carter developed the Trophy Bonded Sledgehammer. It employs a naval bronze jacket with a lead core and a wide, flat meplat. It is a superb solid in every way except one: making it feed smoothly in a magazine rifle can be very difficult. The meplat hangs up on the feed ramp, biting in rather than sliding up. This is not an insoluble problem—it just requires forethought and the making of some dummy cartridges for the gun-maker to work with.

Another company worked along similar lines but with magnified results. GS (for Gerhard Schmidt) of South Africa makes solids of pure copper in a variety of different calibers. These bullets have both a wide meplat and straight, sloped sides, so they look for all the world like an oversized semi-wadcutter. Expansion tests show that they do compress slightly, which makes them not exactly a solid but certainly not a soft.

GS has an enviable collection of testimonials from hunters, both professional and amateur, and I have no doubt that the bullet is effective. But if the shape is exaggerated, the feeding problems are even more so. George Sandmann, at Empire Rifles, told me of making a .458 Lott for a client in Alaska, on Empire's Mauser 98 action. The gun was sent to the client, and Sandmann awaited his reaction. It came in the form of a spluttering phone call, punctuated with ". . . and it won't feed!" Puzzled, since he had tested the feeding himself, George had the rifle returned. He took it to the range with a variety of .458 Lott ammunition and put it through the rifle. All of it fed like a dream. He called the client back. "What ammunition are you using?" he asked.

It turned out to be cartridges loaded by Larry Barnett at Superior in Sturgis (one of the best in the business), using the client's specially ordered GS solids from South Africa. George Sandmann then had some dummy rounds made up, and he sent the rifle back to his gunmaker. Thirty hours of gunsmithing later, the rifle would feed GS bullets smoothly. It was an expensive and time-consuming proposition that could have been avoided if the client had said in the first place that he wanted to use radically different ammunition.

* * *

In the early 1990s, Speer Bullets developed a completely different type of bullet: the tungsten-core solid. Like the Sledgehammer, the Speer African Grand Slam Tungsten-Core Solid (that's its formal name) has a rounded nose with a meplat, but the meplat is considerably smaller than the Sledgehammer's. Ammunition loaded with the tungsten-core feeds quite easily. It has a naval-bronze jacket. Because tungsten is heavier than lead, the TCS is shorter for its weight than a comparable copper-and-lead bullet—the opposite of the Mono-lithic, which is longer than average. And, because tungsten is enormously hard, there is no tendency for the core to squeeze out. One would think that the tungsten-core bullets might present the same (alleged) problems as the Monolithics in thin-walled double-rifle barrels, but I have never heard any complaints.

After testing many solids over the years, I believe the tungsten-core is the best of those available. It feeds beautifully, is practically indestructible, and being short-for-weight, gives no powder-capacity problems. In theory at least (although I have no scientific basis for saying so), its relative density should give it, grain for grain, the best penetration of any solid.

For several years, it has been hard to get tungsten-cores; they have been out of stock and back-ordered, with long waiting lists—and this for a bullet that sells for a couple of dollars apiece. They were in such demand that Larry Barnett took to buying any ammunition he found loaded with tungsten-cores and pulling the bullets for reuse. Then came word, in mid-2005, that Speer has discontinued tungsten-core solids completely. If this is the case (and it has not yet been confirmed), it will be a serious loss. Speer's tungsten-core solid was not only a revolutionary concept, it was (in my opinion) the best solid on the market.

* * *

Finally, there is the Woodleigh solid.

As already noted, Woodleigh bullets are made in Australia and loaded in ammunition from Kynamco and Westley Richards. In all the old nitro-express calibers, Woodleighs are made to the original Kynoch configuration; this allows the ammunition to duplicate the ballistic performance of the original rounds for which old double rifles were regulated. While Woodleigh solids look the same on the outside (even to the point of the .470 having the weird shape that John Taylor disliked), internally they are very close to the famous Rigby, with a lead core inside a steel cup inside a gilding metal jacket. They have a deep, pressed cannelure that allows a vise-like crimp. Altogether, the Woodleigh is a superb solid.

USING THE DANGEROUS-GAME RIFLE

The Custom Rifle

There are many things to be considered before an order should be positively given. What is the rifle wanted for? What is the personal strength of the purchaser? Will he be on foot, or will he shoot from horseback or from an elephant? Will the game be dangerous . . . ?

Sir Samuel White Baker

Almost by definition, the dangerous-game rifle of today is custom or at least semi-custom. In large calibers, even factory rifles usually have a custom element to them—from glass-bedding the stock to having special scope mounts installed.

For obvious reasons, bolt actions, doubles, and single-shots are covered individually, but some principles are common to all three. The purpose of this chapter is not to explain how a custom rifle is made, nor to describe the different types. Rather, it is to explore some of the custom options that are desirable on any dangerous-game rifle and discuss some of the pitfalls that await anyone having a large-bore rifle built.

Two factors set dangerous-game rifles apart: One is their stout recoil and the need to build a rifle that can, itself, withstand the pounding, yet one that will not pound the shooter unduly. Second is the requirement for absolute reliability under all circumstances.

When a hunter decides he needs a new rifle, he can go about it two ways: Pick the rifle type, and then the cartridge, or pick a cartridge and then look for a rifle that is available in that chambering. Everything flows from those decisions, and once they are made, it is not easy to change in mid-construction.

You may ask, why buy a custom rifle at all? Can't I just go out and buy a Ruger 77 in .416 Rigby? Or a Winchester Model 70 in .458? Of course you can, but I have yet to see a factory rifle that would not benefit from about $500 worth of gunsmithing to make it functionally sound, and you will probably want to add a scope as well. On a dangerous-game rifle, a scope demands a hand-detachable mount, and a good mount is not cheap. A little tuning, a scope, mounts, maybe open sights that are better than factory—suddenly you have a customized rifle.

Beside my desk is a .450 Ackley bolt action made in the early 1990s by a fine gunmaker named Siegfried Trillus. It is an attractive rifle with few frills and absolutely no ornamentation. To duplicate that rifle today would cost at least $6,000. It is not a luxurious custom gun; it's a high-quality hunting rifle. The price can be broken down very easily: The action is an FN Supreme, and I paid $700 for modifications in the form of steel bottom metal and a bolt shroud with a three-position safety. (To duplicate the action alone would probably cost $2,000 in 2005.) The barrel and iron sights, with a barrel-band swivel, add $500; a custom stock, fitted to the action, glass bedded, and equpped with a recoil pad and sling swivel increase the price by another $500, at least. The scope is worth $1,000 and the claw mounts almost $2,000. Right there you have $6,000—and not a penny of it for engraving, gold inlay, exhibition-grade walnut, or a fitted case. Or sales tax.

The Custom Double

There are a few factory-made double rifles today, but not many. By the same token, only a relative handful of new custom double rifles are manufactured each year. This is a business that gives fresh meaning to the term "small scale." Holland & Holland is the largest single maker of double rifles in Britain, and it completes ten to twelve rifles annually; if three dozen doubles were produced in a year in all of Britain, with about eight companies supposedly making them, I would be surprised.

The scale may be small, but the money is big: Anyone setting out in search of a custom double rifle in a big caliber from a reputable maker has to be prepared to spend at the absolute minimum $25,000. Double that amount is safer, and most sidelock rifles in Britain (the epicenter of the double-rifle universe) are quoted at starting prices of £55,000; at today's exchange rate, that is about $99,000. H&H's round-action is the notable exception at about $50,000. Rifles are available elsewhere for less, but they are not custom: Merkel offers factory doubles that cost about $11,000 apiece, and the Krieghoff Big Five is still about $12,000—but those are off-the-shelf.

It is obvious, then, that a man who is serious about buying a custom double rifle needs to have a seriously big bank account, a serious love of doubles, and a serious reason *not* to buy a bolt action. Usually, the reason is simply a desire to go hunting with the traditional rifle of Taylor, Sutherland, and J. A. Hunter.

The question of sidelock or boxlock is largely one of economics and availability. The boxlock is certainly less expensive, if you can find someone to make one for you. The problem for the hunter of above-average but not independent means is that custom double rifles are a luxury market and priced accordingly. You may want a plain working double, but the makers are no longer set up to make such a gun. Certainly they can and will make you a "plain working double," but they will charge you the full luxury price for it.

On a custom rifle, whether a double or bolt action, stock dimensions and fit are critical both for handling and reducing felt recoil. This includes making each stock to proper length with cast on or cast off, depending on the client. Here, Holland & Holland stockmaker Chris O'Brien fashions a cheekpiece on a left-handed stock. In the most traditional shops, like H&H, each stock goes to the stocker as a complete blank, to be fashioned one precise gouge at a time. When the stock is completed, it will not only fit the client perfectly, it will have both beautiful grain, and grain that is strong to withstand severe recoil.

Courtesy Holland & Holland

In the early '90s, when he owned Rigby, Paul Roberts tried to make a plain boxlock that would be affordable to the average professional hunter, most of whom are not wealthy. Paul's heart was in the right place, and if anyone could do it, he was the man. He began with the premise that he would buy relatively inexpensive but sound boxlock rifles, in the white, from Italy. The rifles would be brought to London, where they would be stocked in strong walnut, and the barreled actions finished, regulated, and blued. The target price was $10,000. As I recall, Paul found that the lowest price he could possibly manage was $16,000—only half the cost of a Rigby sidelock at the time, but still far out of reach for the average PH. The idea died.

The problem is that a very large percentage of the price of a custom double goes into the internal workings. It is not spent on engraving and exhibition-grade walnut; those are extras. About 950 hours of skilled hand labor go into a H&H game gun, with several hundred more into a rifle. Try as they might with computers and CNC machines, custom gunmakers seem unable to change that. So a double-rifle buyer is playing in a luxury market whether he likes it or not.

After deciding on a boxlock or sidelock, the obvious next question is caliber. When you get above the .470-class cartridges, there is usually a premium. This amounts to several thousand British pounds for a .577 or .600; a .700 H&H is in a class by itself, with the price starting at £110,000 ($190,000). Some companies charge extra for a .500 NE; some don't. Personally, I think it is the best of the bunch and is worth paying for. If one can get a .500 at the base price, it is undoubtedly the best deal.

After that come other basic questions: Barrel length. Stock dimensions. Overall weight. Scope or no scope. Cast on, cast off, or straight stock. Other details of stocking, like cheekpieces and fore-end shape. Sling swivels or not?

All of these are important, but the most vital are barrel length, stock dimensions, and total weight. There is a much greater weight range with a double rifle than with a bolt. A double can weigh from nine pounds for a .375 H&H to nineteen pounds for a .700. At each level there is a generally accepted weight. A .470 should weigh about ten pounds, a .500 no more than eleven. Weight involves more than just how heavy the rifle will be to carry: It absorbs recoil for the shooter and also for the rifle itself. As J. A. Hunter points out, "Makers build these weapons to 'fit the charge.'" This is partly to spare your shoulder, partly to benefit the rifle. It is a serious mistake to make one too light.

Your custom gunmaker may start talking to you about recoil levels, what you can handle, and whether you want recoil reducers of some kind. This vital question needs to be answered right at the beginning, because it is critical to the overall balance of the rifle.

As J.A. Hunter pointed out, balance is essential. So is fit. A rifle that fits properly has better balance and seems to have less recoil than one that does not. With a double rifle, there is as much scope for fitting the gun to the man as there is with a fine English game gun, and the way to go about it is exactly the same. Anyone contemplating the purchase of a double rifle should have himself fitted by a skilled gunfitter who knows rifles as well as shotguns. Length of pull is critical, as is drop at comb and heel. The straighter the stock, the more the rifle will come straight back instead of rearing up in your face when you fire. This increases your control and makes your second shot quicker. The longer the stock, the farther your thumb will be from your nose and also the less likely it is that your middle finger will be bruised by the trigger guard.

Fit is also important for instinctive shooting, when a dangerous animal is bearing down on you at close range and you throw the rifle to your shoulder and

The fitting shop at Dakota Arms, where rifles receive their finishing touches. This vital function is entirely highly skilled hand labor. This is where these fine rifles are made to function perfectly—a trait that cannot be over-emphasized with dangerous game.

Left: A Dakota magnum rifle, the way a pistol grip should be shaped: The very gradual curve keeps your middle finger away from the rear of the trigger guard, preventing bruising and the development of a severe flinch.

Right: Dakota stock finisher Pam Louden, with a stock for a .458 Lott. Note the straight, even grain—chosen for strength primarily, but very attractive nonetheless. This is a combination of qualities possible only in a custom rifle.

Howard Seikkula is in charge of final assembly at Dakota Arms—a vital position related to dangerous-game rifles. Among Seikkula's responsibilities is making each rifle feed flawlessly. Here, he fits a .416 Rigby, a cartridge that is among the most difficult to make feed properly.

shoot without consciously seeing the sights. In these circumstances, you want a rifle that points naturally where you look, like a shotgun.

In the section on recoil, we will examine the beneficial effect on performance of removing the heavy recoil reducers from the stock of my Rigby .500 NE. By making the buttstock lighter, it improved the balance of the gun and actually reduced muzzle jump. Of course, it also changed the point of impact significantly, which brings us to the question of making a double rifle shoot where it is supposed to.

More than any other type, the consistent accuracy of a double depends on the complicated interaction of many factors. The barrels are regulated at the factory for a particular load. The leaf sights are filed to the right depth to put the two bullets on target at set distances. After the rifle is delivered, the owner cannot arbitrarily alter anything about the rifle without running the risk of changing the point of impact. Sometimes, small changes can be accommodated; other times, the change is so great that the rifle needs to be reregulated, which is neither quick nor inexpensive.

Unlike the purchaser of a bolt action or single-shot, the buyer of a double rifle needs to decide early—and once and for all—what load he wants to shoot in his rifle. After the rifle is built, regulated, and delivered, he may want to play around with other bullets or weights, looking for another combination that works. All well and good. But the odds are you will never find another load that works as well as the original one for which the rifle was regulated. For this reason, great care should be taken in specifying your load. If it is some home-brewed combination of a custom-made bullet and oddball powder, will it still be available five or ten years hence? This bears serious consideration. It is not pleasant to find one's self with a $50,000 rifle and no ammunition. Also, keep in mind that you need a load for both softs *and* solids.

The size of your hand is something to consider. Most makers measure your hand to ensure that the triggers are correctly spaced and that your middle finger is not hard up against the trigger guard. Having that finger hammered is a guaranteed flinch inducer.

Of course, this is prevented if you order a single trigger, and that is largely a matter of preference. One of the great advantages of a double rifle, however, is that with two barrels, two locks, and two triggers, you have two rifles in one. Even if something breaks down, you still have one barrel that will shoot. A single trigger potentially negates that. If it is nonselective, you have no choice but to fire the barrels in a set order, which eliminates the option of loading a solid in one barrel, a soft in the other, and having an instant choice. Installing a selective single trigger gives you sort of a choice, but I defy anyone to make an instantaneous decision, under pressure and without thinking, and select a barrel by flicking a switch.

With a single trigger, there is also the little matter of how it sets for the second shot. Is it set mechanically or by inertia? If the latter, it means the recoil of the first shot jars the trigger into position for the second. But what if there is a misfire, and hence no recoil? What then? If you are being charged by a wounded buffalo, you're dead, that's what. As I mentioned previously, when Krieghoff introduced its Classic Big Five in 1996, I shot the prototype, which had a single trigger. I had a misfire, right there on the range in front of everyone, and the second barrel refused to fire. That's why the Big Five in dangerous-game calibers now comes with two triggers.

Double triggers are foolproof, simple, durable, and dependable, and they provide some insurance. Some people tell me they cannot shoot double triggers—that they have been trained from childhood to shoot a single trigger and simply cannot adjust. Maybe. However, I cannot help feeling that anyone who cannot manage to operate double triggers—with a little practice, of course—probably should not be trusted with a firearm.

While on the subject of triggers, my Rigby has trigger pulls of six pounds each (exactly what Henry Holland recommended in 1894, as a matter of fact). The pulls do not feel like six pounds, being very crisp. An acquaintance who wanted to try the rifle loaded two rounds (light practice loads, fortunately) and proceeded to pull both triggers. "This has a hair trigger!" he yelped. Of course, it doesn't. Turns out that he put a finger on each trigger, and when he pulled one, recoil pulled the other. But both triggers release at six pounds. That is about twice what you would want on a shotgun, but, as H. W. H. pointed out, with the weight of the rifle, they won't feel that heavy, and it makes the gun safer. Unless you put a finger on each trigger, of course. Don't.

The choice of a fore end also needs attention. Splinter fore ends are traditional, but modern double rifles are sometimes found with beavertails or semi-beavertails. Both allow a seriously firm grip and protect the lead hand from hot barrels. And those barrels do get hot! It does not take many rounds to heat them up to the point where they are uncomfortable to hold. If you involuntarily relax your grip because the barrels are hot, the next shot will not be pleasant.

Barrel length is less critical than with a big bolt action. Barrels on doubles range from twenty-two to twenty-eight inches (sometimes longer on black-powder rifles), and that is more than sufficient for ballistic performance. Weight, balance, and handiness are the determining factors, not whether there is enough length for efficient powder burning. J. A. Hunter recommended twenty-five inches, and that is still good advice seventy years later.

Traditionally, double rifles come equipped with quarter-ribs and a row of leaf sights—one fixed, the rest folding. These are flipped up according to the range at which you are shooting. Personally, I would skip the rib and the folding leaves, and go with an island rear sight with one fixed blade set for 100 yards.

Regardless of caliber, you will be on target, or close enough, out to 150 yards, and no one ever shoots a .500 beyond that range anyway. Think about it: The bullet will cross the line of sight first at 10 to 15 yards—perfect for close-in shots—rise a couple of inches, and cross the line of sight again at 100 yards. Beyond that range, hold a little high and forget about it. Learn the round's trajectory, learn what 150 yards looks like. Simple.

If you want a scope on your double, the usual way to attach it is with a claw mount. For that you will require a quarter-rib, and there is no way out of it.

We come now to a question that is largely a question of taste when you are looking at a custom double rifle in a display at the Safari Club International convention, but could easily become a question of survival when looking down the barrel at a Cape buffalo. This is the question of gadgets.

Some years ago, I attended the Game Fair, England's annual hunting and shooting extravaganza. There, I had the pleasure of examining an exquisite Purdey double rifle. And I mean exquisite. Beautiful. A work of art. It had one of those little touches that sets a Purdey apart: a tiny détente-equipped latch that swung in front of the safety to prevent its being inadvertently pushed to the "off" position, allowing the gun to be fired accidently. Does a working rifle need such a thing? Does anyone recall an instance when that hypothetical situation actually occurred? I can't. This may, indeed, be a matter of taste, but to me any such gadgetry does not belong on a dangerous-game rifle. To this I would add folding front-sight hoods, multiple front-sight beads, and anything else that adds moving parts to no good purpose.

Custom Bolt Actions

Today, there are very few serious hunters in the United States who do not already have experience with some level of custom bolt action, even if it is only the boyhood sporterizing of an old army rifle.

As with a double rifle, the combination of heavy recoil and situations in which your life may depend on its reliable operation makes the building of a bolt action for dangerous game a whole new proposition. With a bolt, however, the prices are considerably lower and the options vastly greater. As well, American gunmakers are pre-eminent in the field of bolt actions, which means the potential buyer is not at the mercy of export regulations, currency fluctuations, or language difficulties. Americans build the finest bolt actions in the world today— bar none, without exception, and without argument.

Usually, the buyer decides what type of rifle he wants and then what cartridge he prefers. Until the rifle is actually barreled, the caliber can always be changed, and it frequently is.

Barrel length is rarely a huge issue. Anything shorter than twenty-two

On a bolt-action rifle, precise fitting of the extractor is critical to perfect functioning, both in feeding rounds into the chamber and extracting and ejecting them. Custom riflemakers spend considerable time fitting extractors; extractors on production rifles can, almost without exception, benefit from attention by a good gunsmith.

inches costs you ballistically, and anything longer than twenty-four is unwieldy at close quarters.

At this point, the big question is the stock. Walnut? If so, what grade? What about some type of composite? Material such as fiberglass or Kevlar is cheaper, more durable, more accurate under changing conditions, and you will not worry if the stock gets scratched when you are crawling through the buffalo thorns. The only problem is, a composite doesn't feel like wood, it sounds tinny when you cycle the bolt, and it is noisy in the brush. The in-between option, and one that I favor increasingly, is laminated wood. It feels and sounds like traditional wood, it is quiet in thick brush, and it is virtually as strong, stable, and trouble free as any composite. As well, one argument in favor of composites—lighter weight—is not a factor with a big-bore bolt-action rifle, and it may even be a drawback. After all, we want some heft to avoid being beaten to death by recoil.

Still, there is an element that insists a custom rifle should have a beautiful walnut stock. If this is the decision, then choosing the blank will be critical. Strength through the wrist is all important. But let us assume that you know how to pick a blank and have chosen one with nice figure in the butt but straight grain through the wrist and fore end. Depending on your gunmaker, you may run into another obstacle at this point: He may want to inlet the stock carefully in order to display, to you and the world, his virtuosity as a stockmaker. Glass-bed the barrel and action? The horror!

The bald truth is that if you must have real wood in a bolt action intended for dangerous game, it only makes sense to glass-bed the action, not only for stability but also for strength. The alternative is to sink a couple of steel crossbolts through the stock – a feature that certainly gives the gun an air of express-rifle panache. But, glass-bedding is cheaper, easier, stronger, and more dependable.

When confronted by questions such as these, it is helpful to ask yourself, "And how does this help if a wounded buff comes out of the grass . . . ?" I find that works wonders in bringing me back to survival mode.

Wood, either solid or laminated, enjoys one huge advantage: It can be carved to the exact size and shape you want. You are not limited by what molds are available, as you are with composites. You can dictate the length and diameter of the fore end, as well as the length of pull and the size of the butt where it comes in contact with your shoulder.

It is impossible to overstate the importance of stock dimensions in making your rifle comfortable to shoot. The A-Square "Coil-Chek" stock, which Art Alphin designed and which has been standard on his oversized Hannibal rifles, does reduce felt recoil to a remarkable degree. Whether or not you like the look of the Hannibal, you can employ the same principles to make your custom rifle more comfortable to shoot. And, if you tame recoil through stock design, you will not be tempted to try other methods such as muzzle brakes or recoil reducers, both of which have undesirable side effects.

What are the principles you should follow?

- Keep drop to a minimum. A straight stock comes straight back during recoil. This is also better for use with a scope.
- Ensure you have sufficient length of pull. An extra half-inch to an inch will keep the scope away from your eye, move your thumb away from your nose, and help keep your middle finger pulled back from the trigger guard.
- Have a hefty fore end. You want to be able to hold the rifle firmly.
- Make the butt both longer and wider than normal where it meets your shoulder, and install a large, soft recoil pad.
- A pistol grip with a gradual curve rather than a steep one keeps your hand away from the trigger guard.
- A comb that has a wide radius, rather than one that is narrow and sharp, reduces impact on your cheek.

As I have mentioned, for reasons that baffle me, Art Alphin refused to allow checkering on his stocks. His explanation was that, with the heavy recoil of cartridges like the .500 A-Square, checkering could scrape the hand. I can't see it, myself. Particularly in the heat of Africa, with my palms sweaty from heat and tension, I'll take my chances. Because checkering is there for the most functional of reasons, it should not be too fine—certainly no more than twenty-four lines per inch, and twenty or twenty-two is better. If your stock maker is a checkering *artiste*, he may try to talk you into an intricate design with fine lines, but resist the temptation. You want a simple point pattern that gives a firm grip.

The shape of the fore end in cross section also matters. Most fore ends are simply round. Some rifles, like Dakota's Traveler (take-down) model has a vertical oval, which is not as easy to grip. The fore end on the stock that Siegfried Trillus shaped for my .450 Ackley is a faint horizontal oval. You cannot really see it, but you can feel it, and the grip could not be more secure.

When ordering a stock that is custom-made from a blank, one can also specify cast-on or cast-off. Cast is the amount the stock is bent to left or right, depending on whether the shooter is left- or right-handed. Cast-off is a slight bend to the right to accommodate a right-handed shooter. It is usually no more than a fraction of an inch; as well, it can be greater at the toe of the stock than the heel, moving that particular sharp corner away from sensitive areas. Cast is *de rigueur* on custom shotguns and common on double rifles, but it is rare on bolt actions. Probably, this is because most shooters simply don't think about it, and most stock makers in America are unfamiliar with it.

Certainly, building cast into a rifle stock takes more skill and work. Whether it is worth the effort is another question. My .450 Ackley has cast-off, but none of my other bolt action rifles do. When I remove the scope \from the Ackley and shoulder the rifle with my eyes closed, it lines up naturally, like a fine shotgun. This is a trait that could, someday, save my life. Because it makes the rifle feel so good in the hands, it also imparts confidence.

For a good example of how *not* to shape a stock on a bolt rifle for dangerous game, one can look at examples from the English gun trade circa 1920. Invariably, these rifles have skimpy fore ends, excessive drop, and sharp combs. This may be the classic "express" bolt rifle, but rifle makers have learned a lot since then.

* * *

A question that is sure to come up is where to put the front sling swivel. Traditionally it goes on a barrel band two to three inches from the fore-end tip. This serves two valid purposes: First, it protects your lead hand from recoil. Second, when carrying the rifle slung on the shoulder with the muzzle up (as most of us do), it puts the gun lower on the shoulder, making it easier to maneuver in thick brush. A criticism is that using the sling target-style as a shooting aid puts stress on the barrel, but a sling is rarely used that way with a big-bore rifle.

* * *

Several questions arise regarding modifications to the action itself.

For years, it has been standard practice to replace the bolt shroud of a Mauser 98 with one employing the Winchester-style, three-position wing safety. The three-position concept originated with the Mauser, but the original design (which had a bulky catch that swung over in a vertical arc) did not allow the mounting of a scope. It was also slow and awkward. The Winchester version performs the same task but does so in a horizontal front-to-back motion, and it allows the rifle to be switched from "safe" to "fire" with a simple flick of the thumb.

The concept of each is the same: The safety moves a steel ridge into a notch on the striker, camming it back out of contact with the sear and holding it in place regardless of what happens with the trigger or the sear. There are three positions: Fully to the rear locks the striker and the bolt. In the center, the strik-er is still locked, but the bolt can be cycled, allowing the rifle to be unloaded. With the lever all the way forward, the rifle can be fired.

Other safeties, such as those on the Remington 700, block the trigger itself. The striker is still held by the sear, but the trigger is prevented from releasing it. A similar system was used on the FN Supreme Mauser actions and in many other commercial bolt actions.

Generally, such a safety has only two positions. When in the "safe" position, the original design also locked the bolt closed—a great advantage when crawl-ing through the bush. However, because this meant that the safety had to be moved to "fire" in order to cycle the bolt to unload the rifle, it was deemed to be a hazard, so some makers altered the action so the bolt could be cycled with the rifle on "safe." This may or may not make the gun safer, but it seriously degrades performance since it allows the bolt to pop open and eject the round in the chamber accidentally—usually when you least want it to. (Chalk up another tri-umph for litigation lawyers, making the world less safe rather than more so.) It is worth noting that some custom gunmakers who build rifles on Remington 700 actions now use replacement shrouds with three-position wing safeties.

The Enfield P-17 safety has only two positions, but it is very positive. It locks the striker, pulling it back from the sear. Still, one has to move it to "fire" to cycle the bolt and, since the floorplate on the Enfield is quite difficult to open, unloading meant cycling every cartridge through the chamber with the rifle off "safe." Shudder.

A Mauser 98 design that has always been highly regarded by custom gun-makers is the Czech Brno (now CZ). At one time, it had a two-position safety that operated the opposite of everyone else's: To fire, you moved it to the rear, rather than forward. This was justified on the grounds that it simulated a ham-mer being drawn back. Since remarkably few shooters learn to use a hammer gun these days, that argument was never very valid. It was possible for a gun-smith to reverse the safety and make it operate the traditional way, but there were pitfalls.

No feature of a dangerous-game rifle should be radically different than what you are accustomed to. If all your safeties work by pushing them forward to fire, then so should the one on your big-bore rifle. Similarly, if all your bolt actions cock on opening, then you should not get a dangerous-game rifle that cocks on closing instead. This is one of the archaic features of the otherwise excellent P-17, and the means of converting it to cock on opening has been around for years. For a long time, however, A-Square refused to adopt this con-figuration on its Hannibal, which cocked on closing. In 1999, Art Alphin final-ly acknowledged the good sense of switching, and all Hannibal rifles today cock on opening.

But let's get back to safeties.

Because elements of the following story are disputed and because I do not wish to get involved in any lawsuits, I will not name names. However, in 1993, I hunted Cape buffalo in Tanzania with Duff Gifford, a Zimbabwean PH who was the son-in-law of Alan Lowe, a professional hunter who had been killed by an elephant in 1992. Duff was hunting with a .416 built on a Brno action—the same rifle Lowe was carrying the day he was killed. A continuing mystery of Lowe's death was why, with a cartridge in the chamber, he did not shoot the elephant. He was an old hand who knew the ropes, yet when his body was found, his rifle was on "safe."

In time, Duff and I found ourselves facing a charge from a buffalo. As I fired and fired and fired again, Duff got off just one round—and that only after I had already shot twice. Why? He thought the rifle was off "safe," yet it refused to fire. Finally, he switched the safety and got off the one shot.

It turned out that Alan Lowe had not liked way the safety on the Brno operated the reverse of what he was accustomed to, and he had it converted. Somewhere along the line, the conversion mechanism apparently failed, and the rifle reverted to what it had been originally. When he was attacked by the elephant (just as Duff and I were attacked by the buffalo), he may have been trying to shoot but was prevented from doing so by the safety. This theory is contested by the rifle's maker, but that does not change the fact that Alan Lowe is dead and that Duff had great difficulty getting the rifle to fire when, according to the markings, it was off "safe."

Since then, CZ has changed its rifles so that some safeties work its way, and some work our way. I do not see this as progress. Now, you have to look closely to see whether the rifle is or is not "safe," which is not always possible in low light or under stressful conditions. A replacement bolt shroud, installed and blued, costs up to $500, depending on the action. Is the modification worthwhile? You bet. Would I allow this consideration to dictate what action I start with? Absolutely. Every bolt action I own has a three-position wing safety—some factory, some aftermarket—and all work exactly the same way.

* * *

Some actions have floorplates that open easily, with a release; others, like the one on the Enfield P-17, are locked shut and can only be opened with the tip of a military spitzer bullet or similar implement. These can be converted. Still other rifles have floorplates that open too easily. Under heavy recoil, with a magazine full of cartridges exerting maximum downward pressure, the floorplate can fly open, scattering the cartridges on the ground. This embarassing experience is a standing joke with professional hunters, who regale all and sundry with tales of their oafish clients.

There is only one way to know if your rifle is prone to this failing, and that is to fill the magazine and fire some full-house rounds. If the problem has not occurred after a dozen full magazines' worth, then it probably will not happen. But if the floorplate flies open even once, the rifle should go back to the gunmaker to be corrected. There are various ways of doing this—some easier than others, depending on the action. But, it is vital that the problem be fixed.

* * *

The claw extractor found on the Mauser 98 and most of its descendants (the early Model 70 and Enfield P-17) has become an object of reverence to some rifle enthusiasts, especially for big rifles. It was the removal of the claw from the post-'64 Model 70, as much as the rifle's overall tackiness, that caused the great backlash against Winchester's redesign. The claw extractor defines controlled feed: A cartridge rises up from the magazine, and the rim slips in behind the extractor as the cartridge is chambered. Unfortunately, that is the *only* way to chamber a cartridge in the original Mausers.

Other actions, such as the Remington 700 and the Weatherby Mark V, use a "push feed" system in the which the cartridge jumps up loose from the magazine and is "fumbled" into the chamber, as one writer put it. The spring-loaded extractor snaps over the rim as the cartridge is rammed home. The advantage is obvious: In a tight spot, desperately needing to get a round loaded, the hunter can open the bolt, drop a cartridge in, and shove the bolt closed.

Because of the massive size of the claw extractor and the stiffness of the spring steel from which it is made, it is not easy to alter the extractor so that it will snap over a rim—but it can be done. The P-17 was designed with this modification, and it is a common alteration to Mauser 98s; it is standard on Dakota rifles as they come from the factory. All that is required is to bevel the extractor face so that it is cammed outward when it comes in contact with the cartridge head; it is then polished so it presents a slick surface, and *voila!* It is easy to take too much metal off the claw, which compromises its ability to grip the rim, but a good gunmaker will not make this mistake.

* * *

Many hunters are tempted to convert an existing rifle to a dangerous-game caliber.

Probably the simplest project, on paper, is to rechamber a .458 Winchester to .458 Lott, which merely involves lengthening the chamber three-tenths of an inch. Would that it were that easy! Some .458 Winchesters are built on quite short actions that will not accommodate the longer case. Even a rifle with a sufficiently long action may well require some serious gunsmithing to make the Lott feed and eject properly. The magazine box will need alteration to ensure that the longer cartridges fit easily, and it may be necessary to mill a notch in the receiver ring to allow loaded cartridges to be ejected.

If you question whether this step is vital, imagine yourself facing a charging elephant with a chambered cartridge that has misfired, and you are unable to eject it. Or you have a soft in the chamber but urgently need a solid.

Many people believe that the only important factors in rechambering a rifle are whether the action is long enough and whether the cartridge head fits the bolt face. It is just as important that the cartridge fit the magazine and feed properly. An aspect of the Mauser 98 that is not fully appreciated is that Paul Mauser tailored the magazine box to the intended cartridge, the 8x57. Length, width, and the angle of the walls were all fitted to that specific cartridge.

Today, when a rifle manufacturer offers one model in a dozen different calibers, ranging, say, from the .22-250 to the .416 Remington or .458 Winchester, it is no wonder that factory rifles generally do not feed cartridges well (and some don't feed them at all). For example, anyone tempted to convert a .30-06 to a big cartridge with a rebated rim that is deliberately cut small to fit the .30-06 bolt face should think twice or be prepared to spend some money to make it work.

Single-Shot Rifles

Single-shot rifles do not present any particular problem the way doubles or bolt actions do. There is no question of regulating barrels or smooth feeding. A couple of cautions are in order, however.

One is weight. The challenge with a single-shot is making it heavy enough for the cartridge—not just to minimize felt recoil but also to keep the rifle from being jarred into bits and pieces. A major reason that the European break-action, single-barrel stalking rifle is not made in heavy calibers is that it is difficult to make the gun heavy enough.

My Ruger No. 1 .416 Rigby weighs 9 lbs. 9 oz., mainly because its twenty-four-inch barrel is massively heavy from end to end—far more so than you would find on a double rifle and thicker even than on a bolt action. At the muzzle, the barrel measures .840"—almost a full tenth of an inch thicker than even a .458 barrel, which has a larger hole (and therefore less steel). This extra weight out front helps to dampen muzzle jump and makes the rifle quite comfortable to shoot.

Another factor to keep in mind is the relative weakness of most extraction and ejector systems on single-shots. They have no camming power like a bolt—only the rearward push of a small catch. This makes high pressure potentially lethal if a stuck case is not extracted and the hunter is left unarmed. Single-shots can now handle rimless and belted cartridges with aplomb, but it is wise to keep pressures down. Extraction difficulties are bad enough with a double, where you have two shots; with a single-shot, the problem can be fatal.

* * *

Let us end with an object lesson.

Robin Hurt owns several magazine rifles, all built to order on Mauser-type actions. One is a .416 Rigby made by John Rigby & Co. when it was still owned by Paul Roberts. Robin told me:

> *I had trouble with this rifle because the magazine was too short to accommodate the .416 cartridge, and I spent a whole season in CAR* [the Central African Republic] *using this rifle as a single-shot! Paul Roberts corrected the mistake immediately on my return to England. The lesson? Fully test a rifle in every way before taking it into the field.*

How, you might ask, could such a thing happen? Very simple: The rifle was made to accommodate one type of .416 Rigby ammunition, Robin was using another, and somewhere along the line there was a breakdown in communication. George Sandmann at Empire Rifles encountered exactly the same problem with a .416 Rigby he built for a client who wanted to use unusually long (albeit factory) ammunition. Because a magazine needs to be a relatively tight fit to keep the rounds from slamming back and forth, it is all too easy to make it just that little bit too short to handle cartridges loaded with a different bullet.

Again, one *must* tell the gunmaker what ammunition one will be using, and then be prepared to stick with it. And, as Robin says:

Fully test a rifle in every way before taking it into the field.

Loads and Loading

Depend upon it, sir, when a man knows he is to be hanged in a fortnight, it concentrates his mind wonderfully.

Samuel Johnson

Every manual, every text, every treatise on handloading stresses the importance of concentrating on the job at hand. When a man is loading ammunition on which his life will depend, such warnings become—one hopes, at least—redundant.

This section is not a handloading manual, nor does it include favorite loads for any big cartridges. There are many excellent handloading manuals, with a variety of loads for every cartridge—new, old, factory, and wildcat. (Only one manual, A-Square's *Any Shot You Want*, specializes in loads for the big rifles.) Bullet manufacturers publish data for their big bullets, and powder manufacturers usually include data for any cartridge for which their powder may be suitable. As a last resort, *Cartridges of the World* includes basic loading data for almost every caliber it covers, and this provides at least a starting point.

Anyone with experience loading ammunition can do so for a dangerous-game rifle, but it is unwise for a complete novice to begin his handloading career with such rounds. If you are accustomed to buying ammunition for your other rifles, stick with that policy for your .458 or .470. If you have purchased a double in an obscure caliber for which ammunition is not readily available, go to someone like Larry Barnett (Superior Ammunition) and have him do it for you. He will make anything you want in softs, solids, or practice loads. If a well-meaning friend says, "Hey, don't worry, I'll load some up for you," I suggest that you run far and run fast. Either load the ammunition yourself, or have it done by a professional.

This book deals with three types of dangerous-game rifle: doubles, single-shots, and bolt actions. Each has its idiosyncrasies when it comes to ammunition, so this chapter is divided accordingly. As a result, there may be some redundancy, but this makes it simpler for a man with a double to study what he needs, and only what he needs, without having to figure out which advice applies to which rifle. Of the three types, the single-shot is the simplest, since it shares some traits of each of the other two and manages to avoid the worst pitfalls of either.

One caution applies to every shooter, with every type of rifle: Do not procrastinate. Do not leave your loading until the last minute—or even the last month. Assemble the components you need well ahead of time, load your ammunition in a leisurely but fastidious manner, and test it thoroughly at the practice range.

Let's begin with an object lesson: In the fall of 2000, I took delivery of a custom-made sidelock double rifle made by Geoff Miller at John Rigby in California. It is a .500 Nitro Express. I did not fire the rifle until almost two years later. *Two years.* The problem was not the rifle, which is beautifully made, but the ammunition—or rather, the lack of ammunition and dealing with one related problem after another. Remember the "domino effect?" It is alive and well.

The rifle was regulated for Larry Barnett's standard .500 NE load of a 570-grain Woodleigh bullet, powered by IMR 4831 and the Federal 215 primer. Living in Canada, I could not simply have Larry ship me some ammunition because export permits were required and the process was so convoluted and expensive as to be prohibitive. Brass was available from several sources, and since I was not going hunting immediately with the rifle, I did not worry about obtaining Woodleighs. At the time, there was no Woodleigh importer in Canada, but Fred Huntington at Huntington Die Specialties assured me he could get me some bullets. However, export regulations limited the number that could be shipped at any one time.

In expectation of the rifle's arrival, I had begun accumulating the wherewithal to load ammunition. RCBS was prompt in supplying a set of their excellent dies, which also included the oversized shell holder (at the time, a special-order item). The large shell holder did not fit my priming tool, however, and I had to find one that could accommodate it.

Primers were easy, and I ordered a keg of IMR 4831. Keep in mind that in such a large cartridge, eight pounds of powder provides only about six hundred rounds of ammunition. This cartridge swallows powder in great gulps. Brass was slightly more difficult, but I obtained 100 rounds of BELL. For bullets, I gathered a supply of Hawks from Andy Hill, in a variety of weights and configurations, which I assumed would work until I obtained some Woodleighs.

With all the bits and pieces assembled over the course of several months, I loaded my first rounds only to find that the cartridges would not seat properly. . The Rigby has tight chambers that demand cartridges that are crimped. Without the case mouth crimped, the cartridges jam about a quarter-inch from seating completely. Hawks come without cannelures, so I had to obtain a cannelure tool from Dave Corbin to alter them. A machinist friend cut some cannelures on some of the Hawks, which (as I found out in my penetration box) rendered them unfit for hunting, since it weakened the jacket and caused the bullet to go to pieces.

As mentioned, it was two years after the rifle arrived before I pulled the trigger and the gun went *bang*. Had there been a safari in the offing, this process could have been accelerated; as it was, I went about solving one problem after another as they came up, with no sense of urgency. But it would still have taken many months to obtain what I needed to make the rifle work.

With big rifles, we are dealing with cases larger than those that most standard reloading equipment is built to handle. Most presses will accommodate the massive cases, but some of the smaller ones don't do it willingly. Even the arcane problem of the oversized shell holder and the reluctant priming tool was a lesson: *When you start loading for a big rifle, take nothing for granted.* Until you have produced your first round, had it chamber properly, and fire when you pull the trigger, you do not know for certain that you can reload for the rifle. And now to specifics.

Loading for a Double Rifle

As I have said elsewhere, a double rifle is chambered and regulated for one specific load, with one particular bullet. Everything counts: Overall cartridge length, bullet shape, and case diameter from rim to mouth. Because a double rifle has two barrels, it also has two chambers, and these are not always exactly the same. My .500 has a slightly tighter chamber on the right than the left, and a cartridge that will seat nicely in one does not necessarily seat in the other.

Every round of brass should be conditioned before it is used, but even before you do this, you should make a dummy cartridge and check to ensure that it seats properly in both chambers. Once you have ascertained that your ammunition will work, you should condition the new brass by running it into your full-length resizing die, making each flash hole uniform and beveling the edges inside and out, and lightly (!) beveling the case mouth. With a caliper, measure each case to ensure that the length of every cartridge is exactly the same. This is vital, because each case will be crimped. At the same time, it is a good idea to measure rim thickness in every case. Occasionally, brass will slip through with rims that are too thin or too thick; the former can cause a misfire, and the latter can keep the rifle from closing. This is a rare occurrence, but it happens.

For serious hunting ammunition, use either new or once-fired cases; I prefer the latter, but they must be resized over their entire length. It does not hurt to put them in the tumbler and polish them up, but if you do, check each flash hole carefully to ensure that it is not blocked by a particle of polishing grit.

When the case is ready to load, bell the mouth slightly to ensure effortless bullet seating. And slightly means slightly. The case should not be turned into a trumpet. That overworks the brass, which eventually hardens and splits. Unjacketed lead or paper-patched bullets require more belling, but a copper-jacketed bullet needs only enough case expansion to ensure that the lip of the case does not catch on the base of the bullet and get crumpled. Belling (and crimping, for that matter) is rarely done on smaller cartridges these days. Most bullets from .22 up to .375 do not even have cannelures. Boat-tail bullets do not require belling, but most bullets for dangerous-game rifles are not boat-tailed, and even those with a bevelled base benefit from a slight bell in the case.

Priming is standard procedure, but each case should be checked to ensure that the primer was not deformed and is seated three to seven one-thousandths of an inch below flush. Primer pockets are sometimes not as deep as they should be, and a primer that is a few thousandths proud can keep a rifle from closing.

Most powder measures cannot accommodate in one throw the amounts of powder needed for the nitro-express cartridges. The .500, for example, eats 110 grains of IMR 4831, and most measures go up only to 99 grains, so each charge must be weighed.

The specifications of the Sporting Arms and Ammunition Manufacturers' Institute (SAAMI) for nitro-express cartridges are based on the standards developed by Eley Brothers and Kynoch a century ago, and in those days brass was different than it is now. Black-powder ammunition had thinner brass, and since many of the NE cartridges were derived from black-powder rounds, this carried over. Modern brass is thicker, but the case still must fit into the chamber. If outside dimensions are the same but the brass is thicker, then case capacity is reduced. If you chance upon some older, thin brass, it will affect powder capacity and loading pressures; it will also increase the likelihood of a bulged case if you are using a compressed load. Original Kynoch brass was never intended to be reloaded, aside from which, it was Berdan primed. It can be reloaded but it requires special care and attention, and this is not something I would suggest for hunting loads except as a last resort.

With the case belled, primed, and charged, it is time to seat the bullet and crimp the case tightly into the cannelure.

All dangerous-game rounds should be crimped, regardless of rifle type. In a double, with heavy bullets and serious recoil, bullet creep is a potential problem. If the bullets are not gripped firmly, the one in the second barrel can migrate under recoil from the first barrel and jam in the lands of the rifling, making it difficult to unload. If the rifle is fired in this condition, it is unlikely to affect performance particularly, but it will raise pressures. One can come up with all kinds of fanciful scenarios for how a creeping bullet can get you killed. For example, say you tackle a Cape buffalo with both barrels loaded with softs. You fire a shot from the right barrel, and the buff disappears into the bush; you open the rifle and reload. You get another shot and the buff disappears again. Your professional hunter tells you to reload both barrels with solids, but you find that the cartridge in the left barrel is jammed. As you are struggling to free it, the buff boils out of the grass, coming for you, but your rifle is useless because you can neither reload

Dakota Arms' technical director Ward Dobler is in charge of loading custom ammunition for Dakota clients, using such premium game bullets as the Woodleigh WeldCore.

Careful attention to overall cartridge length helps ensure flawless functioning—critical in a dangerous-game rifle.

Larry Barnett of Superior Ammunition, custom-loading big-game cartridges for his clients. Superior will not only load premium game bullets in special ammunition, but they also provide light practice loads in virtually all dangerous-game calibers.

it nor close it. As I say, fanciful—but hunters have been killed in situations more far-fetched than that. Crimping bullets forestalls myriad problems.

Crimping is an art. It is not easily dealt with by specifying measurements. The lip of the case needs to be crimped into the cannelure firmly, but not too firmly, and much depends on the shape of the cannelure itself. Cannelures (also called crimping grooves) come in different depths and profiles. Some are radiused, while others are square, with edges at the front and back. Still others are knurled, and instead of locking into a groove, the case mouth is pressed down into relatively soft brass ridges. The handloader needs to study the configuration of the cannelure carefully.

Loading dies come with instructions on how to adjust the seating die for correct depth and crimping, but essentially here's how it is done: First, we create a cartridge exactly the way we want it, and then use it to set the die and seating rod.

Put the die in the press and screw the seating rod down until the bullet touches it, with the case only partly inserted. This keeps the crimping shoulder well away from the case while we adjust the seating depth. A bit at a time, run the cartridge in, checking frequently. When the bullet is the right depth, and the lip of the case is in line with the deepest part of the cannelure, unscrew the die well out. Raise the ram to the top of the stroke (top dead center). Back the seating rod out as far as it will go so that it will not mess up the bullet seating, then screw the die all the way in, until the crimping shoulder touches the case mouth. Now lower the stroke slightly, screw the die in a half-turn, and crimp it. Check the crimp. If it is not deep enough, screw the die in another quarter-turn and repeat. When the crimp is satisfactory, tighten the locking nut on the die, raise the cartridge back to the top of the stroke so it is all the way in, then tighten the seating rod down until it is firmly in contact with the bullet nose. Now the seating rod and the crimping shoulder are coordinated. Sometimes, tightening the locking nut will change the position of the die slightly, so keep an eye on the first few rounds to make sure that everything is set properly.

As with so many things related to guns and loading, crimping is largely a matter of touch—how the press handle feels as you push the cartridge into the die and how the cartridge feels to your fingertips when you check if over afterward.

It was said of the old gunmakers that they had "eyes in their fingertips," and "feel" is still the best way to check ammunition. Run your index finger over the primer, and you will soon learn to feel the difference between a primer that is recessed three one-thousandths of an inch and one that is recessed eight one-thousandths. Run your finger the length of a loaded case, and you will feel the slightest case bulge, even one that is invisible to the eye. Twirl the case in your fingertips, feeling the crimp, and if there is anything abnormal, you will know.

The final step is to check the case in your rifle. This can be done in your loading room, perfectly safely, by taking the barrels off your rifle. With the extractors pushed in, drop the round *gently* into the left chamber. Then tilt the barrels and let the cartridge drop out, into your hand. Repeat the process with the right chamber. Only when a cartridge falls all the way in and then drops out freely, due only to the force of gravity, is it suitable to hunt with. Every round should be checked in both chambers.

There are pitfalls in seating and crimping bullets. If you have a compressed charge, it may take two strokes of the press handle to seat the bullet fully, and even then the compressed powder may try to push the bullet back out. It is not wise to have powder compressed like that, but sometimes there is no choice. Again, it becomes a matter of touch—feeling the bullet compressing the powder, feeling the degree of resistance, and slowly coaxing the bullet into the case. A solid crimp will then hold it where it belongs.

If powder is compressed too much, however, outward pressure can bulge the case walls, preventing the cartridge from seating in the chamber. This is checked, first with your fingertips, then by chambering each round. Even this is not always enough, however. The pressure does not go away, and bulging can be a delayed reaction. When you get to Africa or wherever, take a few moments to check each round again, in both chambers, and do the same again, each morning, with that day's ammunition. The time to find a bulged case is before you get into the safari car in the morning, not when a wounded buffalo is in your lap.

It is possible to under-crimp, and it is also possible to over-crimp. The former is easy to spot and correct; the latter manifests itself in a case that is either bulged or crumpled like an accordion. This is why it is so important that cases be exactly the same length. Any variation affects the crimp. To ensure perfect crimps, you must have exact, consistent case length.

I like to place the bullet in the belled mouth and guide it into the die, then raise the press until I feel the bullet start to seat. I then lower the press and check to ensure that the bullet is square and has not damaged the lip. With a belled case this is unlikely, but it never hurts to be sure.

Loading for Bolt Actions

Bolt actions have several advantages over doubles. First, there is only one chamber to worry about. Second, with a claw extractor and a turn-bolt, you have a firm grip on the cartridge and considerable camming power to extract a stuck case—and even to seat a cartridge that is a little too snug. These are the worst-case advantages that a bolt enjoys over other types of rifle.

Unlike a double, however, a bolt has a magazine box, and this demands special consideration. First and foremost is overall cartridge length. Each round must be the right length for the magazine, the right length for easy feeding, and the right length to fit the chamber. None of these demands is optional. In the case of some really oversized cartridges, like the .505 Gibbs, you also need to worry about how it fits into the action itself and down into the magazine. All of these concerns largely rule out the kind of load development that bench-rest shooters thrive on and that has become common procedure among hunters who use smaller-caliber rifles. The concept of determining the ideal cartridge length for accuracy, as an example, is either not possible with a big-bore rifle or not desirable because it can compromise reliability.

Often, length will be decided when you choose the bullet. The location of the cannelure will dictate overall cartridge length. If this dimension is too long or too short, you may have to switch to another bullet or add a cannelure. With an overly short cartridge, the rounds in the magazine can charge back and forth under recoil. This can be dealt with by having the magazine altered with an insert, but that is an expensive operation that then limits your options in the future.

A-Square has reduced this problem by making .458 bullets with cannelures in different locations for different cartridges. Some are intended for use in the

.458 Winchester and others for the longer Lott and Ackley. Other manufacturers now provide bullets with two cannelures, and these serve the same purpose.

If you had your bolt-action rifle custom made, a number of decisions will already have been made. Your gunmaker will have asked for dummy rounds loaded with the bullets you intend to use (both softs and solids) so he can ensure that they feed properly and fit the magazine and chamber. The only question then remaining is what powder you intend to use, and how much of it, to get the accuracy and velocity you desire.

Ideally, a cartridge should be about an eighth-inch shorter than the magazine box. This allows space for fast recharging of the magazine, without leaving the cartridges too much room to roam hither and yon.

Almost without exception, big cartridges for bolt actions are rimless or belted. A very few have a rebated rim (such as the .425 Westley Richards and .500 Jeffery), and even fewer have a rim (such as the .600 NE). There is no good reason to chamber a bolt action for a rimmed cartridge and every good reason not to. The main objection is the possibility of the rim of the top cartridge getting behind the rim of the one below it; combined with the upward pressure of the spring and the iron grip of the rails, this will jam a rifle solid.

So, in loading for your bolt action, you will probably be dealing with a rimless cartridge that headspaces on the shoulder, or a belted one that headspaces on the belt. While it has become fashionable in recent years to denigrate belted cartridges, it is really one of the great innovations for dangerous-game rifles. A belt allows the use of a straight, tapered case with all the advantages that affords (easy feeding, low pressures, and efficient powder-burning) without the drawbacks of a rim. And, when reloading, there are no concerns about moving the shoulder too far back.

The comments earlier about case conditioning for doubles apply equally to bolt actions. Because of crimping, cases must be identical. New ones should be run through the resizing die to make the necks perfectly round, then measured with a caliper and trimmed to length; case mouths must be bevelled and belled, and the primer pocket and flash hole conditioned. The next step is to prime carefully, check primer depth, measure each powder charge, and seat the bullet.

With some big rimless and belted cartridges, powder capacity is not an issue. With others, including some of the most popular calibers, it is critical. The .458 Winchester is defined by limitations of powder capacity versus bullet weight. As noted elsewhere in this volume, the .458 Lott was developed specifically to resolve this problem, but even it has limitations if a shooter is determined to get the magical 2,400 fps with a 500-grain bullet. Achieving this velocity with W748, one of the most popular Lott powders, requires severe compression. My preference is to find a load that fills the case almost (but not quite) to the base of the bullet, and take whatever velocity results. For example, 79 grains of H4895 delivers 2,150 fps, nicely fills the case, but leaves enough room to hear the powder rustle when you jiggle the case. This can be reassuring.

If one must compress powder, the same problems occur as mentioned in the previous section. Sometimes it is necessary to use a drop tube to compact the powder as much as possible before seating the bullet; then you will need to double-stroke the press to ease the bullet into place without bulging the case. Finally, a firm crimp clamps the bullet into position.

With a bottleneck case, crimping is even more delicate than with a straight case. If too much pressure is applied, it is possible to compress and slightly expand the entire neck from the shoulder to the mouth. This should be the portion that grips the bullet snugly with friction, while the crimp merely keeps it from moving forward or back. If the neck is enlarged, leaving only the crimp to grip the bullet, it will eventually work itself free to wobble, and if the crimp loosens, the bullet becomes free floating. This is most emphatically not to be desired.

This phenomenon happened a few years ago with some .416 Rigby ammunition used by my friend and Botswana professional hunter Chris Dandridge. As the season wears on in elephant country, ammunition is in and out of the magazine, or a couple of rounds can live in the magazine over the course of several safaris and quite a few shots. In some of Chris's rounds, the bullet was pushed back into the case, while in others the bullets wiggled like toggle switches. During the 2004 season he had a close call with an elephant when bullets did not penetrate, and I expect his well-worn ammunition was the root of the problem. Chris's ammunition supply is a grab bag of factory rounds and handloads of uncertain heritage left by clients. But, in over-regulated Botswana, where ammunition is expensive and hard to come by, he has little choice.

When each cartridge is completed, it should be inspected carefully by eye and fingertip, then run through the chamber. Charge the magazine fully, then cycle the bolt to feed, chamber, and unload every single round.

Some bolt actions will eject an empty case perfectly but be unable to eject a loaded round because the bullet catches on the action ring. The FN Supreme, among others, has a semicircular cut milled into the ring to provide room for ejecting a long cartridge. Sometimes, however, the cut is too small to accommodate a blunt-nosed bullet. If so, it is best to know now (although any problems in this regard should already have been solved by the rifle maker, using your dummy rounds). It is not necessary to go to a range to check ammunition this way. I would not trust a safety, even a three-position Mauser type, when cycling the bolt, but it is possible to remove the bolt shroud and striker altogether and then work the cartridges through the action with no possibility of an accidental discharge.

One point that should be made (and this is as good a place as any to make it) relates to the .458 Lott and .458 Winchester. The Lott is gaining adherents by the day, with factory ammunition and production rifles becoming freely available. Several times I have mentioned the option of shooting .458 Winchester ammunition in a Lott rifle. If this is even a remote possibility, a Lott owner should run some .458 Winchester through his rifle before leaving home and, if possible, see where it groups. If there is a problem, it will most likely be in the feeding, and this is the time to find out.

Loading for Single Shots

In the old days, cartridges for single-shot rifles were exclusively rimmed, but today they are just as likely to be rimless or belted. The Ruger No. 1 is the most commonly seen single-shot in larger calibers, having been made in its "Tropical" guise for decades. It has been available in .375 H&H, .458 Winchester, .416 Rigby, and most recently, .458 Lott.

These cartridges all feature higher pressures than the average rimmed NE, which were most common in Farquharsons. The No. 1 has ample strength to handle them; that is not the problem. What the Ruger lacks is the force required to seat a cartridge that is slightly oversized and the camming power to eject a stuck case.

With the No. 1 and all other single-shot rifles used for dangerous game, it is critical that you avoid excessive pressures that might cause sticky cases, and that means ensuring that you do not load ammunition too hot. A load that works perfectly well on a range in North America in March may be entirely too hot when subjected to the African sun. In developing loads for use in single-shots, whether falling-block or break-action, the shooter should watch closely for any sign of excessive expansion or pressure, and stay well below the maximum loads listed in the reloading manuals. For these cartridges, such loads are usually intended for bolt actions, and while a bolt action may be no stronger than the Ruger No. 1, it is better equipped to cope with sticky cases.

Fraught with Peril–The Unloading Section

Loading data for large cartridges is not as readily available as it is for smaller rounds, nor is there the same wide variety. As already mentioned, only one manual concentrates on the large cartridges and the problems of loading them: A-Square's *Any Shot You Want*. It is billed as both a loading and rifle manual, and it certainly includes a great deal of information on big rifles not found elsewhere.

More common cartridges, such as the .375 H&H, .458 Winchester, and even the .416 Rigby and .470 NE, are now covered in manuals produced by bullet and powder manufacturers. *Cartridges of the World* provides basic loading data for most of the cartridges it covers (which is practically all of them) and can provide at least a starting point. Graeme Wright's *Shooting the British Double Rifle*, published in Australia, has loads for many nitro-express cartridges, large and small, using modern powders.

No specific loads for any cartridges are included here, mainly because the information is available elsewhere. But there is also the liability question. Litigation has come to the hunting and shooting world, with one professional hunter even suing a bullet manufacturer, claiming that the bullet did not perform on a lion. The suit was thrown out, but even so . . .

The one area where information is scarce is for practice loads—light loads for lead bullets, at low velocities, in large cartridges. The need for such loads is dealt with elsewhere in this book, and is something I feel very strongly about. Without suitable loads, most hunters will not get the practice they need to become really proficient with their big rifle. Fortunately, this is a gap that is finally being filled by powder manufacturers, but the options are still not numerous.

Essentially—and this holds true for virtually every dangerous-game cartridge—we are looking for a load that will propel a lead bullet of from 300 to 750 grains at a muzzle velocity of 1,000 to 1,500 fps. Where such loads exist, they go by various names: squib loads, whisper loads, gallery loads. Alas, what little data is available usually applies to cartridges like the .30-06, not the .458 Lott. The Lyman manuals list lead-bullet data to go with specifications for jacketed-bullet hunting loads, but again, not for many dangerous-game cartridges.

In some instances, writers have published information on suitable practice loads that involve small amounts of fast-burning powder, usually requiring some sort of filler like kapok or Styrofoam to take up excess space in the case and hold the powder close to the primer. Many handloaders are not comfortable working with fillers, which get a mixed press at best and complicate the whole process of putting together ammunition in large enough quantities for meaningful practice.

Practice ammunition requires two main components: Lead bullets and suitable powders. Such bullets are available from many sources, and obtaining supplies in common calibers is no problem at all. If you have a .375, .458, .500, or even a .577, getting lead bullets is easy. Oddball calibers are another matter; .416 lead bullets are hard to come by, and getting bullets for a .475 No. 2 Nitro Express (Jeffery), which takes a jacketed bullet of .489, is almost impossible. The same is true for the .476 Westley Richards, .404 Jeffery, and so on. There are small companies that will cast bullets to order if the customer supplies his own mold, and there are firms that will bore a mold to fit your rifle.

Ah, the joys of free enterprise: If there is a demand, a supply can be found (for a price). Personally, the thought of spending a few hundred dollars to get a custom mold and a supply of lead bullets to keep an expensive rifle shooting regularly is not a serious obstacle. At worst, it is still considerably cheaper than buying full-house hunting loads and shooting them in practice.

One caution: If you are starting with an old rifle in an obscure caliber, be sure to slug the bore to determine its exact diameter. (A bore is "slugged" by *carefully* driving a slightly oversized, soft-lead bullet through it with a steel rod, then measuring the resulting bullet across the widest part. This gives you the groove diameter.) For that matter, it is a good idea to do this even with more common cartridges, like the .470 NE. A hundred years ago, exact standards did not exist and many rifle makers had their own ideas about proper bore diameter. We are not concerned with optimum accuracy for practice loads, so we do not need to get into discussions about how oversized a cast bullet should be for best accuracy. Slugging the bore will tell you, however, what diameter you need to get a usable bullet for working practice loads.

As mentioned elsewhere, Larry Barnett at Superior Ammunition loads practice rounds in almost any caliber for which he provides his superb hunting ammunition, so that may solve the problem for most shooters.

* * *

In recent years, gunpowder development has tended toward slower-burning powders for huge magnum cases, but there have been a few powders of the quick-burning, easy-ignition variety suitable for lead bullets and low velocities. Hercules Unique, which has been around for more than a century, is still a standby. I have used Unique in several different cartridges with great success and have had no problems at all. It does not require a filler even with only twenty to twenty-five grains in a voluminous case like the .458 Lott. A Federal 215 primer is hot anyway, and it ignites the powder readily.

Another excellent propellant is Accurate Arms's 5744 (which began life as AA 5744, was changed to XMP 5744, and is now called simply 5744, since AA was acquired by Western Powders of Montana). This is a bulky powder designed specifically for light loads in big rifle cartridges. It was discontinued for a while in the 1990s, then brought back because of the rise of interest in cowboy-action shooting, which demands light loads. It ignites readily and requires no filler of any kind. In the .500 Nitro Express, a charge of 35 grains of 5744, with a 515-grain lead bullet, is a kitten-paw practice load, yet it packs enough punch to be an excellent short-range deer and bear load.

Western Powders has published a special note on 5744, explaining its characteristics and describing the recommended method for developing an appropriate load. This note is reproduced in its entirety in Appendix Two.

* * *

While 5744 has the physical characteristics of a single-base extruded rifle powder, Hodgdon went another direction in developing its new propellant (marketed under the company's subsidiary IMR brand) to fill this niche.

IMR Trail Boss is intended for one purpose and one purpose only: firing lead bullets at low velocities. Hodgdon's engineers looked at the common powders available, recognized that most had one or two drawbacks, and set out to produce a powder that delivered the performance without the pitfalls. For example, wonderful as it is, Hercules Unique is used in such relatively small quantities in a large case that there is the risk of double-charging a cartridge. Trail Boss was deliberately made to be as fluffy as possible and, thus, to occupy a maximum amount of case capacity, virtually eliminating the possibility of an accidental double charge. Other fluffy powders do not measure very well, but Hodgdon ensured that Trail Boss would measure with consistency. To improve it further, they gave it a distinctive shape (little silvery doughnuts) so it would be instantly recognizable. You cannot load a cartridge with Trail Boss thinking it is another powder, or vice versa.

Trail Boss ignites like tinder even with gentle primers, and IMR's loading instructions specifically forbid the use of fillers. Not that any are needed: A charge of nine grains of Trail Boss fills a .30-30 case right to the shoulder. As an added caution, IMR says Trail Boss should not be compressed in any way, and points out that, if you want higher velocity, there are other powders intended for that purpose.

At this writing, loading data for Trail Boss is just being developed, with initial emphasis on old American cartridges like the .38-55 and .45-70, but more loadings are being added all the time. Hodgdon invites shooters with rifles in oddball calibers to call the company for advice on loading with Trail Boss.

* * *

Meanwhile, there are options for many of the common cartridges. For example, if you find a proven light load for the .458 Winchester (and these are widely available), it can quite safely be used exactly as published in a .458 Lott or .450 Ackley.

For nitro-express cartridges, there is another route: If you can find a suitable smokeless-powder equivalent for the original black-powder cartridge, that will give you a perfect load. The ancient .500 BP Express has the exact external case dimensions of the .500 NE 3^1/$_4$"; find a load for the black-powder cartridge, duplicating black-powder ballistics with smokeless powder, and you have a good combination for the modern smokeless round. Needless (I hope!) to say, the reverse is most emphatically *not* the case. Since the .500 BP Express is also remarkably similar to the American .50-140 Sharps (same bullet diameter, same case length), any loading data for the .50-140 can be used in a .500 NE (of either 3" or 3^1/$_4$"). Any modern rifle chambered for the .500 NE is much stronger than the old Sharps action.

Similar situations exist with some .45-caliber cartridges. The .450 Nitro Express and the .45-120 Sharps (3^1/$_4$") are virtually identical cases, and data exists for the latter. Extrapolating loading data from one cartridge to another is never recommended, however, and certainly should not be done without ensuring that your rifle is sound to begin with. Consult a gunsmith and, if possible, a handloading authority to ascertain a safe load.

Some years ago, Hodgdon Powder experimented with different combinations when it was looking for low-velocity, low-recoil loads for standard cartridges. Chris Hodgdon says the company found that the most suitable powder was its old standby, H4895, the original surplus powder that Bruce Hodgdon began selling after the second world war. Originally a .30-06 military powder, H4895 has proven over the years to work very well with large-bore cartridges; it is, for example, my favorite powder for the .458 Lott. Hodgdon says that any H4895 load can be reduced to 60 percent of the published minimum to provide a very mild load in a wide variety of cartridges.

This should *not* be done with slower-burning extruded powders such as the magnum-cartridge standby, H4831. In the 1980s, a phenomenon called a "pressure excursion" was identified with lighter-than-normal loads of slow-burning powders; while this phenomenon was never conclusively explained (or even proven), enough evidence exists to convince me that it is not wise to reduce loads of any powder without guidance from a company like Hodgdon.

With the emergence of Accurate 5744 and IMR Trail Boss, it seems that the problem of light loads for large cartridges has been solved. A measure of the popularity of these two propellants is that, at this writing, Hodgdon is completely sold out of Trail Boss, and Western reports that 5744 is its best-selling powder.

Accuracy

Get as close as ye can, laddie. And then get ten yards closer!
Anonymous

The rifle was born from a desire for long-range accuracy, so it seems strange even to question whether maximum accuracy is desirable in a dangerous-game rifle. In the past twenty years, however, accuracy has become almost an obsession with American riflemen. Every gun is now expected to perform like a benchrest rifle and deliver tiny groups. In the 1960s, when Jack O'Connor was at his peak as the country's most respected gun writer, he considered a hunting rifle acceptable if it delivered two-inch groups at 100 yards; today, a rifle is expected to deliver sub-one-inch groups, and some custom rifle makers such as Kenny Jarrett guarantee accuracy of a half-inch or less.

In a rifle for pronghorns on the plains or white-tailed deer across vast soybean fields in the South, such accuracy is essential for clean kills at 300 yards or more. Even for mountain sheep, where ranges are generally 250 yards or less, precise accuracy is certainly desirable. But every specialized use has its own demands, and often these demands conflict. The rifleman is forced to make a choice: For pronghorns, or shooting across bean fields from a tree stand, rifle weight is not a great consideration; in fact, a heavy, long-barrelled rifle aids in long-range shooting. As well, to really make use of this pinpoint accuracy, you need a powerful, heavy scope. Not so for the sheep rifle, which must be carried over mountains and needs to be light and handy as well as accurate, and usually equipped with a more compact scope.

In the case of a dangerous-game rifle, weight is not a serious concern but handiness certainly is. If a scope is used, it must be compact and low-powered. If the pronghorn rifle is prized for accuracy, and the sheep rifle for light weight, the most desirable quality in a dangerous game rifle is absolute reliability, shot after shot. Unfortunately, the demands of maximum accuracy often lead to reliability being compromised—and this is to be avoided at all costs even if it means using a rifle whose accuracy is, by today's standards, mediocre.

Rifle makers have known for some time that undersizing a bore (by two or three thousandths of an inch) can increase accuracy. Such a barrel squeezes the bullet, presents greater resistance, and increases pressure—but it can deliver tiny groups.

Similarly, a *chamber* that is very tight is an aid to accuracy. The cartridge is more closely aligned with the bore, it does not rattle around, and, thus, the rifle is more consistent from shot to shot. Again, however, a tight chamber increases pressure. Sometimes, it requires an effort even to seat the cartridge because the headspace tolerances are so close. Related to this is the question of relieving the throat. High-intensity cartridges like those in the Weatherby line have long had greater-than-usual freebore in order to reduce pressure spikes at the instant of firing. The bullet jumps across the open space into the rifling, at which point pressure builds up more gradually, as does the bullet's velocity. This jump is not conducive to great accuracy, however (although I have had some Weatherby rifles that left nothing to be desired in that department, in spite of the exaggerated freebore), and it is generally deplored by the super-accuracy crowd.

How does this relate to a dangerous-game rifle? Very simply: All of the above are measures taken to maximize accuracy. However, tight bores, tight chambers, and minimum freebore can lead to difficulties feeding cartridges or extracting cases. In other words, the pursuit of accuracy can result in severely diminished reliability. Such close tolerances can compromise reliability in another way as well: There is no room to accommodate the dirt and dust that inevitably get into the action when hunting. A piece of grit can render a tight mechanism inoperable. For this reason, a little sloppiness is actually desirable, and sloppiness is anathema to the seeker after accuracy.

The argument has been made that a super-accurate dangerous-game rifle increases the chances of a one-shot kill and that, therefore, a second or third shot will be unnecessary. That is a fatuous argument, and every single professional hunter with whom I have discussed this question dismisses it with a wave of the hand. The cult of the one-shot kill—and I plead guilty on all counts—has become as pervasive as the sub-minute accuracy cult. The hunter of dangerous game, especially if he intends to make a career of it, should start immediately to rid himself of such notions.

Today, the Cape buffalo is the most widely hunted of Africa's Big Five. It is the toughest to kill, can be the most dangerous, and is hunted under the widest range of conditions. Because the buffalo is the most numerous and the least expensive to hunt, it is the animal that the first-time safari hunter is most likely to pursue.

One-shot kills on Cape buffalo are more good luck than good shooting. Two animals, shot with the same rifle under identical conditions, taking the bullet in the same place, can react quite differently. One will drop like a stone, the other will plunge into the brush, keep breathing, start to pump adrenalin, and turn into a completely different beast altogether. No one knows why this happens. Could it

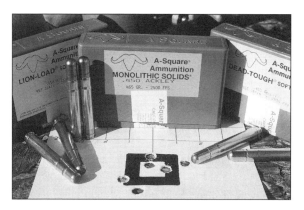

A-Square's Triad system provides three types of ammunition (Monolithic solids, Dead Tough expanding bullets, and ultra-soft Lion Loads) that are guaranteed to shoot to the same point of impact—as the target, shot with a .450 Ackley at 100 yards, clearly shows. Six shots, three different bullet types, factory ammunition, in a group slightly more than two inches. This is fine performance, and more than adequate accuracy for a dangerous-game rifle.

---

be a slight difference in the bullet's angle of entry or a difference in temperament between the two animals? Perhaps one was inhaling when the bullet struck, while the other was exhaling. Who knows? The end result is that no matter how well placed a shot might be, there is no guarantee of a one-shot kill.

As well, a frequent complaint of professional hunters is that Americans tend to take a shot and then watch the animal's reaction rather than immediately chamber a round and plant another bullet after the first. In many cases, this is due to a desire to record a one-shot kill, as if this were somehow a feather in the cap. I have known hunters who will proudly come up to you and exclaim that they have just completed a safari, recorded seven one-shot kills, and are now running a string of twenty-three such kills in a row. This is all well and good, as long as it does not lead to neglecting your primary duty as a hunter, which is to finish off the animal as quickly and humanely as possible, and to do everything you can to ensure that you do not create a situation in which you, your professional hunters, or your trackers may get savaged by a wounded buffalo.

Derek Hurt, with whom I hunted Cape buffalo in Tanzania, says his rule is that as long as the buffalo is on his feet and in sight, the client should keep pumping bullets into him. This is a good rule to follow. On that particular safari, one bull died with four bullets in him, the other with six. In both cases, the first bullet would have killed the bull in a few minutes, but we took no chances.

Obviously, being able to chamber one round after another, quickly and effortlessly, and to keep shooting as long as necessary, is the most desirable quality in a dangerous-game rifle.

* * *

So how accurate should your rifle be? Or to put it another way, how inaccurate can it be and still be acceptable?

Consistent two-inch groups at 100 yards are, in my opinion, more than adequate. A double rifle that will plant bullets from both barrels, shot after shot, into a four-inch group at 50 yards is just fine.

Elephants are shot, generally, at 25 yards or less. So are leopards from a blind, and the range is considerably closer if they are tracked on foot. Cape buffalo can be shot at long range, but a professional hunter will try to get the client to within 75 yards. The longest shot I have ever taken on a Cape buffalo was 175 yards, and the shortest was four feet (and closing). That long shot was highly unusual and would not even have been attempted had I not had supreme confidence in my rifle, which was a .458 Lott on a Dakota action, with a Leupold 1.5-5X scope. That rifle shoots two-inch groups consistently at 100 yards with 500-grain bullets.

With the exception of leopards, dangerous game animals are quite large and have commensurately large vital regions at which to aim. The combination of short range and large targets means that pinpoint accuracy in a rifle is superfluous—and absolutely undesirable if attaining it means compromising the rifle's operation and reliability.

Sights and Sighting

Tear off all the other sighting leaves. They only put you off or get pushed up by accident at the wrong moment, or persuade you that you can kill farther than you thought.

Major H.C. Maydon

The sights on dangerous-game rifles are descended directly from the most basic types first used on muzzleloaders more than a century ago, and for most rifles, these are still about the best: an open rear and a bead front, with the rear a very shallow "V." From there, however, depending on the nature, temperament, and experience of your gunmaker—to say nothing of your willingness to write a check—the sky is the limit.

Given the range of rifles and sights on the market today, the possible combinations are almost endless. Double rifles and bolt actions accommodate (or require) different systems. There are open sights, scopes, a few receiver (aperture) sights, and quick-detachable mounts that allow the shooter to have both available.

Like most shooting tools, sights evolved over many years, their design dictated partly by technology and partly by the demands of the hunter. Anyone outfitting a dangerous-game rifle needs to keep in mind the possibility of a worst-case scenario (a charging animal, in close, in thick bush) and ignore the siren song of long-range capability. Dangerous game is not shot at long range. As Elmer Keith points out, when the animal is at long range, it is not dangerous. A professional hunter will get his client as close as humanly possible to a potentially dangerous animal in order to ensure that the shot goes where it is supposed to. Under normal circumstances, one should consider 150 yards the upper limit. Unless you have very bad eyes, such a shot is possible even with the simplest iron sights.

There is also the consideration that a rifle such as a .375 H&H may be used for more than lions or Cape buffalo and needs to be outfitted accordingly. But, if this is one's primary dangerous-game rifle, its suitability for that task should not be compromised in the interests of shooting, say, elk at long range. Not if one values one's skin.

Open Sights

Open sights are absolutely essential. Every dangerous-game rifle should have them. Some should have nothing else.

As already noted, in their simplest form, open sights consist of a bead front and a "V" rear. At their most complex, the front sight has a large white bead that flips up in front of the small brass bead, for shooting in low light. The sight may have a hood over it to protect it from knocks. The rear sight may have as many as five folding leaves for different distances and be mounted on a quarter-rib that extends along the barrel from the receiver. These are immensely stylish, especially on custom single-shots, and when you marry a quarter-rib to a barrel-band and hooded ramp front sight, the rifle veritably screams "nitro express!"

Is any of this necessary, except to separate the client from his money or to qualify the rifle to win best-of show at an exhibition? No. What's more, a feature that can look absolutely ingenious when you are handling a rifle in a booth at the Safari Club convention can become an irritation and distraction in the bush.

Let us look at all the things that can go wrong. To do this, I will draw on my own experience because, at some point (usually on a shooting range, thank goodness) I have had almost everything happen at least once. I am now to the point where I would like to reduce all my open sights to the simplest possible and then weld the things in place. As long as they direct the bullet reliably out to seventy-five yards, I am more than happy.

To begin with the front bead, hoods are wonderful things and I admire them deeply. I prefer to have them because they do protect the bead. Some criticize hoods because they block out light, which is bad in the bush near darkness (hence the larger folding bead, but we'll get to that). Because of this, hoods are made to be removable, and because they are removable they have a lamentable tendency to flee the scene under stiff recoil.

Faced with this, some sight makers put detents behind the sliding hood, and some of these even work. Other makers merely rely on friction. I have put my faith in epoxy, and it has never let me down, but it does eliminate the removability feature. But then, I have never felt the urge to remove the hood.

The flip-up white bead came along largely to counter the light-blocking tendency of hoods. I remember the first one of these gadgets I ever saw, but I cannot tell you where it is today because it is one of the many bits and pieces that have flown off one of my hard-recoiling rifles, never to be seen again. The sight had a tendency to flip up on its own, and since the bead was held only by a copper band, when it struck the fixed bead it popped out and sailed away. A replacement was epoxied in place, the maker was informed of the problem, and the deficiency was fixed on future rifles by replacing the ring-like band with a copper cup to hold the ivory bead. A better solution is to forget the whole idea.

Well 'nigh perfect: The island rear sight on a Dakota. The 'V' is broad, shallow and fast; the base is simple, and the dovetail for the sight blade wide and solid, with a firm set-screw to ensure it stays in place.

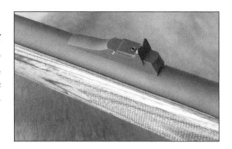

Three approaches to front sights: In the foreground, a Dakota with ramp but no shroud, and a flip-up, large, white bead (partly raised) for low light. The center rifle has a single bead, with a shroud that gives it ample protection yet allows enough to protrude that it catches any light available. The shroud, having parted company with the rifle several times, is now epoxied in place. In the rear, another Dakota with a barrel-band ramp, detachable hood, and flip-up bead. Note the white bead is contained by a copper cup, to keep the insert from being punched out under recoil. The shroud is partly removed to show the bead. The detente holds it firmly in place, even with the jarring recoil of a .458 Lott. Flip-up beads should be tested with full-power loads, to ensure they stay where they are set.   *Photo by Sallie*

Similar problems arise with folding rear leaves. To keep them from flipping up, sight makers install little springs and detents. Generally these work, but they also increase cost substantially. Look at the price of a quarter-rib and folding leaves, and you will see what I mean.

On my .450 Ackley, seeking to maximize durability and minimize expense, I had my gunmaker install a solid-steel rear sight with a blade in a double dovetail with both windage and elevation adjustment. About the third shot, the blade sailed off, and there followed a long process of drilling and tapping for progressively larger set screws until we found one that could be torqued down hard enough to hold the slide in place. So, even choosing a single blade is no guarantee.

The reality of heavy recoil should make you view any intricate adjustment mechanism with infinite suspicion, and you should trust it only after it has been proven to hold up under the recoil of at least fifty full-house rounds. A sight that stands up well on a stalking rifle in 7x65 may have great difficulty withstanding the eyeball-jarring jolt of a big .450.

On its new round-action double rifle, seeking to reduce manufacturing costs to keep the price down to $50,000 (!), Holland & Holland simplified the open sights and, in my opinion, ended up with the perfect arrangement: A fixed-bead front and one solid, fixed-blade rear. The rifle is regulated, the sights are adjusted, and the shooter takes it from there. Solid as a rock, ultra-dependable, and without distractions.

Most blade rear sights depend for windage adjustment on simply tapping the blade back and forth in a dovetail, which works well until you have done it so much that the slide becomes loose. At that point, you need to pay your gunmaker to install a set screw to hold it firmly in place. The moral of this story is, find your heavy load, set your sight in place, and don't fiddle with it unless absolutely necessary.

The same applies to the bead front. These always have dovetails but should never be adjusted. Fix them in the center by whatever means, including solder, epoxy, or electro-welding, and do all your adjustments with the rear sight.

Aperture Sights

Aperture sights are not common on big rifles these days, but there are a few available and some professional hunters prefer them to a scope. They are used almost exclusively on bolt actions and single-shots. The old Lyman 48 and Redfield receiver sights, made for the Winchester Model 70 and various Mausers (and now in serious demand as collector's items) are attached to the side of the receiver and provide fine windage and elevation adjustment. Because of their location, they generally preclude the use of a scope. The shooter must choose one or the other.

The other type of aperture sight is the tang sight commonly seen on Winchester 94s and old black-powder single-shots. These are most emphatically not advised for hard-recoiling rifles, even if you could find one to fit.

If you install an aperture sight, remove the open sight on the barrel. Here, too, you need one or the other, not both. Some old-time hunters said having both made for more exact sighting. The double-sight configuration does not do that, and even if it did, you don't need it. The key to any receiver sight is that you look through the aperture, then simply place the front bead on the target and pull the trigger. The eye automatically centers the bead in the aperture, regardless of how large it is. When receiver sights were in common use, many of the screw-in apertures got lost, and hunters found the sights worked just fine—faster and better, in fact—without them. Jack O'Connor advised readers to throw away the apertures and just look through the large, threaded hole.

Quarter rib with folding leaf sights on a John Rigby & Co. .500 Nitro Express. Such sights are traditional on "best" double rifles.

Front sight of Rigby .500 NE double: Elegantly simple and simply elegant, as well as sturdy, effective, and fast.

New England Custom Gunmaking (NECG) has a receiver sight of its own design, one that fits a Weaver base mounted on the receiver of a bolt-action rifle or into the factory dovetail on a Ruger No. 1. It works quite well. The only problem I have with it (on a No. 1) is that the sight places the aperture too far from the eye for really fast shooting. And because tightening the aperture secures the elevation adjustment, you cannot simply remove it.

Another type of aperture sight, rarely seen today but common years ago, is one that is attached to the end of the striker on a bolt action. Some of these were hinged, and they flipped down out of the way. Others screwed up into position for the range at which one wished to shoot. German gunmakers were particularly fond of these gadgets. They were usually a third sight; the rifle would have open sights for close-range emergencies, a scope for longer ranges under good conditions, and the aperture sight for situations where the scope could not be used, whatever those might be. Such sights led a rough life, since they were hammered every time the rifle was fired and the striker slammed forward. I doubt that this would affect their usefulness, but perhaps that is because I question their usefulness to begin with. The one need they satisfy, as far as I can see, is the deep-seated tribal need of Teutonic gunmakers to complicate things unmercifully.

Scopes

At one time, mounting a scope on a dangerous-game rifle was not only unusual, it was highly suspect. Many professional hunters refused to countenance the idea for a variety of reasons: scopes were simply too fragile; they would either not stand up to recoil or were unable to tolerate the abuse of safari life. Some PHs found them too difficult to put onto the target quickly, because of a small field of view or too much magnification.

With modern scopes, few of these reasons are valid, although many PHs (and not all of them old ones) stick to iron sights. Today, a good scope is every bit as durable as most iron sights, provided—and this is the key—*provided* they are fastened securely in a good scope mount.

A rifle scope for dangerous game should be either a low-power fixed or a low-range variable. If the scope cannot be adjusted down to at least 2X, then it needs to be detachable. Everything is subject to argument, but I believe most professional hunters would agree on that. This is one area where a rifle used by a client for dangerous game and the rifle used by a PH for backing up the client might be considerably different. The client will use a scoped rifle for his first shot on an animal that is relaxed and not expecting trouble, whereas the PH will use his on an animal that has already been shot and is either not down, not going down, on his way into thick bush, or on his way out of thick bush with mayhem in mind.

For a client, a 1-4X scope might serve just fine, and many hunters have them installed on bolt-action rifles, single-shots—even doubles. Many clients are older men whose eyes are not what they used to be; if they are younger, chances are they learned to shoot a rifle with a scope and really don't know any other way. If that is the case, there is every good reason for using a scope and no good reason not to. With the excellent scopes available today, there is certainly no technical reason not to.

But once you have an animal wounded in the bush, the game changes. You then need to be able either to turn the scope to a low power to get onto a charging animal quickly or be able to remove it altogether and use iron sights. Whether the animal will afford you the luxury of doing either is another question.

In terms of dangerous-game rifles, there is no situation I can think of where one might want or need a scope that is greater than 4X, and many situations where 1X or 1.5X would be infinitely preferable. Power aside, a scope should be as light and compact as possible, yet be durable. If there is a better dangerous-game scope than the Leupold Vari-X 1.5-5X, I have yet to see it. It is a compact scope with a one-inch tube, it has a good, simple duplex reticle, and it sits low on the rifle. It is durable to a fault.

Although there is a growing range of scopes with larger-diameter, 30mm tubes—the European favorite—there is rarely any need for one. Their primary virtue is the ability to see the target in low light, when hunting in near-darkness. This situation is highly uncommon in African hunting. Nor is there a need for modern "conveniences" like illuminated reticles with batteries, adjustable lumination, and so on. The one situation where such features *might* be useful is hunting leopards at night in those few places where hunting these animals with lights is permitted. Even this is questionable. If you have a light and it is switched on, then you can place a conventional reticle on the animal as if it were daylight. No illuminated reticle is likely to be useful. No professional hunter will go into the bush after a wounded animal in the dark, and the next day you will not be pursuing your prey with a scoped rifle anyway (assuming you are invited along at all, which is doubtful with a leopard).

Illuminated reticles of various types have become common. The problem they address is the difficulty of making out the reticle in low light. While good optics and a large objective lens can turn near-darkness into near-daylight, it is still hard to see a black reticle against a dark animal. An illuminated reticle seems like a logical answer. Unfortunately, the early ones glowed so brightly that they ruined the shooter's night vision, and the result was that you could see the glowing reticle but nothing else. Today's illuminated reticles are much dimmer—you don't need to be able to read by them, after all—and they are all adjustable. Some of the more esoteric and expensive European creations even have automatic brightness controls that brighten or dim the reticle as the ambient light changes. It all becomes very complicated and is not something I want to depend on if my life is on the line. Fortunately, most of these contraptions are limited to high-power scopes intended for long-range shooting.

When you analyze it, you realize that the chances of needing such a reticle when hunting dangerous game are almost nonexistent to begin with. A PH will not let a client take a shot too close to dark. It is always better to wait until tomorrow. And, as noted earlier, if the animal is wounded and in the bush, you will not go in after it until the next day. The only time an illuminated reticle might be useful is if the animal has a bullet in it, the light is fading, and you have one last shot as it disappears. Weighing that against the need for batteries, adjustments, and the added distraction for the hunter when he should be thinking about seeing the animal and making that last shot count, I would opt for simplicity and a good duplex reticle every time.

The best choice is the reticle you can see most clearly, the one that is least confusing. I prefer a medium-weight duplex, although I have used the European variation, which has thick bars coming in from three or four sides (sometimes they leave out the upper vertical) and features a crosshair in the center. A dot is also good. It depends entirely on what you are comfortable with and can see clearly. The mil-spec reticles that are all the rage, with their rangefinders and scales for calling in air strikes, belong on sniper rifles, not dangerous-game rifles.

In the early '90s, when Swarovski introduced its PH series of scopes, the company equipped its 1.25-4X with a reticle that was both interesting and useful. It consisted of a heavy crosshair inside a circle. The reticle became larger or smaller as the scope's power was changed. At high power, you used the crosshair for exact sighting; at low power, the circle contracted until it appeared to the eye as a heavy dot. The idea was ingenious, and it worked well. The members of the Swarovski family have been serious hunters for many years, and it shows.

So much for functioning on game. What about functioning on your rifle?

There is one excellent reason for using a small, light scope: Recoil. The heavier a scope is, the more it is affected by inertia under recoil. The rifle moves but the scope wants to stay put. Immediately, this applies bending, tearing stress to the scope mounts. They become levers, with the inertia of the scope applying the force. Naturally, the heavier the scope, the greater the force. If the scope has a thick tube and a big objective lens, it sits that much higher above the action. The higher the scope, the longer the lever, and the greater the force. In other words, a big, heavy scope is much more likely to be damaged or flung off your rifle than a smaller, lighter scope that can ride it out.

One of my favorite scopes is an ancient Swarovski 1.5X fixed-power scope with a steel 26mm tube; it is a true oddball, but the optics are clear as a crystal. Some years ago, I got into difficulty with a load for my .450 Ackley using 500-grain bullets and unwise amounts of that most mercurial of powders, H335. It is not recommended for heavy bullets, although it is fine with lighter ones. I did not know that then, but I do now. One shot caused the rifle's floorplate to fly open; the second shot also shook the reticle loose in the scope. It was a crosshair, and when I looked again it was a fine line flanked by two dangling wires. A trip to Swarovski and several months later, I got my scope back and it has worked beautifully ever since. This episode shows what recoil can do to even the best rifle scope.

What about the question of variable versus fixed power? I like fixed-power scopes, but here's the situation: Scope technology has progressed immensely in the last twenty years, but has been applied almost exclusively to variables. The progress that has made scopes lighter, stronger, more durable, waterproof, fog-proof—everything-proof—has not really been applied to fixed-power scopes. Everything being equal, a fixed-power is optically superior and more durable, but in reality everything is not equal.

One bright spot on the horizon is the increasing use of scopes on shotguns, and the ever-expanding number of jurisdictions that demand shotguns for deer hunting. Shotguns use heavy slugs, which, in a seven-pound gun, create some very hefty recoil. Manufacturers are trying to make scopes suitable for the short ranges at which deer and turkey hunters shoot, while allowing for stiff recoil at the same time. Some of these scopes may work well on a big-bore rifle.

Having said all that, the simplest and smallest variable is still preferable for dangerous game. Parallax correction is not needed, nor is a rangefinder. Any kind of complicated reticle, or illuminated reticle, is not necessary, and you should eschew anything that requires a battery. The new scopes that offer a choice of four settings for four different loads, or that allow the scope to be moved among

The EAW swing mount has many of the virtues of the claw, at less than half the cost. It can be removed easily with one hand, without looking down, by lifting the small lever and swinging the scope 90 degrees to release the front dovetail. Return to zero is excellent, and it is very strong.

The rear base of a classic German claw. The knurled catch slides to the rear to release the claw, which lifts up and allows the front claw to pull free. This can be done without looking, and really without thought. It can be replaced the same way almost as easily.

four different rifles without resighting belong many places, but your dangerous-game rifle is not one of them. They are too complicated, and they offer too much of an opportunity to choose the wrong setting at the wrong time.

Detachable Scope Mounts

Think of a spear, that most basic of hunting implements. Think of the joint between the spearhead and the shaft. That joint is the weak link in the system and one that Man, over thousands of years, strove to perfect. Now, try to imagine a configuration that is strong enough to withstand being flung, thrust, stepped on by mammoths, and chewed by saber-toothed tigers, *and* is easily detached so the spear heads can be interchanged.

That is essentially the problem faced by makers of scope mounts, particu-

DANGEROUS-GAME RIFLES

larly those who make detachables. Today's rifle scope is every bit as durable and dependable as any iron sight—more so in some cases—but the Achilles heel is the mount. While manufacturers can create mounts strong enough for big rifles, it is difficult to create one that is both detachable and strong.

The word "detachable" means different things to different people. On a big rifle, you need a mount that allows you to remove your scope and put it back on, easily, with a return to zero every time—no adjustments, no fiddling, no sighting shots. This is the principle behind the king of detachable mounts, the German claw mount, as well as Holland & Holland's own system for bolt actions.

Not all so-called "detachable" mounts work that way.

When I first began investigating detachable mounts in the late 1980s, there were only four or five types available. Since then, as they have become increasingly popular, variations have sprouted like daisies in May. Some work well, others not so well. Some are suited to heavy recoil, but most are not. Finally, when my first articles about detachable mounts were published, a few makers wrote to insist that their mounts should have been included because they were detachable. This they were, as long as you had a screwdriver and were prepared to scratch reference marks on the mount so you could put the scope back on and line it up. This is the kind of blurring of the term that has occurred, and if you have your gunmaker install detachable mounts on your rifle, it is worth as much attention as choosing the caliber.

One of the simplest, strongest, and cheapest mounts ever developed is the Weaver, and because of this, it is the most common. It could be argued that it is a detachable mount, since the large screws that clamp the rings to the base can be turned with a coin or a cartridge rim. Certainly the scope can be taken off in a hurry, if you have a suitable coin, but it cannot be reaffixed with any certainty that the zero has not changed, because once it is off the rifle the clamping screws are free to get completely out of whack. This is what I mean about the variable definition of "detachable."

Now consider the opposite case.

The German claw mount, developed originally for drillings, has hefty steel claws on each ring—one pair facing forward, the other aft. The front set fits into matching slots on a base, clamped securely by a steel shelf; the rear set presses down into another set of slots with a spring-loaded catch very much like the sliding bolt with a set of Purdey underlugs. The scope can be removed easily by feel without even looking at it and can be replaced on the rifle exactly the same way. A good claw mount snaps into place with a solid *thunk*.

Claw mounts have been around since prehistory, in gun terms. For a double rifle, they are the only real option. Single-shots also use them (especially the elegant Continental break-action stalking rifles), and they are available for bolt actions. The drawback to the claw mount is cost. Today (2005), a set of claw

— 298 —

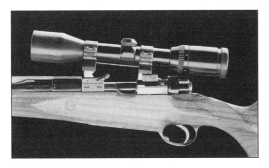

H&H detachable scope mount. Similar in operation to the German claw mount, the H&H variation uses one large lug front and back, and the bases are attached to the side of the receiver rather than the top. It is extremely strong, dependable, and returns to zero almost perfectly. This mount has become standard among British makers of large-bore bolt actions, but is rarely seen elsewhere—largely because it is very expensive and difficult to make. *Courtesy Holland & Holland*

mounts installed on a rifle will cost between $1,500 and $2,000. A portion of this is the parts, but most is labor. Installing claw mounts is a job for the skilled gunmaker, not the local mechanic. The first set I ever had was installed by my old German gunmaker, Siegfried Trillus, who silver-soldered the bases to the receiver as well as screwing them into place. Those mounts are going nowhere. Most gunsmiths are aghast at this practice, insisting that the heat involved in silver soldering will soften and ruin the action. Siegfried dismissed this, saying that if you knew how to use heat sinks there was no problem.

That mount has been on my FN Supreme-actioned .450 Ackley for fifteen years with nary a problem. Were I able to afford it, I would put claw mounts on every rifle I own, but they are just too expensive. If money is no object, however, claw mounts are definitely the way to go.

The H&H system mentioned above is derived from the claw mount, adapted to the Mauser 98. It uses one heavy claw front and back, and the bases are installed on the side of the receiver. Instead of a spring-loaded catch at the rear, it uses a swinging lever to lock the scope firmly into place. The whole mechanism is a masterpiece of the gunmaker's art. Unfortunately, this fine system is available only on custom rifles, either from H&H or a handful of top-notch independent custom makers.

The first such mount I ever saw was on Tony Henley's .375 H&H rifle, which he used as a professional hunter for thirty or forty years. At that point, it was as solid as the day he took delivery, although there was not a trace of bluing left.

Each of these systems works the same way: You move just one catch, then lift to remove the scope and press down to reinstall it. By the way, claw mounts are made in a variety of configurations to accommodate all kinds of actions and scopes. A scope with a large objective lens out front cannot pivot down very far, so sometimes the ring is put on the objective lens itself rather than the tube, and the base is located out on the barrel; other times the system can be reversed so that the scope lifts up from the front. None of these variations is as good for a danger-ous-game rifle, but it shows that the basic claw principle can accommodate almost any combination of gun and scope. All it takes is a skilled gunmaker.

The other common German approach, and the one usually chosen for a custom rifle where the buyer wants to avoid the expense of a claw, is the EAW swing mount. There are other makes that are similar, but the design is associat-ed with EAW. It combines a front dovetail with a locking mechanism on the rear base, controlled by a little spring-loaded lever. To remove the scope, you lift the lever to unlock the rear and rotate the scope ninety degrees, freeing the front dovetail. This system is neither as elegant nor convenient as the claw, but it works well and returns the scope to zero every time—or at least as close as you need for a big rifle.

Some accuracy-obsessed rifle smiths insist that no detachable mount returns absolutely to zero, and a few have gone to great pains to prove this with extensive tests. Fine, I have no argument with this position. But the point is, on a dangerous-game rifle, there are bigger considerations than a return to absolute zero and shooting tiny groups. For our purposes, these are as close as one needs.

Even the EAW swing mount is not cheap, and for those who want a sim-ilar system at lower cost, there is one readily available: the basic Leupold dove-tail combined with a Pilkington lever. Cliff Pilkington is the gunsmith who developed this variation. The scope attaches front and back with standard Leupold bases. The rear base, which has a screw on either side to adjust for windage, is altered. The left screw is replaced by a lever with one flat side, while the right screw is pinned in place to keep it from moving when the scope is off the rifle. To remove the scope, the lever is rotated 180 degrees, allowing the scope to swing out over the flat side of the lever. This frees the dovetail, in a manner similar to that of the EAW mounts.

Looking at the Pilkington lever, one might think it is not very strong. After all, the scope is held at the rear by nothing more than the thin lips of two screws (or a screw and a lever) that slide over a shallow groove in the stem of the ring. The secret is that this fastening point is not where stress occurs, and so it does not need to be Herculean to work well. I had a Pilkington lever on a .416 Weatherby, with a muzzle brake, and it held up just fine. It is not a good system for a professional hunter's working rifle, but for the sport hunter of dangerous game it is adequate.

The reason I would not recommend it for a hard-working rifle is that the parts, especially the lever, are vulnerable when the scope is off the rifle. This is a factor that should be taken into account in assessing any system: Does it have moving parts that can go out of adjustment, or delicate parts that can be damaged by wear and tear when the scope is bouncing around in the glove box, or the rifle is being carried through the bush? If so, it may be fine for occasional use but is not a good long-term investment for a professional.

* * *

This brings us to the second group of detachable mounts, which share one feature: Each ring is released separately, either from a Weaver-style base or a rail or an individual base like the Leupold. Typically, a little lever is used to lock each ring in place, so two separate movements are required to release the scope. Replacing the scope generally requires that the shooter look down as he positions the ring posts in the bases, or slides the scope onto the rail, before tightening down each lever. As well, when the scope is off the rifle, the levers should be either tightened up to keep them from coming off, or at least turned to a position where they are out of the way.

Talley mounts are the most common of the type, and are found on many fine rifles—Dakota and Empire, to name two. The most recent Talleys have a rail-type base with a solid bar that prevents movement forward and aft under recoil if, for some reason, the fasteners come loose. The scope does not slide onto the rail, it rocks on from the side, like a Weaver.

Leupold came out with its own detachable rings in the late 1980s. These had small posts on the rings that fit into matching holes in the bases, and a short (very short!) lever tightened them down. I had this system on a .458 Winchester, hunting Cape buffalo in Tanzania in 1993, and discovered an unfortunate trait of such mounts: Under recoil, the levers tightened themselves to the point where it was impossible to loosen them with finger pressure to remove the scope. Pliers would do it, but not everyone carries pliers when hunting. I found myself facing a charging buffalo with the scope still on the rifle, but since that ended with me shooting from the hip, it was not a factor. Since then, Leupold has lengthened the levers to make them easier to manipulate.

For sheer looks, Conetrol mounts are the most elegant available for a fine custom rifle. They are finicky in the extreme to install, but once you get them right, they are smooth and sleek. Conetrols are also very strong. The company now makes a hand-detachable model, but removal of the scope requires a small screwdriver or key. For a dangerous-game rifle, that alone rules them out.

There are other detachable scope mounts, but the vast majority are intended for rifles of relatively light recoil. Anyone intending to use such a mount on a dangerous-game gun should investigate thoroughly before doing so, then very carefully test the whole assembly before departing for Africa or Alaska. If a scope is going to part company with your rifle under recoil, it will generally give some indication in the first five or ten shots; if it withstands fifty full-house rounds with no sign of stress, it will probably handle the next five hundred with aplomb.

Scope mounts are the weak link in the whole system, but when you analyze it, you will see that the problem is even more exact than that. The rings themselves fasten very securely to the scope and almost become part of it. The bases fasten likewise to the rifle. The weak point is where the rings fasten to the bases. Really strong systems, like dovetails, are of limited use here if you want instant detachability. If, for whatever reason, a shooter wants a rock-solid, nondetachable base that is as strong as possible, the Leupold double-dovetail is the ticket. With a dovetail front and back, and the scope fitted after the rings are installed, nothing will move it.

To see where the stress occurs on a scope mount, imagine riding in a car and slamming on the brakes. The front end rocks forward and down, and the rear lifts up; as the car settles back, the sequence occurs in reverse. This is exactly the same motion a scope wants to make as the rifle recoils to the rear beneath it. There is then stress in the other direction as the reaction sets in. This is why the most important fastening point is under the front ring and why the rear ring on a Leupold mount can be held securely with relatively light tackle.

In case anyone thinks equipping a rifle with a muzzle brake (which reduces felt recoil) will make it easier on the scope, think again: In fact, the brake increases the stress on the scope mounts. The rifle still recoils, but instead of completing that motion and then settling back, the gases jetting out of the brake jerk the rifle forward almost instantly. Only after this motion subsides does the rifle finally settle back to the rear. So, with a brake there are three distinct stress motions, not just two, and the second is almost as violent as the first. It is a good scope mount indeed that will cheerfully cope with life on a hard-recoiling, fully braked rifle.

For this reason, bases must be securely screwed (or silver soldered) to the receiver, with the screws very snug and held in place with Loctite. When you return from the range after the first session of shooting with a newly installed scope, take it off and check every base screw to see if they have loosened in the least. This should be a periodic habit henceforth. Loctite is generally not recommended for the screws that hold the rings on the scope itself, because they need to be carefully tightened, alternately and a bit at a time, to prevent uneven stresses on the tube. Still, they should be very snug and should be checked regularly. When you prepare your cleaning kit for your hunting trip, make sure you have the right screwdrivers to check all the screws in your scope mount when you reach your destination. Do not depend on your professional hunter to have the right tools.

In Africa one time, another client's rifle suddenly went strange, not putting subsequent bullets within six inches of each other. It was a tried-and-true .375 H&H, and he was at his wit's end. As it turned out, the scope rings were loose, and the scope was free to slide back and forth, twisting and turning as it went. We then had to find a screwdriver to fit.

The front sight of a Heym double rifle. Hoods are not uncommon, although opinion on their utility is mixed. Criticism generally centers on the reduced visibility and difficulty seeing the bead in low light. Sometimes they are removable; sometimes they remove themselves when you least desire it. Either way, they require some attention to ensure they function dependably

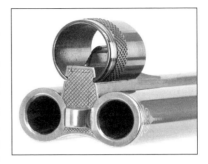

under heavy recoil. On balance, I like hoods because they do protect the bead.

RCMP Photo

Two basic, simple, sturdy front sights on Merkel double rifles. For sheer dependability, such sights are hard to beat. The sight on the right has a luminous plastic insert for increased visibility in low light. Not traditional, but certainly functional.

Photo courtesy GSI

A simple, sturdy leaf rear sight on a quarter rib, standard on all Merkel double rifles. The standing leaf is regulated for 50 meters, the folding leaf for 100.

If you run into a situation where your scope rings simply will not stay tight and you have no Loctite, a drop of some cola product works wonders, as does hot urine. Don't ask me how I know this. When you get home, though, you will probably need the services of a gunsmith to get the screws out. And it's not pretty.

* * *

In the early years of telescopic sights, they were generally fragile and their optical quality was poor except in good light. Iron sights were used all the time, while the telescope was carried separately in a leather case and installed only under certain conditions.

As scopes became better, manufacturers developed alternate methods that still allowed the use of iron sights. There were see-through mounts, with the scope mounted high so the shooter could see beneath it. There were hinged mounts that swung out of the way and side mounts that put the scope off center, leaving a clear view of the iron sights. Occasionally one still sees such rigs on old rifles in Africa—a testament to their durability, at least—but they have all but disappeared on modern rifles.

The most usual arrangement today is a scope that is left on the rifle all the time and is removed only under special circumstances. The iron sights are for emergency use—either when the scope breaks or is unsuitable for the conditions (such as a wounded animal in thick brush, with ranges short and visibility limited).

With a good detachable mount, a hunter can remove the scope for traveling, wrapping it in thick cushioning and packing it separately from the rifle. I believe this is a good idea, as it effectively precludes the possibility that a jarring fall of the gun case will cause the scope to go out of whack. This is rare today anyway—the scope going out of whack, that is, not the flinging of gun cases by airline handlers.

One approach that is becoming common is to have two scopes for the same rifle, each mounted in its own rings. One might be of lower power. This is a sound idea, especially for a more versatile rifle like a .375 H&H. When you arrive in camp, your professional hunter will want you to check your sighting. He will wedge a piece of cardboard into an anthill and drive off about a hundred yards, put the seat cushion over the hood of the safari car, and invite you to have at it. Two things to remember: First, all it takes is one shot to show that your scope has not been jarred out of alignment; second, such confirmation is strictly secondary in the eyes of the PH. His real reason for having you do this is to see how you handle your rifle.

In the unlikely event that your scope has been jarred out of alignment, it will be off by a lot, not just by an inch or two. So, if your shot is a few inches off center, do not start adjusting your settings; more than likely it is just rifle wobble or a slight flinch. To be on the safe side, however, always pack enough ammunition that you can, in a genuine emergency, resight the rifle.

If a young and overzealous PH tries to grab your rifle and start fiddling with the scope adjustments, either shoot him or brain him with it. It's your rifle, your life, and—if you are properly prepared—your territory. Relations with one's professional hunter could fill a book, but when it comes to your rifle, keep a firm grip on it. Just because some teenaged farm boy from Namibia has been given a PH license does not make him a gunsmith (although most think they are). One hopes you will not be hunting anything dangerous with such a professional anyway, but . . .

There are tales of clients who arrive in safari camps with brand-new rifles and boxes containing new scopes and mounts. They ask their long-suffering professional to mount the scopes for them because they did not have time or because the rifle arrived late. It is one thing to do this while hunting pronghorns and quite another if you are hunting grizzly bears or elephants. Mounting a scope on a hard-bucking, big-bore rifle and having it stay put is a painstaking task and not one to be left until the last minute.

Recoil, Weight, and Balance

In selecting a heavy calibre rifle, it is most essential to see that the rifle is well balanced. If not, you will never like it or shoot to do you justice. It will always have that "crowbar" feeling about it and appear to be pounds heavier than it really is.

J. A. Hunter

With a heavy rifle, the greatest enemy of good shooting is recoil—the equal and opposite reaction dictated by the laws of physics when a heavy bullet is ejected from the muzzle at high speed. The bullet goes one way, the rifle goes the other. The heavier the bullet and the higher its velocity, the greater the recoil energy that must be absorbed by the rifle and the man holding it.

I say "by the rifle" because the gun can absorb a certain amount of recoil energy if it is heavy enough. The heavier the rifle, the less recoil is felt by the shooter.

There are many aspects to recoil. There is the thrust that punches the rifle into the shooter's shoulder. There is muzzle jump, which throws the end of the barrel into the air and slams the shooter's cheekbone with the comb of the stock. Sometimes the trigger guard will punish the second finger of the trigger hand hard enough to cause bone bruises, swelling, and lifelong sensitivity. Finally, there is noise. The *crash* of a heavy rifle, especially in a confined area, causes headaches, permanent hearing loss, and an almost painful gun-shyness. Muzzle blast, as it is called, is the forgotten villain of recoil—underestimated in its effect, and often exacerbated by efforts to reduce recoil itself.

Throughout the history of hunting—especially in Africa, where big guns have been the order of the day since Europeans encountered the first elephant—there are stories of horrendous recoil wreaking havoc with a man's shooting. The most famous case of injury caused by recoil—physical and psychological—is Frederick Courteney Selous. Selous arrived in Africa with a rifle made by the well-known London gunsmith, E. M. Reilly. It was stolen, so Selous was forced to make do with one he bought locally, and he took such a pounding from the ill-fitting gun that he developed a flinch that plagued him the rest of his life. Selous was frank about the affliction. He saw no shame in it (unlike many today, who would sooner admit to pederasty than confess to a flinch). Late in life, he gave up "big" rifles in favor of a smaller one—a .505 Gibbs built on a single-shot Farquharson action, made by George Gibbs of Bristol. If that was Selous's idea of a light rifle, he was certainly entitled to a flinch.

The word "flinch" covers a multitude of shooting sins. While a flinch may be induced by a few shots of great recoil, it can also result from hundreds of shots of relatively light recoil. Trap shooters understand this, and they go to great lengths to reduce recoil. One flinch resulting in one lost bird can lose a match and thousands of dollars. Hence the determination to forestall it. Trap guns are heavy and trap loads are light, so recoil is relatively tame. Yet hundreds of rounds, day after day, can induce a flinch that becomes a lifelong affliction, sometimes ending in the complete inability to pull a trigger.

Shooting a heavy rifle usually induces the kind of flinch that causes a shooter to cringe away from the gun at the instant of firing and to yank the trigger rather than squeezing it smoothly. Jerking the trigger in this way almost always pulls the muzzle off-target, and cringing at the moment of firing does the same thing. Once a flinch has a hold on you, it is difficult to reverse.

* * *

There are two types of recoil. The laws of physics may not admit them, but practical shooters are well aware of them, and this is why formulae that reduce recoil to foot-pounds are less than helpful. Aside from being extraordinarily complicated, there are so many variables in the formulae that they are unlikely to give any meaningful number. A difference of two pounds in rifle weight makes the result look completely different, as does a change in muzzle velocity.

However:

- A 570-grain bullet fired at 2,150 fps from a .500 NE will generate 74 ft. lbs. of recoil.
- A 500-grain bullet fired at 2,600 fps from a .460 Weatherby will generate 100 ft. lbs. of recoil.

There is only an 8 percent difference in muzzle energy (7,000 ft. lbs. versus 7,500) but a 33 percent increase in recoil energy. If you reduce bullet weight further, to 300 grains, and increase velocity to 2,900 fps, as in the .378 Weatherby, muzzle energy drops, as does calculated recoil energy. That said, the .378 has (to me) the most unpleasant recoil of the three. Why? Because the bullet is moving *faster*. The recoil is compressed into a shorter space of time, making it much more jarring. This is why a .300 Weatherby firing a 150-grain bullet at 3,500 fps has more unpleasant recoil than the same rifle firing a 220-grain bullet at 2,700 fps.

What we see, comparing the .500 NE, .460 Weatherby, and .378 Weatherby, is a simultaneous reduction in bullet weight, an increase in velocity, and a *drastic* increase in discomfort level.

By controlling velocity, we can limit recoil to some extent. Every rifle has a threshold beyond which recoil becomes seriously unpleasant. Keep velocity below that threshold and you have a relatively comfortable load to shoot. In the case of the .458 Lott or .450 Ackley (the two dangerous-game cartridges with which I have the most experience) this threshold is about 2,250 fps with a 500-grain bullet. Certainly, both rifles can be stoked to much higher velocities, but do the benefits outweigh the drawbacks? Personally, I do not think so, and I keep my loads below that level.

Every rifle and cartridge combination has its own threshold that can be identified only by shooting it, but it is worthwhile to find out exactly what that threshold is and then keep your standard load just below it. It is much easier on the rifle, it reduces the chance of a malfunction such as a stuck bolt, and it allows more precise shooting.

As far as the rifle itself is concerned, there are two major factors that govern recoil. First is weight. To me, no dangerous-game rifle should weigh less than nine pounds, or (with a couple of exceptions) more than eleven pounds. Nine pounds fully loaded with scope and sling is just about perfect for a .375 H&H. A .500 Nitro Express double should weigh, ideally, ten and a half pounds, give or take an ounce. Everything else should fall in between. The exceptions are the seriously big doubles—the .577 NE and .600 NE. A .577 generally weighs twelve to fourteen pounds, while a .600 is fourteen to sixteen. Holland's huge .700 usually weighs nineteen pounds, but that behemoth (expensive though it is) hardly qualifies as a hunting rifle.

The other major factor in recoil is fit. An ill-fitting rifle, with a stock that is too short or bent to the wrong side, or that features too much drop, can become a kicking monster that will induce a flinch in record time, regardless of weight.

John Taylor had this to say about the relationship between rifle balance, stock fit, and felt recoil:

> Balance . . . minimizes to an enormous extent the degree to which recoil is felt, because no effort is required to hold the rifle at your shoulder and therefore your own muscles act as the finest of all recoil pads. In the same way, if the stock is of the right length and bend it permits you to mount the rifle correctly for every shot so that the butt beds properly into your shoulder. If the butt is well into your shoulder the rifle can't kick you; it can only shove—a shove can't hurt.

In 1993, I had a graphic demonstration of this at the Holland & Holland shooting ground when I was test-firing some double rifles. They included a .375 H&H, a .500/465, a .500 NE, and a .700. According to folklore, the .500/465 has less recoil than a .470 (although the two are ballistically identical) and considerably less than the .500. In this case, the .500/465 had a kick that was jarring and unpleasant. I then fired the .500, which was quite comfortable. I thought perhaps it was all relative—that after firing the .700, anything would seem tame. Yet, when I fired them both a second time, the .500/465 was still very unpleasant, while the .500 was still very nice. The difference was stock fit. Both were custom rifles, but the .500 was being made for a client just about my size. It fit me, and rifle and body absorbed the recoil without a murmur.

We have all heard of shotguns that are apparently identical, yet one kicks like the devil while the other is a pussycat. The same is true of double rifles. London gunmakers understand how to fit a double rifle so that recoil is reduced to a minimum without resorting to other means (which we shall get to shortly). Not all makers of double rifles, however, have this understanding of fit and recoil.

A lesser factor with recoil is barrel length. A longer barrel adds weight both overall and at the muzzle, reducing muzzle jump and helping to absorb recoil. It also moves the muzzle blast farther away from the shooter's ears, making it seem less severe. Obviously, one can carry this too far in both directions, but it is something to keep in mind when specifying barrel length. To my mind, twenty-two inches is about ideal for most bolt actions, while twenty-six inches is good for a double rifle. As always, there are exceptions. The .378 Weatherby, for example, would be an utter beast with a twenty-two-inch barrel, aside from failing to deliver anything near its alleged ballistics. A bottleneck case that size requires a barrel twenty-six inches long in order to ensure complete powder ignition. If you insist on a shorter barrel, you might as well go to a more compact cartridge.

While on the subject of rifle fit, three other design features can make recoil seem less severe. One is a longer length of pull. The average American factory rifle has a length of pull of less than fourteen inches. Increasing this to fourteen inches-plus moves your trigger hand farther from your face; it also moves the scope farther from the eye. The longer pull, combined with a more gradual pistol grip, keeps the second finger away from the trigger guard, reducing the chance of it being whacked. The third design feature is a comparatively straight stock, rather than the exaggerated drop seen on early bolt actions (which were a holdover from black-powder days). Excessive drop aggravates muzzle jump, whereas a straight stock minimizes the fulcrum effect and causes the rifle to recoil more in a straight line. Most of us would rather absorb recoil with our shoulder than our jaw or cheekbone, so a straight stock makes recoil feel more comfortable even if, mathematically, it does not reduce recoil one whit.

Adding a recoil pad goes without saying, but recoil pads are not all created equal. They can be thick, thin, wide, narrow, hard, or soft. The butt of a big-bore rifle should be wider than normal, deeper than normal (from heel to toe), with a thicker-than-normal recoil pad. This spreads the impact over a larger area. Many custom rifles have stocks that are very slim and elegant—beautiful in a .270 but not so wonderful in a .458. By increasing the dimensions of the butt-stock, the gunmaker can make the comb wider, with a broad, smooth radius that is easy on the cheek even when muzzle jump is severe. Having a sharp comb—narrow, coming almost to a point—is a guaranteed flinch inducer.

One more note on recoil pads: Rubber deteriorates over time, and sunshine is particularly damaging. If you buy a used rifle that is more than a few years old, give some thought to replacing the recoil pad with a new one. Not only are today's recoil pads vastly better than the old ones (the Pachmayr Decelerator is an excellent example of improved design), but also fresh rubber is softer and rebounds better. And if you are replacing the pad, you can use that opportunity to adjust the length of pull to whatever suits you. This step alone can make a world of difference.

All of these factors can, when put together by a good gunmaker, add up to a level of *felt* recoil that is neither unduly disturbing nor likely to induce a flinch.

A rifle that attempts to include all of the above (and more) and uses reduced recoil as a selling point is the A-Square Hannibal. It is fitted with a stock that is massive to the point of awkwardness. The Hannibal's stock more closely resembles that of an offhand target rifle than one made for hunting. It is broad, long, and deep. The butt is deep and wide, with a thick, soft recoil pad; recoil to the rear is almost in a straight line. Altogether, recoil is reduced by every means possible short of a muzzle brake or stock insert, and the result is a rifle that is relatively comfortable to shoot even in calibers like the .416 Rigby. The catch is that the rifle itself is heavy and awkward—like a gas pipe lashed to a railroad tie. The Hannibals are indisputably accurate and reliable, with minimal recoil, but the handling is anything but dynamic—and to me, dynamic handling is an essential quality in a dangerous-game rifle.

But there are hunters, including many professionals, who own A-Square Hannibal rifles and swear by them, and I cannot argue with that.

Muzzle Brakes

There have been several trends in rifles over the past twenty years. One is to lighter weight, another is to higher velocities. A third is to the creation of factory and wildcat big-bore cartridges that shade even the old nitro-express rounds in terms of power. Obviously, if all of these trends converge in one rifle, you will have a beast with recoil that is almost unbearable. Even the *thought* of shooting a .458 Lott in a six-pound rifle makes me flinch.

Makers of light rifles have tried two approaches to reducing recoil. The

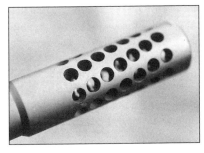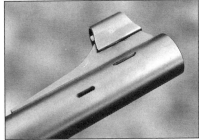

Two approaches to muzzle brakes: Left is a detachable brake on a Kenny Jarret rifle, typical of the most common type. While felt recoil is reduced, muzzle blast is increased dramatically and point of impact can change significantly when the brake is removed. On the right is a Mag-Na-Port modified system of two slots on each side of the front sight. These do not increase muzzle blast noticeably, nor do they reduce straight-back recoil; their purpose (and they do it well) is to moderate the muzzle jump. This reduces the flinch-inducing impact on the cheek, and allows the shooter to get back on target more quickly.

most common is the muzzle brake. As well, different types of recoil-absorbing inserts are put into the buttstock to act as shock absorbers.

Muzzle brakes work by redirecting gases from the burning gunpowder out of the muzzle at an angle—upward, to reduce muzzle jump, and slightly to the rear, to counter the backward movement of the rifle itself. There is no doubt that a muzzle brake can reduce felt recoil to almost nothing, depending on the rifle and cartridge in question. In ballistics, however, there is never—repeat, *never*— a free lunch. What you receive over here, you must pay for over there. A 500-grain bullet exiting the muzzle at 2,250 fps generates a certain amount of energy and an equal and opposite reaction. That reaction has to go somewhere. If it does not go here, it must go there.

Muzzle brakes have been common on target pistols—even .22 rimfire pistols with minuscule recoil—since the 1950s, but they really became a factor on big rifles in the mid-1980s. They were touted as the ultimate answer to the recoil problem. As with most such developments, they did not live up to the early promises; what's more, as shooters gained experience with them, unexpected new problems were identified.

The major drawback to any muzzle brake is dramatically increased muzzle blast. The noise generated by a big rifle with a muzzle brake must be heard to be believed. In an enclosed space, it can be physically painful, even with the finest hearing protection.

In 1990, I obtained one of the first .416 Weatherby rifles to come out of

South Gate, California, and took it to Africa to hunt Cape buffalo. The rifle had a detachable muzzle brake, but I left it on the rifle throughout load development, sighting in, and practice. Shooting the rifle from a bench on a covered firing line was seriously disconcerting for those around me, and I tried to ensure that I was alone on the line before firing. In Tanzania, hunting without ear protection, the blast was deafening. Robin Hurt, Finn Aagaard, and I all experienced ringing in our ears after I pulled the trigger—the unmistakable indication that we had just destroyed a bit of our hearing. That was in 1990. By 1996, muzzle brakes had become common, but so had damaged hearing among the African trackers and gun bearers, who are usually off to the side when the rifle is fired. Now, many professional hunters are insisting that their clients either bring a rifle without a muzzle brake or remove it when hunting, in order to protect their hearing and that of their men.

Almost all muzzle brakes are removable, but even this does not solve all the problems. Some hunters do load development and practice with the brake on, then remove it when hunting. Anyone who follows this procedure *must* check the sighting of his rifle with the brake off, because removing it can cause the center of impact to shift dramatically. The muzzle begins to rise the instant the bullet starts to move; reducing that muzzle movement obviously changes the point of impact. I have seen an impact change of up to eight inches at 100 yards, and I have heard of others experiencing a change of eighteen inches! A lesser problem may be groups opening up. A barrel vibrates differently without a brake than with it, and this may cause a group to get larger; conversely (if you are lucky), it may get smaller. Either way, the result without the brake will not be the same as with it.

Recognizing this problem, some rifle makers now claim that their brakes reduce recoil without increasing muzzle blast, but I have never seen a device that actually lived up to the marketing hype.

There is a middle ground, which is a brake that only partially redirects recoil. Years ago, Mag-Na-Port introduced a system (non-removable) consisting of two small slots milled into each side of the muzzle behind the front sight. This was intended only to reduce muzzle jump, not to reduce recoil itself, and it did so with minimal increase in muzzle blast. I installed this system on a .450 Ackley and can attest to the fact that muzzle jump was substantially reduced. Whether blast increased or not I cannot say; it does not seem any worse than it was before, nor any worse than a comparable .458 Lott that has no brake at all.

A final note on muzzle brakes: Not one of them actually reduces recoil. How could they? Energy cannot be destroyed. What they do is redirect it or reconfigure it so that it *seems* less. In reconfiguring recoil, the brake may actually increase the stress on the rifle or, more particularly, the scope mount. The scope mount on a hard-recoiling rifle is the most fragile and vulnerable part of the whole system. As the rifle tries to kick out from under the scope, and inertia forces the scope to resist movement, it is up to the scope mount to hold it all together through the stress of recoil and the anti-recoil that follows—a process that can be likened to whiplash. Add the effect of a muzzle brake, and you turn whiplash into a three-part (rather than two-part) stress of the scope mount as the rifle moves back, is jerked forward by the brake, and then relaxes.

Recoil Reducers

Trap shooters have for years used different types of inserts in buttstocks and have even used stocks in two pieces connected by a shock absorber. Most of the inserts consist of a cylinder filled with mercury, which presents great resistance to movement. The inertia of the mercury supposedly absorbs recoil energy or at least spreads it out over a longer period of time. Perhaps the sophisticated measuring instruments of a ballistic laboratory could prove that these things work, but I am unable to see it in practical terms. The fact that the inserts themselves weigh about a pound apiece suggests to me that any real effect on recoil is achieved by increasing the weight of the rifle, not through the inertia of the mercury.

Over the years, I have had two rifles with such inserts. One was a bolt-action .375 H&H; the other a .500 Nitro Express double. I did not ask for the insert with either rifle, and eventually got rid of them in both. I found the gurgling sound of the mercury to be profoundly irritating, but that was the least of the problem.

In the .500, the inserts not only increased the weight of the rifle from just under eleven pounds to twelve and a half pounds, they also drastically altered the balance of the gun. The rifle was unnaturally butt-heavy. When I took the rifle apart, the buttstock practically plunged to the floor because of almost two pounds of steel and mercury contained therein. At the same time, the recoil was unpleasant—far more so than it should have been in such a heavy-for-caliber rifle. I was in the process of preparing said rifle for an expedition to Tanzania when I happened to find myself in England, at the Holland & Holland Shooting Ground, with an hour to spare and access to one of the new H&H round-action .500s and a dozen rounds of ammunition.

I doubt that there is any company in the world that knows more about double rifles, recoil, and balance than Holland & Holland. The round-action rifle weighed almost exactly 10.5 pounds—precisely what John Taylor says a .500 should weigh. Yet it seemed lighter. It was well-balanced but slightly muzzle heavy—just the way I like it. What's more, it had a very thin recoil pad of quite hard rubber, not more than a half-inch thick. After a dozen shots, I was still pulling the trigger with relatively little jerking, my middle finger had not started to swell, and my cheek was not red and puffy. Yet, this rifle was almost two pounds lighter than my own .500. What was the difference? Balance. When I got home, I immediately took my .500 to my friendly rifle maker, Edwin von Atzigen, and had him remove the two recoil reducers.

My Rigby .500 now weighed eleven pounds—not quite what I wanted, but still a vast improvement. Most important, the balance had shifted dramatically to the muzzle. On the range, it was significantly more comfortable to shoot than it had been, in spite of the weight reduction. I concluded that the extra weight in the buttstock actually increased muzzle jump because of the fulcrum effect. The butt wanted to drop. When the rifle was fired, it would pivot in the hands, with the muzzle jump accentuated by the plunging buttstock. With the weight gone from the butt, the weight of the barrels worked in my favor. Physicists may tell me that I am wrong and that what I have described is not possible. All I know is what I felt, and with recoil, what you feel is more important than what a physicist tells you.

Before anyone asks, the answer is yes, the point of impact changed noticeably, as should be expected with a double rifle when you make a significant alteration. With the reducers gone, it grouped about six inches low at 50 yards. I compensated by using the 100-yard leaf sight even for close shots. It seemed a small price to pay.

Properly used, in moderation, recoil reducers can and do work. Paul Roberts at W. J. Jeffery has installed recoil reducers in the stocks of lighter rifles, on the order of the 9.3x74R, and says they reduce recoil and muzzle jump significantly. Certainly Roberts would know. The point is, such devices are not a panacea. They must be used properly, in conjunction with other aspects of stock fit, in order to accomplish their purpose.

* * *

There is an inherent contradiction in much of what we attempt to do with dangerous-game rifles: We try to squeeze more power from them while simultaneously reducing their weight to make them easier to carry and then taking all kinds of measures to make the recoil at least bearable.

While all this is going on, one fact should never be forgotten: At some point in your hunting career, you may call upon your rifle to save your life. How well you handle it—instinctively, in an emergency—may determine whether you live or die. A dangerous-game rifle should handle with all the balanced grace and easy "pointability" of a fine English game gun. It does not matter whether the rifle is a bolt action or a double: Any rifle can and should have dynamic handling that allows you to shoot accurately without even noticing the sights, reload rapidly, and fire again.

As the immortal Major Maydon put it, "There is a certain feel about a nice rifle; you love to handle it." That is precisely the quality you want in your big rifle, and such handling results from a combination of things, including overall weight, weight distribution, stock dimensions, and stock shape. A good rifle maker—and there are many in the world—knows how to produce a gun that has these dynamic qualities. Most hunters, while they may recognize these qualities in a rifle when they pick it up, shoulder it, and swing it, do not know how to build them into the gun. In ordering a rifle, they may insist on features that detract from these qualities, rather than enhance them.

In my vault I have two .458 Lotts. One is built on the standard Dakota action tailored for the .375 H&H, with a magazine capacity of three rounds; the other is the magnum Dakota action, and the magazine holds four rounds. There is not much difference in size, but there is a world of difference in handling. The smaller gun handles like a *rifle*; the larger one handles like a railroad tie. Which would I want to have in my hands in a tight spot? Obviously, the smaller one.

In our relentless drive toward greater power, heavier bullets, and higher velocities, we sometimes lose sight of the fact that a bullet will kill only when it hits the right place, and whether or not it accomplishes that has less to do with inherent accuracy than it does with the natural pointing and handling qualities of the rifle itself.

As I pointed out earlier, in ballistics there is no free lunch. Every gain must be paid for. Some things work. Others do not.

Above all, a dangerous-game rifle should be as simple a mechanism as possible. The fewer adjustments there are to make, the fewer distractions there will be in a tight situation. As I have said elsewhere, I do not even like the two- or three-leaf folding sights that are common on doubles. If a man is going to shoot a big rifle such as a .470 or .500, he must accept two things: First, the gun must have a certain minimum weight. This has nothing to do with the effect of recoil on the shooter and everything to do with the effect of recoil on the mechanism itself. A .500 Nitro Express that weighed five pounds would, in all likelihood, pound itself into oblivion in a few dozen shots. For this reason, you simply must accept that a rifle of a certain power will have to be of a certain heft. Second, if you are not comfortable carrying that weight, then either get in shape to do so, hire a gunbearer, or go to a smaller cartridge. That sounds like a harsh prescription, but I see no alternative.

Having obtained a rifle that fits you well, one with which you are comfortable, you are then in a position to take said rifle and, through practice, make it a part of your body, a part that you can manipulate with the skill and unthinking dexterity of your right hand.

Practice with a Heavy Rifle

I want you to own a rifle that it is a joy to shoot with, the sort of gun that you will pick up daily to drop a guinea-fowl or bustard or to pepper an ant-hill. Thus are made the master shots.

Major H. C. Maydon

It was late afternoon in the Great Rift Valley. Two Cape buffalo were safely in the bag, and Derek Hurt and I were driving, looking, and chatting. Our second bull had gone to his reward off the end of my .500 and Derek's .470, and we were discussing the impact of those bullets relative to my earlier buffalo, which was taken with a .458 Lott. Then the topic turned to recoil and different rifles.

"Have you ever fired a .505 Gibbs?" Derek asked. I had and told him my thoughts on it.

"I had a client last year with a new .505," Derek said. "A custom rifle. Very expensive. He asked me to sight it in for him. Refused to shoot it until we were actually hunting." The client felt he was only up to one or two shots from such a rifle, and he wanted those to be at a Cape buffalo. It was a somewhat nervous hunt from all perspectives.

If such tales were rare, they would be amusing; unfortunately, they are common and, it seems, becoming more so. Big-game hunters are buying rifles that are bigger and more powerful than at any time in hunting history, yet they are shooting them less and, in some alarming cases, not at all.

In the 1930s, the .505 Gibbs acquired a fearsome reputation for recoil, partly due to Ernest Hemingway. When Hemingway was getting ready for his first safari in 1933, he haunted the Abercrombie & Fitch store in Manhattan, which had a shooting range in the basement. Hemingway shot a .505 there himself and watched with great amusement as another unsuspecting soul pulled the trigger on it and practically dislocated his shoulder. This is according to legend, which—true or not—helped promote the idea that anyone who shot a .505 and lived deserved a medal. Of course, Hemingway later cemented the .505's reputation by arming a professional hunter with one in his great short story, *The Short Happy Life of Francis Macomber*. Probably more significant were references to the .505 in Phil Sharpe's *Complete Guide to Handloading*, which dwells on this caliber's horrific recoil.

Such tales are not terribly helpful in encouraging hunters to actually shoot their rifles. It makes them approach their big gun as if it were a crouching beast just waiting for the chance to pound them into oblivion. While many big rifles have recoil that is decidedly unpleasant, not all of them do, and practicing with one does not necessarily mean subjecting yourself to an endless succession of jackhammer blows and deafening muzzle blast. To get meaningful practice with a big rifle, however—by which I mean practice that makes you a better shot and pays off in the field—requires thought and preparation.

First of all, you need some practice ammunition. Second, you need a place to shoot in your own way. Third, you need to make the time to do it, not just once or twice before you leave, but a couple of times a week for several months prior to boarding the plane. Most important, you need a practice regime that is *fun*. Not an ordeal, not painful, not forced, but fun to the point of being addictive.

Assuming that you are already an accomplished hunter and familiar with rifles, you should plan to shoot a minimum of 300 rounds through your dangerous-game rifle before you leave. Of these, probably 50 should be full-power loads (not counting load development). The rest should be low-power practice loads that are not damaging to your nerves, your shoulder, or your hearing.

Practice Ammunition

Some hunters are enthusiastic handloaders, but others are not. None of the ammunition companies make real practice loads. Some produce "utility" rounds—low-priced, if not low-powered—but these are generally unsuitable for the purposes outlined here. What you need is low-velocity ammunition loaded with a lead bullet. Lead is not only inexpensive, it is also delightfully adaptable to low velocities.

For example, the .500 NE normally fires a 570-grain bullet at 2,100 fps. The recoil is severe even in an eleven-pound rifle, but it is not unbearable. When I was playing with the new H&H round-action .500 a few years ago, I shot a half-dozen rounds as quickly as I could in a series of left-and-rights, holding spare cartridges between my fingers. By the time I pulled the triggers the fifth and sixth time, I'd had enough. The rapid succession of blows, shooting with the rifle thrown to my shoulder rather than carefully tucked in, combined with the muzzle blast, made me feel pretty well knocked around.

Certainly you need to fire full-power loads to see what the rifle feels like, to accustom yourself to it as much as possible, and to ensure that it functions properly. But for day-after-day practice, you need a different load. For the .500 NE, a good one is a 515-grain lead bullet exiting the muzzle at about 1,200 fps. I was given this formula by Larry Barnett at Superior Ammunition a few years ago. It calls for 35 grains of Accurate Arms' 5744, which is a superb powder for the purpose because it ignites readily and requires no filler to take up extra room in these large cases. As a result, loading is extremely simple.

This is a light load, but it is no powder puff. Figure it out: a 515-grain bullet at 1,200 fps has 1,800 ft. lbs. at the muzzle. You could hunt big bears with it; I would even hunt Cape buffalo with it, under strict rules of engagement. Derek and I shot such a round into a dead buffalo to see how it performed, and it penetrated two feet-plus of ribs, just behind the shoulder. Yet, in terms of recoil, this load is so mild it defies belief. The muzzle jumps a couple of inches, and that's all. There is no straight-back thrust to speak of.

It is important to find a lead bullet that closely resembles your hunting bullet, so that it will feed properly. One factor that is definitely not important is accuracy. Find a load that works in your rifle, but do not waste a lot of time looking for one that shoots minute-of-angle groups. Your practice sessions will be at ranges of ten feet to forty yards, and few if any of your shots will be at paper, as we'll discuss in a moment. Once you have your practice load, check to see where it is shooting (with both your scope and iron sights) and let it go at that. Once I have a heavy rifle sighted in with my hunting loads, I leave the sights alone because each day I will fire a few full-power loads, and I want them to go where they are supposed to. With the practice loads I can make allowances, but at such short ranges it is rarely necessary.

And if you do not load your own? The easiest course is to go to Larry Barnett at Superior Ammunition, tell him what cartridge you are using, and ask him to load some practice ammunition for you that will approximate the point of impact of your hunting loads at short range. "More and more people are asking me for that," Larry told me, "So I stock lead bullets and 5744 powder. It's a growing part of the business."

Targets for Practice

Now, what to shoot at?

Anything that is available, safe, and expendable will do, but I have three favorites: Steel plates, plastic jugs filled with water, and clay pigeons.

If your range does not have a steel-plate layout, you can easily cobble one together if you have some property where you can shoot. Round plates of quarter-inch or three-eighths-inch steel, six to ten inches in diameter, with bases welded on, can be set up on a rail or placed on the ground. These go over with a gratifying *whang*, and a half-dozen provide a good shooting exercise. My usual routine is to set them up, load the rifle, and begin at a hundred yards, shooting from a variety of normal hunting positions: offhand, kneeling, sitting, or using whatever rest happens to be available. When I hit one, I run in ten paces, reloading as I go, knock down another, and so on.

Clay pigeons are useful in a different way. An earth bank is ideal because it allows you to see where your bullet goes if you miss. Place some clay pigeons on the bank and shoot them one at a time.

Water jugs are spectacular when hit, and they are ideal at twenty-five to fifty yards when practicing a "left and right" with your double rifle. Whacking two jugs of water as the climax of a day's practice, using full-power loads, is exhilarating and does wonders for your self-confidence.

The only real requirement for targets (aside from safety) is that they be cheap or reusable. Also, you want to see an instant reaction when you shoot—the plate keel over, the clay explode, or the jug erupt in a geyser. Instant gratification is the name of the game.

Today, many shooting ranges have "practical" shooting courses for handguns and shotguns, and a few can accommodate a low-powered rifle shooting lead. If there is such a range nearby, it might solve the problem—provided you can get the kind of practice you want. In the absence of such a facility, an informal range set up on a friend's farm works best. The old standby—an unused gravel pit—is still first-rate if there is one in your neighborhood and the owner is a shooter.

Off the Bench

Shooting benches are wonderful things, but for the purpose of practicing with a dangerous-game rifle they have severe limitations. They provide no meaningful hunting experience and, since they accentuate recoil, they can really contribute to a flinch. Except for prone (definitely not recommended with a .505 Gibbs), there is no more uncomfortable shooting position than hunched down behind a rifle, on a rest, at a bench. A bench should be used for two purposes only: load development and sighting in. Once that is done, find another way to shoot. Any shots you fire from a bench beyond the minimum serve no useful purpose and can actually hurt your shooting. But, since some bench work is required, here are a few suggestions to minimize the damage.

Forget the classic bench-rest position with your left hand (assuming you are right-handed) squeezing the sandbag under the buttstock. Your left hand should grip the fore end firmly, holding it down and pulling the rifle back into your shoulder. Gunmakers who shoot a variety of big-bore rifles, day after day, sometimes use sandbags between the butt and their shoulder, but I have found that for a few shots this precaution is not necessary. In fact, such devices force me into an unnatural position where I cannot see the sights properly. I would rather nestle down with the rifle in a normal way, hold on tight, and keep the shots to a minimum.

If you have a scope on your dangerous-game rifle, this is a good way to make sure that you have maximum eye relief, too. And if the middle finger of your trigger hand is sensitive to being whacked by the trigger guard, either wear a glove or place some padding in between. Except for a scope-cut over the eye, nothing is more flinch-inducing than a bone bruise on a swollen middle finger.

Serious target shooters wear shooting coats with integral recoil pads and elbow pads, and if you have one, it will certainly help. Naturally, you should also wear both eye and ear protection. With a big rifle, especially one equipped with a muzzle brake, ear protection is absolutely essential—not just to prevent hearing loss but also to minimize flinching. The blast from something like a .416 Weatherby with a muzzle brake, especially on a covered shooting line, must be experienced to be believed. To get an idea of the forces involved, fire a shot from one and immediately look down the line, up at the rafters. You will see a rain of dust and debris, vibrated loose. Imagine what such shock will do to your eardrums. The best protection is *both* earplugs and ear muffs, and preferably plugs that are custom-molded to fit you.

Even when shooting for load development, it is a good idea to fill your magazine, work the bolt smartly each time, and eject the brass with abandon. Why? Partly to make sure it works and partly to avoid bad habits. Devoted handloaders are especially bad in this regard, and I plead guilty on all counts. Since we treat our brass with loving care, we don't want it coated with sand, dented, or the mouth crushed, so we open our bolts carefully and pluck the case out before it is ejected. If you get into the habit of doing this, however, you will unconsciously do it after you have just shot a buffalo or elephant, with the wounded animal heading toward the thick bush and your professional hunter yelling at you to shoot him again. When the PH looks over and sees you carefully picking out the case and pocketing it, you will hear some choice words and very likely a few shots as he takes over to finish off the animal himself.

Get in the habit of working the bolt with authority and letting the cases land where they may. Sand can be cleaned off, and dented case mouths can be repaired. I now try to do this with every rifle I shoot, regardless of the circumstances.

Filling the magazine every time accomplishes two things: First, it accustoms you to doing it, getting the feel of the cartridges as they go in. Large cases always present problems with bolt-action magazines; they are a tight fit and many rifles require that cartridges be placed in and pressed down just so. Apply pressure in the wrong place, or with the cartridge not positioned correctly, and you can cause a jam.

The second benefit of filling the magazine is ensuring that it works properly. Everyone has heard the horror stories about the sportsman who gets to Africa, fires his first shot, and has the floorplate fly open, dropping his remaining rounds in the dirt at his feet. This actually happens, and it does so for a reason: A full magazine puts maximum pressure on the follower spring and the floorplate latch. If the latter is not secure, this pressure—combined with the shock of recoil—can fling the floorplate open. In 1990, I found myself in Africa with a .416 Weatherby whose floorplate had to be wedged shut with a match-stick and secured with some electrical tape, precisely because I did not follow this rule at the range.

Speaking of Weatherby, the big rifles (.378, .416, and .460) have two-round magazines with the cartridges sitting atop one another, held with spring-steel lips like those in the clip of a .45 Auto. They are very finicky and difficult to load without looking, but you want to be able to recharge the magazine without taking your eyes off the brush where the buffalo disappeared. Only practice allows you to do this.

Human nature being what it is, preparing your big-bore rifle and practicing with it are two of the most important things to be done before a safari, yet these tasks are the most likely to be left to the last minute. When that happens, we pack too much shooting into too little time; if something goes wrong with the load, scope, or sights, a hunter can find himself backed into a corner, firing too many shots with the clock ticking down.

I have found that, from a bench, I can shoot no more than eight or nine full-power .458 Lott loads at a sitting. I may keep shooting after that, but I won't accomplish anything. For other people, the limit may be more, or it may be less. Learn what your tolerance is, schedule your practice sessions accordingly, and always allow more sessions than you think you need.

Fire and Movement

The goal is *meaningful* practice. In this regard, what I am recommending is much like IPSC or cowboy-action shooting, or any of the other "practical" shooting disciplines. You will be using your hunting equipment, under hunting conditions (insofar as that is possible) without having fire-breathing Cape buffalo in the underbrush.

Now you have your rifle and practice ammunition and targets of some sort scattered around a makeshift hunting ground. If possible, wear what you will have on in Africa or Alaska, along with the same ammunition pouches on your belt. Fill them up in order to get used to the weight, and if you carry a knife, put it on, too. If something is likely to get in the way, now is the time to find out. Wear your hunting boots. Put the sling on your rifle and fill the magazine. Chamber a round and add one to the magazine, if that is your practice. Put the safety on.

The only concession to reality that I make at this point is eye and ear protection, solely in the interests of still being able to listen to Debussy when my hunting days are done.

At this point, I can only tell you what I do. The magazine of my .458 Lott holds four rounds, and my ammunition pouch nine more, so a practice session is thirteen rounds. I scatter clay targets on the faces of both banks of a narrow ravine, toss a coin to see if I approach it from east or west, then trot the first fifty yards to get into position and stalk through the woods. As I come up to the ravine, I look for the first clay. As soon as I see it, I shoot from wherever I am. If there is a handy rest, I use it. If I can drop to my knees to shoot, that's allowed; if not, I shoot offhand. When the first clay is dust, I move on, looking for the next. When my magazine is empty, I refill it. When it is empty the second time, I remove the scope and expend the last ammunition using iron sights, shooting as quickly as I can. The purpose of all this physical activity is to get my heart pumping and my hands shaking. Realism is everything.

I then do it all again from the other side of the ravine. At the end of the session, I've fired about twenty-five shots. I never take the same path twice. The clays get scattered in different spots each time. I deliberately look for a difficult way through the brush, then negotiate it as quietly as possible.

If I am using a double rifle, the procedure is similar, although a typical session is eight rounds—two in the chambers, two between the fingers, and two each in two Keith "double-duty" belt pouches. I learned the hard way that Bill Keith's neat invention works, but that it takes practice to access it without thinking—and without spilling the two rounds onto the ground.

Occasionally, to vary things, I even remove the sling in the middle of the exercise as one might if going into thick bush after a wounded animal. At other times, I start with the scope off and put it back on the rifle in mid-session, as one might if a wounded animal suddenly appeared in a clearing a hundred yards off.

Always, *always* work the bolt smartly and eject the cases into the long grass. As I have said, dents are easy to fix, but bad habits are hard to break. If you lose a few cases, that's even more like hunting.

It is more beneficial, by far, to spread out many short practice rounds over a couple of months than to try to pack all your practice into two or three sessions the week before you leave. When I was preparing for two trips to Africa in 2004, I went to the range two or three times a week, and several times I shot on five or six consecutive days. Each session consisted of a few shots off the bench for load development and sighting in, then a practice round. My biggest day consisted of thirty-six practice shots from the .500 and thirteen from the .458 Lott, plus a half-dozen full-power loads from the bench. That was a lot of shooting, but I was feeling frisky.

Full-Power Practice

Practice with full-powered hunting loads and jacketed bullets, especially solids, is more difficult. The absolute paramount concern is safety, and for this reason I do not shoot jacketed bullets at high velocities at hard objects like steel plates. The ideal target is a water-filled plastic jug, with a high earth bank behind it. There is no danger of a ricochet and the effect is spectacular. If plastic jugs are in short supply, a scattering of clay targets works very well.

A practice session of one full magazine in a bolt action or a half-dozen rounds with a double is all that is needed to ensure that the rifle functions smoothly and shoots where it is supposed to, and to give the shooter the feel of the real thing. The best position is offhand, because it allows you to roll with the punches. A rifle that is painful off the bench may be quite manageable offhand, and just knowing that the recoil is not so bad is beneficial.

If you are going to carry both softs and solids, practice with both. If you like to keep a couple of solids in the bottom of the magazine, with two softs on top, practice exactly that way.

Shooting Sticks

African shooting sticks are one of the great home-remedy inventions of the shooting world. They are simplicity itself: three poles, each about six feet long and an inch thick, lashed together six inches from one end with a Gordian knot of rubber strips cut from an inner tube. They open into a tripod that provides a shooting platform almost as stable as a shooting bench.

Shooting sticks usually have the ends sharpened to dig into the ground. The more sophisticated ones have little refinements. Sometimes one stick will be shorter than the other two so that its flat end is enclosed by the rubber knot. The rubber is wrapped up around the other two ends, providing a flat, padded rest for the rifle's fore end. At the stake end, one stick will be a few inches longer than the other two. This ensures that when the tripod is planted in the ground, the sticks open the same way each time.

Sometimes, shooting sticks will even be carved with images and totems, or notched like a gunfighter's Colt. Generally, the professional hunter carries the shooting sticks. When you see him suddenly plant the sticks and spread them open, you know he has spotted your animal and it's time to shoot. After you've seen this often enough, just thinking about it will give you a rush of adrenalin.

As is the case with all shooting equipment, using sticks effectively requires practice. It is easy to buy three pieces of dowel and lash them together with an inner tube, thereby creating your own shooting sticks to play with. This is immensely useful. I particularly like using them when it is time to shoot full-power ammunition on the practice range, because it gives you the feel of what it will be like in the field. They are most often used for shooting standing, but shooting sticks can be spread wider to provide a stable rest for sitting or kneeling. Kneeling is particularly good because you can prop your right elbow on your

African shooting sticks are the most useful field aid to stable shooting ever invented, but most client hunters do not know how to use them correctly. Practice before you leave home is extremely helpful, and coordination with your PH when you get there can pay huge dividends. Here, Finn Aagaard demonstrates the correct way to shoot from sticks. The rifle is placed firmly in the crook and the left hand grips the fore end. Robin Hurt and Finn combine to show an even more stable approach, where the PH grasps the stick to make them rock-steady, and offers his back as a rest for the trigger-hand elbow. Sticks can be spread wide to shoot from sitting or kneeling or, another approach, you can leave them upright and grasp one leg at any height to provide a solid rest.

knee and literally have a rest as good as a bench, yet be above the grass for a clear shot. I have used shooting sticks on flat ground, hillsides, in the bush, and—on one memorable occasion—with the ends wedged among the rocks on a ledge part way up a cliff.

The correct technique with a hard-kicking rifle is to place the fore end in the "V" of the sticks just forward of the floorplate, reach around the sticks, and grasp the fore end firmly to pull it down and into your shoulder.

On your first morning in Africa, ask your professional hunter about his shooting sticks. Have him demonstrate his technique, and practice a bit to ensure that when he opens them, they will be the correct height for you. Having the sticks too high almost guarantees a miss, and the time to get it straight is *before* you go hunting, not when your animal is right there with his head up, looking at you.

* * *

The object of all this is not just to make you a better rifle shot, although that will be one result.

The real goal is to make your dangerous-game rifle an extension of your arm and your mind—to give you the means to manipulate it, handle it, operate it, load it, aim it, and shoot it, all without conscious thought. When, after a few sessions, you find yourself walking back with the rifle riding easily in your hand, as if it belonged there, you will know that you are making progress.

Ultimately, this will help your shooting because, when you get to Africa and find yourself in the long grass with a herd of Cape buffalo working their way toward you and your professional hunter puts his hand on your shoulder and whispers, *"That one! There! On the left!"* and you look through the scope, it will seem as natural as gazing at a sunset. The rifle will be at home in your hand. Knowing its capabilities—and, more important, what you are capable of doing with it—the worst of the quivers will flutter away and you will center the crosshairs and squeeze. *Mbogo piga. Mbogo kufa.*

Section VII

APPENDIX ONE
APPENDIX TWO
BIBLIOGRAPY
INDEX

BALLISTICS FOR A-SQUARE AMMUNITION

Cartridge	Bullet Weight	Type	Velocity (fps) Mzl.	100	200	300	400
9.3X62	286	Triad	2360	2089	1844	1623	
9.3X64	286	Triad	2700	2391	2103	1835	
9.3X74R	286	Triad	2360	2089	1844	1623	
.375 H&H	300	Triad	2550	2251	1973	1717	
.375 Weatherby	300	Triad	2700	2391	2103	1835	
.378 Weatherby	300	Triad	2900	2577	2276	1997	
.450/.400 (3")	400	Triad	2150	1910	1690	1490	
.450/.400 (3¼")	400	Triad	2150	1910	1690	1490	
.400 A-Square DPM	400	Triad	2400	2146	1909	1689	1490
.416 Taylor	400	Triad	2350	2093	1853	1634	
.416 Remington	400	Triad	2380	2122	1879	1658	
.416 Rigby	400	Triad	2400	2140	1897	1673	
.416 Weatherby	400	Triad	2600	2328	2073	1834	
.404 Jeffery	400	Triad	2150	1901	1674	1468	
.458 Winchester	465	Triad	2220	1999	1791	1601	
.450 NE (3¼")	465	Triad	2190	1970	1765	1577	
.450 #2	465	Triad	2190	1970	1765	1577	
.458 Lott	465	Triad	2380	2150	1932	1730	
.450 Ackley	465	Triad	2400	2169	1950	1747	
.460 Sh. A-Sq.	500	Triad	2420	2198	1987	1789	
.460 Weatherby	500	Triad	2580	2349	2131	1923	
.500/.465 NE	480	Triad	2150	1928	1722	1533	
.470 NE	500	Triad	2150	1912	1693	1494	
.470 Capstick	500	Triad	2400	2172	1958	1761	
.475 #2 NE	480	Triad	2200	1964	1744	1544	
.475 #2 Jeffery	500	Triad	2200	1966	1748	1550	
.505 Gibbs	525	Triad	2300	2063	1840	1637	
.500 NE (3")	570	Triad	2150	1928	1722	1533	
.495 A-Square	570	Triad	2350	2117	1896	1693	
.500 A-Square	600	Triad	2470	2235	2013	1804	
.577 NE	750	Triad	2050	1811	1595	1401	
.577 Tyrannosaur	750	Triad	2400	2141	1898	1675	
.600 NE	900	Triad	1950	1680	1452	1336	
.700 NE	1000	Monolithic	1900	1669	1461	1288	

BALLISTICS FOR A-SQUARE AMMUNITION

	Energy (ft. lbs.)						Bullet Path		
Mzl.	100	200	300	400	Mzl.	100	200	300	400
3538	2771	2157	1670		-1.50	+3.04	Zero	-13.12	
4629	3630	2808	2139		-1.50	+2.33	Zero	-10.11	
3538	2771	2157	1670		-.90	+3.61	Zero	-14.02	
4331	3375	2592	1964		-1.50	+2.71	Zero	-11.72	
4856	3808	2946	2243		-1.50	+2.33	Zero	-10.11	
5602	4424	3452	2656		-1.50	+1.87	Zero	-8.69	
4105	3241	2537	1972		-.90	+4.39	Zero	-16.52	
4105	3241	2537	1972		-.90	+4.39	Zero	-16.52	
5116	4092	3236	2533	1972	-1.50	+2.78	Zero	-10.02	-29.16
4905	3892	3049	2371		-1.50	+3.19	Zero	-13.62	
5031	3998	3136	2440		-1.50	+3.08	Zero	-13.22	
5115	4069	3194	2487		-1.50	+3.02	Zero	-12.95	
6004	4813	3816	2986		-1.50	+2.49	Zero	-10.49	
4105	3211	2489	1915		-1.50	+4.14	Zero	-16.45	
5088	4127	3312	2646		-1.50	+3.57	Zero	-14.69	
4952	4009	3216	2567		-.90	+4.33	Zero	-15.40	
4952	4009	3216	2567		-.90	+4.33	Zero	-15.40	
5848	4773	3855	3091		-1.50	+2.99	Zero	-12.46	
5947	4857	3927	3150		-1.50	+2.93	Zero	-12.17	
6501	5362	4385	3553		-1.50	+2.87	Zero	-11.59	
7389	6126	5040	4107		-1.50	+2.43	Zero	-9.96	
4926	3960	3160	2505		-.90	+4.28	Zero	-16.03	
5132	4058	3182	2478		-.90	+4.38	Zero	-16.48	
6394	5236	4255	3445		-1.50	+2.91	Zero	-11.88	
5158	4109	3240	2539		-.90	+4.09	Zero	-15.63	
5373	4291	3392	2666		-.90	+4.07	Zero	-15.58	
6166	4962	3948	3122		-.90	+3.61	Zero	-14.18	
5850	4703	3752	2975		-.90	+4.28	Zero	-16.03	
6989	5671	4552	3629		-1.50	+3.10	Zero	-13.02	
8127	6654	5397	4336		-1.50	+2.74	Zero	-11.29	
6998	5463	4234	3267		-.90	+4.94	Zero	-18.48	
9591	7633	5996	4671		-1.50	+3.02	Zero	-12.94	
7596	5634	4212	3564		-.90	+5.61	Zero	-20.74	
8015	6188	4740	3685		-.90	+5.74	Zero	-22.22	

BALLISTICS FOR WESTLEY RICHARDS AMMUNITION

Caliber	Bullet	Barrel L	Vel Muzzle ft/sec	Vel 100Y ft/sec	E Muzzle ft/lb	E 100Y ft/lb
.375 H&H Mag	300g	24"	2280	2050	3485	2815
.400 H&H Mag Belted	400g	26"	2374	2145	5043	4115
.450/400 NE	400g	24"	2100	1870	3940	3125
.416 RM	410g	23.5"	2330	2100	4961	4031
.416 Rigby	410g	26"	2330	2100	4961	4031
.500/.416	410g	23.5"	2296	2067	4822	3906
.404	400g	26"	2165	1936	4190	3463
.425 WR	410g	26"	2350	2119	5045	4107
.450 NE	480g	25"	2130	1903	4862	4005
.500/.450	480g	25"	2150	1921	4861	4006
.500/.465	480g	25"	2160	1931	4982	4115
.470	500g	23.5"	2100	1871	4880	4147
.475 No. 2	500g	25"	2181	1952	5300	4218
.500	570g	23.5"	2116	1886	5680	4518
.500J	535g	23.5"	2280	2050	6196	5011
.505G	525g	25"	2315	2083	6256	5075
.577	750g	23.5"	1984	1771	6582	5244
.600	900g	23.5"	1968	1755	7768	6176

Note: 0.5 inch barrel length will result in 20.8 ft/sec more or less
Temperature: 60 degrees Fahrenheit to 120 degrees Fahrenheit will result in 10% pressure plus and about 5% increased bullet speed

BALLISTICS FOR KYNAMCO AMMUNITION

Caliber	Bullet	Barrel	Pressure at 15YC tons per sq. in.	Muzzle Vel ft/sec	E ft/lb	50 Yards Vel ft/sec	E ft/lb	100 Yards Vel ft/sec	E ft/lb
.700 Nitro	1000g S/SN	28"	9	2000	8900				
.600 Nitro	900g S/SN	28"	11	1950	7600	1807	6530	1676	5620
.577 3"	750g S/SN	28"	14	2050	7010	1960	6400	1874	5860
.577 2³/4" (*special order*)	750g S/SN	28"	12.5	1800	5400	1711	4880	1626	4410
.577 Snider	480g Lead	36"		1250	1660	1124	1350	1034	1140
.500 3"	570g S/SN	28"	16	2150	5850	2048	5300	1948	4800
.500 3¹/4"	570g S/SN	28"	15.5	2125	5720	2022	5180	1923	4690
.500 3" N for B	440g SN	28"		1900	3530	1747	2990	1617	2560
.500 3¹/4" N for B	440g SN	28"		1900	3530	1747	2990	1617	2560
.500 Jeffery	535g S/SN	28"	16	2400	6800				
.505 Gibbs	525g S/SN	28"	16	2300	6180				
.476 Nitro	520g S/SN	28"	16	2100	5090	2000	4620	1903	4180
.475 Nitro	480g S/SN	28"	15	2175	5050	2065	4550	1959	4090
.475 No. 2 Jeffery	500g S/SN	28"	14	2120	5000	2023	4550	1930	4130
.475 No. 2 Eley	480g S/SN	28"	15.5	2200	5170	2084	4640	1974	4160
.470 Nitro	500g S/SN	31"	14	2125	5030	2023	4650	1923	4120
.470 Capstick	500g S/SN	27"	20	2150	5050	2030	4700	1950	4200
.500/.465	480g S/SN	28"		2150	4930	2054	4490	1962	4100
.500/.450 3¹/4" Case	480g S/SN	28"	14	2175	5050	2078	5610	1987	4220
.458 Lott	480g S/SN	26"	15.5	2200	5170	2084	4640	1974	4160
.450 Rigby	480g S/SN	26"	18.5	2378	6288	2366	5353	2118	4802
.577/.450 MH	480g Lead	33"	18	1350	1945	1273	1730	1201	1535
.450 No. 2 NE	480g S/SN	28"		2175	5050	2038	4430	1904	3700
.450 3¹/4" N for B	350g SN	28"	13	1700	2340	1540	1920	1415	1620
.450 3¹/4" NE	480g S/SN	28"		2150	4930	2050	4490	1960	4100
.425 WR	410g S/SN	32"	17	2350	5022				
.416 Rigby	410g S/SN	26"	18.5	2300	4702	2200	4302	2110	3957
.450/.400 3"	400g S/SN	30"	18	2125	4010	2033	3668	1946	3361
.450/.400 3¹/4"	400g S/SN	26"	16	2150	4110	2060	3780	1980	3490
.405 Winchester	300g SN	24"	16.5	2220	3240	2090	2890	1970	2570
.404	400g S/SN	28"	16.5	2125	4010	1996	3540	1872	3115
.400 Purdey 3"	230g SN	26.5"	16	2050	2148	1855	1759	1687	1455
.375 Flanged	300g S/SN	28"	14	2425	3930	2300	3526	2183	3180
.375 Flanged	270g SN	28"	18	2600	4060	2482	3700	2367	3362
.375 Flanged	235g SN	28"	18	2750	3950	2615	3571	2489	3240
.375 Belted Mag	300g SN	28"	18	2500	4070	2370	3744	2253	3390
.375 Belted Mag	270g SN	28"	19.5	2650	4210	2531	3837	2415	3496
.375 Belted Mag	235g SN	28"	19.5	2800	4090	2660	3695	2535	3360

Addendix Two: Practice Loads with 5744 Powder

Special note on ACCURATE 5744 powder, provided by Western Powders' ballistician Johan Loubser.

Accurate 5744 is a unique product.

It can best be described as a fast-burning rifle or slow-burning magnum-handgun double-base "hybrid" powder, having the typical chemical composition of handgun powders—i.e., 20 percent nitroglycerine—and the geometry of a typical extruded, single-perforated rifle powder.

Rifle Applications

The characteristics of 5744, cited above, result in the powder's being very ignitable, as well as bulky. This makes it ideal for low loading-density applications such as reduced loads in bottleneck rifle calibers and low performance "straight case" designs, such as the old "black-powder" calibers such as the 45-70, 45-110, 50-110, etc. This powder is virtually insensitive to powder position, and there is no need for "fillers." It will deliver consistent results at low performance levels. Although there will be some unburned powder (see paragraph below), performance will remain consistent.

Unburned Powder Granules

Although 5744 is recommended for reduced- or low-performance loads, it cannot be completely efficient (clean burning) at very low pressures of less than 18,000 psi. It is still a modern, high-density, smokeless powder, with limitations regarding complete combustion at very low chamber pressures. With nitrocellulose-based "modern" powders, burn rate and pressure are directly proportional. This means that some level of unburned powder will be present, constituting the remainder of some of the granules. This cannot be improved with primers or crimp; the only way to eliminate it is to increase chamber pressure.

Determining the Charge

We have a very simple method to determine a reduced load in any caliber using 5744 powder.

- Determine the maximum charge per volume by filling the case to the base of the seated bullet.
- Multiply that value by 0.40 (40 percent).

For example, a charge of 5744 that fills a .416 Rigby case to the base of the bullet weighs 102 grains. Multiplying this by 0.40 (40 percent) gives a load of 40 grains. That will be a good, safe, reduced load that will produce velocities of between 40 and 50 percent of a full-power load. One can then load up to 48 percent for maximum lead-bullet velocity. If you wanted to obtain the maximum possible velocity and pressure with jacketed bullets, it would be between 60 and 65 percent of full case-capacity.

Bibliography

Literally hundreds of books about rifles and cartridges have been written over the past hundred and fifty years. Listed here are those the author feels are particularly relevant to the subject at hand or those from which he has drawn significant information.

* * *

Alphin, Col. Arthur B., et al
Any Shot You Want (The A-Square Handloading and Rifle Manual). A-Square, 1996. Contributors: Finn Aagaard, Col. Craig T. Boddington, Dr. Gary Minton, Terry Wieland.

Baker, Sir Samuel White.
The Nile Tributaries of Abyssinia, 1867.
Wild Beasts and Their Ways, 1890.

Barnes, Frank C., et al.
Cartridges of the World (Ed. 1-10, 1965-2003) Gun Digest Books and successors.

Boddington, Craig.
Safari Rifles. Safari Press, 1990.

Dallas, Donald.
Holland & Holland. The Quiller Press, 2003.

Gray, Alexander R.
The Hammerless Double Rifle. Wolfe Publishing, 1994.

Gresham, Grits, and Gresham, Tom.
Weatherby. Cane River Publishing, 1992.

de Haas, Frank.
> *Bolt Action Rifles.* DBI Books, 1971, 1984.

King, Peter.
> *The Shooting Field—One hundred and fifty years with Holland & Holland.* The Quiller Press, 1985

Matthews, Paul.
> *The Paper Jacket.* Wolfe Publishing, 1991.

Maydon, Major H.C.
> *Big Game of Africa.* Scribner's, 1935.

McIntosh, Michael.
> *The Big-Bore Rifle.* Countrysport Press, 1990.

Olson, Ludwig.
> *Mauser Bolt Rifles.* Brownell & Sons, 1976.

Phillipps-Wolley, Clive, et al.
> *Big Game Shooting.* Anthology published by *The Badminton Library* in two volumes. Longmans, Green, and Co., London, 1894.

Taylor, John.
> *African Rifles and Cartridges.* Originally published, 1948. Reprinted by The Gun Room Press, 1977.
>
> *Big Game and Big Game Rifles.* Originally published, 1948; facsimile reprint by Trophy Room Books, 1986.

Wieland, Terry
> *The Magic of Big Game.* Countrysport Press, 1999.

Wright, Graeme.
> *Shooting the British Double Rifle.* Published privately in Australia, 1996.

Index

A

Martini-Henry, 36, 63, 130
Mathieu action, 119
Matthews, Paul, 201-2, 335
Mauser, Peter Paul, 39, 89
Mauser
    Model 93/95, 89, 122
    Model 94/96, 89, 122; strength of,
        123-5
    Model 98, *3A, 13A,* 15*A, 39,* 50-1,
        66, 74, 87-96, 97-9, 100, 112,
        122, 143, 173, , 268,
        33/40, 93
    Magnum action, 51, 87
    "Double Square-Bridge", 87, 173
Mauserwerke Oberndorf, 121
Maydon, Major H.C., 65, 79, 129,
    289, 314, 316, 335
McDonald, Geoff, 211, 222
McIntosh, Michael, 335
Medwell & Perrett, 64
Merkel, *6A, 16A, 33,* 52, 67-8, 256,
    303
MidwayUSA, 156
Miller, David, xi, *3A, 13A, 95*
Miller, Geoffrey, xi, *6A,* 52, 67-8
Minié ball, 196
Minton, Dr. Gary, 334
Mitchell, Roger, 45
Moore, David, 74-6, 78, 80
Moore, William & Grey, 62
Moore, William Larkin, 74, 76, 78,
    80, 83
Mortimer, Thomas, 82
Muil, Rory, *245*
Muzzle brakes, 302, 320
Muzzleloaders
    2-bore, 22, 27, 129
    3-bore, 25
    4-bore, 22-*3,* 27, 129
    8-bore, 27
    10-bore, 129
    16-bore, *63*
    24-bore, 167

N
Nelson, Peter, 66-7
New England Custom Gunmaking
    (NECG), 293
Newton, Charles, 235-6
Nobel Industries, 170
Norma Projektilfabrik, 103
Nosler Bullets, 205
    Partitition, 206, 238

O
O'Brien, Chris, *257*
O'Connor, Jack, xvi, 68-9, 87, 94-5,
    100, 111-12, 180, 233, 239, 285,
    292
Old Western Scrounger (OWS), 154
Olson, Ludwig, 89, 335
Osborne, Mark, 60-1

P
Palmer, Lionel, 178, 240, 242
Pape, William Rochester, 59
Paper-patched bullets, 198-202, 207-8
Parker-Hale, 53, 88, 179
Perodeau, J.J., 83
Phillipps-Wolley, Clive, 335
Pilkington lever, 300-1
Piotti, 80
Powell, William, 53
Pressure excursion, 284
Purdey, James & Sons, xvi, 23, 26-7,
    43, 62, 64, 80, 159, 169, 233, 262
Purdey double underlug, 27, *33*

R
Reed, Lee, 211
Reilly, E.M., 82, 129, 306
Remington, 94-5, 105, 205
    Model 30, 96
    Model 30S, 96
    Model 700, 101-2, 122, 266
    Model 720, 96
    Model 721, 96, 100-01